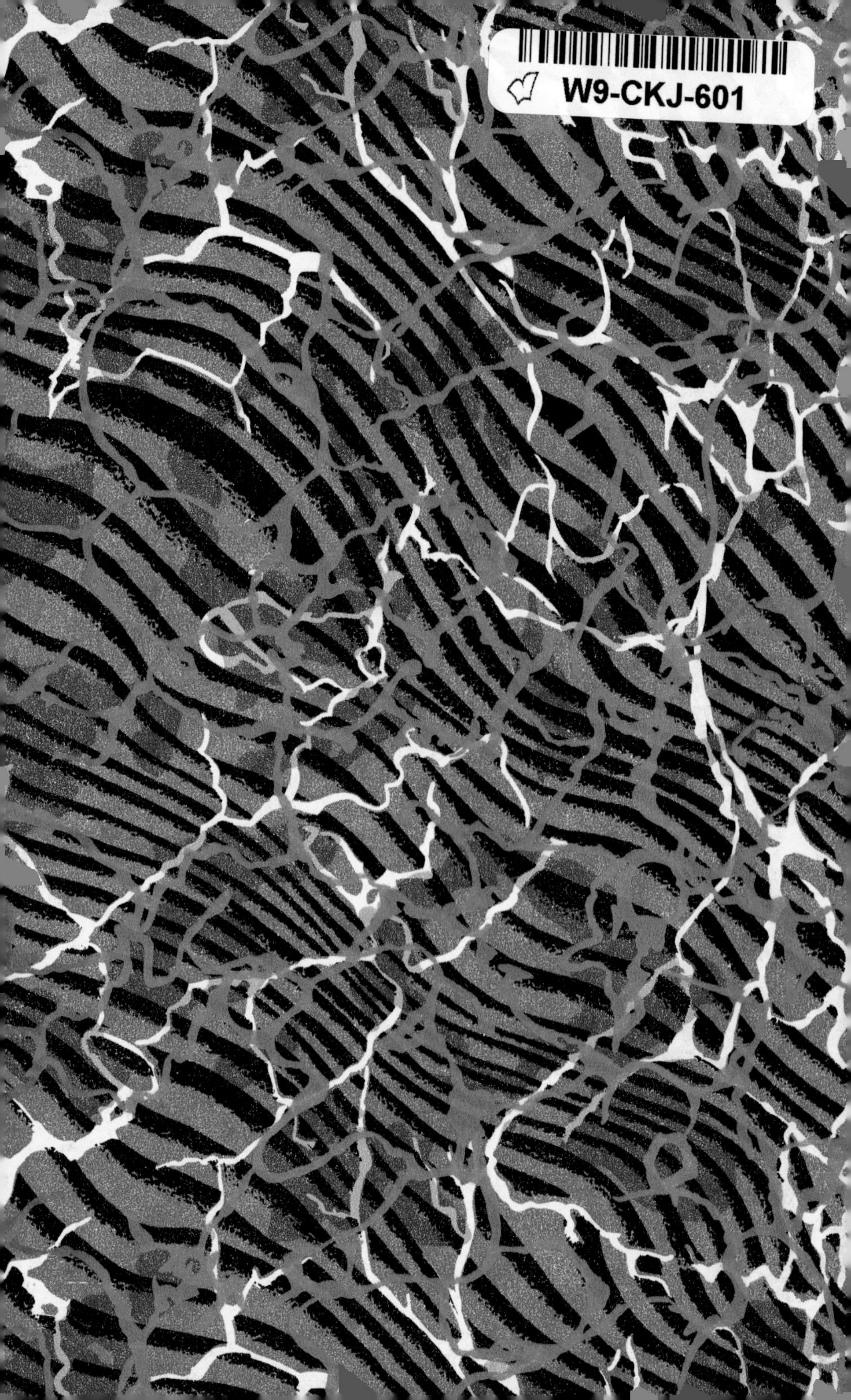
W9-CKJ-601

THE
HARVARD CLASSICS

Registered Edition

The Five-Foot Shelf of Books

The Captives of Babylon
From the painting by Herbert Schmalz —*Page 318*

THE HARVARD CLASSICS
EDITED BY CHARLES W. ELIOT, LL.D.

Sacred Writings

IN TWO VOLUMES
VOLUME I

Confucian · Hebrew
Christian, *Part I*

With Introductions and Notes

Volume 44

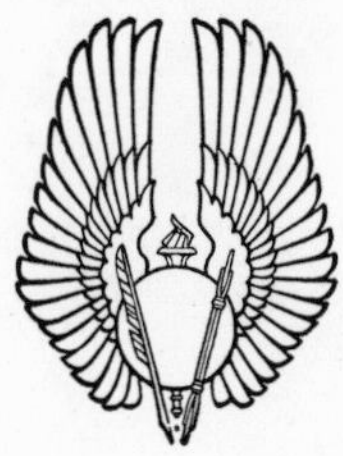

P. F. Collier & Son Corporation
NEW YORK

Fifty-Fifth Printing, 1963

Manufactured in U. S. A.

CONTENTS

INTRODUCTORY NOTE

THE name Confucius is the Latinized form of the Chinese characters, K'ung Foo-tsze, meaning "The master, K'ung." The bearer of this name was born of an ancient and distinguished family in the district of Tsow, in the present province of Shentung, China, B. C. 551. His father was a soldier of reputation and governor of Tsow, but not a man of wealth. Confucius married at nineteen, and in his early manhood held a minor office; but within a few years he became a public teacher, and soon attracted numerous disciples. Rising in reputation, he was invited to the court of Chow, where he investigated the traditional ceremonies and maxims of the ruling dynasty; and in the following year visited another state where he studied the ancient music. When he was nearly fifty, in the year 500 B. C., he again took office, becoming in turn chief magistrate of the town of Chung-too, Assistant-Superintendent of Works to the Ruler of Loo, and finally Minister of Crime. In spite of almost miraculous efficiency, he lost the support of his ruler in 496 B. C.; and until his death in 478 B. C., he wandered from state to state, sometimes well-treated, sometimes enduring severe hardships, always saddened by the refusal of the turbulent potentates to be guided by his beneficent counsels. No sooner was he dead, however, than his wisdom was recognized by peasant and emperor alike; admiration rose to veneration, veneration to worship. Sacrifices were offered to him, temples built in his honor, and a cult established which has lasted almost two thousand years.

Confucius did not regard himself as an innovator, but as the conservator of ancient truth and ceremonial propriety. He dealt with neither theology nor metaphysics, but with moral and political conduct.

The Lun Yu, Analects or Sayings of Confucius, were probably compiled, says Legge, "by the disciples of the disciples of the sage, making free use of the written memorials concerning him which they had received, and the oral statements which they had heard, from their several masters. And we shall not be far wrong, if we determine its date as about the beginning of the third, or the end of the fourth century before Christ."

THE SAYINGS OF CONFUCIUS

I

[1]

THE Master said: "In learning and straightway practising is there not pleasure also? When friends gather round from afar do we not rejoice? Whom lack of fame cannot vex is not he a gentleman?"

[2] Yu-tzu[1] said: "A dutiful son and brother is seldom fond of thwarting those over him: a man unwilling to thwart those over him is never given to crime. A gentleman nurses the roots: when the root has taken, the truth will grow; and what are the roots of love, but the duty of son and of brother?"

[3] The Master said: "Honeyed words and flattering looks seldom speak of love."

[4] Tseng-tzu[1] said: "Thrice daily I ask myself: 'Have I been unfaithful in dealing for others? Have I been untrue to friends? Do I practise what I preach?'"

[5] The Master said: "To guide a land of a thousand chariots, honour business, be true and sparing, love the people, and time thy claims upon them."

[6] The Master said: "The young should be dutiful at home, modest abroad, heedful and true, full of goodwill for the many, close friends with love; and should they have strength to spare, let them spend it upon the arts."

[7] Tzu-hsia[1] said: "If a man honour worth and forsake lust, serve father and mother with all his strength, be ready to give his life for the king, and keep faith with his friends; though men may call him rude, I call him learned."

[8] The Master said: "Of a gentleman who is frivolous none stand in awe, nor can his learning be sound. Make faithfulness and truth

[1] Disciples.

thy masters: have no friends unlike thyself: be not ashamed to mend thy faults."

[9] Tseng-tzu[1] said: "Respect death and recall forefathers, the good in men will again grow sturdy."

[10] Tzu-ch'in[1] said to Tzu-kung[1]: "The Master, on coming to a country, learns all about the government: does he ask, or is it told him?"

Tzu-kung said: "The Master learns it by his warmth and honesty, by politeness, modesty, and yielding. The way that the Master asks is unlike other men's asking."

[11] The Master said: "As long as his father lives a son should study his wishes; after he is dead, he should study his life. If for three years he do not forsake his father's ways, he may be called dutiful."

[12] Yu-tzu[1] said: "In daily courtesy ease is of price. This was the beauty of the old kings' ways; this they followed in small and great. But knowing this, it is not right to give way to ease, unchecked by courtesy. This also is wrong."

[13] Yu-tzu said: "If promises hug the right, word can be kept: if attentions are bounded by courtesy, shame will be banished: heroes may be worshipped, if we choose them aright."

[14] The Master said: "A gentleman who is not a greedy eater, nor a lover of ease at home, who is earnest in deed and careful of speech, who seeks the righteous and profits by them, may be called fond of learning."

[15] Tzu-kung said: "Poor, but no flatterer; rich, but not proud. How were that?"

"Good," said the Master; "but better still were poor, yet merry; rich, yet courteous."

Tzu-kung said: "Where the poem says:

'If ye cut, if ye file,
If ye polish and grind';

is that what is meant?"

The Master said: "Now I can talk of poetry to thee, Tz'u. Given a clue, thou canst find the way."

[1] Disciples.

[16] The Master said: "Not to be known should not grieve you: grieve that ye know not men."

II

[1] The Master said: "In governing, cleave to good; as the north star holds his place, and the multitude of stars revolve upon him."

[2] The Master said: "To sum up the three hundred songs in a word, they are free from evil thought."

[3] The Master said: "Guide the people by law, subdue them by punishment; they may shun crime, but will be void of shame. Guide them by example, subdue them by courtesy; they will learn shame, and come to be good."

[4] The Master said: "At fifteen, I was bent on study; at thirty, I could stand; at forty, doubts ceased; at fifty, I understood the laws of Heaven; at sixty, my ears obeyed me; at seventy, I could do as my heart lusted, and never swerve from right."

[5] Meng Yi asked the duty of a son.

The Master said: "Obedience."

As Fan Ch'ih[1] was driving him, the Master said: "Mengsun[2] asked me the duty of a son; I answered 'Obedience.'"

"What did ye mean?" said Fan Ch'ih.

"To serve our parents with courtesy whilst they live," said the Master; "to bury them with all courtesy when they die; and to worship them with all courtesy."

[6] Meng Wu asked the duty of a son.

The Master said: "What weighs on your father and mother is concern for your health."

[7] Tzu-yu[3] asked the duty of a son.

The Master said: "To-day a man is called dutiful if he keep his father and mother. But we keep both our dogs and horses, and unless we honour parents, is it not all one?"

[8] Tzu-hsia asked the duty of a son.

The Master said: "Our manner is the hard part. For the young to be a stay in toil, and leave the wine and cakes to their elders, is this to fulfil their duty?"

[1] A disciple. [2] Meng Yi. [3] A disciple.

[9] The Master said: "If I talk all day to Hui,[4] like a dullard, he never stops me. But when he is gone, if I pry into his life, I find he can do what I say. No, Hui is no dullard."

[10] The Master said: "Look at a man's acts; watch his motives; find out what pleases him: can the man evade you? Can the man evade you?"

[11] The Master said: "Who keeps the old akindle and adds new knowledge is fitted to be a teacher."

[12] The Master said: "A gentleman is not a vessel."

[13] Tzu-kung asked, What is a gentleman?

The Master said: "He puts words into deed first, and sorts what he says to the deed."

[14] The Master said: "A gentleman is broad and fair: the vulgar are biassed and petty."

[15] The Master said: "Study without thought is vain: thought without study is dangerous."

[16] The Master said: "Work on strange doctrines does harm."

[17] The Master said: "Yu,[5] shall I teach thee what is understanding? To know what we know, and know what we do not know, that is understanding."

[18] Tzu-chang[6] studied with an eye to pay.

The Master said: "Listen much, keep silent when in doubt, and always take heed of the tongue; thou wilt make few mistakes. See much, beware of pitfalls, and always give heed to thy walk; thou wilt have little to rue. If thy words are seldom wrong, thy deeds leave little to rue, pay will follow."

[19] Duke Ai[7] asked: "What should be done to make the people loyal?"

Confucius answered: "Exalt the straight, set aside the crooked, the people will be loyal. Exalt the crooked, set aside the straight, the people will be disloyal."

[20] Chi K'ang[8] asked how to make the people lowly, faithful, and willing.

The Master said: "Behave with dignity, they will be lowly: be

[4] The Master's favourite disciple, Yen Yüan.

[5] The disciple, Tzu-lu. [6] A disciple. [7] Duke of Lu, during Confucius' closing years. [8] Head of the Chi clan during Confucius' closing years.

pious and merciful, they will be faithful: exalt the good, teach the unskilful, they will grow willing."

[21] One said to Confucius: "Why are ye not in power, Sir?"

The Master answered: "What does the book say of a good son? 'An always dutiful son, who is a friend to his brothers, showeth the way to rule.' This also is to rule. What need to be in power?"

[22] The Master said: "Without truth I know not how man can live. A cart without a crosspole, a carriage without harness, how could they be moved?"

[23] Tzu-chang asked whether we can know what is to be ten generations hence.

The Master said: "The Yin[9] inherited the manners of the Hsia;[9] the harm and the good that they wrought them is known. The Chou[9] inherited the manners of the Yin; the harm and the good that they wrought them is known. And we may know what is to be, even an hundred generations hence, when others follow Chou."

[24] The Master said: "To worship the ghosts of strangers is fawning. To see the right and not do it is want of courage."

III

[1] Of the Chi having eight rows of dancers[1] in his hall, Confucius said: "If this is to be borne, what is not to be borne?"

[2] At the end of worship, the Three Clans made use of the Yung hymn.[1]

The Master said:

"'The dukes and princes assist,
Solemn is the Son of Heaven;'

what sense has this in the hall of the Three Clans?"

[3] The Master said: "A man without love, what is courtesy to him? A man without love, what is music to him?"

[4] Lin Fang asked, What is the life of ceremony?

The Master said: "A great question! At hightides, waste is worse than thrift: at burials, grief outweighs nicety."

[9] The three dynasties that had ruled China up till the time of Confucius.
[1] An imperial prerogative.

[5] The Master said: "The wild tribes have kings; whilst the realm of Hsia[2] is without!"

[6] The Chi worshipped on Mount T'ai.[3]

The Master said to Jan Yu[4]: "Canst thou not stop this?"

He answered: "I cannot."

"Alas!" said the Master; "dost thou set Mount T'ai below Lin Fang?"

[7] The Master said: "A gentleman has no rivalries—except perhaps in archery; and then, as bowing he joins the winners, or steps down to see the loser drink, throughout the struggle he is still the gentleman."

[8] Tzu-hsia asked: "What is the meaning of:

'Her cunning smiles,
Her dimples light,
Her lovely eyes,
So clear and bright,
The ground, not yet
With colours dight'?"

The Master said: "Colouring follows groundwork."

"Then does courtesy follow after?" said Tzu-hsia.

"Shang,"[5] said the Master, "thou hast hit my meaning! Now I can talk of poetry to thee."

[9] The Master said: "I can speak of the manners of Hsia; but for Chi witnesses fail. I can speak of the manners of Yin; but for Sung witnesses fail. This is due to their dearth of books and great men. Were there enough of these, they would witness for me."

[10] The Master said: "After the drink offering at the Great Sacrifice, I have no wish to see more."

[11] One asked about the words of the Great Sacrifice.

The Master said: "I do not understand them. Could one understand them, he would overlook the world as I this"—and he pointed to his palm.

[12] Worship as though those ye worship stood before you; worship the spirits, as though they stood before you.

The Master said: "If I take no part in the sacrifice, it is none to me."

[2] China. [3] A prerogative of the Duke of Lu. [4] A disciple, in the service of the Chi.
[5] Tzu-hsia.

[13] Wang-sun Chia[6] said: "What is the meaning of 'it is better to court the Kitchen God than the God of the Home'?"

"Not at all," said the Master. "A sin against Heaven is past praying for."

[14] The Master said: "Two lines of kings have passed beneath the ken of Chou. How rich in art is Chou! It is Chou I follow."

[15] On entering the Great Temple, the Master asked how each thing was done.

One said: "Who says that the man of Tsou's son has a knowledge of ceremony? On entering the Great Temple, he asked how each thing was done!"

On hearing this, the Master said: "Such is the ceremony."

[16] The Master said: "To pierce through the target does not score in archery; because men differ in strength. This was the old rule."

[17] Tzu-kung wished to do away with the sheep offering at the new moon.

The Master said: "Thou lovest the sheep, Tz'u: I love the rite."

[18] The Master said: "Treat the king with all courtesy, men call it fawning."

[19] Duke Ting asked how a king should behave to his ministers; how ministers should serve their king?

Confucius answered: "A king should behave with courtesy to his ministers; ministers should serve their king faithfully."

[20] The Master said: "The poem 'The Osprey' is glad, but not wanton; it is sad, but not morbid."

[21] Duke Ai asked Tsai Wo[7] about the shrines of the guardian spirits.

Tsai Wo answered: "The Hsia Emperors grew firs round them; the men of Yin grew cypress; the men of Chou grew chestnut, meaning '*jest not* over holy matters.'"[8]

6 Wang-sun Chia was minister of Wei, and more influential than his master. The Kitchen God is less honourable than the God of the Home (the Roman *lares*), but since he sees all that goes on in the house, and ascends to Heaven at the end of the year to report what has happened, it is well to be on good terms with him.

7 A disciple of Confucius.

8 *Literally* "to cause the people to be in awe." The commentators are more than usually learned over the Master's anger. I attribute it to the foolishness of the pun, and translate accordingly.

On hearing this, the Master said: "I do not speak of what is ended, chide what is settled, or find fault with what is past."

[22] The Master said: "How shallow was Kuan Chung!"[9]

"But," said one, "was not Kuan Chung thrifty?"

"Kuan owned San Kuei, and in his household none doubled offices," said the Master; "was that thrift?"

"At least Kuan Chung was versed in courtesy."

The Master said: "Kings screen their gates with trees; Kuan, too, had trees to screen his gate. When two kings make merry together, they have a stand for the turned-down cups; Kuan had a turned-down cup-stand too! If Kuan were versed in courtesy, who is not versed in courtesy?"

[23] The Master said to the chief musician of Lu: "How to play music may be known. At first each part in unison; then, a swell of harmony, each part distinct, rolling on to the finish."

[24] The warden of Yi asked to see Confucius, saying: "No gentleman has ever come here, whom I have failed to see."

The followers presented him.

On leaving he said: "My lads, why lament your fall? The world has long been astray. Heaven will make of the Master a warning bell."

[25] The Master said: "All beautiful and noble is the music of Shao! The music of Wu is as beautiful, but less noble."

[26] The Master said: "Rank without bounty; ritual without reverence; mourning without grief, why should I cast them a glance?"

IV

[1] The Master said: "Love makes a spot beautiful: who chooses not to dwell in love, has he got wisdom?"

[2] The Master said: "Loveless men cannot bear need long, they cannot bear fortune long. Loving hearts find peace in love; clever heads find profit in it."

[3] The Master said: "Love can alone love others, or hate others."

[9] Kuan Chung (+B.C. 645), a famous man in his day, was chief minister to the Duke of Ch'i, whom he raised to such wealth and power, that he became the leading prince of the empire. His chief merit lay in crushing the barbarous frontier tribes. The rest of his work, being founded in the sand, died with him.

[4] The Master said: "A heart set on love will do no wrong."

[5] The Master said: "Wealth and honours are what men desire; but abide not in them by help of wrong. Lowliness and want are hated of men; but forsake them not by help of wrong.

"Shorn of love, is a gentleman worthy the name? Not for one moment may a gentleman sin against love; not in flurry and haste, nor yet in utter overthrow."

[6] The Master said: "A friend to love, a foe to evil, I have yet to meet. A friend to love will set nothing higher. In love's service, a foe to evil will let no evil touch him. Were a man to give himself to love, but for one day, I have seen no one whose strength would fail him. Such men there may be, but I have not seen one."

[7] The Master said: "A man and his faults are of a piece. By watching his faults we learn whether love be his."

[8] The Master said: "To learn the truth at daybreak and die at eve were enough."

[9] The Master said: "A scholar in search of truth who is ashamed of poor clothes and poor food it is idle talking to."

[10] The Master said: "A gentleman has no likes and no dislikes below heaven. He follows right."

[11] The Master said: "Gentlemen cherish worth; the vulgar cherish dirt. Gentlemen trust in justice; the vulgar trust in favour."

[12] The Master said: "The chase of gain is rich in hate."

[13] The Master said: "What is it to sway a kingdom by courteous yielding? Who cannot by courteous yielding sway a kingdom, what can he know of courtesy?"

[14] The Master said: "Be not concerned at want of place; be concerned that thou stand thyself. Sorrow not at being unknown, but seek to be worthy of note."

[15] The Master said: "One thread, Shen,[1] runs through all my teaching."

"Yes," said Tseng-tzu.

After the Master had left, the disciples asked what was meant.

Tseng-tzu said: "The Master's teaching all hangs on faithfulness and fellow-feeling."

[1] The disciple Tseng-tzu.

[16] The Master said: "A gentleman considers what is right; the vulgar consider what will pay."

[17] The Master said: "At sight of worth, think to grow like it. When evil meets thee, search thine own heart."

[18] The Master said: "A father or mother may be gently chidden. If they will not bend, be the more lowly, but persevere; nor murmur if trouble follow."

[19] The Master said: "Whilst thy father and mother live, do not wander afar. If thou must travel, hold a set course."

[20] The Master said: "If for three years a son do not forsake his father's ways, he may be called dutiful."

[21] The Master said: "A father's and a mother's age must be borne in mind; with joy on the one hand, fear on the other."

[22] The Master said: "Men of old were loth to speak; lest a word that they could not make good should shame them."

[23] The Master said: "Who contains himself goes seldom wrong."

[24] The Master said: "A gentleman wishes to be slow to speak and quick to act."

[25] The Master said: "Good is no hermit. It has ever neighbours."

[26] Tzu-yu said: "Preaching to princes brings disgrace, nagging at friends estrangement."

V

[1] Of Kung-yeh Ch'ang the Master said: "A girl might marry him. In him was no crime, though he has been in bonds."

He gave him his daughter to wife.

Of Nan Jung the Master said: "When right prevails, he will not be neglected: when wrong prevails, he will escape law and punishment."

He gave him his brother's daughter to wife.

[2] Of Tzu-chien[1] the Master said: "What a gentleman he is! But could he have grown to be a man like this were there no gentlemen in Lu?"

[3] Tzu-kung asked: "And what of me?"

"Thou art a vessel," said the Master.

"What kind of vessel?"

[1] A disciple, born in Lu.

"A rich temple vessel."

[4] "Yung,"[2] said one, "has love, but he has not a glib tongue."

The Master said: "What is the good of a glib tongue? Fighting men with tongue-craft breeds much bitterness. Whether love be his I do not know, but what is the good of a glib tongue?"

[5] The Master moved Ch'i-tiao K'ai[3] to take office.

He answered: "For this I lack confidence."

The Master was pleased.

[6] The Master said: "Truth makes no way. Let me go afloat and scour the sea! and Yu[4] shall follow me."

When Tzu-lu heard this he was glad.

The Master said: "Yu is more venturesome than I, but he does not know how to take things."

[7] Meng Wu asked whether Tzu-lu had love?

The Master said: "I do not know."

He asked again.

The Master said: "A land of a thousand chariots might give Yu charge of its levies; but whether he have love, I do not know."

"And how about Ch'iu?"[5]

"A town of a thousand households, a clan of an hundred chariots might make Ch'iu governor; but whether he have love, I do not know."

"And how about Ch'ih?"[6]

"Girt with his sash, erect in the court, Ch'ih might entertain the guests; but whether he have love, I do not know."

[8] The Master said to Tzu-kung: "Who is abler, thou or Hui?"[7]

He answered: "How dare I aspire to Hui? If he hear one thing, Hui understands ten; when I hear one thing, I understand two."

The Master said: "Thou art not his peer. I grant, thou art not his peer."

[9] Tsai Yü[8] slept in the daytime.

The Master said: "Rotten wood cannot be carved, nor are dung walls plastered. Why chide with Yü?"

The Master said: "In my first dealings with men, I hearkened to their words, and took their deeds on trust. Now, in dealing with

[2] The disciple Chung-kung. [3] A disciple. [4] The disciple Tzu-lu.
[5] The disciple Jan Yu. [6] The disciple Kung-hsi Hua. [7] The disciple Yen Yüan.
[8] The disciple Tsai Wo.

men, I hearken to their words, and watch their deeds. I righted this on Yü."

[10] The Master said: "I have met no firm man."

One answered. "Shen Ch'ang."

The Master said: "Ch'ang is passionate: how can he be firm?"

[11] Tzu-kung said: "What I do not wish to have done unto me, I likewise wish not to do unto others."

The Master said: "That is still beyond thee, Tz'u."

[12] Tzu-kung said: "We may listen to the Master's culture; but on life and the ways of Heaven his words are denied us."

[13] Until Tzu-lu could carry out what he heard, he only dreaded to hear more.

[14] Tzu-kung asked: "Why was K'ung-wen styled cultured?"

The Master said: "He was quick and fond of learning, not ashamed to ask those beneath him. That is why he was called cultured."

[15] Of Tzu-ch'an the Master said: "In four ways he was a gentleman. His own life was modest; he honoured the man whom he served; he was kind in rearing the people; he was just in his calls upon them."

[16] The Master said: "Yen P'ing was versed in friendship. Familiarity bred courtesy."

[17] The Master said: "Tsang Wen lodged his tortoise with hills on the pillars, reeds on the uprights. Was this his good sense?"

[18] Tzu-chang said: "Tzu-wen was thrice made minister without show of gladness, and thrice left office with unmoved face. He was careful to unfold his rule to the new minister. What do ye think of him?"

"He was faithful," said the Master.

"But had he love?"

"I do not know," said the Master: "how should this amount to love?"

"When Ts'ui slew the King of Ch'i, Ch'en Wen forsook ten teams of horses, and left the land. On coming to another kingdom, he said, 'Like my lord Ts'ui,' and left it. On coming to a second kingdom, he said, 'Like my lord Ts'ui,' and left it. What do ye think of him?"

"He was pure," said the Master.

"But had he love?"

"I do not know," said the Master: "how should this amount to love?"

[19] Chi Wen thought thrice before acting.

On hearing this, the Master said: "Twice, that is enough."

[20] The Master said: "Whilst peace reigned in the land Ning Wu[9] showed understanding: when troubles came he turned simpleton. His understanding is within our reach; such simplicity is beyond our reach."

[21] When he was in Ch'en the Master said: "Home, I must go home! My batch of boys, ambitious and hasty, their minds cultured, their schooling ended, know not what needs fashioning!"

[22] The Master said: "As Po-yi[10] and Shu-ch'i never recalled past wickedness the foes they made were few."

[23] The Master said: "Who would call Wei-sheng Kao straight? A man begged him for vinegar. He begged it from a neighbour and gave it."

[24] The Master said: "Honeyed words, flattering looks and overdone humility, Tso Ch'in-ming thought shameful, and so do I. To hide ill-will and ape friendship, Tso Ch'in-ming thought shameful, and so do I."

[25] As Yen Yüan and Chi-lu[11] were sitting with him, the Master said: "Why not each of you tell me his wishes?"

Tzu-lu said: "Carriages and horses I would have, and robes of fine fur to share with my friends, and would wear them out all free from care."

[9] Ning Wu was minister to the Duke of Wei, in the middle of the seventh century B.C. The duke was driven from his throne, and deserted by the wise and prudent; but Ning Wu, in his simplicity, followed his master everywhere, and finally effected his restoration.

[10] Po-yi and Shu-ch'i were sons of the King of Ku-chu. Their father left the throne to the younger of the two; but he would not supplant the elder, nor would the elder act against his father's wishes. So they both retired into obscurity. When King Wu overthrew the tyrant Chou (B.C. 1122), rather than live under a new dynasty, they starved to death. Of Po-yi, Mencius tells us (V. B. 1): "His eyes could not look on evil, nor his ears listen to evil. He would serve none but his own king, lead none but his own people. He took office when order reigned, and left it when times grew turbulent. He could not bear to live under lawless rulers, or amongst a lawless people. To stand by the side of a countryman he thought like sitting, in court dress, in the midst of dust and ashes. Through Chou's day he dwelt on the shores of the North Sea, waiting till the world grew clean. So when men hear tell of Po-yi, fools grow honest, weak wills grow strong."

[11] Tzu-lu.

Yen Yüan said: "To make no boast of talent. nor show of merit, were my wish."

Tzu-lu said: "We should like to hear your wishes, Sir."

The Master said: "To make the old folk happy, to be true to friends, to have a heart for the young."

[26] The Master said: "It is finished! I have met no one who can see his own faults, and arraign himself within."

[27] The Master said: "In a hamlet of ten households there must be men faithful and true as I: why is there no one as fond of learning?"

VI

[1] THE Master said: "Yung[1] might fill the seat of a prince."

"And might Tzu-sang Po-tzu?" asked Chung-kung.

"Yes," said the Master: "but he is lax."

"To be lax in his claims on the people might be right," said Chung-kung, "were he stern to self; but to be lax to self and lax to others must surely be over-lax."

The Master said: "What Yung says is true."

[2] Duke Ai asked which disciples were fond of learning.

Confucius answered: "Yen Hui[2] loved learning. His anger fell not astray; he made no mistake twice. By ill-luck his life was cut short. Now that he is gone, I hear of no one who is fond of learning."

[3] Tzu-hua[3] having been sent to Ch'i, the disciple Jan asked for grain to give to his mother.

The Master said: "Give her a bushel."

He asked for more.

The Master said: "Give her half a quarter."

Jan gave her twenty-five quarters.

The Master said: "On his way to Ch'i, Ch'ih[4] was drawn by sleek horses, clad in fine furs. A gentleman, I have heard, helps the needy: he does not swell riches."

When Yüan Ssu[5] was governor his pay was nine hundred measures of grain. On his refusing it, the Master said: "Not so. Why not take it and give it to thy neighbours and country-folk?"

[1] The disciple Chung-kung. [2] The disciple Yen Yüan. [3] The disciple Kung-hsi Hua, or Kung-hsi Ch'ih.

[4] The disciple Kung-hsi Hua, or Kung-hsi Ch'ih. [5] A disciple.

[4] Of Chung-kung the Master said: "If the calf of a brindled cow be red and horned, though men be shy to offer him, will the hills and streams disdain him?"

[5] The Master said: "For three months together Hui's[6] heart never sinned against love. The others may hold out for a day, or a month; but no more."

[6] Chi K'ang[7] asked whether Chung-yu[8] were fit for power.

The Master said: "Yu[8] has character; what would governing be to him?"

"And Tz'u,[9] is he fit for power?"

"Tz'u is intelligent; what would governing be to him?"

"And Ch'iu,[10] is he fit for power?"

"Ch'iu has ability; what would governing be to him?"

[7] The Chi sent to make Min Tzu-ch'ien[11] governor of Pi.

Min Tzu-ch'ien said: "Make some good excuse for me. If he send again, I must be across the Wen."

[8] When Po-niu[11] was ill the Master went to ask after him. Grasping his hand through the window, he said: "He is dying. It is our lot. But why this man of such an illness? why this man of such an illness?"

[9] The Master said: "What a man was Hui![12] A dish of rice, a gourd of water, in a low alleyway; no man can bear such misery! Yet Hui never fell from mirth. What a man he was!"

[10] Jan Ch'iu[13] said: "Pleasure in the Master's path I do not lack: I lack strength."

The Master said: "Who lacks strength faints by the way; thou puttest a curb upon thee."

[11] The Master said to Tzu-hsia: "Read to become a gentleman; do not read as the vulgar do."

[12] When Tzu-yu was governor of Wu-ch'eng,[14] the Master said: "Hast thou gotten any men?"

He answered: "I have Tan-t'ai Mieh-ming. When walking he will not take a short-cut; he has never come to my house except on business."

[6] The disciple Yen Yüan. [7] Head of the Chi clan after the death of Chi Huan.
[8] The disciple Tzu-lu. [9] The disciple Tzu-kung. [10] The disciple Jan Yu.
[11] A disciple. [12] The disciple of Yen Yüan. [13] The disciple Jan Yu.
[14] A town in Lu, belonging to the Chi.

[13] The Master said: "Meng Chih-fan never bragged. He was covering the rear in a rout; but when the gate was reached, he whipped up his horse and cried: 'Not courage kept me behind; my horse won't go!'"

[14] The Master said: "Unless glib as the reader T'o, and handsome as Chao of Sung, escape is hard in the times that be!"

[15] The Master said: "Who can go out except by the door? Why is it no one keeps to the way?"

[16] The Master said: "Nature outweighing art begets roughness; art outweighing nature begets pedantry. Art and nature well blent make a gentleman."

[17] The Master said: "Man is born upright. If he cease to be so and live, he is lucky to escape!"

[18] The Master said: "Who knows does not rank with him who likes, nor he who likes with him who is glad therein."

[19] The Master said: "To men above the common we may speak of things above the common. To men below the common we must not speak of things above the common."

[20] Fan Ch'ih[15] asked, What is wisdom?

The Master said: "To foster right amongst the people; to honour the ghosts of the dead, whilst keeping aloof from them, may be called wisdom."

He asked, What is love?

The Master said: "To rank the effort above the prize may be called love."

[21] The Master said: "Wisdom delights in water; love delights in hills. Wisdom is stirring; love is quiet. Wisdom enjoys life; love grows old."

[22] The Master said: "By one revolution Ch'i might grow as Lu: by one revolution Lu might win to truth."

[23] The Master said: "A drinking horn that is no horn! What a horn! What a drinking horn!"

[24] Tsai Wo[16] said: "Were a man who loves told that there is a man in a well, would he go in after him?"

The Master said: "Why should he? A gentleman might be brought to the well, but not entrapped into it. He may be cheated; he is not to be fooled."

[15] A disciple. [16] A disciple.

[25] The Master said: "By breadth of reading and the ties of courtesy a gentleman will also keep from error's path."

[26] The Master saw Nan-tzu.[17] Tzu-lu was displeased. The Master took an oath, saying: "If there were sin in me may Heaven forsake me, may Heaven forsake me!"

[27] The Master said: "The highest goodness is to hold fast the golden mean. Amongst the people it has long been rare."

[28] Tzu-kung said: "To treat the people with bounty and help the many, how were that? Could it be called love?"

The Master said: "What has this to do with love? Would it not be holiness? Both Yao and Shun[18] still yearned for this. In seeking a foothold for self, love finds a foothold for others; seeking light for itself, it enlightens others also. To learn from the near at hand may be called the key to love."

VII

[1] THE Master said: "A teller and not a maker, one who trusts and loves the past; I may be likened to our old P'eng."[1]

[2] The Master said: "A silent communer, an ever hungry learner, a still unflagging teacher; am I any of these?"

[3] The Master said: "Neglect of what is good in me; want of thoroughness in study; failure to do the right when told me; lack of strength to overcome faults, these are my sorrows."

[4] In his free moments the Master was easy and cheerful.

[5] The Master said: "How deep is my decay! It is long since I saw the Duke of Chou[2] in a dream."

[6] The Master said: "Will the right; hold to good won; rest in love; move in art."

[7] The Master said: "From the man who paid in dried meat upwards, I have withheld teaching from no one."

[8] The Master said: "Only to those fumbling do I open, only for those stammering do I find the word. From him who cannot turn the whole when I lift a corner I desist."

[17] The dissolute wife of Duke Ling of Wei. [18] Two emperors of the golden age.

[1] Of old P'eng we should be glad to know more, but "the rest is silence."

[2] Died B.C. 1105. He was the younger brother of King Wu, the founder of the Chou dynasty, as great in peace as the king in war. He was so anxious to carry out olden principles, "that when aught he saw did not tally with them, he would look up in thought, till day gave way to night; and if by good luck he found the answer, would sit on waiting for dawn" (Mencius, IV. B. 20).

[9] When eating beside a mourner the Master never ate his fill. On days when he had been wailing, the Master did not sing.

[10] The Master said to Yen Yüan: "I and thou alone can both fill a post when given one and live unseen when passed by."

Tzu-lu said: "Had ye to command three armies, Sir, who should go with you?"

"No man," said the Master, "ready to fly unarmed at a tiger, or plunge into a river and die without a pang should be with me; but one, rather, who is wary before a move and gains his end by well-laid plans."

[11] The Master said: "Were shouldering a whip a sure road to riches, I would turn carter: but since there is no sure road, I tread the path I love."

[12] The Master gave heed to devotions, war, and sickness.

[13] When the Master was in Ch'i for three months after hearing the Shao played he knew not the taste of meat.

"I did not suppose," he said, "that music could touch such heights."

[14] Jan Yu said: "Is the Master for the King of Wei?"[3]

"I will ask him," said Tzu-kung.

He went in, and said: "What kind of men were Po-yi[4] and Shu-ch'i?"

"Worthy men of yore," said the Master.

"Did they rue the past?"

"They sought love and found it; what had they to rue?"

Tzu-kung went out, and said: "The Master is not on his side."

[15] The Master said: "Living on coarse rice and water, with bent arm for pillow, mirth may be ours; but ill-gotten wealth and honours are to me a wandering cloud."

[16] The Master said: "Given a few more years, making fifty for the study of the Yi,[5] I might be purged from gross sin."

[17] The Master liked to talk of poetry, history, and the upkeep of courtesy. Of all these he was fond of talking.

[18] The Duke of She asked Tzu-lu about Confucius.

[3] The grandson of Duke Ling, husband of Nan-tzu. His father had been driven from the country for planning to kill Nan-tzu. When Duke Ling died, he was succeeded by his grandson, who opposed by force his father's attempts to seize the throne. [4] See note to v. 22.

[5] An abstruse, ancient classic, usually called the Book of Changes.

Tzu-lu did not answer.

The Master said: "Why couldst thou not say: 'He is a man so eager that he forgets to eat, whose cares are lost in triumph, unmindful of approaching age'?"

[19] The Master said: "I was not born to understanding. I loved the past, and questioned it earnestly."

[20] The Master never spake of ghosts or strength, crime or spirits.

[21] The Master said: "Walking three together I am sure of teachers. I pick out the good and follow it; I see the bad and shun it."

[22] The Master said: "Heaven planted worth in me; what harm can come of Huan T'ui?"[6]

[23] The Master said: "My boys, do ye think that I hide things from you? I hide nothing. One who keeps from his boys nought that he does, such is Ch'iu."[7]

[24] The four things the Master taught were culture, conduct, faithfulness, and truth.

[25] The Master said: "A holy man I shall not live to see; enough could I find a gentleman! A good man I shall not live to see; enough could I find a steadfast one! But when nothing poses as something, cloud as substance, want as riches, steadfastness must be rare."

[26] The Master angled, but did not fish with a net; he shot, but not at birds sitting.

[27] The Master said: "There may be men who act without understanding why. I do not. To listen much, pick out the good and follow it; to see much and ponder it: this comes next to understanding."

[28] It was ill talking to the Hu villagers. A lad having been admitted, the disciples wondered.

The Master said: "I allow his coming, not what is to come. Why be so harsh? If a man cleanse himself to gain admission, I admit his cleanness, but go not bail for his past."

[29] The Master said: "Is love so far a thing? I yearn for love, and lo! love is come."

[30] A judge of Ch'en asked whether Duke of Chao[8] knew courtesy.

[6] In B.C. 495, during Confucius' wanderings, Huan T'ui was an officer of Sung. He sent a band of men to kill Confucius; but why he did so is not clear.

[7] Confucius. [8] Duke Chao of Lu (+B.C. 510) was the duke who first employed Confucius. It is contrary to Chinese custom for a man to marry a girl of the same surname as himself.

Confucius answered: "He knew courtesy."

After Confucius had left, the judge beckoned Wu-ma Ch'i[9] to his side, and said: "I had heard that gentlemen are of no party, but are they too for party? The prince married a Wu, of the same name as himself, and called her Miss Tzu of Wu. If the prince knew courtesy, who does not know courtesy?"

When Wu-ma Ch'i told this to the Master, he said: "How lucky I am! If I make a slip, men are sure to know it!"

[31] When any one sang to the Master, and sang well, he would make him repeat it and join in.

[32] The Master said: "I have no more culture than others: to live as a gentleman is not yet mine."

[33] The Master said: "How dare I lay claim to holiness or love? A man of endless craving I might be called, an unflagging teacher; but nothing more."

"That is just what we disciples cannot learn," said Kung-hsi Hua.

[34] The Master being very ill, Tzu-lu asked leave to pray.

The Master said: "Is it the custom?"

"It is," answered Tzu-lu. "The Memorials say, 'Pray to the spirits in heaven above and on earth below.'"

The Master said: "Long lasting has my prayer been."

[35] The Master said: "Waste begets self-will; thrift begets meanness: but better be mean than self-willed."

[36] The Master said: "A gentleman is calm and spacious: the vulgar are always fretting."

[37] The Master was friendly, yet dignified; he inspired awe, but not fear; he was respectful, yet easy.

VIII

[1] The Master said: "T'ai-po[1] might indeed be called a man of highest worth. Thrice he gave up the throne. Men were at a loss how to praise him."

[9] A disciple of Confucius.

[1] T'ai-po was the eldest son of the King of Chou. The father wished his third son to succeed him, in order that the throne might pass through him to his famous son, afterwards known as King Wen. To facilitate this plan T'ai-po and his second brother went into voluntary exile.

[2] The Master said: "Without a sense of courtesy, attentions grow into fussiness, heed turns to fearfulness, courage becomes unruliness, uprightness turns to harshness. When the gentry are true to kinsmen, love will thrive among the people. If they do not forsake old friends, the people will not be selfish."

[3] When Tseng-tzu lay sick he summoned his disciples and said: "Uncover my feet, uncover my arms. The poem says:

'As though a deep gulf
Were yawning below,
As crossing thin ice,
Take heed how ye go.'

Till this day, and beyond, I have walked unscathed, my boys."[2]

[4] When Tseng-tzu lay sick Meng Ching[3] came to ask after him.

Tseng-tzu said: "When a bird is to die, his note is sad; when a man is to die, his words are true. There are three duties that a gentleman prizes: to banish from his bearing violence and levity; to sort his face to the truth; to purge his speech of the low and unfair. As for temple matters there are officers to mind them."

[5] Tseng-tzu said: "Out of knowledge to learn from ignorance, out of wealth to learn from penury; having to seem wanting, real to seem shadow; when gainsaid never answering back: I had once a friend who would act thus."[4]

[6] Tseng-tzu said: "A man to whom an orphan stripling or the fate of an hundred townships may be entrusted, and whom no crisis can corrupt, is he not a gentleman, a gentleman indeed?"

[7] Tseng-tzu said: "The scholar had need be strong and bold; for his burden is heavy, the road is far. His burden is love, is it not a heavy one? Death is the goal, is that not far?"

[8] The Master said: "Poetry rouses, courtesy upholds us, music is our crown."

[9] The Master said: "The people may be made to follow: they cannot be made to understand."

[10] The Master said: "Love of daring, inflamed by poverty, leads to crime: a man without love, if deeply ill-treated, will turn to crime."

[2] The Chinese say: "The body is born whole by the mother; it is for the son to return it again whole." [3] Head of the Meng clan, minister of Lu.

[4] This is believed to refer to Yen Yüan.

[11] The Master said: "All the glorious gifts of the Duke of Chou,[5] if coupled with pride and meanness, would not be worth one glance."

[12] The Master said: "A man to whom three years of study have borne no fruit would be hard to find."

[13] The Master said: "A man who loves learning with simple faith, who to mend his life is content to die, will not enter a tottering kingdom, nor stay in a land distraught. When right prevails below heaven, he is seen; when wrong prevails, he is unseen. When right prevails, he would blush to be poor and lowly; when wrong prevails, wealth and honours would shame him."

[14] The Master said: "When not in office, discuss not policy."

[15] The Master said: "In the first days of the music master Chih how grand was the ending of the Kuan-chü! How it filled the ear!"

[16] The Master said: "Of such as are eager, but not straight; shallow, but not simple; dull, but not truthful, I will know nothing."

[17] The Master said: "Study as though the time were short, as one who fears to lose."

[18] The Master said: "It was sublime how Shun and Yü swayed the world and made light of it!"

[19] The Master said: "How great was Yao in kingship! Sublime! Heaven alone is great; Yao alone was patterned on it! Boundless! Men's words failed them. Sublime the work he did, dazzling the wealth of his culture!"

[20] Shun had five ministers, and order reigned below heaven.

King Wu said: "Ten in number are my able ministers."

Confucius said: " 'The dearth of talent,' is not that the truth? The days when Yü[6] succeeded T'ang[7] were rich in talent; yet there were but nine men in all, and one of these was a woman. The utmost worth was the worth of Chou![8] Lord of two-thirds of the earth, he submitted all to Yin."

[21] The Master said: "I find no flaw in Yü. Frugal in eating and drinking, he was lavish to the ghosts of the dead: ill-clad, he was gorgeous in cap and gown: his home a hovel, he poured out his strength upon dikes and ditches. No kind of flaw can I find in Yü."

[5] See note to vii. 5. [6] Shun. [7] Yao. [8] King Wen, Duke of Chou.

IX

[1] THE Master seldom spake of gain, doom, or love.

[2] A man from the Ta-hsiang village said: "The great Confucius, with his vast learning, has made no name in anything."

When the Master heard it, he said to his disciples: "What shall I take up? Shall I take up charioteering? Shall I take up bowmanship? I must take up charioteering."

[3] The Master said: "A linen cap is correct: to-day silk is worn. It is cheap, and I follow the many. To bow below is correct: to-day it is done above. This is overweening, and, despite the many, I bow below."

[4] From four things the Master was quite free. He had no by-views; he knew not "must," or "shall," or "I."

[5] When the Master was affrighted in K'uang,[1] he said: "Since the death of King Wen, is not this the home of culture? Had Heaven condemned culture, later mortals had missed their share in it. If Heaven uphold culture, what can the men of K'uang do to me?"

[6] A high minister said to Tzu-kung: "The Master must be a holy man, he can do so many things!"

Tzu-kung said: "Heaven has indeed well-nigh endowed him with holiness, and he is many-sided too."

When the Master heard it, he said: "Does the minister know me? Being lowly born, I learned many an humble trade in my youth. But has a gentleman skill in many things? No, in few things."

Lao said that the Master would say: "Having no post, I learned a craft."

[7] The Master said: "Have I in truth understanding? I have no understanding. But if a yokel ask me aught in an empty way, I tap it on this side and that, and sift it to the bottom."

[8] The Master said: "The phœnix comes not, nor does the river give forth a sign. All is over with me!"

[9] When the Master saw folk clad in mourning, or in robes of

[1] During the Master's wanderings. K'uang is said to have been a small state near Lu, that had been oppressed by Yang Huo. Confucius resembled him, and the men of K'uang set upon him, mistaking him for their enemy. The commentators say that the Master was not affrighted, only "roused to a sense of danger." I cannot find that the text says so.

state, or else a blind man, he made a point of rising—even for the young—or, if he were passing by, of quickening his step.

[10] Yen Yüan heaved a sigh and said: "As I gaze it grows higher, more remote as I dig! I sight it in front, next moment astern! The Master tempts men forward deftly bit by bit. He widened me with culture, he bound me with courtesy. Until my strength was spent I had no power to stop. The goal seemed at hand: I longed to reach it, but the way was closed."

[11] When the Master was very ill, Tzu-lu moved the disciples to act as ministers.

During a better spell the Master said: "Yu has long been feigning. This show of ministers, when I have no ministers, whom can it deceive? Will it deceive Heaven? Moreover, is it not better to die in your arms, my boys, than to die in the arms of ministers? And if I lack a grand burial, shall I die by the roadside?"

[12] Tzu-kung said: "Were a beauteous jadestone mine, ought I to hide it away in a case, or seek a good price and sell it?"

The Master said: "Sell it, sell it! I tarry for my price."

[13] The Master wished to make his home among the nine tribes.[2]

One said: "They are low, how could ye?"

The Master said: "Where a gentleman has his home, can aught live that is low?"

[14] The Master said: "After I came back from Wei to Lu the music was set straight and each song found its place."

[15] The Master said: "To serve men of high rank when abroad, and father and brothers when at home; to dread slackness in graveside duties, and be no thrall to wine: to which of these have I won?"

[16] As he stood by a stream, the Master said: "Hasting away like this, day and night without stop!"

[17] The Master said: "I have found none who love good as they love women."

[18] The Master said: "In making a mound, if I stop when one basketful more would end it, it is I that stop. In levelling ground, if I go on after throwing down one basketful, it is I that proceed."

[2] The half-barbarous tribes in the mountainous, eastern districts of the present province of Shantung.

[19] The Master said: "Never listless when spoken to, such was Hui!"[3]

[20] Speaking of Yen Yüan, the Master said: "The pity of it! I have seen him go on, but never have I seen him stop."

[21] The Master said: "Some sprouts do not blossom, some blossoms bear no fruit."

[22] The Master said: "Awe is due to youth. May not to-morrow be bright as to-day? To men of forty or fifty, who are unknown still, no awe is due."

[23] The Master said: "Who would not give ear to a downright word? But to mend is of price. Who would not be pleased by a guiding word? But to ponder the word is of price. With such as give ear, but will not mend; who are pleased, but will not ponder, I can do nothing."

[24] The Master said: "Make faithfulness and truth thy masters: have no friends unlike thyself: be not ashamed to mend thy faults."

[25] The Master said: "Three armies may be robbed of their leader, no wretch can be robbed of his will."

[26] The Master said: "Clad in a tattered, quilted cloak, Yu[4] will stand unabashed amidst robes of fox and badger.

'Void of hatred and greed,
What but good does he do?' "

But when Tzu-lu was ever humming these words, the Master said: "This is the way: but is it the whole of goodness?"

[27] The Master said: "Erst the cold days show how fir and cypress are last to fade."

[28] The Master said: "The wise are free from doubt; love is never vexed; the bold have no fears."

[29] The Master said: "With some we can join in learning, but not in aims; with others we can join in aims, but not in standpoint; and with others again in standpoint, but not in measures."

[30] " The flowers overhead
Are dancing in play;
My thoughts are with thee,
In thy home far away."

[3] Yen Yüan. [4] Tzu-lu.

The Master said: "Her thoughts were not with him, or how could he be far away?"

X

[1] Amongst his own country folk Confucius wore a homely look, like one who has no word to say.

In the ancestral temple and at court his speech was full, but cautious.

[2] At court, he talked frankly to men of low rank, winningly to men of high rank.

In the king's presence he looked intent and solemn.

[3] When the king bade him receive guests, his face seemed to change, his knees to bend. He bowed left and right to those beside him, straightened his robes in front and behind, and sped forward, his elbows spread like wings. When the guest had left, he always reported it, saying: "The guest has ceased to look back."

[4] Entering the palace gate he stooped, as though it were too low for him. He did not stand in the middle of the gate, nor step on the threshold.

Passing the throne, his face seemed to change, his knees to bend, he spake with bated breath.

Mounting the daïs, he lifted his robes, bowed his back and masked his breathing, till it seemed to stop.

Coming down, his face relaxed below the first step, and bore a pleased look. From the foot of the steps he sped forward, his elbows spread like wings; and when again in his seat he looked intent as before.

[5] When bearing the sceptre, his back bent, as under too heavy a burden. He held his hands not higher than in bowing, nor lower than in giving a present. He wore an awed look and dragged his feet, as though they were fettered.

When presenting royal gifts his manner was formal; but he was cheerful at the private audience.

[6] This gentleman was never arrayed in maroon or scarlet; even at home he would not don red or purple.

In hot weather he wore unlined linen clothes, but always over other garments.

Over lamb-skin he wore black, over fawn he wore white, over fox-skin he wore yellow. At home he wore a long fur robe, with the right sleeve short.

He always had his nightgown half as long again as his body.

In the house he wore fox or badger skin for warmth.

When out of mourning there was nothing wanting from his girdle.

Except for court dress, he was sparing of stuff.

He did not wear lamb's fur, or a black cap, on a visit of condolence.

On the first day of the moon he always went to court in court dress.

[7] On fast days he always donned clothes of pale hue, changed his food, and moved from his wonted seat.

[8] He did not dislike his rice cleaned with care, nor his hash chopped small.

He did not eat sour or mouldy rice, putrid fish, or tainted meat. Aught discoloured, or high, badly cooked, or out of season, he would not eat. He would not eat what was badly cut, or a dish with the wrong sauce. A choice of meats could not tempt him to eat more than he had a relish for. To wine alone he set no limit, but he did not drink till he got fuddled.

He did not drink bought wine, or eat ready-dried market meat.

Ginger was never missing at table.

He did not eat much.

After sacrifice at the palace he would not keep the meat over night, at home not more than three days. If kept longer it was not eaten.

He did not talk at meals, nor speak when in bed.

Though there were but coarse rice and vegetable soup, he made his offering with all reverence.

[9] If his mat were not straight, he would not sit down.

[10] When drinking with the villagers, as those with staves left, he left too.

At the village exorcisms he donned court dress, and stood on the eastern steps.

[11] When sending inquiries to another land, he bowed twice and saw his messenger out.

On K'ang making him a gift of medicine, he accepted it with a bow, saying: "I do not know it: I dare not taste it."

[12] His stables having been burnt, the Master, on his return from court, said: "Is any one hurt?" He did not ask after the horses.

[13] When the king sent him bake-meat, he set his mat straight, and tasted it first. When the king sent him raw meat, he had it cooked for sacrifice. When the king sent a living beast, he had him reared.

When dining in attendance on the king, the king made the offering, Confucius ate of things first.

On the king coming to see him in sickness, he turned his face to the east and had his court dress spread across him, with the girdle over it.

When summoned by the king, he walked, without waiting for his carriage.

[14] On entering the Great Temple he asked how each thing was done.

[15] When a friend died who had no home to go to, he said: "It is for me to bury him."

When a friend sent a gift, even of a carriage and horses, he did not bow. He only bowed for sacrificial meat.

[16] He did not sleep like a corpse. At home he unbent.

On meeting a mourner, and were he a friend, his face changed. Even in everyday clothes, when he met any one in full dress, or a blind man, his face grew staid.

When he met men in mourning he bowed over the cross-bar; to the census-bearers he bowed over the cross-bar.

Before choice meats he rose with changed look. At sharp thunder, or fierce wind, his look changed.

[17] In mounting his chariot he stood straight and grasped the cord. When in his chariot he did not look round, speak fast, or point.

[18] Seeing a man's face, she rose, flew round and settled.

The Master said: "Hen pheasant on the ridge, it is the season, it is the season."

He and Tzu-lu got on the scent thrice and then she rose.

XI

[1] The Master said: "Those who led the way in courtesy and music are deemed rude, and elegant the later school of courtesy and music. My wont is to follow the leaders."

[2] The Master said: "None of the men who were with me in Ch'en or Ts'ai come any more to my door! Of noble life were Yen Yüan, Min Tzu-ch'ien, Jan Po-niu, and Chung-kung; Tsai Wo and Tzu-kung were the talkers; statesmen Jan Yu and Chi-lu. Tzu-yu and Tzu-hsia were men of culture."

[3] The Master said: "I get no help from Hui.[1] No word I say but delights him!"

[4] The Master said: "How good a son was Min Tzu-ch'ien! In all that parents and brethren said of him no hole was picked."

[5] Nan Jung would thrice repeat "The sceptre white."[2]

Confucius gave him his niece to wife.

[6] Chi K'ang asked which of the disciples loved learning.

Confucius answered: "Yen Hui[3] loved learning. By ill luck his life was cut short. Now there is no one."

[7] When Yen Yüan died, Yen Lu[4] asked for the Master's chariot to furnish an outer coffin.

The Master said: "Whether gifted or not, each one speaks of his son. When Li[5] died he had an inner but not an outer coffin. I would not walk on foot to furnish an outer coffin. Following in the wake of the ministry, it would ill become me to walk on foot."

[8] When Yen Yüan died the Master cried: "Woe is me! I am undone of Heaven! I am undone of Heaven!"

[9] When Yen Yüan died the Master gave way to grief.

Those with him said: "Sir, ye are giving way."

The Master said: "Am I giving way? If for this man I did not give way to grief, for whom should I give way?"

[10] When Yen Yüan died the disciples wished to bury him in state.

The Master said: "This must not be."

The disciples buried him in state.

The Master said: "Hui treated me as a father: I have failed to treat him as a son. No, not I: it was your doing, my boys."

[1] Yen Yüan. [2] The verse runs—

"A flaw can be ground
From a sceptre white;
A slip of the tongue
No man can right."

[3] Yen Yüan. [4] The father of Yen Yüan. [5] Confucius' son.

[11] Chi-lu[6] asked what is due to the ghosts of the dead.

The Master said: "We fail in our duty to the living; can we do our duty to the dead?"

He ventured to ask about death.

"We know not life," said the Master, "how can we know death?"

[12] Seeing the disciple Min standing at his side in winning strength, Tzu-lu with war-like front, Jan Yu and Tzu-kung fresh and rank, the Master's heart was glad.

"A man like Yu,"[7] he said, "dies before his day."

[13] The men of Lu were building the Long Treasury.

Min Tzu-ch'ien said: "Would not the old one do? Why must a new one be built?"

The Master said: "That man does not talk: when he speaks, he hits the mark."

[14] The Master said: "What has the lute of Yu[8] to do twanging at my door!"

But when the disciples began to look down on Tzu-lu, the Master said: "Yu has climbed to the hall, though he has not passed the closet door."

[15] Tzu-kung asked whether Shih[9] or Shang[10] were the better man.

The Master said: "Shih goes too far: Shang goes not far enough."

"Then Shih is the better man," said Tzu-kung.

"Too far," replied the Master, "is no better than not far enough."

[16] The Chi was richer than the Duke of Chou: Ch'iu[11] added to his wealth by becoming his tax-gatherer.

The Master said: "He is no disciple of mine. Sound your drums to the attack, my boys!"

[17] Ch'ai[12] is simple, Shen[13] is dull, Shih[14] is smooth, Yu[15] is coarse.

[6] Tzu-lu. [7] Tzu-lu. This prophecy came true. Tzu-lu and Tzu-kao were officers of Wei when troubles arose. Tzu-lu hastened to the help of his master. He met Tzu-kao withdrawing from the danger, and was advised to follow suit. But Tzu-lu refused to desert the man whose pay he drew. He plunged into the fight and was killed. [8] Tzu-lu. [9] The disciple Tzu-chang. [10] The disciple Tzu-hsia.

[11] The disciple Jan Yu. [12] The disciple Kao Ch'ai.

[13] The disciple Tseng-tzu. [14] The disciple Tzu-chang. [15] Tzu-lu.

[18] The Master said: "Hui[16] is well-nigh faultless, and ofttimes empty. Tz'u[17] will not bow to fate, and hoards up substance; but his views are often sound."

[19] Tzu-chang asked, What is the way of a good man?

The Master said: "He does not tread in footprints; neither can he gain the closet."

[20] The Master said: "Commend a man for plain speaking: he may prove a gentleman, or else but seeming honest."

[21] Tzu-lu asked: "Shall I do all I am taught?"

The Master said: "Whilst thy father and elder brothers live, how canst thou do all thou art taught?"

Jan Yu asked: "Shall I do all I am taught?"

The Master said: "Do all thou art taught."

Kung-hsi Hua said: "Yu[18] asked, 'Shall I do all I am taught?' and ye spake, Sir, of father and elder brothers. Ch'iu[19] asked, 'Shall I do all I am taught?' and ye answered, 'Do all thou art taught.' I am puzzled, and make bold to ask you, Sir."

The Master said: "Ch'iu is bashful, so I egged him on: Yu has the pluck of two, so I held him back."

[22] When fear beset the Master in K'uang, Yen Yüan fell behind.

The Master said: "I held thee as dead."

He answered: "Whilst my Master lives durst I brave death?"

[23] Chi Tzu-jan[20] asked whether Chung Yu[21] or Jan Ch'iu[22] could be called statesmen.

The Master said: "I thought ye would ask me some riddle, Sir, and your text is Yu[21] and Ch'iu.[22] A minister who does his duty to the king, and withdraws rather than do wrong, is called a statesman. As for Yu and Ch'iu, I should call them tools."

"Who would do one's bidding then?"

"Neither would they do your bidding," said the Master, "if bidden slay king or father."

[24] Tzu-lu had Tzu-kao made governor of Pi.

The Master said: "Thou art undoing a man's son."

[16] The disciple Yen Yüan.
[17] The disciple Tzu-kung. [18] Tzu-lu.
[19] Jan Yu. [20] The younger brother of Chi Huan, head of the Chi clan.
[21] Tzu-lu. He and Jan Yu had taken office under the Chi. [22] Jan Yu.

Tzu-lu said: "What with the people and the guardian spirits must a man read books to come by knowledge?"

The Master said: "This is why I hate a glib tongue."

[25] The Minister said to Tzu-lu, Tseng Hsi,[23] Jan Yu, and Kung-hsi Hua as they sat beside him: "I may be a day older than you, but forget that. Ye are wont to say, 'I am unknown.' Well, had ye a name, what would ye do?"

Tzu-lu lightly answered: "Give me charge of a land of a thousand chariots, crushed between great neighbours, overrun by soldiery and searched by famine, in three years' time I could put courage into the people and high purpose."

The Master smiled.

"What wouldst thou do, Ch'iu?"[24] he said.

He answered: "Had I charge of sixty or seventy square miles, or from fifty to sixty square miles, in three years' time I would give the people plenty. As for courtesy, music, and the like, they would wait the rise of a gentleman."

"And what wouldst thou do, Ch'ih?"[25]

He answered: "I speak of the things I fain would learn, not of what I can do. At service in the Ancestral Temple, or at the Grand Audience, clad in black robe and cap, I fain would fill a small part."

"And what wouldst thou do, Tien?"[26]

Tien ceased to play, pushed his still sounding lute aside, rose and answered: "My choice would be unlike those of the other three."

"What harm in that?" said the Master. "Each but spake his mind."

"In the last days of spring, all clad for the season, with five or six grown men and six or seven lads, I would bathe in the Yi, be fanned by the breeze in the Rain God's glade, and wander home with song."

The Master sighed and said: "I hold with Tien."

Tseng Hsi stayed after the other three had left, and said: "What did ye think of what the others said, Sir?"

"Each but spake his mind," said the Master.

"Why did ye smile at Yu,[27] Sir?"

"Lands are swayed by courtesy, but what he said was not modest. That was why I smiled."

[23] A disciple: the father of Tseng-tzu. [24] Jan Yu. [25] Kung-hsi Hua.
[26] Tseng Hsi. [27] Tzu-lu.

"But did not Ch'iu, too, speak of a state?"

"Where could sixty or seventy square miles be found, or from fifty to sixty, that are not a state?"

"And did not Ch'ih, too, speak of a state?"

"Who but great vassals would there be in the Ancestral Temple, or at the Grand Audience? But if Ch'ih were to play a small part, who could fill a big one?"

XII

[1] Yen Yüan asked, What is love?

The Master said: "Love is to conquer self and turn to courtesy. Could we conquer self and turn to courtesy for but one day, all mankind would turn to love. Does love flow from within, or does it flow from others?"

Yen Yüan said: "May I ask what are its signs?"

The Master said: "To be ever courteous of eye and ever courteous of ear; to be ever courteous in word and ever courteous in deed."

Yen Yüan said: "Dull as I am, I hope to live by these words."

[2] Chung-kung asked, What is love?

The Master said: "Without the door to behave as though a great guest were come; to treat the people as though we tendered the high sacrifice; not to do unto others what we would not they should do unto us; to breed no wrongs in the state and breed no wrongs in the home."

Chung-kung said: "Dull as I am, I hope to live by these words."

[3] Ssu-ma Niu[1] asked, What is love?

The Master said: "Love is slow to speak."

"To be slow to speak! Can that be called love?"

The Master said: "That which is hard to do, can it be lightly spoken?"

[4] Ssu-ma Niu asked, What is a gentleman?

The Master said: "A gentleman knows neither sorrow nor fear."

"No sorrow and no fear! Can that be called a gentleman?"

The Master said: "He finds no sin in his heart, so why should he sorrow, what should he fear?"

[1] A disciple.

[5] Ssu-ma Niu cried sadly: "All men have brothers, I alone have none!"

Tzu-hsia said: "I have heard that life and death are allotted, that wealth and honours are in Heaven's hand. A gentleman is careful and does not trip; he is humble towards others and courteous. All within the four seas are brethren; how can a gentleman mourn his lack of them?"

[6] Tzu-chang asked, What is insight?

The Master said: "To be unmoved by lap and wash of slander, or by plaints that pierce to the quick, may be called insight. Yea, whom lap and wash of slander, or plaints that pierce to the quick cannot move may be called far-sighted."

[7] Tzu-kung asked, What is kingcraft?

The Master said: "Food enough, troops enough, and a trusting people."

Tzu-kung said: "Were there no help for it, which could best be spared of the three?'

"Troops," said the Master.

"And were there no help for it, which could better be spared of the other two?"

"Food," said the Master. "From of old all men die, but without trust a people cannot stand."

[8] Chi Tzu-ch'eng[2] said: "A gentleman is all nature: what can art do for him?"

"Alas! my lord," said Tzu-kung, "how ye speak of a gentleman! No team overtakes the tongue! Nature is no more than art; art is no more than nature. Without the fur, a tiger or a leopard's hide is as the hide of a dog, or goat."

[9] Duke Ai said to Yu Jo[3]: "In this year of dearth I have not enough for my wants; what should be done?"

"Ye might tithe the people," answered Yu Jo.

"A fifth is all too little," said the duke; "how could a tenth avail?"

"When the people all live in plenty," answered Yu Jo, "will the king alone be in want? If the people are all in want, can the king alone live in plenty?"

[10] Tzu-chang asked how to raise the mind and scatter delusions.

[2] Minister of Wei. [3] A disciple of Confucius.

The Master said: "Make faithfulness and truth thy masters, and follow the right; the mind will be raised. We wish life to things we love, death to things we hate. To wish them both life and death is a delusion.

'Whether prompted by wealth,
Yet ye made a distinction.' "

[11] Ching,[4] Duke of Ch'i asked Confucius, What is kingcraft?

Confucius answered: "When the king is king and the minister is minister; when the father is father and the son is son."

"True indeed!" said the duke. "Were the king no king and the minister no minister, were the father no father and the son no son, could I get aught to eat, though the grain were there?"

[12] The Master said: "To stint a quarrel with half a word Yu[5] is the man."

Tzu-lu never slept over a promise.

[13] The Master said: "At hearing lawsuits I am no better than another. What is needed is to stay lawsuits."

[14] Tzu-chang asked, What is kingcraft?

The Master said: "To be tireless of spirit and faithful at work."

[15] The Master said: "Breadth of reading and the ties of courtesy will also keep a man from error's path."

[16] The Master said: "A gentleman shapes the good in man; he does not shape the bad in him. Contrariwise the vulgar."

[17] Chi K'ang[6] asked Confucius how to rule.

Confucius answered: "To rule is to set straight. If we give an upright lead, sir, who will dare walk crooked?"

[18] Chi K'ang being vexed by robbers spake of it to Confucius.

Confucius answered: "But for your greed, sir, though ye rewarded thieves, no man would steal."

[19] Chi K'ang, speaking of kingcraft, said to Confucius: "To help the good, should we kill the bad?"

Confucius answered: "Sir, what need has a ruler to kill? Were ye set on good, sir, your people would do good. The king's mind is

[4] Confucius was in Ch'i in B.C. 517. The duke was overshadowed by his ministers, and contemplated setting aside his eldest son. [5] Tzu-lu.

[6] On the death of Chi Huan, Chi K'ang set aside his infant nephew and made himself head of the clan.

the wind, and grass are the minds of the people: whither the wind blows, thither the grass bends."

[20] Tzu-chang asked, When may a scholar be called eminent?

The Master said: "What dost thou mean by eminence?"

Tzu-chang answered: "To be famous in the state, and famous in his home."

The Master said: "That is fame, not eminence. The eminent man is plain and straight. He loves right, weighs men's words, and scans their looks. At pains to step down to them, he will be eminent in the state, and eminent in his home. The famous man wears a mask of love, but his deeds belie it. He knows no misgivings, and fame will be his in the state and fame be his in his home."

[21] Whilst wandering through the Rain God's glade with the Master, Fan Ch'ih said to him: "May I ask how to raise the mind, amend evil, and scatter errors?"

The Master said: "A good question! Rate the task above the prize; will not the mind be raised? Fight thine own faults, not the faults of others; will not evil be mended? One angry morning to forget both self and kin, is that no error?"

[22] Fan Ch'ih asked, What is love?

The Master said: "To love mankind."

He asked, What is wisdom?

The Master said: "To know mankind."

Fan Ch'ih did not understand.

The Master said: "Exalt the straight, put aside the crooked; the crooked will grow straight."

Fan Ch'ih withdrew, and meeting Tzu-hsia, said to him: "I was received by the Master and asked him 'What is wisdom?' The Master answered: 'Exalt the straight, put aside the crooked; the crooked will grow straight.' What did he mean?"

"How rich a saying!" said Tzu-hsia. "When Shun[7] was lord of the earth, he chose Kao-yao from the many, exalted him, and evil vanished. When T'ang[8] was lord of the earth, he chose Yi-yin[9] from

[7] An emperor of the golden age. [8] The founder of the Shang, or Yin, dynasty.
[9] T'ang's chief minister. "Yi-yin said: 'Is he whom I serve not my king? Are they whom I lead not my people?' In quiet times he took office and in lawless times he took office. He said: 'Heaven begat mankind, meaning those who are quick learners to teach those slow to learn, and those who are quick-sighted to teach those slow to

the many, exalted him, and evil vanished."

[23] Tzu-kung asked about friends.

The Master said: "Talk faithfully to them: guide them with skill. If this prove vain, stop. Do not court shame."

[24] Tseng-tzu said: "A gentleman gathers friends by culture and props love with friendship."

XIII

[1] Tzu-lu asked how to rule.

The Master said: "Lead the way: take pains."

Asked to add more, he said: "Never flag."

[2] When steward of the Chi, Chung-kung asked how to rule.

The Master said: "Let officers act first: overlook small faults: raise worth and talent."

Chung-kung said: "How shall I learn to know the worth and talent I have to raise?"

"Raise those thou dost know," said the Master; "and those unknown to thee, will other men pass by?"

[3] Tzu-lu said: "The King of Wei[1] looks to you, Sir, to govern. How shall ye begin?"

"If need were," said the Master, "by putting names right."

"Indeed," said Tzu-lu, "that is far fetched, Sir! Why put them right?"

"Yu," said the Master, "thou art ill-bred. On matters beyond his ken a gentleman speaks with caution. If names are not right, words are misused. When words are misused, affairs go wrong. When affairs go wrong, courtesy and music droop. When courtesy and music droop, law and justice fail. And when law and justice fail them, a people can move neither hand nor foot. So a gentleman must be ready to put names into speech, to put words into deed. A gentleman is nowise careless of words."

[4] Fan Ch'ih asked to be taught husbandry.

---

see. I am one of Heaven's men whose sight is quick: it falls to me to show the way to the people.' Were there man or wife below heaven, who had missed his share in the heritage of Yao and Shun, it was to him as though his hand had pushed him into the ditch; for the burden he took upon him was the weight of all below heaven." (Mencius, V. B. 1.)

[1] See note to vii. 14. Tzu-lu was his officer.

The Master said: "I cannot rank with an old husbandman."

He asked to be taught gardening.

The Master said: "I cannot rank with an old gardener."

After Fan Ch'ih had left, the Master said: "How small a man! If those above love courtesy, none will dare to slight them: if those above love right, none will dare to disobey: if those above love truth, none will dare to hide the heart. Then, from the four corners of the earth, folk will gather, their children on their backs; what need will there be for husbandry?"

[5] The Master said: "Though a man have conned three hundred poems; if he stand helpless when put to govern; if he cannot answer for himself, when sent to the four corners of the earth; despite their number, what have they done for him?"

[6] The Master said: "The man of upright life is obeyed before he speaks: commands even go unheeded where the life is crooked."

[7] The Master said: "The governments of Lu and Wei are brothers."

[8] Speaking of Ching, of the ducal house of Wei, the Master said: "He was wise in his private life. When he had begun saving, he said, 'This is much.' When he grew better off, he said 'Now we lack nothing.' And when he was rich, he said 'We live in splendour.' "

[9] Whilst Jan Yu was driving him on the road to Wei, the Master said: "What numbers!"

Jan Yu said: "Since numbers are here, what next is needed?"

"Wealth," said the Master.

"And after wealth, what next were needed?"

"Teaching," said the Master.

[10] The Master said: "Had I power for a twelvemonth only, much could be done. In three years all were ended."

[11] The Master said: " 'Could good men govern for an hundred years, cruelty would be vanquished, putting to death an end.' How true are these words!"

[12] The Master said: "Had we a king among men, a lifetime would pass ere love dawned!"

[13] The Master said: "What is governing to him who can rule himself? Who cannot rule himself, how should he rule others?"

[14] As the disciple Jan[2] came back from court, the Master said to him: "Why so late?"

"Business of state kept me," he answered.

"Household business," said the Master. "Though I am out of office, I had heard were there business of state."

[15] Duke Ting asked: "Is there any one saying that can prosper a kingdom?"

Confucius answered: "That is more than words can do. But a proverb says 'Hard it is to be king, nor yet light to be minister.' And did one know how hard it is to be king, might not this saying all but prosper a kingdom?"

"And is there any one saying that can wreck a kingdom?"

"That is more than words can do," Confucius answered. "But a proverb says 'My one joy as king is that none withstand what I say.' Now if none withstand him when right, will it not be well? But if none withstand him when wrong, might not this saying all but wreck a kingdom?"

[16] The Duke of She asked, What is kingcraft?

The Master said: "To gladden those around us and draw men from afar."

[17] Tzu-hsia, when governor of Chü-fu, asked how to rule.

The Master said: "Never be in a hurry: shut thine eyes to small gains. Nought done in a hurry is thorough, and an eye for small gain means big things undone."

[18] The Duke of She told Confucius: "Among the upright men of my home if the father steal a sheep his son will bear witness."

Confucius answered: "Our people's uprightness is unlike that. The father screens his son, the son screens his father. There is uprightness in this."

[19] Fan Ch'ih asked, What is love?

The Master said: "To be respectful at home, painstaking at work, faithful to all. Even among savages none of this may be dropped."

[20] Tzu-kung asked, When can a man be called a good crown servant?

The Master said: "In private life he wants a sense of shame: if sent

[2] Jan Yu. He was in the service of the Chi, not of the Duke of Lu.

to the four corners of the earth he must not disgrace the king's commands."

"May I ask who would rank second?"

"A man who his clansmen call dutiful, and his neighbours call modest."

"May I ask who would rank next?"

"A man who clings to his word and sticks to his course, a flinty little fellow, would perhaps come next."

"And how are the crown servants of to-day?"

"What! The weights and measures men!" said the Master. "Are they worth reckoning?"

[21] The Master said: "As followers of the golden mean are not to be found, I have to work with ambitious and headstrong men. Ambitious men push ahead, and there are things that headstrong men will not do."

[22] The Master said: "The men of the south say, 'Unless steadfast a man will make neither a wizard nor a leech.' This is true. 'A falling off in merit will reap disgrace.'"

The Master said: "Neglect of the omens, that is all."

[23] The Master said: "A gentleman is pleasant, not fulsome: the vulgar are fulsome, but not pleasant."

[24] Tzu-kung said: "Would it be right if a man were liked by all his neighbours?"

"No," said the Master.

"And would it be right if a man were hated by all his neighbours?"

"No," said the Master. "It would be better if the good men of the neighbourhood liked him, and the bad men of the neighbourhood hated him."

[25] The Master said: "A gentleman is easy to serve, and hard to please. Nought but what is right pleases him: he fits his behests to the man. The vulgar are hard to serve, and easy to please. What is wrong may yet please them: but of their men they expect all things."

[26] The Master said: "A gentleman is high-minded, not proud: the vulgar are proud, but not high-minded."

[27] The Master said: "Strength and courage, simplicity and meekness are akin to love."

[28] Tzu-lu asked, When can a man be called educated?

The Master said: "A man who is earnest, encouraging, and kind may be called educated. Earnest with friends and encouraging; kind towards his brothers."

[29] The Master said: "Could a good man teach the people for seven years, they would be fit for arms also."

[30] The Master said: "To take untaught men into battle is to cast them away."

XIV

[1] Hsien[1] asked, What is shame?

The Master said: "Hire when right prevails, hire when wrong prevails, hire is always shame."

[2] "To eschew strife and boasting, spite and greed, can that be called love?"

The Master said: "I call that hard to do: I do not know that it is love."

[3] The Master said: "A scholar who loves comfort is not worthy the name."

[4] The Master said: "When right prevails, be fearless of speech and fearless in deed: when wrong prevails, be fearless in deed but soft of speech."

[5] The Master said: "A man of worth can always talk, but talkers are not always men of worth. Love is always bold, though boldness is found without love."

[6] Nan-kung Kuo said to Confucius: "Yi[2] was good at archery, Ao could push a boat overland; each died before his time. Yü and Chi toiled at their crops, and won the world."

The Master did not answer.

But when Nan-kung Kuo had left, the Master said: "What a gentleman he is! How he prizes worth!"

[7] The Master said: "Gentlemen without love there may be, but the vulgar must ever be strangers to love."

[8] The Master said: "Can one love, yet take no pains? Can he be faithful who gives no counsel?"

[1] The disciple Yüan Ssu.

[2] Yi was killed by his best pupil, who thought within himself, "In all the world Yi alone shoots better than I," and so he slew him.

[9] The Master said: "The decrees were drafted by P'i Shen, criticised by Shih-shu, polished by the Foreign Minister Tzu-yü, and given the final touches by Tzu-ch'an of Tung-li."

[10] Being asked what he thought of Tzu-ch'an, the Master said: "A kind-hearted man."

Asked what he thought of Tzu-hsi, the Master said: "Of him! What I think of him!"

Asked what he thought of Kuan Chung,[3] the Master said: "He was the man who drove the Po from the town of Pien and its three hundred households, to end his days on coarse rice, and no word of wrong could he find to say."

[11] The Master said: "It is hard not to chafe at poverty, a light thing not to be proud of wealth."

[12] The Master said: "Meng Kung-ch'o is more than fit to be steward to Chao or Wei, but is not fit to be minister of T'eng or Hsieh."

[13] Tzu-lu asked what were a full-grown man.

The Master said: "A man wise as Tsang Wu-chung, greedless as Kung-ch'o, bold as Chuang of Pien, skilful as Jan Ch'iu, and graced with courtesy and music, might be called a full-grown man. But to-day who asks the like of a full-grown man? Who in sight of gain remembers right, in face of danger will risk his life, and cleaves to his word for a lifetime, however old the bond, him we must call a full-grown man."

[14] Speaking of Kung-shu Wen, the Master said to Kung-ming Chia: "Is it true that thy master does not speak, nor laugh, nor take a gift?"

Kung-ming Chia answered: "That is saying too much. My master speaks when it is time to speak, so none weary of his speaking: he laughs when he is merry, so none weary of his laughter: he takes what it is right to take, so none weary of his taking."

"It may be so," said the Master; "but is it?"

[15] The Master said: "When Tsang Wu-chung holding Fang asked Lu to appoint an heir, though he said that he was not forcing his prince, I cannot believe it."

[3] See note to iii. 22.

[16] The Master said: "Duke Wen of Chin was deep, but dishonest: Duke Huan of Ch'i was honest, but shallow."

[17] Tzu-lu said: "When Duke Huan slew the young duke Chiu, Shao Hu died with him, but not Kuan Chung, was this not want of love?"[4]

The Master said: "Duke Huan gathered the nobles together, without help from chariots of war, through the might of Kuan Chung. What can love do more? What can love do more?"

[18] Tzu-kung said: "In becoming minister, instead of dying with the young duke Chiu, when he was slain by Duke Huan, Kuan Chung showed want of love, it would seem."

The Master said: "Through Kuan Chung helping Duke Huan to bend the nobility, and tame the world, men have fared the better from that day unto this. But for Kuan Chung we should wear our hair down our backs and the left arm bare: or should he, like the ploughboy and his lass, their troth to keep, have drowned in a ditch, no man the wiser?"

[19] The minister Hsien, once steward to Kung-shu Wen, went to audience of the duke together with Wen.

When the Master heard of this, he said: "He is rightly called Wen (cultured)."

[20] The Master spake of the wickedness of Ling, Duke of Wei.

K'ang[5] said: "If that be so, how does he escape ruin?"

Confucius answered: "With Chung-shu Yü in charge of the guests, the reader T'o in charge of the Ancestral Temple, and Wang-sun Chia in charge of the troops, how should he come to ruin?"

[21] The Master said: "If the tongue have no fear, words are hard to make good."

[4] Huan and Chiu were brothers, sons of the Duke of Ch'i. When the father died, their uncle seized the throne. To preserve the rightful heirs Shao Hu and Kuan Chung fled with Chiu to Lu, whilst Huan escaped to another state. The usurper having subsequently been murdered, Huan returned to Ch'i and secured the throne. He then required the Duke of Lu to kill his brother and deliver up to him Shao Hu and Kuan Chung. This was done. But on the way to Ch'i, Shao Hu cut his throat. Kuan Chung, on the other hand, took service under Duke Huan, became his Prime Minister, and raised the state to greatness (see note to iii. 22).

[5] Chi K'ang.

[22] Ch'en Ch'eng murdered Duke Chien.[6]

Confucius cleansed himself, went to court, and told Duke Ai, saying: "Ch'en Heng has murdered his prince. Pray chastise him."

The duke said: "Tell the three chiefs."

Confucius said: "Following in the wake of the ministry I dared not leave this untold; but the prince says, 'Tell the three chiefs.'"

He told the three chiefs. It was vain.

Confucius said: "Following in the wake of the ministry I dared not leave this untold."

[23] Tzu-lu asked how to serve the king.

The Master said: "Never cheat him: withstand him to the face."

[24] The Master said: "A gentleman's life leads upwards; a vulgar life leads down."

[25] The Master said: "Men of old learned for their own sake: the men of to-day learn for show."

[26] Ch'ü Po-yü sent an envoy to Confucius.

As they sat together, Confucius asked him: "How is your lord busied?"

He answered: "My lord tries to pare his faults, and tries in vain."

When the envoy had left, the Master said: "An envoy, an envoy indeed!"

[27] The Master said: "When not in office discuss not policy."

[28] Tseng-tzu said: "A gentleman is bent on keeping his place."

[29] The Master said: "A gentleman is shamefast of speech: his deeds go further."

[30] The Master said: "In three ways I fall short of a gentleman. Love is never vexed; wisdom has no doubts; courage is without fear."

Tzu-kung replied: "That is what ye say, Sir."

[31] Tzu-kung would compare one man with another.

The Master said: "What talents Tz'u has! Now I have no time for this."

[32] The Master said: "Sorrow not at being unknown: sorrow for thine own shortcomings."

[6] B.C. 481, two years before the death of Confucius, who was not at the time in office. Chien was Duke of Ch'i, a state bordering on Lu. The three chiefs were the heads of the three great clans, all powerful in Lu.

[33] The Master said: "Not to expect falsehood, nor look for mistrust, and yet to forestall them, shows worth in a man."

[34] Wei-sheng Mou said: "How dost thou still find roosts to roost on, Ch'iu, unless by wagging a glib tongue?"

Confucius answered: "I dare not wag a glib tongue; but I hate stubbornness."

[35] The Master said: "A steed is not praised for his strength, but praised for his mettle."

[36] One said: "To mete out good for evil, how were that?"

"And how would ye meet good?" said the Master. "Meet evil with justice: meet good with good."

[37] The Master said: "Alas! no man knows me!"

Tzu-kung said: "Why do ye say, Sir, that no man knows you?"

The Master said: "Never murmuring against Heaven, nor finding fault with men; learning from the lowest, cleaving the heights. I am known but to one, but to Heaven."

[38] Liao, the duke's uncle, spake ill of Tzu-lu to Chi-sun.[7]

Tzu-fu Ching-po told this to Confucius, saying: "My lord's mind is surely being led astray by the duke's uncle, but strength is yet mine to expose his body in the market-place."

The Master said: "The doom has fallen if truth is to win: it has fallen if truth is to lose. Can Liao, the duke's uncle, fight against doom?"

[39] The Master said: "Men of worth shun the world; the next best shun the land. Then come men who go at a look, then men who go at speech."

[40] The Master said: "Seven men did so."

[41] Tzu-lu spent a night at Shih-men.

The gate-keeper asked him: "Whence comest thou?"

"From Confucius," he answered.

"The man who knows it is vain, yet cannot forbear to stir?" said the gate-keeper.

[42] When the Master was chiming his sounding stones in Wei, a basket-bearer said, as he passed the door: "His heart is full, who chimes those stones!" But then he added: "For shame! What a tinkling note! If no one heed thee, have done!

[7] The head of the Chi clan, in whose service Tzu-lu was.

'Wade the deep places,
Lift thy robe through the shallows.' "

The Master said: "Where there's a will, that is lightly done."

[43] Tzu-chang said: "What does the book mean by saying that Kao-tsung,[8] when mourning his predecessor, did not speak for three years?"

The Master said: "Why pick out Kao-tsung? Men of old were all thus. For three years after the king had died, the hundred officers acted each for himself, and obeyed the chief minister."

[44] The Master said: "When those above love courtesy, the people are easy to lead."

[45] Tzu-lu asked, What is a gentleman?

The Master said: "A man bent on shaping his mind."

"Is that all?" said Tzu-lu.

"On shaping his mind to give happiness to others."

"And is that all?"

"On shaping his mind to give happiness to the people," said the Master. "To shape the mind and give happiness to the people, for this both Yao and Shun still pined."

[46] Yüan Jang awaited the Master squatting.

The Master said: "Unruly when young, unmentioned as man, undying when old, spells good-for-nothing!" and hit him on the leg with his staff.

[47] When a lad from the village of Ch'üeh was made message-bearer, some one asked, saying: "Is it because he has made progress?"

The Master said: "I have seen him sitting in a man's seat, seen him walking abreast of his elders. This shows no wish to improve, only hurry to be a man."

XV

[1] Ling, Duke of Wei, asked Confucius about the line of battle.

Confucius answered: "Of temple ware I have learned: arms I have not studied."

On the morrow he went his way.

In Ch'en grain ran out. His followers grew too ill to rise. Tzu-lu could not hide his vexation.

[8] An emperor of the house of Yin.

"Must gentlemen also face misery?" he said.

"Of course a gentleman must face misery," said the Master. "It goads the vulgar to violence."

[2] The Master said: "Dost thou not think, Tz'u,[1] that I am a man who learns much, and bears it in mind?"

"Yes," he answered: "is it not so?"

"No," said the Master. "I string all into one."

[3] The Master said: "Yu,[2] how few know what is worthy!"

[4] The Master said: "To rule doing nothing, that was Shun's way. What need to be doing? Self-respect and a kingly look are all."

[5] Tzu-chang asked how to get on.

The Master said: "Be faithful and true of word; let thy walk be plain and lowly: thou wilt get on, though in savage land. If thy words be not faithful and true, thy walk plain and lowly, wilt thou get on, though in thine own home? Standing, see these words ranged before thee; driving, see them written upon the yoke. Then thou wilt get on."

Tzu-chang wrote them upon his girdle.

[6] The Master said: "Straight indeed was the historian Yü! Straight as an arrow when right prevailed, and straight as an arrow when wrong prevailed! What a gentleman was Ch'ü Po-yü! When right prevailed he took office: when wrong prevailed he rolled himself up in thought."

[7] The Master said: "To keep silence to him who has ears to hear is to spill the man. To speak to a man without ears to hear is to spill thy words. Wisdom spills neither man nor word."

[8] The Master said: "A high will, or a loving heart, will not seek life at cost of love. To fulfil love they will kill the body."

[9] Tzu-kung asked how to practise love. The Master said: "A workman bent on good work will first sharpen his tools. In the land that is thy home, serve the best men in power, and get thee friends who love."

[10] Yen Yüan asked how to rule a kingdom.

The Master said: "Follow the Hsia seasons; drive in the chariot

[1] Tzu-kung.

[2] Tzu-lu: believed to have been said to him on the occasion mentioned above in xv. 1.

of Yin; wear the head-dress of Chou; choose for music the Shao and its dance. Banish the strains of Cheng, and shun men of glib tongue; for wanton are the strains of Cheng; there is danger in a glib tongue."

[11] The Master said: "Without thought for far off things, there will be troubles near at hand."

[12] The Master said: "It is finished! I have met no one who loves good as he loves women!"

[13] The Master said: "Did not Tsang Wen filch his post? He knew the worth of Liu-hsia Hui,[3] and did not stand by him."

[14] The Master said: "By asking much of self, and throwing little on others, ill feeling is put to flight."

[15] The Master said: "Unless a man ask, 'Will this help? will that help?' I know not how to help him."

[16] The Master said: "When all day long there is no talk of right, and sharp moves find favour, the company is in hard case."

[17] The Master said: "A gentleman makes right his base. Done with courtesy, spoken with deference, rounded with truth, right makes a gentleman."

[18] The Master said: "His unworthiness vexes a gentleman: to live unknown cannot vex him."

[19] The Master said: "A gentleman fears lest his name should die when life is done."

[20] The Master said: "A gentleman looks within: the vulgar look unto others."

[21] The Master said: "A gentleman is firm, not quarrelsome; a friend, not a partisan."

[22] The Master said: "A gentleman does not raise a man for his words, nor scorn what is said for the speaker."

[23] Tzu-kung asked: "Can one word cover the whole duty of man?"

[3] Another of these *seigneurs du temps jadis* who is more to us than a dim shadow, still living on in the pages of Mencius. There we learn that "He was not ashamed of a foul king, nor scorned a small post. He hid not his worth in office, but held his own way. Dismissal did not vex him; want did not make him sad. If thrown together with countrymen he felt so much at ease that he could not bear to leave them. 'Thou art thou,' he said, 'and I am I. Standing beside me with shoulders bare, or body naked, how canst thou defile me?' (V. B. 1). When pressed to stay, he stayed; for he set no store on going" (II. A. 9).

The Master said: "Fellow-feeling, perhaps. Do not do unto others what thou wouldst not they should do unto thee."

[24] The Master said: "Of the men that I meet, whom do I decry? whom do I flatter? Or if I flatter, it is after trial. Because of this people three lines of kings followed the straight road."

[25] The Master said: "Even in my time an historian would leave a blank in his text, an owner of a horse would lend him to others to ride. To-day it is so no more."

[26] The Master said: "Honeyed words confound goodness: impatience of trifles confounds great projects."

[27] The Master said: "The hatred of the many calls for search: the favour of the many calls for search."

[28] The Master said: "The man can exalt the truth: truth cannot exalt the man."

[29] The Master said: "The fault is to cleave to a fault."

[30] The Master said: "In vain have I spent in thought whole days without food, whole nights without sleep! Study is better."

[31] The Master said: "A gentleman aims at truth; he does not aim at food. Ploughing may end in famine; study may end in pay. But a gentleman pines for truth: he is not pined with poverty."

[32] The Master said: "What the mind has won will be lost again, unless love hold it fast. A mind to understand and love to hold fast, without dignity of bearing, will go unhonoured. A mind to understand, love to hold fast and dignity of bearing are incomplete, without courteous ways."

[33] The Master said: "A gentleman has no skill in trifles, but has strength for big tasks: the vulgar are skilled in trifles, but have no strength for big tasks."

[34] The Master said: "Love is more to the people than fire and water. I have known men come to their death by fire and water: I have met no man whom love brought unto death."

[35] The Master said: "When love is at stake yield not to an army."

[36] The Master said: "A gentleman is consistent, not changeless."

[37] The Master said: "A servant of the king honours work and rates pay last."

[38] The Master said: "All educated men are peers."

[39] The Master said: "Mingle not in projects with men whose ways are not thine."

[40] The Master said: "The whole end of speech is to be understood."

[41] When the music-master Mien was presented, the Master, on coming to the steps, said: "Here are the steps." On reaching the mat, the Master said: "Here is the mat." When all were seated, the Master told him: "Such an one is here, and such an one is here."

After the music-master had left, Tzu-chang said: "Is this the way to speak to a music-master?"

The Master said: "Surely it is the way to help a music-master."[4]

XVI

[1] The Chi was about to chastise Chuan-yü.[5]

Jan Yu and Chi-lu,[6] being received by Confucius, said to him: "The Chi is going to deal with Chuan-yü."

Confucius said: "After all, Ch'iu,[7] are ye not in the wrong? The kings of old made Chuan-yü lord of Tung Meng.[8] It is within the borders of the realm, moreover, and a vassal state. Ought it to be chastised?"

Jan Yu said: "Our lord wishes it. We, his ministers, are both against it."

Confucius said: "Ch'iu, Chou Jen was wont to say, 'Put forth thy strength in the ranks; leave them rather than do wrong.' Who would choose as guide one that is no prop in danger, who cannot lift him when fallen? Moreover, what thou sayest is wrong. If a tiger or a buffalo escape from the pen, if tortoiseshell or jade be broken in the case, who is to blame?"

Jan Yu said: "But Chuan-yü is strong, and close to Pi;[9] if not seized to-day, it will bring sorrow in after times on our sons and grandsons."

[4] The man being blind, like most musicians in the East.

[5] A small feudatory state of Lu.

[6] Tzu-lu. He and Jan Yu were at the time in the service of the Chi. [7] Jan Yu.

[8] A mountain in Chuan-yü. The ruler of that state, having received from the emperor the right to sacrifice to its mountains, had some measure of independence, though the state was feudatory to Lu, and within its borders.

[9] A town belonging to the Chi.

Confucius said: "To make excuses instead of saying 'I want it' is hateful, Ch'iu, to a gentleman. I have heard that unlikeness of lot grieves a king or a chief, not fewness of men. Unrest grieves him, not poverty. Had each his share there would be no poverty. In harmony is number: peace prevents a fall. So if far off tribes will not bend, win them by encouraging worth and learning; and when they come in, give them peace. But now, when far off tribes will not bend, ye two, helpers of your lord, cannot win them. The kingdom is rent asunder; ye are too weak to defend it. Yet spear and shield ye would call up through the land! The sorrows of Chi's grandsons, I fear, will not rise in Chuan-yü: they will rise within the palace wall."

[2] Confucius said: "When right prevails below heaven, courtesy, music and punitive wars flow from the Son of Heaven. When wrong prevails below heaven, courtesy, music, and punitive wars flow from the feudal princes. When they flow from the feudal princes they will rarely last for ten generations. When they flow from the princes' ministers they will rarely last for five generations. When courtiers sway a country's fate, they will rarely last for three generations. When right prevails below heaven power does not lie with ministers. When right prevails below heaven common men do not argue."

[3] Confucius said: "For five generations its income has passed from the ducal house;[10] for four generations power has lain with ministers: and humbled, therefore, are the sons and grandsons of the three Huan."

[4] Confucius said: "There are three friends that do good, and three friends that do harm. The friends that do good are a straight friend, a sincere friend, and a friend who has heard much. The friends that do harm are a smooth friend, a fawning friend, and a friend with a glib tongue."

[5] Confucius said: "There are three joys that do good, and three joys that do harm. The joys that do good are joy in dissecting courtesy and music, joy in speaking of the good in men, and joy in a number of worthy friends. The joys that do harm are joy in pomp, joy in roving, and joy in the joys of the feast."

[10] Of Lu.

[6] Confucius said: "Men who wait upon princes fall into three mistakes. To speak before the time has come is rashness. Not to speak when the time has come is secrecy. To speak heedless of looks is blindness."

[7] Confucius said: "A gentleman has three things to guard against. In the days of thy youth, ere thy strength is steady, beware of lust. When manhood is reached, in the fulness of strength, beware of strife. In old age, when thy strength is broken, beware of greed."

[8] Confucius said: "A gentleman holds three things in awe. He is in awe of Heaven's doom: he is in awe of great men: he is awed by the speech of the holy.

"The vulgar are blind to doom, and hold it not in awe. They are saucy towards the great, and of the speech of the holy they make their game."

[9] Confucius said: "The best men are born wise. Next come those who grow wise by learning: then, learned, narrow minds. Narrow minds, without learning, are the lowest of the people."

[10] Confucius said: "A gentleman has nine aims. To see clearly; to understand what he hears; to be warm in manner, dignified in bearing, faithful of speech, painstaking at work; to ask when in doubt; in anger to think of difficulties; in sight of gain to remember right."

[11] Confucius said: "In sight of good to be filled with longing; to regard evil as scalding to the touch: I have met such men, I have heard such words.

"To dwell apart and search the will; to unriddle truth by righteous life: I have heard these words, but met no such men."

[12] Ching, Duke of Ch'i, had a thousand teams of horses; but the people, on his death day, found nought in him to praise. Po-yi[11] and Shu-ch'i starved at the foot of Shou-yang, and men to-day still sound their praises.

Is not this the clue to that?

[13] Ch'en K'ang[12] asked Po-yü:[13] "Apart from us, have ye heard aught, Sir?"

He answered: "No. Once as I sped across the hall, where my father stood alone, he said to me: 'Dost thou study poetry?' I

[11] See note to v. 22. [12] The disciple Tzu-ch'in. [13] Confucius' son.

answered, 'No.' 'Who does not study poetry,' he said, 'has no hold on words.' I withdrew and studied poetry.

"Another day as I sped across the hall, where he stood alone, he said to me: 'Dost thou study courtesy?' I answered, 'No.' 'Who does not study courtesy,' he said, 'loses all foothold.' I withdrew and studied courtesy. These two things I have heard."

Ch'en K'ang withdrew and cried gladly: "I asked one thing and get three! I hear of poetry: I hear of courtesy: and I hear, too, that a gentleman keeps aloof from his son."

[14] A king speaks of his wife as "my lady." She calls herself "handmaid." Her subjects call her "our royal lady." Speaking to foreigners they say, "our little queen." Foreigners also call her "the royal lady."

XVII

[1] Yang Huo[1] wished to see Confucius. Confucius did not visit him. He sent Confucius a sucking pig. Confucius chose a time when he was out, and went to thank him. They met on the road.

He said to Confucius: "Come, let us speak together. To cherish a gem and undo the kingdom, is that love?"

"It is not," said Confucius.

"To be fond of power and let each chance of office slip, is that wisdom?"

"It is not," said Confucius.

"The days and months glide by; the years do not tarry for us."

"True," said Confucius; "I must take office."

[2] The Master said: "Men are near to each other at birth: the lives they lead sunder them."

[3] The Master said: "Only the wisest and the stupidest of men never change."

[4] As the Master drew near to Wu-ch'eng[2] he heard sounds of lute and song.

"Why use an ox-knife to kill a fowl?" said the Master, with a pleased smile.

Tzu-yu answered: "Master, I have heard you say of yore: 'A

[1] The all-powerful, unscrupulous minister of the Chi.

[2] A very small town, of which the disciple Tzu-yu was governor.

gentleman who has conned the truth will love mankind; poor folk who have conned the truth are easy to rule.' "

"My boys," said the Master, "Yen[3] is right. I spake before in play."

[5] Kung-shan Fu-jao[4] held Pi in rebellion. He summoned the Master, who fain would have gone.

Tzu-lu said in displeasure: "This cannot be. Why must ye go to Kung-shan?"

The Master said: "This lord summons me, and would that be all? Could I not make an Eastern Chou[5] of him that employed me?"

[6] Tzu-chang asked Confucius, What is love?

"Love," said Confucius, "is to mete out five things to all below heaven."

"May I ask what they are?"

"Modesty and bounty," said Confucius, "truth, earnestness, and kindness. Modesty escapes insult; bounty wins the many; truth gains men's trust; earnestness brings success; kindness is the key to men's work."

[7] Pi Hsi summoned the Master, who fain would have gone.

Tzu-lu said: "Master, I have heard you say of yore: 'When the man in touch with the soul does evil, a gentleman stands aloof.' Pi Hsi holds Chung-mou in rebellion: how, Sir, could ye join him?"

"Yes, I said so," answered the Master. "But is not a thing called hard that cannot be ground thin; white, if steeping will not turn it black? and am I a gourd? can I hang without eating?"

[8] The Master said: "Hast thou heard the six words, Yu,[6] or the six they sink into?"

He answered: "No."

"Sit down that I may tell thee. The thirst for love, without love of learning, sinks into fondness. Love of knowledge, without love of learning, sinks into presumption. Love of truth, without love of learning, sinks into cruelty. Love of uprightness, without love of learning, sinks into harshness. Love of courage, without love of learning, sinks into turbulence. Love of strength, without love of learning, sinks into oddity."

[3] Tzu-yu. [4] Steward of the Chi and a confederate of Yang Huo.

[5] A kingdom in the east to match Chou in the west, the home of Kings Wen and Wu. [6] Tzu-lu

[9] The Master said: "My boys, why do ye not study poetry? Poetry would ripen you; teach you insight, fellow-feeling, and forbearance; show you first your duty to your father, then your duty to the king; and would teach you the names of many birds and beasts, plants and trees."

[10] The Master said to Po-yü[7]: "Hast thou conned the Chou-nan[8] and Shao-nan?[8] Who has not conned the Chou-nan and Shao-nan is as a man standing with his face to the wall."

[11] The Master said: "'Courtesy, courtesy,' is the cry: but are jade and silk the whole of courtesy? 'Harmony, harmony,' is the cry: but are bells and drums the whole of harmony?"

[12] The Master said: "A fierce outside and a weak core, is it not like a paltry fellow, like a thief who crawls through a hole in the wall?"

[13] The Master said: "The bane of all things noble is the pattern citizen."

[14] The Master said: "To proclaim each truth, as soon as learned to the highwayside, is to lay waste the soul."

[15] The Master said: "How can one serve the king with a sordid colleague, itching to get what he wants, trembling to lose what he has? This trembling to lose what he has may lead him anywhere."

[16] The Master said: "Men of old had three failings, which have, perhaps, died out to-day. Ambitious men of old were not nice: ambitious men to-day are unprincipled. Masterful men of old were rough: masterful men to-day are quarrelsome. Simple men of old were straight: simple men to-day are false. That is all."

[17] The Master said: "Honeyed words and flattering looks seldom speak of love."

[18] The Master said: "I hate the ousting of scarlet by purple. I hate the strains of Cheng, confounders of sweet music. I hate a sharp tongue, the ruin of kingdom and home."

[19] The Master said: "I long for silence."

Tzu-kung said: "If ye, Sir, were silent, what would your disciples have to tell?"

The Master said: "Does Heaven speak? The seasons four revolve, and all things multiply. Does Heaven speak?"

[7] His son. [8] The first two books of the "Book of Poetry."

[20] Ju Pei wished to see Confucius. Confucius excused himself on the plea of sickness. As the messenger went out, Confucius took a lute and sang to it, so that he should hear.

[21] Tsai Wo[9] asked about the three years' mourning. He thought one enough.

"If for three years pomp is scouted by the gentry, will not courtesy suffer? If music stop for three years, will not music decay? The old grain vanishes, the new springs up; the round of woods for the fire-drill is ended in one year."

The Master said: "Feeding on rice, clad in brocade, couldst thou feel happy?"

"I could feel happy," he answered.

"Then do what makes thee happy. A gentleman, when in mourning, has no taste for sweets, no ear for music; he is unhappy in his home. And so he forsakes these things. But since thou art happy in them, keep them."

When Tsai Wo had left, the Master said: "A man without love! At the age of three a child first leaves his parents' arms, and three years is the time for mourning everywhere below heaven. But did Yü[10] enjoy for three years a father's and a mother's love?"

[22] The Master said: "Bad it is when a man eats his fill all day, and has nought to task the mind! Could he not play at chequers? Even that were better."

[23] Tzu-lu said: "Does a gentleman honour courage?"

The Master said: "Right comes first for a gentleman. Courage, without sense of right, makes rebels of the great, and robbers of the poor."

[24] Tzu-kung said: "Does a gentleman also hate?"

"He does," said the Master. "He hates the sounding of evil deeds; he hates men of low estate who slander their betters; he hates courage without courtesy; he hates daring matched with blindness."

"And Tz'u," [11] he added, "dost thou hate too?"

"I hate those who mistake spying for wisdom. I hate those who take want of deference for courage. I hate evil speaking, cloaked as honesty."

[9] A disciple. [10] Tsai Wo. [11] Tzu-kung.

[25] The Master said: "Only girls and servants are hard to train. Draw near to them, they grow unruly; hold them off, they pay you with spite."

[26] The Master said: "When a man of forty is hated, it will be so to the end."

XVIII

[1] THE lord of Wei[1] went into exile, the lord of Ch'i became a slave, Pi-kan[1] died for his reproofs.

Confucius said: "In three of the Yin there was love."

[2] When Liu-hsia Hui[2] was judge he was thrice dismissed.

Men said: "Why not leave, Sir?"

He answered: "Whither could I go and not be thrice dismissed for upright service? To do crooked service what need to leave the land of my forefathers?"

[3] Ching, Duke of Ch'i, speaking of how to treat Confucius, said: "I could not treat him as I do the Chi. I should set him between Chi and Meng."

Again he said: "I am old: I have no use for him."

Confucius went his way.

[4] Chi Huan accepted a gift of singing girls from the men of Ch'i.[3] For three days no court was held.

Confucius went his way.

[5] Chieh-yü, the mad-head of Ch'u, as he passed Confucius sang:—

"Phœnix, bright phœnix,
    Thy glory is ended!
Think of the future:
    The past can't be mended.
Up and away!
The court is to-day
    With danger attended."

Confucius alighted and fain would have spoken with him. But hurriedly he made off: no speech was to be had of him.

[1] Kinsman of Chou, the last tyrannical emperor of the house of Yin.

[2] See note to XV. 13.

[3] B.C. 497. The turning point in Confucius' career. Sorrowfully the Master left office and his native land and went forth to twelve years of wandering in exile.

[6] Ch'ang-chü and Chieh-ni were working together in the fields. Confucius, as he passed by, sent Tzu-lu to ask after a ford.

Ch'ang-chü said: "Who is that holding the reins?"

"K'ung Ch'iu,"[4] answered Tzu-lu.

"What, K'ung Ch'iu of Lu?"

"The same," said Tzu-lu.

"He knows the ford," said Ch'ang-chü.

Tzu-lu asked Chieh-ni.

"Who are ye, sir?" he answered.

"I am Chung Yu."

"The disciple of K'ung Ch'iu of Lu?"

"Yes," said Tzu-lu.

"The world is one seething torrent," answered Chieh-ni, "what man can guide it? Were it not better to choose a master who flees the world, than a master who flees this man and that man?"

And he went on hoeing without stop.

Tzu-lu went back and told the Master, whose face fell.

"Can I herd with birds and beasts?" he said. "Whom but these men can I choose as fellows? And if all were right with the world, I should have no call to set it straight."

[7] Tzu-lu having fallen behind met an old man bearing a basket on his staff.

Tzu-lu asked him: "Have ye seen the Master, Sir?"

The old man answered: "Thou dost not toil with thy limbs, nor canst thou tell one grain from another; who is thy Master?"

And planting his staff in the ground, he began weeding.

Tzu-lu bowed and stood before him.

He kept Tzu-lu for the night, killed a fowl, prepared millet, feasted him, and presented his two sons.

On the morrow Tzu-lu went to the Master, and told what had happened.

The Master said: "He is in hiding."

He sent Tzu-lu back to see him; but when he reached the house the man had left.

Tzu-lu said: "Not to take office is wrong. If the ties of old and young are binding, why should the claim of king on minister be

[4] Confucius.

set aside? Wishing to keep his person clean, he flouts a foremost duty. A gentleman takes office at the call of right, aware though he be, that the cause is lost."

[8] Po-yi, Shu-ch'i, Yü-chung, Yi-yi, Chu-chang, Liu-hsia Hui and Shao-lien were men who fled the world.

The Master said: "Po-yi[5] and Shu-ch'i would not bend the will, or shame the body.

"We can but say that Liu-hsia Hui[6] and Shao-lien bent the will and shamed the body. Their words jumped with duty; their deeds answered our hopes.

"We may say of Yü-chung and Yi-yi that they lived in hiding, but gave the rein to the tongue. They were clean in person: their retreat was timely.

"But I am unlike all of these: I know not 'must' or 'must not.' "

[9] Chih, the chief Musical Conductor, went to Ch'i; Kan, the Conductor at the second meal, went to Ch'u; Liao, the Conductor at the third meal, went to Ts'ai; Chüeh, the Conductor at the fourth meal, went to Ch'in. The drum master Fang-shu crossed the river; the tambourine master Wu crossed the Han; Yang, the assistant Bandmaster, and Hsiang, who played the sounding stones, crossed the sea.

[10] The Duke of Chou[7] said to the Duke of Lu:[8] "A prince does not forsake kinsmen, nor offend great vassals by neglect. He will not discard an old servant, unless he have big cause. He asks perfection of no man."

[11] Chou had eight officers: Po-ta and Po-kuo, Chung-tu and Chung-hu, Shu-yeh and Shu-hsia, Chi-sui and Chi-kua.

XIX

[1] Tzu-chang said: "The scholar who in danger will stake his life, who in sight of gain remembers right, who is lowly in heart at worship, and sad at heart when mourning, may pass muster."

[2] Tzu-chang said: "Goodness blindly clutched, faith that lacks simplicity, can they be said to be, or said not to be?"

[3] The disciples of Tzu-hsia asked Tzu-chang about friendship.

[5] See note to v. 22. [6] See note to xv. 13. [7] See note to vii. 5. [8] His son.

Tzu-chang said: "What does Tzu-hsia say?"

They answered: "Tzu-hsia says: 'Cling to worthy friends; push the unworthy away.'"

Tzu-chang said: "I was taught otherwise. A gentleman honours worth, and bears with the many. He applauds goodness, and pities weakness. Am I a man of great worth, what could I not bear with in men? Am I a man without worth, men will push me away. Why should I push others away?"

[4] Tzu-hsia said: "Though there is no trade without interest, a gentleman will not follow one, lest it clog the mind at length."

[5] Tzu-hsia said: "Who recalls each day what fails him, who each month forgets nothing won, he may indeed be called fond of learning!"

[6] Tzu-hsia said: "Through wide learning and singleness of aim, through keen questions and searchings of heart we come to love."

[7] Tzu-hsia said: "To learn their trade apprentices work in a shop: by study a gentleman reaches the truth."

[8] Tzu-hsia said: "The vulgar always gloss their faults."

[9] Tzu-hsia said: "A gentleman alters thrice. Seen from afar he looks stern: as we draw near, he thaws: but the sound of his words is sharp."

[10] Tzu-hsia said: "A gentleman lays no burdens on the people until they have learned to trust him. Unless they trusted him they would think him cruel. Until he is trusted he does not reprove. Unless he were trusted it would seem fault-finding."

[11] Tzu-hsia said: "If we keep within the bounds of honour, we may step to and fro through propriety."

[12] Tzu-yu said: "The disciples, the boys of Tzu-hsia, can sprinkle and sweep the floor, answer when spoken to, and enter or leave a room; but what can come of branches without root?"

When Tzu-hsia heard this, he said: "Yen Yu[1] is wrong. In training a gentleman, because we teach one thing first, shall we flag before reaching the next? Thus plants and trees vary in size. Should a gentleman's training bewilder him? To absorb it first and last none but the holy are fit."

[13] Tzu-hsia said: "Crown servants should use their spare

[1] Tzu-yu.

strength for study. A scholar with his spare strength should serve the crown."

[14] Tzu-yu said: "Mourning should stretch to grief, and stretch no further."

[15] Tzu-yu said: "My friend Chang[2] can do things that are hard, but he is void of love."

[16] Tseng-tzu said: "So magnificent is Chang that to do as love bids is hard when at his side."

[17] Tseng-tzu said: "I have heard the Master say: 'Man never shows what is in him unless when mourning one near to him.' "

[18] Tseng-tzu said: "I have heard the Master say: 'In all else we may rival the piety of Meng Chuang, but in not changing his father's ministers, or his father's rule, he is hard to rival.' "

[19] The Meng[3] made Yang Fu[4] criminal judge, who asked Tseng-tzu about his duties.

Tseng-tzu said: "The gentry have lost their way, and the people long been distraught. When thou dost get at the heart of a crime, be moved to pity, not puffed with joy."

[20] Tzu-kung said: "The wickedness of Chou[5] was not so great. Thus let princes beware of living in a sink, where the filth of the world all streams together!"

[21] Tzu-kung said: "The faults of a prince are like the darkening of sun or moon. The fault is seen of all, and when he breaks free all men admire."

[22] Kung-sun Ch'ao of Wei asked Tzu-kung: "Where did Chung-ni[6] get his learning?"

Tzu-kung said: "The lore of Wen and Wu has not fallen into ruin, but lives in men: the big in big men, the small in small men. No man is empty of the lore of Wen and Wu. How should the Master not learn it? What need had he for a set teacher?"

[23] Shu-sun Wu-shu,[7] talking to some lords at court, said: "Tzu-kung is a greater man than Chung-ni."[8]

Tzu-fu Ching-po told this to Tzu-kung.

Tzu-kung said: "This is like the palace and its wall. My wall reaches to the shoulder. Peeping over one sees the goodly home

[2] Tzu-chang. [3] The chief of the Meng clan, powerful in Lu.
[4] A disciple of Tseng-tzu. [5] The foul tyrant, last of the house of Yin.
[6] Confucius. [7] Head of the Meng clan. [8] Confucius.

within. The Master's wall is many fathoms high. Unless he enter the gate, no man can see the beauty of the Ancestral Temples, the wealth of the hundred officers. And if but few men gain the gate, is my lord not right to speak as he does?"

[24] Shu-sun Wu-shu decried Chung-ni.

Tzu-kung said: "It is labour lost. Chung-ni cannot be cried down. The greatness of other men is a mound that can be overleaped. Chung-ni is the sun or moon that no man can overleap. To run into death though a man were ready, how could he hurt the sun or moon? His want of sense would but show the better!"

[25] Ch'en Tzu-ch'in[9] said to Tzu-kung: "Sir, your humility is overdone. In what way is Chung-ni your better?"

Tzu-kung said: "By a word a gentleman betrays wisdom, by a word his want of wisdom. Words are not to be lightly spoken. None can come up to the Master, as heaven is not to be climbed by steps. Had the Master power in the land, the saying would come true: 'All that he plants takes root; whither he leads men follow. The peace he brings draws men; his touch tunes them to harmony: honored in life, he is mourned when dead.' Who can come up to him?"

XX

[1][1] Yao said: "Hail to thee, Shun! The number that the Heavens are telling falls on thee. Keep true hold of the golden mean. Should there be stress or want within the four seas, the gift of Heaven will pass for ever."

Shun laid the same commands on Yü.

T'ang said: "I, Thy child Li, make bold to offer this black steer, and make bold to proclaim before Thee, Almighty Lord, that I dare not forgive sin, nor hold down Thy servants. Search them, oh Lord, in Thine heart. Visit not my sins on the ten thousand hamlets: the sins of the ten thousand hamlets visit upon my head."

Chou bestowed great gifts, and good men grew rich.

[9] The disciple Tzu-ch'in.

[1] This chapter shows the principles on which China was governed in ancient days. Yao and Shun were the legendary founders of the Chinese Empire. Yü, T'ang, and Chou were the first emperors of the houses of Hsia, Shang, and Chou, which had ruled China up to the time of Confucius.

"Loving hearts are better than men that are near of kin. All the people throw the blame upon me alone."[2]

He attended to weights and measures, revised the laws, and restored broken officers. On all sides order reigned. He revived states that had perished, and gave back fiefs that had reverted. He called forth men from hiding. All hearts below heaven turned to him. The people's food, burials, and worship he held to be of moment. His bounty gained the many; his truth won the people's trust; his earnestness brought success; his justice made men glad.

[2] Tzu-chang asked Confucius: "How should men be governed?"

The Master said: "He who would govern men must honour the five graces, spurn the four vices."

Tzu-chang said: "What are the five graces?"

The Master said: "A gentleman is kind, but not wasteful; he burdens, but does not embitter; he is covetous, not sordid; high-minded, not proud; he inspires awe, and not fear."

Tzu-chang said: "What is meant by kindness without waste?"

The Master said: "To further what furthers the people, is not that kindness without waste? If burdens be sorted to strength, who will grumble? To covet love and win love, is that sordid? Few or many, small or great, all is one to a gentleman: he dare not slight any man. Is not this to be high-minded and not proud? A gentleman straightens his robe and settles his face. He is stern, and men look up to him with dread. Is not this to inspire awe, and not fear?"

Tzu-chang said: "What are the four vices?"

The Master said: "To leave untaught and then kill is cruelty: to ask full tale without warning is tyranny: to give careless orders, and be strict when the day comes is robbery: to be stingy in rewarding men is littleness."

[3] The Master said: "A man who is blind to doom can be no gentleman. Without a knowledge of courtesy we must want foothold. Without a knowledge of words there is no understanding men."

[2] Said by King Wu (Chou). The people blamed him for not dethroning at once the infamous tyrant Chou Hsin.

(HEBREW)

THE BOOK OF JOB

INTRODUCTORY NOTE

THE Book of Job is one of the great masterpieces, not only of Hebrew, but of all literature. The vividness of its pictures, the rapidity of its narrative, the poignancy of its lyric passages, the passionate boldness of its attack on one of the great universal problems of human life, all raise it to the level of the highest achievements in the literature of any tongue.

As a book, it is difficult to classify. Its prologue and epilogue are narrative prose; and though the poetical dialogue of the central part of the work at first suggests drama, there is no action portrayed in the speeches, and they are in themselves sometimes didactic and argumentative, often lyrical, hardly at all strictly dramatic. There can scarcely be any doubt that the author's main interest was in the solution of the problem suggested by the spectacle of the righteous man in distress.

Of the authorship, nothing is known. Moses, Solomon, Isaiah, Job himself, and many others have been suggested, but none of them on grounds worthy of consideration. It has been thought that the story of Job's experiences may have long existed in popular form; and that this old folk-tale may have been taken up by some unknown author who saw its possibilities, and who, with superb artistic power and a profound sense of the mystery of life, retold the incidents and added the elaborate speeches of Job, of his friends, and finally of the Almighty.

Job himself is pictured as belonging to patriarchal times, and living, not in Palestine, but in the land of Uz, probably to the east, on the borders of Arabia. The period of the author has been very variously conjectured, and may have been as late as 400 B. C.

The authenticity of several parts of the work has been disputed, the speech of Elihu especially being regarded by many modern scholars for various and weighty reasons as a later interpolation.

THE BOOK OF JOB

I

[1]
THERE was a man in the land of Uz, whose name was[1]
Job; and that man was perfect and upright, and one that
feared God, and turned away from evil. [2] And there
were born unto him seven sons and three daughters. [3] His[2] substance also was seven thousand sheep, and three thousand camels,
and five hundred yoke of oxen, and five hundred she-asses, and a
very great household; so that this man was the greatest of all the
children of the east. [4] And his sons went and held a feast in the
house of each one upon his day; and they sent and called for their
three sisters to eat and to drink with them. [5] And it was so, when
the days of their feasting were gone about, that Job sent and sanctified them, and rose up early in the morning, and offered burnt-offerings according to the number of them all: for Job said, It may be
that my sons have sinned, and renounced[3] God in their hearts. Thus
did Job continually.

[6] Now it came to pass on the day when the sons of God came
to present themselves before Jehovah, that Satan[4] also came among
them. [7] And Jehovah said unto Satan, Whence comest thou?
Then Satan answered Jehovah, and said, From going to and fro in
the earth, and from walking up and down in it. [8] And Jehovah
said unto Satan, Hast thou considered my servant Job? for[5] there is
none like him in the earth, a perfect and an upright man, one that
feareth God, and turneth away from evil. [9] Then Satan answered
Jehovah, and said, Doth Job fear God for nought? [10] Hast not
thou made a hedge about him, and about his house, and about all
that he hath, on every side? thou hast blessed the work of his hands,
and his substance is increased in the land. [11] But put forth thy

[1] Heb. *Iyob.* [2] Or, *cattle.* [3] Or, *blasphemed.* So ver. 11; ch. 2. 5, 9.
[4] That is, *the Adversary.* [5] Or, *that.*

hand now, and touch all that he hath, and he will renounce thee to thy face. [12] And Jehovah said unto Satan, Behold, all that he hath is in thy power;[6] only upon himself put not forth thy hand. So Satan went forth from the presence of Jehovah.

[13] And it fell on a day when his sons and his daughters were eating and drinking wine in their eldest brother's house, [14] that there came a messenger unto Job, and said, The oxen were plowing, and the asses feeding beside them; [15] and the[7] Sabeans fell *upon them,* and took them away: yea, they have slain the servants[8] with the edge of the sword; and I only am escaped alone to tell thee. [16] While he was yet speaking, there came also another, and said, The fire of God is fallen from heaven, and hath burned up the sheep and the servants,[8] and consumed them; and I only am escaped alone to tell thee. [17] While he was yet speaking, there came also another, and said, The Chaldeans made three bands, and fell[9] upon the camels, and have taken them away, yea, and slain the servants[8] with the edge of the sword; and I only am escaped alone to tell thee. [18] While he was yet speaking, there came also another, and said, Thy sons and thy daughters were eating and drinking wine in their eldest brother's house; [19] and, behold, there came a great wind from[10] the wilderness, and smote the four corners of the house, and it fell upon the young men, and they are dead; and I only am escaped alone to tell thee.

[20] Then Job arose, and rent his robe, and shaved his head, and fell down upon the ground, and worshipped; [21] and he said, Naked came I out of my mother's womb, and naked shall I return thither: Jehovah gave, and Jehovah hath taken away; blessed be the name of Jehovah. [22] In all this Job sinned not, nor charged[11] God foolishly.

II

[1] Again it came to pass on the day when the sons of God came to present themselves before Jehovah, that Satan came also among them to present himself before Jehovah. [2] And Jehovah said unto Satan, From whence comest thou? And Satan answered Jehovah,

[6] Heb. *hand.* [7] Heb. *Sheba.* [8] Heb. *young men.* [9] Or, *made a raid.* [10] Or, *over.* [11] Or, *attributed folly to God.*

and said, From going to and fro in the earth, and from walking up and down in it. [3] And Jehovah said unto Satan, Hast thou considered my servant Job? for[1] there is none like him in the earth, a perfect and an upright man, one that feareth God, and turneth away from evil: and he still holdeth fast his integrity, although thou movedst me against him, to[2] destroy him without cause. [4] And Satan answered Jehovah, and said, Skin for skin, yea, all that a man hath will he give for his life. [5] But put forth thy hand now, and touch his bone and his flesh, and he will renounce thee to thy face. [6] And Jehovah said unto Satan, Behold, he is in thy hand; only spare his life.

[7] So Satan went forth from the presence of Jehovah, and smote Job with sore boils from the sole of his foot unto his crown. [8] And he took him a potsherd to scrape himself therewith; and he sat among the ashes. [9] Then said his wife unto him, Dost thou still hold fast thine integrity? renounce God, and die. [10] But he said unto her, Thou speakest as one of the foolish[3] women speaketh. What? shall we receive good at the hand of God, and shall we not receive evil? In all this did not Job sin with his lips.

[11] Now when Job's three friends heard of all this evil that was come upon him, they came every one from his own place: Eliphaz the Temanite, and Bildad the Shuhite, and Zophar the Naamathite; and they made an appointment together to come to bemoan him and to comfort him. [12] And when they lifted up their eyes afar off, and knew him not, they lifted up their voice, and wept; and they rent every one his robe, and sprinkled dust upon their heads toward heaven. [13] So they sat down with him upon the ground seven days and seven nights, and none spake a word unto him: for they saw that his grief[4] was very great.

III

[1] After this opened Job his mouth, and cursed his day.
[2] And Job answered and said:
[3] Let the day perish wherein I was born,
And the night which said, There is a man-child conceived.

[1] Or, *that*. [2] Heb. *to swallow him up*. [3] Or, *impious*. [4] Or, *pain*.

[4] Let that day be darkness;
Let not God from above seek for it,
Neither let the light shine upon it.
[5] Let darkness and the[1] shadow of death claim it for their own;
Let a cloud dwell upon it;
Let all that maketh black the day terrify it.
[6] As for that night, let thick darkness seize upon it:
Let it not rejoice among the days of the year;
Let it not come into the number of the months.
[7] Lo, let that night be barren;[2]
Let no joyful voice come therein.
[8] Let them curse it that curse the day,
Who are ready[3] to rouse up leviathan.
[9] Let the stars of the twilight thereof be dark:
Let it look for light, but have none;
Neither let it behold the eyelids of the morning:
[10] Because it shut not up the doors of my *mother's* womb,
Nor hid trouble from mine eyes.
[11] Why died I not from the womb?
Why did I not give up the ghost when my mother bare me?
[12] Why did the knees receive me?
Or why the breasts, that I should suck?
[13] For now should I have lain down and been quiet;
I should have slept; then had I been at rest,
[14] With kings and counsellors of the earth,
Who built[4] up waste places for themselves;
[15] Or with princes that had gold,
Who filled their houses with silver:
[16] Or as a hidden untimely birth I had not been;
As infants that never saw light.
[17] There the wicked cease from troubling;[5]
And there the weary are at rest.
[18] There the prisoners are at ease together;
They hear not the voice of the taskmaster.

[1] Or, *deep darkness* (and so elsewhere).
[2] Or, *solitary.* [3] Or, *skilful.* [4] Or, *built solitary piles.* [5] Or, *raging.*

[19] The small and the great are there;
And the servant is free from his master.

[20] Wherefore is light given to him that is in misery,
And life unto the bitter in soul;
[21] Who long[6] for death, but it cometh not,
And dig for it more than for hid treasures;
[22] Who rejoice exceedingly,[7]
And are glad, when they can find the grave?
[23] *Why is light given* to a man whose way is hid,
And whom God hath hedged in?
[24] For my sighing cometh before[8] I eat,
And my groanings[9] are poured out like water.
[25] For the[10] thing which I fear cometh upon me,
And that which I am afraid of cometh unto me.
[26] I am[11] not at ease, neither am I quiet, neither have I rest;
But trouble cometh.

IV

[1] Then answered Eliphaz the Temanite, and said,
[2] If one assay to commune with thee, wilt thou be grieved?
But who can withhold himself from speaking?
[3] Behold, thou hast instructed many,
And thou hast strengthened the weak hands.
[4] Thy words have upholden him that was falling,
And thou hast made firm the feeble[1] knees.
[5] But now it is come unto thee, and thou[2] faintest;
It toucheth thee, and thou art troubled.
[6] Is not thy fear *of God* thy confidence,
And the integrity of thy ways thy hope?
[7] Remember, I pray thee, who *ever* perished, being innocent?
Or where were the upright cut off?
[8] According as I have seen, they that plow iniquity,
And sow trouble,[3] reap the same.

[6] Heb. *wait.* [7] Or, *unto exultation.* [8] Or, *like my food.*
[9] Heb. *roarings.* [10] Or, *the thing which I feared is come, &c.*
[11] Or, *was not at ease . . . yet trouble came.*
[1] Heb. *bowing.* [2] Or, *art grieved.* [3] Or, *mischief.*

[9] By the breath of God they perish,
And by the blast of his anger are they consumed.
[10] The roaring of the lion, and the voice of the fierce lion,
And the teeth of the young lions, are broken.
[11] The old lion perisheth for lack of prey,
And the whelps of the lioness are scattered abroad.

[12] Now a thing was secretly[4] brought to me,
And mine ear received a whisper thereof.
[13] In thoughts from the visions of the night,
When deep sleep falleth on men,
[14] Fear came upon me, and trembling,
Which made all my bones to shake.
[15] Then a[5] spirit passed before my face;
The hair of my flesh stood up.
[16] It stood still, but I could not discern the appearance thereof;
A form was before mine eyes:
There[6] *was* silence, and I heard a voice, *saying,*
[17] Shall mortal man be[7] more just than God?
Shall a man be[8] more pure than his Maker?
[18] Behold, he putteth no trust in his servants;
And his angels he chargeth with folly:
[19] How much more them that dwell in houses of clay,
Whose foundation is in the dust,
Who are crushed before[9] the moth!
[20] Betwixt[10] morning and evening they are destroyed:[11]
They perish for ever without any regarding it.
[21] Is[12] not their tent-cord plucked up within them?
They die, and that without wisdom.

V

[1] CALL now; is there any that will answer thee?
And to which of the holy ones wilt thou turn?

[4] Heb. *brought by stealth.* [5] Or, *a breath passed over.*
[6] Or, *I heard a still voice.* [7] Or, *be just before God.*
[8] Or, *be pure before his Maker.* [9] Or, *like.*
[10] Or, *From morning to evening.* [11] Heb. *broken in pieces.*
[12] Or, *Is not their excellency which is in them removed?*

[2] For vexation killeth the foolish man,
And jealousy[1] slayeth the silly one.
[3] I have seen the foolish taking root:
But suddenly I cursed his habitation.
[4] His children are far from safety,
And they are crushed in the gate,
Neither is there any to deliver them:
[5] Whose harvest the hungry eateth up,
And taketh it even out of the thorns;
And the[2] snare gapeth for their substance.
[6] For affliction[3] cometh not forth from the dust,
Neither doth trouble spring out of the ground;
[7] But man is born unto trouble,
As the[4] sparks fly upward.

[8] But as for me, I would seek unto God,
And unto God would I commit my cause;
[9] Who doeth great things and unsearchable,
Marvellous things without number:
[10] Who giveth rain upon the earth,
And sendeth waters upon the fields;
[11] So that he setteth up on high those that are low,
And those that mourn are exalted to safety.
[12] He frustrateth the devices of the crafty,
So that their hands cannot[5] perform their enterprise.
[13] He taketh the wise in their own craftiness;
And the counsel of the cunning is carried headlong:
[14] They meet with darkness in the day-time,
And grope at noonday as in the night.
[15] But he saveth from the sword of[6] their mouth,
Even the needy from the hand of the mighty.
[16] So the poor hath hope,
And iniquity stoppeth her mouth.

[17] Behold, happy is the man whom God correcteth:[7]

[1] Or, *indignation.* [2] Acc. to Vulg., *the thirsty swallow up.*
[3] Or, *iniquity.* See ch. 4. 8. [4] Heb. *the sons of flame* (or, *of lightning*).
[5] Or, *can perform nothing of worth.* [6] Heb. *out of their mouth.*
[7] Or, *reproveth.*

Therefore despise not thou the chastening of the Almighty.
[18] For he maketh sore, and bindeth up;
He woundeth, and his hands make whole.
[19] He will deliver thee in six troubles;
Yea, in seven there shall no evil touch thee.
[20] In famine he will redeem thee from death;
And in war from the power of the sword.
[21] Thou shalt be hid from the scourge of the tongue;
Neither shalt thou be afraid of destruction when it cometh.
[22] At destruction and dearth thou shalt laugh;
Neither shalt thou be afraid of the beasts of the earth.
[23] For thou shalt be in league with the stones of the field;
And the beasts of the field shall be at peace with thee.
[24] And thou shalt know that thy tent is in peace;
And thou shalt visit thy fold,[8] and shalt[9] miss nothing.
[25] Thou shalt know also that thy seed shall be great,
And thine offspring as the grass of the earth.
[26] Thou shalt come to thy grave in a full age,
Like as a shock of grain cometh in in its season.
[27] Lo this, we have searched it, so it is;
Hear it, and know thou it for[10] thy good.

VI

[1] THEN Job answered and said,
[2] Oh that my vexation were but weighed,
And all my calamity laid in the balances!
[3] For now it would be heavier than the sand of the seas:
Therefore have my words been rash.
[4] For the arrows of the Almighty are within me,
The poison whereof my spirit drinketh up:
The terrors of God do set themselves in array against me.
[5] Doth the wild ass bray when he hath grass?
Or loweth the ox over his fodder?
[6] Can that which hath no savor be eaten without salt?
Or is there any taste in the[1] white of an egg?

[8] Or, *habitation.* [9] Or, *shalt not err.* [10] Heb. *for thyself.*
[1] Or, *the juice of purslain.*

[7] My[2] soul refuseth to touch *them;*
They are as loathsome food to me.

[8] Oh that I might have my request;
And that God would grant *me* the thing that I long for!
[9] Even that it would please God to crush me;
That he would let loose his hand, and cut me off!
[10] And be it still my consolation,
Yea,[3] let me exult[4] in pain that[5] spareth not,
That I have not denied[6] the words of the Holy One.
[11] What is my strength, that I should wait?
And what is mine end, that I should be patient?
[12] Is my strength the strength of stones?
Or is my flesh of brass?
[13] Is it not that I have no help in me,
And that wisdom is driven quite from me?

[14] To him that is ready to faint kindness *should be showed* from his friend;
Even[7] to him that forsaketh the fear of the Almighty.
[15] My brethren have dealt deceitfully as a brook,
As the channel of brooks that pass away;
[16] Which are black by reason of the ice,
And wherein the snow hideth itself:
[17] What time they wax[8] warm, they vanish;
When it is hot, they are consumed out of their place.
[18] The[9] caravans *that travel* by the way of them turn aside;
They go up into the waste, and perish.
[19] The caravans of Tema looked,
The companies of Sheba waited for them.
[20] They were put to shame because they had hoped;
They came thither, and were confounded.
[21] For now ye are[10] nothing;
Ye see a terror, and are afraid.

[2] Or, What things *my soul refused to touch, these are as my loathsome food.*
[3] Or, *Though I shrink back.* [4] Or, *harden myself.* [5] Or, *though he spare not.*
[6] Or, *concealed.* [7] Or, *Else might he forsake.* Or, *But he forsaketh.* [8] Or, *shrink.*
[9] Or, *The paths of their way are turned aside.* [10] Another reading is, *are* like *thereto.*

[22] Did I say, Give unto me?
Or, Offer a present for me of your substance?
[23] Or, Deliver me from the adversary's hand?
Or, Redeem me from the hand of the oppressors?

[24] Teach me, and I will hold my peace;
And cause me to understand wherein I have erred.
[25] How forcible are words of uprightness!
But your reproof, what doth it reprove?
[26] Do ye think to reprove words,
Seeing that the speeches of one that is desperate are as[11] wind?
[27] Yea, ye would cast *lots* upon the fatherless,
And make merchandise of your friend.
[28] Now therefore be pleased to look upon me;
For[12] surely I shall not lie to your face.
[29] Return, I pray you, let there be no injustice;
Yea, return again, my[13] cause is righteous.
[30] Is there injustice on my tongue?
Cannot my taste discern mischievous things?

VII

[1] Is there not a warfare[1] to man upon earth?
And are not his days like the days of a hireling?
[2] As a servant that earnestly desireth the shadow,
And as a hireling that looketh for his wages:
[3] So am I made to possess months of misery,
And wearisome nights are appointed to me.
[4] When I lie down, I say,
When shall I arise, and the night be gone?
And I am full of tossings to and fro unto the dawning of the day.
[5] My flesh is clothed with worms and clods of dust;
My skin closeth[2] up, and breaketh out afresh.
[6] My days are swifter than a weaver's shuttle,
And are spent without hope.

[11] Or, *for the wind.* [12] Or, *And it will be evident unto you if I lie.*
[13] Heb. *my righteousness is in it.* [1] Or, *time of service.*
[2] Or, *is broken and become loathsome.*

[7] Oh remember that my life is a breath:
Mine eye shall no more see good.
[8] The eye of him that seeth me shall behold me no more;
Thine eyes shall be upon me, but I shall not be.
[9] As the cloud is consumed and vanisheth away,
So he that goeth down to Sheol shall come up no more.
[10] He shall return no more to his house,
Neither shall his place know him any more.

[11] Therefore I will not refrain my mouth;
I will speak in the anguish of my spirit;
I will complain in the bitterness of my soul.
[12] Am I a sea, or a sea-monster,
That thou settest a watch over me?
[13] When I say, My bed shall comfort me,
My couch shall ease my complaint;
[14] Then thou scarest me with dreams,
And terrifiest me through visions:
[15] So that my soul chooseth strangling,
And death rather than *these* my bones.
[16] I[3] loathe *my life;* I would[4] not live alway:
Let me alone; for my days are vanity.[5]
[17] What is man, that thou shouldest magnify him,
And that thou shouldest set thy mind upon him,
[18] And that thou shouldest visit him every morning,
And try him every moment?
[19] How long wilt thou not look away from me,
Nor let me alone till I swallow down my spittle?
[20] If I have sinned, what do[6] I unto thee, O thou watcher[7] of men?
Why hast thou set me as a mark for thee,
So that I am a burden to myself?
[21] And why dost thou not pardon my transgression, and take away mine iniquity?
For now shall I lie down in the dust;
And thou wilt seek me diligently, but I shall not be.

[3] Or, *I waste away.* [4] Or, *shall*
[5] Or, *as a breath.* [6] Or, *can I do.* [7] Or, *preserver.*

VIII

[1] THEN answered Bildad the Shuhite, and said,
[2] How long wilt thou speak these things?
And *how long* shall the words of thy mouth be *like* a mighty wind?
[3] Doth God pervert justice?
Or doth the Almighty pervert righteousness?
[4] If[1] thy children have sinned against him,
And he hath delivered them into the hand of their transgression;
[5] If thou wouldest seek diligently unto God,
And make thy supplication to the Almighty;
[6] If thou wert pure and upright:
Surely now he would awake for thee,
And make the habitation of thy righteousness prosperous.
[7] And though thy beginning was small,
Yet thy latter end would greatly increase.

[8] For inquire, I pray thee, of the former age,
And apply thyself to that which their fathers have searched out:
[9] (For we are but of yesterday, and know nothing,
Because our days upon earth are a shadow:)
[10] Shall not they teach thee, and tell thee.
And utter words out of their heart?

[11] Can the rush[2] grow up without mire?
Can the flag[3] grow without water?
[12] Whilst it is yet in its greenness, *and* not cut down,
It withereth before any *other* herb.
[13] So are the paths of all that forget God;
And the hope of the godless man shall perish:
[14] Whose confidence shall break[4] in sunder,
And whose trust is a spider's web.[5]
[15] He shall lean upon his house, but it shall not stand:
He shall hold fast thereby, but it shall not endure.

[1] Or, *If thy children sinned . . . he delivered &c.* [2] Or, *papyrus.*
[3] Or, *reed-grass.* [4] Or, *be cut off.* [5] Heb. *house.*

[16] He is green before the sun,
And his shoots go forth over his garden.
[17] His roots are wrapped about[6] the *stone*-heap,
He beholdeth the place of stones.
[18] If he be destroyed from his place,
Then it shall deny him, *saying,* I have not seen thee.
[19] Behold, this is the joy of his way;
And out of the earth[7] shall others spring.
[20] Behold, God will not cast away a perfect man,
Neither will he uphold the evil-doers.
[21] He[8] will yet fill thy mouth with laughter,
And thy lips with shouting.
[22] They that hate thee shall be clothed with shame;
And the tent of the wicked shall be no more.

IX

[1] THEN Job answered and said,
[2] Of a truth I know that it is so:
But[1] how can man be just with[2] God?
[3] If[3] he be pleased to contend with him,
He cannot answer him one of a thousand.
[4] *He is* wise in heart, and mighty in strength:
Who hath hardened himself against him, and prospered?—
[5] *Him* that removeth the mountains, and they know it not,
When he overturneth them in his anger;
[6] That shaketh the earth out of its place,
And the pillars thereof tremble;
[7] That commandeth the sun, and it riseth not,
And sealeth up the stars;
[8] That alone stretcheth out the heavens,
And treadeth upon the waves[4] of the sea;
[9] That maketh the Bear, Orion, and the Pleiades,
And the chambers of the south;
[10] That doeth great things past finding out,
Yea, marvellous things without number.

[6] Or, *beside the spring.* [7] Or, *dust.*
[8] Or, *Till he fill.* [1] Or, *For.* [2] Or, *before.* [3] Or, *If one should desire . . . he could not &c.* [4] Heb. *high places.*

[11] Lo, he goeth by me, and I see him not:
He passeth on also, but I perceive him not.
[12] Behold, he seizeth *the prey,* who can hinder[5] him?
Who will say unto him, What doest thou?
[13] God will not withdraw his anger;
The helpers of Rahab[6] do[7] stoop under him.
[14] How much less shall I answer him,
And choose out my words *to reason* with him?
[15] Whom, though I were righteous, yet would I not answer;
I would make supplication to my judge.
[16] If I had called, and he had answered me,
Yet would I not believe that he hearkened unto my voice.
[17] For[8] he breaketh me with a tempest,
And multiplieth my wounds without cause.
[18] He will not suffer me to take my breath,
But filleth me with bitterness.
[19] If *we speak* of strength, lo,[9] *he is* mighty!
And if of justice, Who, *saith he,* will summon me?
[20] Though I be righteous, mine own mouth shall condemn me:
Though I be perfect, it[10] shall prove me perverse.
[21] I[11] am perfect; I regard not myself;
I despise my life.
[22] It is all one; therefore I say,
He destroyeth the perfect and the wicked.
[23] If the scourge slay suddenly,
He will mock at the trial[12] of the innocent.
[24] The earth is given into the hands of the wicked;
He covereth the faces of the judges thereof:
If *it be* not *he,* who then is it?

[25] Now my days are swifter than a post:[13]
They flee away, they see no good.
[26] They are passed away as the swift[14] ships;
As the eagle that swoopeth on the prey.

[5] Or, *turn him back.* [6] Or, *arrogancy.* See Is. 30. 7. [7] Or, *did.* [8] Heb. *He who.*
[9] Or, *Lo,* here am I, saith he; *and if of justice, Who &c.* [10] Or, *he.*
[11] Or, *Though I be perfect, I will not regard &c.* [12] Or, *calamity.*
[13] Or, *runner.* [14] Heb. *ships of reed.*

[27] If I say, I will forget my complaint,
I will put off my *sad* countenance, and be[15] of good cheer;
[28] I am afraid of all my sorrows,
I know that thou wilt not hold me innocent.
[29] I shall be condemned;
Why then do I labor in vain?
[30] If I wash myself with[16] snow water,
And make[17] my hands never so clean;
[31] Yet wilt thou plunge me in the ditch,
And mine own clothes shall abhor me.
[32] For he is not a man, as I am, that I should answer him,
That we should come together in judgment.
[33] There is no umpire betwixt us,
That might lay his hand upon us both.
[34] Let him take his rod away from me,
And let not his terror make me afraid:
[35] Then would I speak, and not fear him;
For I am not so in myself.

X

[1] My soul is weary of my life;
I will give free course to my complaint;
I will speak in the bitterness of my soul.
[2] I will say unto God, Do not condemn me;
Show me wherefore thou contendest with me.
[3] Is it good unto thee that thou shouldest oppress,
That thou shouldest despise the work[1] of thy hands,
And shine upon the counsel of the wicked?
[4] Hast thou eyes of flesh?
Or seest thou as man seeth?
[5] Are thy days as the days of man,
Or thy years as man's days,
[6] That thou inquirest after mine iniquity,
And searchest after my sin,

15 Heb. *brighten up.* 16 Another reading is, *with snow.* 17 Heb. *cleanse my hands with lye.* 1 Heb. *labor.*

[7] Although thou knowest that I am not wicked,
And there is none that can deliver out of thy hand?

[8] Thy hands have framed me and fashioned me
Together round about; yet thou dost destroy me.
[9] Remember, I beseech thee, that thou hast fashioned me as clay;
And wilt thou bring me into dust again?
[10] Hast thou not poured me out as milk,
And curdled me like cheese?
[11] Thou hast clothed me with skin and flesh,
And knit me together with bones and sinews.
[12] Thou hast granted me life and lovingkindness;
And thy visitation[2] hath preserved my spirit.
[13] Yet these things thou didst hide in thy heart;
I know that this is with thee:
[14] If I sin, then thou markest me,
And thou wilt not acquit me from mine iniquity.
[15] If I be wicked, woe unto me;
And if I be righteous, yet shall I not lift up my head;
Being[3] filled with ignominy,
And looking upon mine affliction.
[16] And if *my head* exalt itself, thou huntest me as a lion;
And again thou showest thyself marvellous upon me.
[17] Thou renewest thy witnesses against me,
And increasest thine indignation upon me:
Changes[4] and warfare are with me.

[18] Wherefore then hast thou brought me forth out of the womb?
I had given up the ghost, and no eye had seen me.
[19] I should have been as though I had not been;
I should have been carried from the womb to the grave.
[20] Are not my days few? cease[5] then,
And let me alone, that I may take[6] comfort a little,
[21] Before I go whence I shall not return,
Even to the land of darkness and of the shadow of death;

[2] Or, *care.* [3] Or, *I am filled with ignominy, but look thou . . . for it increaseth: thou &c.* [4] Or, *Host after host is against me.*
[5] Another reading is, *let him cease, and leave me alone.* [6] Heb. *brighten up.*

[22] The land dark as midnight;[7]
The land of the shadow of death, without any order,
And where the light is as midnight.[7]

XI

[1] THEN answered Zophar the Naamathite, and said,
[2] Should not the multitude of words be answered?
And should a man full of talk be justified?
[3] Should thy boastings make men hold their peace?
And when thou mockest, shall no man make thee ashamed?
[4] For thou sayest, My doctrine is pure,
And I am clean in thine eyes.
[5] But oh that God would speak,
And open his lips against thee,
[6] And that he would show thee the secrets of wisdom!
For he is manifold in understanding.
Know therefore that God exacteth[1] of thee less than thine iniquity deserveth.

[7] Canst[2] thou by searching find out God?
Canst thou find out the Almighty unto perfection?
[8] It[3] is high as heaven; what canst thou do?
Deeper than Sheol; what canst thou know?
[9] The measure thereof is longer than the earth,
And broader than the sea.
[10] If he pass through, and shut up,
And call[4] unto judgment, then who can hinder him?
[11] For he knoweth false men:
He seeth iniquity also, even[5] though he consider it not.
[12] But[6] vain man is void of understanding,
Yea, man is born *as* a wild ass's colt.

[7] Heb. *thick darkness.*
[1] Or, *remitteth* (Heb. *causeth to be forgotten*) *unto thee of thine iniquity.*
[2] Or, *Canst thou find out the deep things of God?*
[3] Heb. *The heights of heaven.* [4] Heb. *call an assembly.*
[5] Or, *and him that considereth not.*
[6] Or, *But an empty man will get understanding, when a wild ass's colt is born a man.*

[13] If thou set thy heart aright,
And stretch out thy hands toward him;
[14] If iniquity be in thy hand, put it far away,
And let not unrighteousness dwell in thy tents.
[15] Surely then shalt thou lift up thy face without spot;
Yea, thou shalt be stedfast, and shalt not fear:
[16] For thou shalt forget thy misery.
Thou shalt remember it as waters that are passed away.
[17] And *thy* life shall be[7] clearer than the noonday;
Though there be darkness, it shall be as the morning.
[18] And thou shalt be secure, because there is hope;
Yea, thou shalt search *about thee,* and shalt take thy rest in safety.
[19] Also thou shalt lie down, and none shall make thee afraid;
Yea, many shall make suit unto thee.
[20] But the eyes of the wicked shall fail,
And they[8] shall have no way to flee;
And their hope shall be the giving up of the ghost.

XII

[1] THEN Job answered and said,
[2] No doubt but ye are the people,
And wisdom shall die with you.
[3] But I have understanding as well as you;
I am not inferior to you:
Yea, who knoweth not such things as these?
[4] I am as one that is a laughing-stock to his neighbor,
I who called upon God, and he answered:
The just, the perfect man is a laughing-stock.
[5] In the thought of him that is at ease there is contempt for misfortune;
It is ready for them whose foot slippeth.
[6] The tents of robbers prosper,
And they that provoke God are secure;
Into[1] whose hand God bringeth *abundantly.*

[7] Or, *arise above.* [8] Heb. *refuge is perished from them.*
[1] Or, *That bring* their *god in their hand.*

[7] But ask now the beasts, and they shall teach thee;
And the birds of the heavens, and they shall tell thee:
[8] Or speak to the earth, and it shall teach thee;
And the fishes of the sea shall declare unto thee.
[9] Who knoweth not in[2] all these,
That the hand of Jehovah hath wrought this,
[10] In whose hand is the soul of every living thing,
And the breath[3] of all mankind?
[11] Doth not the ear try words,
Even as the palate tasteth its food?
[12] With[4] aged men is wisdom,
And in length of days understanding.

[13] With *God*[5] is wisdom and might;
He hath counsel and understanding.
[14] Behold, he breaketh down, and it cannot be built again;
He shutteth up a man, and there can be no opening.
[15] Behold, he withholdeth the waters, and they dry up;
Again, he sendeth them out, and they overturn the earth.
[16] With him is strength and wisdom;
The deceived and the deceiver are his.
[17] He leadeth counsellors away stripped,
And judges maketh he fools.
[18] He looseth the bond of kings,
And bindeth their loins with a girdle.
[19] He leadeth priests away stripped,
And overthroweth the mighty.
[20] He removeth the speech of the trusty,
And taketh away the understanding of the elders.
[21] He poureth contempt upon princes,
And looseth the belt of the strong.
[22] He uncovereth deep things out of darkness,
And bringeth out to light the shadow of death.
[23] He increaseth the nations, and he destroyeth them:
He enlargeth the nations, and he leadeth them captive.

[2] Or, *by*. [3] Or, *spirit*. [4] Or, *With aged men*, ye say, *is wisdom*.
[5] Heb. *him*.

[24] He taketh away understanding from the chiefs of the people of the earth,[6]
And causeth them to wander in a wilderness where there is no way.
[25] They grope in the dark without light;
And he maketh them to stagger[7] like a drunken man.

XIII

[1] Lo, mine eye hath seen all *this,*
Mine ear hath heard and understood it.
[2] What ye know, *the same* do I know also:
I am not inferior unto you.

[3] Surely I would speak to the Almighty,
And I desire to reason with God.
[4] But ye are forgers of lies;
Ye are all physicians of no value.
[5] Oh that ye would altogether hold your peace!
And it would be your wisdom.
[6] Hear now my reasoning,
And hearken to the pleadings of my lips.
[7] Will ye speak unrighteously for God,
And talk deceitfully for him?
[8] Will ye show partiality to him?
Will ye contend for God?
[9] Is it good that he should search you out?
Or as one deceiveth[1] a man, will ye deceive[2] him?
[10] He will surely reprove you,
If ye do secretly show partiality.
[11] Shall not his majesty make you afraid,
And his dread fall upon you?
[12] Your memorable sayings are proverbs of ashes,
Your defences are defences of clay.

[13] Hold your peace, let me alone, that I may speak;
And let come on me what will.

[6] Or. *land.* [7] Heb. *wander.* [1] Or, *mocketh.* [2] Or, *mock.*

[14] Wherefore[3] should I take my flesh in my teeth,
And put my life in my hand?
[15] Behold,[4] he will slay me; I have no hope:
Nevertheless I will maintain[5] my ways before him.
[16] This also shall be my salvation,
That a godless man shall not come before him.
[17] Hear diligently my speech,
And let my declaration be in your ears.
[18] Behold now, I have set my cause in order;
I know that I am[6] righteous.
[19] Who is he that will contend with me?
For then would[7] I hold my peace and give up the ghost.

[20] Only do not two things unto me;
Then will I not hide myself from thy face:
[21] Withdraw thy hand far from me;
And let not thy terror make me afraid.
[22] Then call thou, and I will answer;
Or let me speak, and answer thou me.
[23] How many are mine iniquities and sins?
Make me to know my transgression and my sin.
[24] Wherefore hidest thou thy face,
And holdest me for thine enemy?
[25] Wilt thou harass a driven leaf?
And wilt thou pursue the dry stubble?
[26] For thou writest bitter things against me,
And makest me to inherit the iniquities of my youth:
[27] Thou puttest my feet also in the stocks,
And markest all my paths;
Thou settest a bound to the soles of my feet:
[28] Though[8] I am like a rotten thing that consumeth,
Like a garment that is moth-eaten.

[3] Or, *At all adventures I will take &c.*
[4] Or, *Though he slay me, yet will I wait for him.* [5] Heb. *argue.*
[6] Or, *shall be justified.* [7] Or, *if I hold my peace, I shall give up &c.*
[8] Heb. *And he is like.*

XIV

[1] Man, that is born of a woman,
Is of few days, and full of trouble.
[2] He cometh forth like a flower, and is[1] cut down:
He fleeth also as a shadow, and continueth not.
[3] And dost thou open thine eyes upon such a one,
And bringest me into judgment with thee?
[4] Who[2] can bring a clean thing out of an unclean? not one.
[5] Seeing his days are determined,
The number of his months is with thee,
And thou hast appointed his bounds that he cannot pass;
[6] Look away from him, that he may rest,[3]
Till he shall accomplish,[4] as a hireling, his day.

[7] For there is hope of a tree,
If it be cut down, that it will sprout again.
And that the tender branch thereof will not cease.
[8] Though the root thereof wax old in the earth,
And the stock thereof die in the ground;
[9] Yet through the scent of water it will bud,
And put forth boughs like a plant.
[10] But man dieth, and is laid low: Yea, man giveth up the ghost,
and where is he?
[11] *As* the waters fail[5] from the sea,
And the river wasteth and drieth up;
[12] So man lieth down and riseth not:
Till the heavens be no more, they shall not awake,
Nor be roused out of their sleep.

[13] Oh that thou wouldest hide me in Sheol,
That thou wouldest keep me secret, until thy wrath be past,
That thou wouldest appoint me a set time, and remember me!
[14] If a man die, shall he live *again?*
All the days of my warfare would[6] I wait,
Till my release[7] should come.

[1] Or, *withereth.* [2] Or, *Oh that a clean thing could come out of an unclean! not one* can. [3] Heb. *cease.* [4] Or, *have pleasure in.* [5] Heb. *are gone.*
[6] Or, *will . . . shall come.* [7] Or, *change.*

[15] Thou wouldest[8] call, and I would answer thee:
Thou wouldest have a desire to the work of thy hands.
[16] But now thou numberest my steps:
Dost thou not watch over my sin?
[17] My transgression is sealed up in a bag,
And thou fastenest up mine iniquity.

[18] But the mountain falling cometh[9] to nought;
And the rock is removed out of its place;
[19] The waters wear the stones;
The overflowings thereof wash away the dust of the earth:
So thou destroyest the hope of man.
[20] Thou prevailest for ever against him, and he passeth;
Thou changest his countenance, and sendest him away.
[21] His sons come to honor, and he knoweth it not;
And they are brought low, but he perceiveth it not of them.
[22] But[10] his flesh upon him hath pain,
And his soul within him mourneth.

XV

[1] THEN answered Eliphaz the Temanite, and said,
[2] Should a wise man make answer with vain[1] knowledge,
And fill himself with the east wind?
[3] Should he reason with unprofitable talk,
Or with speeches wherewith he can do no good?
[4] Yea, thou doest away with fear,
And hinderest[2] devotion[3] before God.
[5] For thine[4] iniquity teacheth thy mouth,
And thou choosest the tongue of the crafty.
[6] Thine own mouth condemneth thee, and not I;
Yea, thine own lips testify against thee.

[7] Art thou the first man that was born?
Or wast thou brought forth before the hills?

[8] Or, *shalt call, and I will &c.* [9] Heb. *fadeth away.*
[10] Or, *Only for himself his flesh hath pain, and for himself his soul mourneth.*
[1] Heb. *knowledge of wind.* [2] Heb. *diminishest.* [3] Or, *meditation.*
[4] Or, *thy mouth teacheth thine iniquity.*

[8] Hast[5] thou heard the secret counsel of God?
And dost thou limit wisdom to thyself?
[9] What knowest thou, that we know not?
What understandest thou, which is not in us?
[10] With us are both the gray-headed and the very aged men,
Much elder than thy father.
[11] Are the consolations of God too small for thee,
Even[6] the word that is gentle toward thee?
[12] Why doth thy heart carry thee away?
And why do thine eyes flash,
[13] That against God thou turnest thy spirit,
And lettest words go out of thy mouth?
[14] What is man, that he should be clean?
And he that is born of a woman, that he should be righteous?
[15] Behold, he putteth no trust in his holy ones;
Yea, the heavens are not clean in his sight:
[16] How much less one[7] that is abominable and corrupt,
A man that drinketh iniquity like water!

[17] I will show thee, hear thou me;
And that which I have seen I will declare:
[18] (Which wise men have told
From their fathers, and have not hid it;
[19] Unto whom alone the land was given,
And no stranger passed among them):
[20] The wicked man travaileth with pain all his days,
Even[8] the number of years that are laid up for the oppressor.
[21] A sound of terrors is in his ears;
In prosperity the destroyer shall come upon him:
[22] He believeth not that he shall return out of darkness,
And he is waited for of the sword:
[23] He wandereth abroad for bread, *saying,* Where is it?
He knoweth that the day of darkness is ready at his hand.
[24] Distress and anguish make him afraid;
They prevail against him, as a king ready to the battle.

[5] Or, *Dost thou hearken in the council.*
[6] Or, *Or is there any secret thing with thee?* [7] Or, *that which is.*
[8] Or, *And years that are numbered are laid up &c.*

[25] Because he hath stretched out his hand against God,
And behaveth[9] himself proudly against the Almighty;
[26] He runneth upon him with a *stiff* neck,
With[10] the thick bosses of his bucklers;
[27] Because he hath covered his face with his fatness,
And gathered fat upon his loins;
[28] And he hath dwelt in desolate[11] cities,
In houses which no man inhabited,[12]
Which were ready to become heaps;
[29] He shall not be rich, neither shall his substance continue,
Neither shall their[13] possessions be extended on the earth.
[30] He shall not depart out of darkness;
The flame shall dry up his branches,
And by the breath of *God's*[14] mouth shall he go away.
[31] Let him not trust in vanity, deceiving himself;
For vanity shall be his recompense.
[32] It shall be accomplished[15] before his time,
And his branch shall not be green.
[33] He shall shake off his unripe grape as the vine,
And shall cast off his flower as the olive-tree.
[34] For the company of the godless shall be barren,
And fire shall consume the tents of bribery.
[35] They conceive mischief, and bring forth iniquity,
And their heart prepareth deceit.

XVI

[1] THEN Job answered and said,
[2] I have heard many such things:
Miserable[1] comforters are ye all.
[3] Shall vain[2] words have an end?
Or what provoketh thee that thou answerest?
[4] I also could speak as ye do;
If your soul were in my soul's stead,
I could join words together against you,
And shake my head at you.

[9] Or, *biddeth defiance to.* [10] Or, *Upon.* [11] Heb. *cut off.* [12] Or, *would inhabit.*
[13] Or, *their produce bend to the earth.* [14] Heb. *his.* [15] Or, *paid in full.*
[1] Or, *Wearisome.* [2] Heb. *words of wind.*

[5] *But* I would strengthen you with my mouth,
And the solace of my lips would assuage *your grief*.

[6] Though I speak, my grief is not assuaged;
And though I forbear, what[3] am I eased?
[7] But now he hath made me weary:
Thou hast made desolate all my company.
[8] And thou hast laid[4] fast hold on me, *which* is a witness *against me:*
And my leanness riseth up against me,
It testifieth to my face.
[9] He hath torn me in his wrath, and persecuted[5] me;
He hath gnashed upon me with his teeth:
Mine adversary sharpeneth his eyes upon me.
[10] They have gaped upon me with their mouth;
They have smitten me upon the cheek reproachfully:
They gather themselves together against me.
[11] God delivereth me to the ungodly,
And casteth me into the hands of the wicked.
[12] I was at ease, and he brake me asunder;
Yea, he hath taken me by the neck, and dashed me to pieces:
He hath also set me up for his mark.
[13] His archers[6] compass me round about;
He cleaveth my reins asunder, and doth not spare;
He poureth out my gall upon the ground.
[14] He breaketh me with breach upon breach;
He runneth upon me like a giant.[7]
[15] I have sewed sackcloth upon my skin,
And have laid[8] my horn in the dust.
[16] My face is red with weeping,
And on my eyelids is the shadow of death;
[17] Although there is no violence in my hands,
And my prayer is pure.
[18] O earth, cover not thou my blood,
And let my cry have[9] no *resting*-place.

[3] Heb. *what departeth from me?* [4] Or, *shrivelled me up.* [5] Or, *hated.*
[6] Or, *arrows.* Or, *mighty ones.* [7] Or, *mighty man.* [8] Or, *defiled.*
[9] Or, *have no more place.*

[19] Even now, behold, my witness is in heaven,
And he that voucheth for me is on high.
[20] My friends scoff at me:
But mine eye poureth out tears unto God;
[21] That[10] he would maintain the right of a man with God,
And of a son of man with his neighbor!
[22] For when a few years are come,
I shall go the way whence I shall not return.

XVII

[1] My spirit is consumed, my days are extinct,
The grave is *ready* for me.
[2] Surely there are mockers[1] with me,
And mine eye dwelleth upon their provocation.

[3] Give now a pledge, be surety for me with thyself;
Who is there that will strike hands with me?
[4] For thou hast hid their heart from understanding:
Therefore shalt thou not exalt *them*.
[5] He that denounceth his friends for a prey,[2]
Even the eyes of his children shall fail.

[6] But he hath made me a byword of the people;
And they spit in my face.
[7] Mine eye also is dim by reason of sorrow,
And all my members are as a shadow.
[8] Upright men shall be astonished at this,
And the innocent shall stir up himself against the godless.
[9] Yet shall the righteous hold on his way,
And he that hath clean hands shall wax stronger and stronger.
[10] But as for you all, come on now again;
And[3] I shall not find a wise man among you.
[11] My days are past, my purposes are broken off,
Even the thoughts[4] of my heart.

[10] Or, *That one might plead for a man with God. As a son of man* pleadeth *for his neighbor.* [1] Heb. *mockery.* [2] Heb. *portion.* [3] Or, *For I find not.* [4] Heb. *possessions.*

[12] They change the night into day:
The light, *say they,* is near unto[5] the darkness.
[13] If I look[6] for Sheol as my house;
If I have spread my couch in the darkness;
[14] If I have said to corruption,[7] Thou art my father;
To the worm, *Thou art* my mother, and my sister;
[15] Where then is my hope?
And as for my hope, who shall see it?
[16] It shall go down to the bars of Sheol,
When once there is rest in the dust.

XVIII

[1] THEN answered Bildad the Shuhite, and said,
[2] How long will ye hunt for words?
Consider, and afterwards we will speak.
[3] Wherefore are we counted as beasts,
And are become unclean in your sight?
[4] Thou that tearest thyself in thine anger,
Shall the earth be forsaken for thee?
Or shall the rock be removed out of its place?

[5] Yea, the light of the wicked shall be put out,
And the spark[1] of his fire shall not shine.
[6] The light shall be dark in his tent,
And his lamp above[2] him shall be put out.
[7] The steps of his strength shall be straitened,
And his own counsel shall cast him down.
[8] For he is cast into a net by his own feet,
And he walketh upon the toils.
[9] A gin shall take *him* by the heel,
And a snare shall lay hold on him.
[10] A noose is hid for him in the ground,
And a trap for him in the way.
[11] Terrors shall make him afraid on every side,
And shall chase him at his heels.

[5] Or, *because of.* [6] Or, *hope, Sheol is my house; I have spread . . . I have said . . . and where now is my hope?* [7] Or, *the pit.* [1] Or, *flame.* [2] Or, *beside.*

[12] His strength shall be hunger-bitten,
And calamity shall be ready at[3] his side.
[13] The members[4] of his body shall be devoured,
Yea, the first-born of death shall devour his members.
[14] He shall be rooted out of his tent wherein he trusteth;
And he[5] shall be brought to the king of terrors.
[15] There[6] shall dwell in his tent that which is none of his;
Brimstone shall be scattered upon his habitation.
[16] His roots shall be dried up beneath,
And above shall his branch be[7] cut off.
[17] His remembrance shall perish from the earth,
And he shall have no name in the street.
[18] He shall be driven from light into darkness,
And chased out of the world.
[19] He shall have neither son nor son's son among his people,
Nor any remaining where he sojourned.
[20] They[8] that come after shall be astonished at his day,
As they that went before were[9] affrighted.
[21] Surely such are the dwellings of the unrighteous,
And this is the place of him that knoweth not God.

XIX

[1] THEN Job answered and said,
[2] How long will ye vex my soul,
And break me in pieces with words?
[3] These ten times have ye reproached me:
Ye are not ashamed that ye deal hardly with me.
[4] And be it indeed that I have erred,
Mine error remaineth with myself.
[5] If[1] indeed ye will magnify yourselves against me,
And plead against me my reproach;
[6] Know now that God hath subverted[2] me *in my cause,*
And hath compassed me with his net.

[3] Or, *for his halting.* [4] Heb. *bars of his skin.* [5] Heb. *it shall* (or, *thou shalt*) *bring him.* [6] Or, *It shall dwell in his tent, that it be no more his* (or, *because it is none of his*). [7] Or, *wither.* [8] Or, *They that dwell in the west are . . . as they that dwell in the east are &c.* [9] Heb. *laid hold on horror.*

[1] Or, *Will ye indeed . . . reproach?* [2] Or, *overthrown me.*

[7] Behold, I cry[3] out of wrong, but I am not heard:
I cry for help, but there is no justice.
[8] He hath walled up my way that I cannot pass,
And hath set darkness in my paths.
[9] He hath stripped me of my glory,
And taken the crown from my head.
[10] He hath broken me down on every side, and I am gone;
And my hope hath he plucked up like a tree.
[11] He hath also kindled his wrath against me,
And he counteth me unto him as *one of* his adversaries.
[12] His troops come on together,
And cast up their way against me,
And encamp round about my tent.

[13] He hath put my brethren far from me,
And mine acquaintance are wholly estranged from me.
[14] My kinsfolk have failed,
And my familiar friends have forgotten me.
[15] They that dwell[4] in my house, and my maids, count me for a stranger:
I am an alien in their sight.
[16] I call unto my servant, and he giveth me no answer,
Though I entreat him with my mouth.
[17] My breath is strange to my wife,
And my[5] supplication to the children of[6] mine own mother.
[18] Even young children despise me;
If I arise, they speak against me.
[19] All my[7] familiar friends abhor me,
And they whom I loved are turned against me.
[20] My bone cleaveth to my skin and to my flesh,
And I am escaped with the skin of my teeth.
[21] Have pity upon me, have pity upon me, O ye my friends;
For the hand of God hath touched me.
[22] Why do ye persecute me as God,
And are not satisfied with my flesh?

[3] Or, *cry out, Violence!* [4] Or, *sojourn.* [5] Or, *I make supplication.* Or, *I am loathsome.* [6] Or, *of my body.* [7] Heb. *the men of my council.*

[23] Oh that my words were now written!
Oh that they were inscribed in a book!
[24] That with an iron pen and lead
They were graven in the rock for ever!
[25] But[8] as for me I know that my Redeemer[9] liveth,
And at last he will stand up upon the earth:[10]
[26] And[11] after my skin, *even* this *body,* is destroyed,
Then without my flesh shall I see God;
[27] Whom I, even I, shall see, on[12] my side,
And mine eyes shall behold, and not as a stranger.
My heart[13] is consumed within me.
[28] If ye say, How we will persecute him!
And that the root of the matter is found in me;
[29] Be ye afraid of the sword:
For wrath[14] *bringeth* the punishments of the sword,
That ye may know there is a judgment.

XX

[1] THEN answered Zophar the Naamathite, and said,
[2] Therefore do my thoughts give answer to me,
Even[1] by reason of my haste that is in me.
[3] I have heard the reproof which putteth me to shame;
And[2] the spirit of my understanding answereth me.
[4] Knowest thou *not* this of old time,
Since man was placed upon earth,
[5] That the triumphing of the wicked is short,
And the joy of the godless but for a moment?
[6] Though his height mount up to the heavens,
And his head reach unto the clouds;
[7] Yet he shall perish for ever like his own dung:
They that have seen him shall say, Where is he?
[8] He shall fly away as a dream, and shall not be found:
Yea, he shall be chased away as a vision of the night.

[8] Or, *For.* [9] Or, *vindicator.* Heb. *goel.* [10] Heb. *dust.* [11] Or, *And after my skin hath been thus destroyed, yet from my flesh shall I see God.* [12] Or, *for myself.* [13] Heb. *reins.* [14] Or, *wrathful are.* [1] Or, *And by reason of* this *my haste is within me.* [2] Or, *But out of my understanding* my *spirit answereth me.*

[9] The eye which saw him shall see him no more;
Neither shall his place any more behold him.
[10] His[3] children shall seek the favor of the poor,
And his hands shall give back his wealth.
[11] His bones are full of his youth,
But it shall lie down with him in the dust.

[12] Though wickedness be sweet in his mouth,
Though he hide it under his tongue,
[13] Though he spare it, and will not let it go,
But keep it still within his mouth;
[14] Yet his food in his bowels is turned,
It is the gall of asps within him.
[15] He hath swallowed down riches, and he shall vomit them up again;
God will cast them out of his belly.
[16] He shall suck the poison of asps:
The viper's tongue shall slay him.
[17] He shall not look upon the rivers,
The flowing streams of honey and butter.
[18] That which he labored for shall he restore, and shall not swallow it down;
According to the substance that[4] he hath gotten, he shall not rejoice.
[19] For he hath oppressed and forsaken the poor;
He hath violently taken away a house, and[5] he shall not build it up.

[20] Because he knew no quietness within[6] him,
He shall not save aught of that wherein he delighteth.
[21] There was nothing left that he devoured not;
Therefore his prosperity shall not endure.
[22] In the fulness of his sufficiency he shall be in straits:
The hand of every one that is in misery shall come upon him.

[3] Or, as otherwise read, *The poor shall oppress his children.* [4] Heb. *of his exchange.*
[5] Or, *which he builded not.* [6] Or, *in his greed.* Heb. *in his belly.*

[23] When[7] he is about to fill his belly,
God will cast the fierceness of his wrath upon him,
And will rain it upon him while[8] he is eating.
[24] He shall flee from the iron weapon,
And the bow of brass shall strike him through.
[25] He draweth it forth, and it cometh out of his body;
Yea, the glittering point cometh out of his gall:
Terrors are upon him.
[26] All darkness is laid up for his treasures:
A fire not blown *by man* shall devour him;
It[9] shall consume that which is left in his tent.
[27] The heavens shall reveal his iniquity,
And the earth shall rise up against him.
[28] The increase of his house shall depart;
His goods shall flow away in the day of his wrath.
[29] This is the portion of a wicked man from God,
And the heritage appointed unto him by God.

XXI

[1] THEN Job answered and said,
[2] Hear diligently my speech;
And let this be your consolations.
[3] Suffer me, and I also will speak;
And after that I have spoken, mock[1] on.
[4] As for me, is my complaint to[2] man?
And why should I not be impatient?
[5] Mark[3] me, and be astonished,
And lay your hand upon your mouth.
[6] Even when I remember I am troubled,
And horror taketh hold on my flesh.
[7] Wherefore do the wicked live,
Become old, yea, wax mighty in power?
[8] Their seed is established with them in their sight,
And their offspring before their eyes.

[7] Or, *Let it be for the filling of his belly that* God *shall cast &c.* [8] Or, *as his food.*
[9] Or, *It shall go ill with him that is left.*
[1] Or, *thou shalt mock.* [2] Or, *of.* [3] Heb. *Look unto me.*

[9] Their houses are safe[4] from fear,
Neither is the rod of God upon them.
[10] Their bull gendereth, and faileth not;
Their cow calveth, and casteth not her calf.
[11] They send forth their little ones like a flock,
And their children dance.
[12] They sing[5] to the timbrel and harp,
And rejoice at the sound of the pipe.
[13] They spend their days in prosperity,
And in a moment they go down to Sheol.
[14] And they say unto God, Depart from us;
For we desire not the knowledge of thy ways.
[15] What is the Almighty, that we should serve him?
And what profit should we have, if we pray unto him?
[16] Lo,[6] their prosperity is not in their hand:
The counsel of the wicked is far from me.

[17] How[7] oft is it that the lamp of the wicked is put out?
That their calamity cometh upon them?
That *God* distributeth sorrows in his anger?
[18] That they are as stubble before the wind,
And as chaff that the storm carrieth away?
[19] *Ye*[8] *say,* God layeth up his iniquity for his children.
Let him recompense it unto himself, that he may know it:
[20] Let his own eyes see his destruction,
And let him drink of the wrath of the Almighty.
[21] For what careth he for his house after him,
When the number of his months is cut off?
[22] Shall any teach God knowledge,
Seeing he judgeth those that are high?
[23] One dieth in his full strength,
Being wholly at ease and quiet:

[4] Or, *in peace, without fear.*
[5] Heb. *lift up* the voice.
[6] Or, Ye say, *Lo &c.* [7] Or, *How oft is the lamp of the wicked put out, and* how oft *cometh their calamity upon them!* God *distributeth sorrows in his anger. They are as stubble . . . away.* [8] Or, *God layeth up his iniquity for his children: He rewardeth him, and he shall know it. His eyes shall see his destruction, and he shall drink &c.*

[24] His pails are full of milk,
And the marrow of his bones is moistened.
[25] And another dieth in bitterness of soul,
And never tasteth of good.
[26] They lie down alike in the dust,
And the worm covereth them.

[27] Behold, I know your thoughts,
And the devices wherewith ye would wrong me.
[28] For ye say, Where is the house of the prince?
And where is the tent wherein the wicked dwelt?
[29] Have ye not asked wayfaring men?
And do ye not know their evidences,
[30] That the evil man is reserved[9] to the day of calamity?
That they are led[10] forth to the day of wrath?
[31] Who shall declare his way to his face?
And who shall repay him what he hath done?
[32] Yet[11] shall he be borne to the grave,
And men shall keep watch over the tomb.
[33] The clods of the valley shall be sweet unto him,
And all men shall draw after him,
As there were innumerable before him.
[34] How then comfort ye me in[12] vain,
Seeing in your answers there remaineth *only* falsehood?[13]

XXII

[1] THEN answered Eliphaz the Temanite, and said,
[2] Can a man be profitable unto God?
Surely he that is wise is profitable unto himself.
[3] Is it any pleasure to the Almighty, that thou art righteous?
Or is it gain *to him,* that thou makest thy ways perfect?
[4] Is it for[1] thy fear *of him* that he reproveth thee,
That he entereth with thee into judgment?

[9] Or, *spared in &c.* [10] Or, *led away in &c.* [11] Or, *Moreover he is borne to the grave, and keepeth watch over his tomb. The clods of the valley are sweet unto him; And all men draw &c.* [12] Or, *with vanity.* [13] Or, *faithlessness.*

[1] Or, *for fear of thee.*

[5] Is not thy wickedness great?
Neither is there any end to thine iniquities.
[6] For thou hast taken pledges of thy brother for nought,
And stripped the naked of their clothing.
[7] Thou hast not given water to the weary to drink,
And thou hast withholden bread from the hungry.
[8] But as for the[2] mighty man, he had the earth;[3]
And the[4] honorable man, he dwelt in it.
[9] Thou hast sent widows away empty,
And the arms of the fatherless have been broken.
[10] Therefore snares are round about thee,
And sudden fear troubleth thee,
[11] Or[5] darkness, so that thou canst not see,
And abundance of waters cover thee.

[12] Is not God in the height of heaven?
And behold the height[6] of the stars, how high they are!
[13] And thou sayest, What doth God know?
Can he judge through the thick darkness?
[14] Thick clouds are a covering to him, so that he seeth not;
And he walketh on the vault of heaven.
[15] Wilt[7] thou keep the old way
Which wicked men have trodden?
[16] Who were snatched away before their time,
Whose foundation was poured out as a stream,
[17] Who said unto God, Depart from us;
And, What can the Almighty do for[8] us?[9]
[18] Yet he filled their houses with good things:
But the counsel of the wicked is far from me.
[19] The righteous see it, and are glad;
And the innocent laugh them to scorn,
[20] *Saying,* Surely they that did rise up against us are cut off,
And the[10] remnant of them the fire hath consumed.

[2] Heb. *the man of arm.* [3] Or, *land.*
[4] Heb. *he whose person is accepted.*
[5] Or, *Or dost thou not see the darkness, and the flood of waters that covereth thee?* [6] Heb. *head.* [7] Or, *Dost thou mark.* [8] Or, *to.* [9] Heb. *them.*
[10] Or, *that which remained to them.* Or, *their abundance.*

[21] Acquaint now thyself with him, and be at peace:
Thereby[11] good shall come unto thee.
[22] Receive, I pray thee, the[12] law from his mouth,
And lay up his words in thy heart.
[23] If thou return to the Almighty, thou shalt be built up,
If[13] thou put away unrighteousness far from thy tents.
[24] And lay thou *thy* treasure[14] in[15] the dust,
And *the gold of* Ophir among the stones of the brooks;
[25] And the Almighty will be thy treasure,[14]
And precious[16] silver unto thee.
[26] For then shalt thou delight thyself in the Almighty,
And shalt lift up thy face unto God.
[27] Thou shalt make thy prayer unto him, and he will hear thee;
And thou shalt pay thy vows.
[28] Thou shalt also decree a thing, and it shall be established unto thee;
And light shall shine upon thy ways.
[29] When they cast[17] *thee* down, thou shalt say, *There is* lifting up;
And the[18] humble person he will save.
[30] He will deliver *even* him that is not innocent:
Yea, he shall be delivered through the cleanness of thy hands.

XXIII

[1] THEN Job answered and said,
[2] Even to-day is my complaint rebellious:[1]
My stroke is heavier than my groaning.
[3] Oh that I knew where I might find him!
That I might come even to his seat!
[4] I would set my cause in order before him,
And fill my mouth with arguments.
[5] I would know the words which he would answer me,
And understand what he would say unto me.
[6] Would he contend with me in the greatness of his power?
Nay; but[2] he would give heed unto me.

[11] Or, as otherwise read, *Thereby shall thine increase be good.* [12] Or, *instruction.* [13] Or, *Thou shalt put away . . . And shalt lay up.* [14] Heb. *ore.* [15] Or, *on the earth.* [16] Or, *precious silver shall be thine.* [17] Or, *are made low.* [18] Heb. *him that is lowly of eyes.* [1] Or, *bitter.* Or, accounted *rebellion.* [2] Or, *he would only give heed.*

[7] There the upright might reason with him;
So should I be delivered for ever from my judge.
[8] Behold, I go forward, but he is not *there;*
And backward, but I cannot perceive him;
[9] On the left hand, when he doth work, but I cannot behold him;
He hideth[3] himself on the right hand, that I cannot see him.

[10] But[4] he knoweth the[5] way that I take;
When he hath tried me, I shall come forth as gold.
[11] My foot hath held fast to his steps;
His way have I kept, and turned not aside.
[12] I have not gone back from the commandment of his lips;
I have treasured up the words of his mouth more[6] than my necessary[7] food.
[13] But he[8] is in one *mind,* and who can turn him?
And what his soul desireth, even that he doeth.
[14] For he performeth that which is appointed for me:
And many such things are with him.
[15] Therefore am I terrified at his presence;
When I consider, I am afraid of him.
[16] For God hath made my heart faint,
And the Almighty hath terrified me;
[17] Because[9] I was not cut off before the darkness,
Neither did he cover the thick darkness from my face.

XXIV

[1] Why[1] are times not laid up by the Almighty?
And why do not they that know him see his days?
[2] There are that remove the landmarks;
They violently take away flocks, and feed them.
[3] They drive away the ass of the fatherless;
They take the widow's ox for a pledge.
[4] They turn the needy out of the way:
The poor[2] of the earth all hide themselves.

[3] Or, *turneth himself to . . . him, but.* [4] Or, *For.* [5] Heb. *the way* that is *with me.*
[6] Or, *more than my own law.* [7] Or, *portion.* See Prov. 30. 8. [8] Or, *he is one.*
[9] Or, *For I am not dismayed because of the darkness, Nor because thick darkness covereth my face.*
[1] Or, *Why is it, seeing times are not hidden from the Almighty, that they who know him see not his days?* [2] Or, *meek.*

[5] Behold, as wild asses in the desert
They go forth to their work, seeking diligently for food;[3]
The wilderness *yieldeth* them bread for their children.
[6] They cut their[4] provender in the field;
And they glean the vintage of the wicked.
[7] They lie all night naked without clothing,
And have no covering in the cold.
[8] They are wet with the showers of the mountains,
And embrace the rock for want of a shelter.
[9] There are that pluck the fatherless from the breast,
And take[5] a pledge of the poor;
[10] *So that* they go about naked without clothing,
And being hungry they carry the sheaves.
[11] They make oil within the walls of these men;
They tread *their* winepresses, and suffer thirst.
[12] From out of the populous[6] city men groan,
And the soul of the wounded crieth out:
Yet God regardeth not the folly.

[13] These are of them that rebel against the light;
They know not the ways thereof,
Nor abide in the paths thereof.
[14] The murderer riseth with the light;
He killeth the poor and needy;
And in the night he is as a thief.
[15] The eye also of the adulterer waiteth for the twilight,
Saying, No eye shall see me:
And he disguiseth[7] his face.
[16] In the dark they dig through houses:
They[8] shut themselves up in the day-time;
They know not the light.
[17] For the[9] morning is to all of them as thick darkness;
For they know the terrors of the thick darkness.

[18] Swiftly[10] they *pass away* upon the face of the waters;
Their portion is cursed in the earth:

[3] Heb. *prey.* [4] Or, *his.* [5] Or, *take in pledge that which is on the poor.*
[6] Heb. *city of men.* [7] Or, *putteth a covering on his face.* [8] Or, Which *they had marked for themselves.* [9] Or, *thick darkness is to all of them as the morning; For they &c.* [10] Or, Ye say, *Swiftly &c.* Heb. *Swift is he &c.*

They turn not into the way of the vineyards.
[19] Drought and heat consume[11] the snow waters:
So doth Sheol *those that* have sinned.
[20] The womb shall forget him;
The worm shall feed sweetly on him;
He shall be no more remembered;
And unrighteousness shall be broken as[12] a tree.
[21] He devoureth the barren that beareth not,
And doeth not good to the widow.
[22] Yet *God* preserveth the mighty by his power:
He riseth up that hath no assurance of life.
[23] *God* giveth them to be in security, and they rest thereon;
And[13] his eyes are upon their ways.
[24] They are exalted; yet a little while, and they are gone;
Yea,[14] they are brought low, they are taken[15] out of the way as all others,
And are cut off as the tops of the ears of grain.
[25] And if it be not so now, who will prove me a liar,
And make my speech nothing worth?

XXV

[1] THEN answered Bildad the Shuhite, and said,
[2] Dominion and fear are with him;
He maketh peace in his high places.
[3] Is there any number of his armies?
And upon whom doth not his light arise?
[4] How then can man be just with[1] God?
Or how can he be clean that is born of a woman?
[5] Behold, even the moon hath no brightness,
And the stars are not pure in his sight:
[6] How much less man, that is a worm!
And the son of man, that is a worm!

[11] Heb. *violently take away.* [12] Or, *as a tree; even he that devoureth &c.*
[13] Or, *But.* [14] Or, *And when they are &c.* [15] Or, *gathered in.* [1] Or, *before.*

XXVI

[1] THEN Job answered and said,
[2] How hast thou helped him that is without power!
How hast thou saved the arm that hath no strength!
[3] How hast thou counselled him that hath no wisdom,
And plentifully declared sound knowledge!
[4] To whom hast thou uttered words?
And whose spirit[1] came forth from thee?

[5] They[2] that are deceased tremble
Beneath the waters and the inhabitants thereof.
[6] Sheol is naked before *God,*[3]
And Abaddon[4] hath no covering.
[7] He stretcheth out the north over empty space,
And hangeth the earth upon[5] nothing.
[8] He bindeth up the waters in his thick clouds;
And the cloud is not rent under them.
[9] He incloseth the face of his throne,
And spreadeth his cloud upon it.
[10] He hath described a boundary upon the face of the waters,
Unto the confines of light and darkness.
[11] The pillars of heaven tremble
And are astonished at his rebuke.
[12] He stirreth[6] up the sea with his power,
And by his understanding he smiteth through Rahab.
[13] By his Spirit the heavens are garnished;[7]
His hand hath pierced the swift[8] serpent.
[14] Lo, these are but the outskirts of his ways:
And how[9] small a whisper do[10] we hear of him!
But the thunder of his power[11] who can understand?

[1] Heb. *breath.* [2] Or, *The shades.* Heb. *The Rephaim.* [3] Heb. *him.* [4] Or, *Destruction.* [5] Or, *over.* [6] Or, *stilleth.* [7] Heb. *beauty.* [8] Or, *fleeing.* Or, *gliding.* [9] Or, *how little a portion.* [10] Or, *is heard.* [11] Or, *mighty deeds.*

XXVII

[1] And Job again took up his parable, and said,
[2] As God liveth, who hath taken away my right,
And the Almighty, who hath vexed[1] my soul;
[3] (For[2] my life is yet whole in me,
And the Spirit of God is in my nostrils);
[4] Surely my lips shall[3] not speak unrighteousness,
Neither shall[4] my tongue utter deceit.
[5] Far be it from me that I should justify you:
Till I die I will not put away mine integrity from me.
[6] My righteousness I hold fast, and will not let it go:
My heart shall[5] not reproach *me* so long as I live.
[7] Let mine enemy be as the wicked,
And let him that riseth up against me be as the unrighteous.

[8] For what is the hope of the godless, though[6] he get him gain,
When God taketh away his soul?
[9] Will God hear his cry,
When trouble cometh upon him?
[10] Will he delight himself in the Almighty,
And call upon God at all times?
[11] I will teach you concerning the hand of God;
That which is with the Almighty will I not conceal.
[12] Behold, all ye yourselves have seen it;
Why then are ye become altogether vain?

[13] This is the portion of a wicked man with God,
And the heritage of oppressors, which they receive from the Almighty:
[14] If his children be multiplied, it is for the sword;
And his offspring shall not be satisfied with bread.
[15] Those that remain of him shall be buried in death,
And his widows shall make no lamentation.

[1] Heb. *made my soul bitter.* [2] Or, *All the while my breath is in me . . . nostrils; surely.* [3] Or, *do.* [4] Or, *doth.*
[5] Or, *doth not reproach* me for *any of my days.*
[6] Or, *when God cutteth him off, when he taketh &c.*

[16] Though he heap up silver as the dust,
And prepare raiment as the clay;
[17] He may prepare it, but the just shall put it on,
And the innocent shall divide the silver.
[18] He buildeth his house as the moth,
And as a booth which the keeper maketh.
[19] He lieth down rich, but he shall not be gathered *to his fathers;*
He openeth his eyes, and he is not.
[20] Terrors overtake him like waters;
A tempest stealeth him away in the night.
[21] The east wind carrieth him away, and he departeth;
And it sweepeth him out of his place.
[22] For *God* shall hurl at him, and not spare:
He would fain flee out of his hand.
[23] Men shall clap their hands at him,
And shall hiss him out of his place.

XXVIII

[1] SURELY[1] there is a mine for silver,
And a place for gold which they refine.
[2] Iron is taken out of the earth,[2]
And copper is molten out of the stone.
[3] *Man* setteth an end to darkness,
And searcheth out, to the furthest bound,
The stones of obscurity and of thick darkness.
[4] He[3] breaketh open a shaft away from where men sojourn;
They are forgotten of the foot;
They hang afar from men, they swing[4] to and fro.
[5] As for the earth, out of it cometh bread;
And underneath it is turned up as it were by fire.
[6] The stones thereof are the place of sapphires,
And[5] it hath dust of gold.
[7] That path no bird of prey knoweth,
Neither hath the falcon's eye seen it:

[1] Or, *For.* [2] Or, *dust.*
[3] Or, *The flood breaketh out from where men sojourn;* Even the waters *forgotten of the foot: They are diminished, they are gone away from man.* [4] Or, *flit.*
[5] Or, *And he winneth lumps of gold.*

[8] The proud[6] beasts have not trodden it,
Nor hath the fierce lion passed thereby.
[9] He putteth forth his hand upon the flinty rock;
He overturneth the mountains by the roots.
[10] He cutteth out channels[7] among the rocks;
And his eye seeth every precious thing.
[11] He bindeth the streams that[8] they trickle not;
And the thing that is hid bringeth he forth to light.
[12] But where shall wisdom be found?
And where is the place of understanding?
[13] Man knoweth not the price thereof;
Neither is it found in the land of the living.
[14] The deep saith, It is not in me;
And the sea saith, It is not with me.
[15] It cannot be gotten for gold,[9]
Neither shall silver be weighed for the price thereof.
[16] It cannot be valued with the gold of Ophir,
With the precious onyx,[10] or the sapphire.
[17] Gold and glass cannot equal it,
Neither shall it be exchanged for jewels[11] of fine gold.
[18] No mention shall be made of coral or of crystal:
Yea, the price of wisdom is above rubies.[12]
[19] The topaz of Ethiopia shall not equal it,
Neither shall it be valued with pure gold.
[20] Whence then cometh wisdom?
And where is the place of understanding?
[21] Seeing it is hid from the eyes of all living,
And kept close from the birds of the heavens.
[22] Destruction[13] and Death say,
We have heard a rumor thereof with our ears.

[23] God understandeth the way thereof,
And he knoweth the place thereof.
[24] For he looketh to the ends of the earth,
And seeth under the whole heaven;

[6] Heb. *sons of pride.* [7] Or, *passages.* [8] Heb. *from weeping.*
[9] Or, *treasure.* [10] Or, *beryl.* [11] Or, *vessels.*
[12] Or, *red coral.* Or, *pearls.* [13] Heb. *Abaddon.*

[25] To[14] make a weight for the wind:
Yea, he meteth out the waters by measure.
[26] When he made a decree for the rain,
And a way for the lightning of the thunder;
[27] Then did he see it, and declare[15] it;
He established it, yea, and searched it out.
[28] And unto man he said,
Behold, the fear of the Lord, that is wisdom;
And to depart from evil is understanding.

XXIX

[1] And Job again took up his parable, and said,
[2] Oh that I were as in the months of old,
As in the days when God watched over me;
[3] When his lamp shined upon[1] my head,
And by his light I walked through darkness;
[4] As I was in the[2] ripeness of my days,
When the friendship[3] of God was upon my tent;
[5] When the Almighty was yet with me,
And my children were about me;
[6] When my steps were washed with butter,
And the rock poured me out streams of oil!
[7] When I went forth to the gate unto the city,
When I prepared my seat in the street,[4]
[8] The young men saw me and hid themselves,
And the aged rose up and stood;
[9] The princes refrained from talking,
And laid their hand on their mouth;
[10] The voice of the nobles was hushed,[5]
And their tongue cleaved to the roof of their mouth.
[11] For when the ear heard *me,* then it blessed me;
And when the eye saw *me,* it gave witness unto me:
[12] Because I delivered the poor that cried,
The fatherless also, that[6] had none to help him.
[13] The blessing of him that was ready to perish came upon me;
And I caused the widow's heart to sing for joy.

[14] Or, *When he maketh.* [15] Or, *recount.* [1] Or, *above.* [2] Heb. *my days of autumn.* [3] Or, *counsel.* [4] Or, *broad place.* [5] Heb. *hid.* [6] Or, *and* him *that had &c.*

[14] I put on righteousness, and it clothed[7] me:
My justice was as a robe and a diadem.[8]
[15] I was eyes to the blind,
And feet was I to the lame.
[16] I was a father to the needy:
And the[9] cause of him that I knew not I searched out.
[17] And I brake the jaws[10] of the unrighteous,
And plucked the prey out of his teeth.
[18] Then I said, I shall die in[11] my nest,
And I shall multiply my days as the sand:
[19] My root is spread[12] out to[13] the waters,
And the dew lieth all night upon my branch:
[20] My glory is fresh in me,
And my bow is renewed in my hand.
[21] Unto me men gave ear, and waited,
And kept silence for my counsel.
[22] After my words they spake not again;
And my speech distilled upon them.
[23] And they waited for me as for the rain;
And they opened their mouth wide *as* for the latter rain.
[24] I smiled on them, when they had no confidence;
And the light of my countenance they cast not down.
[25] I chose out their way, and sat *as* chief,
And dwelt as a king in the army,
As one that comforteth the mourners.

XXX

[1] But now they that are younger than I have me in derision,
Whose fathers I disdained to set with the dogs of my flock.
[2] Yea, the strength of their hands, whereto should it profit me?
Men in whom ripe[1] age is perished.
[3] They are gaunt with want and famine;
They[2] gnaw the dry ground, in[3] the gloom of wasteness and desolation.

[7] Or, *clothed itself with me.* [8] Or, *turban.* [9] Or, *the cause which I knew not.* [10] Heb. *great teeth.* [11] Or, *beside.* Heb. *with.* [12] Heb. *opened.* [13] Or, *by.* [1] Or, *vigor.* [2] Or, *They flee into the wilderness, into &c.* [3] Or, which *yesternight* was. Or, *on the eve of.*

[4] They pluck salt-wort by the bushes;
And the roots of the broom are their[4] food.
[5] They are driven forth from the midst *of men;*
They cry after them as after a thief;
[6] So that they dwell in frightful valleys,
In holes of the earth and of the rocks.
[7] Among the bushes they bray;
Under the nettles[5] they are[6] gathered together.
[8] *They are* children of fools, yea, children of base[7] men;
They were[8] scourged out of the land.

[9] And now I am become their song,
Yea, I am a byword unto them.
[10] They abhor me, they stand aloof from me,
And spare not to spit in[9] my face.
[11] For he hath loosed his[10] cord, and afflicted me;
And they have cast off the bridle before me.
[12] Upon my right hand rise the rabble;[11]
They thrust aside my feet,
And they cast up against me their ways of destruction.
[13] They mar[12] my path,
They set forward my calamity,
Even men that have no helper.
[14] As[13] through a wide breach they come:
In the midst of the ruin they roll themselves *upon me.*
[15] Terrors are turned upon me;
They[14] chase mine[15] honor as the wind;
And my welfare is passed away as a cloud.

[16] And now my soul is poured out within[16] me;
Days of affliction have taken hold upon me.
[17] In the night season my bones are pierced[17] in[18] me,
And the[19] *pains* that gnaw me take no rest.

[4] Or, *to warm them.* [5] Or, *wild vetches.* [6] Or, *stretch themselves.* [7] Heb. men of *no name.* [8] Or, *are outcasts from the land.* [9] Or, *at the sight of me.* [10] According to another reading, *my cord* (or, *bowstring*). [11] Or, *brood.* [12] Or, *break up.* [13] Or, *As a wide breaking in* of waters. [14] Or, *Thou chasest.* [15] Or, *my nobility.* [16] Heb. *upon.* [17] Or, *corroded* and drop *away from me.* [18] Heb. *from off.* [19] Or, *my sinews take &c.*

[18] By *God's* great force is my garment disfigured;
It bindeth me about as the collar of my coat.
[19] He hath cast me into the mire,
And I am become like dust and ashes.
[20] I cry unto thee, and thou dost not answer me:
I stand up, and thou gazest at me.
[21] Thou art turned to be cruel to me;
With the might of thy hand thou persecutest me.
[22] Thou liftest me up to the wind, thou causest me to ride *upon it;*
And thou dissolvest me in the storm.
[23] For I know that thou wilt bring me to death,
And to the[20] house appointed for all living.

[24] Howbeit doth not one stretch out the hand in his fall?
Or in his calamity therefore cry for help?
[25] Did not I weep for him that was in trouble?
Was not my soul grieved for the needy?
[26] When I looked for good, then evil came;
And when I waited for light, there came darkness.
[27] My heart is troubled, and resteth not;
Days of affliction are come upon me.
[28] I go mourning[21] without the sun:
I stand up in the assembly, and cry for help.
[29] I am a brother to jackals,
And a companion to ostriches.
[30] My skin is black, *and falleth* from me,
And my bones are burned with heat.
[31] Therefore is my harp *turned* to mourning,
And my pipe into the voice of them that weep.

XXXI

[1] I MADE a covenant with mine eyes;
How then should I look upon a virgin?
[2] For[1] what is the portion from God above,
And the heritage from the Almighty on high?

[20] Or, *the house of meeting for &c.* [21] Or, *blackened, but not by the sun.*
[1] Or, *For what portion* should I have *of God . . . and what heritage &c. Is there not calamity &c.?*

[3] Is it not calamity to the unrighteous,
And disaster to the workers of iniquity?
[4] Doth not he see my ways,
And number all my steps?

[5] If I have walked with falsehood,
And my foot hath hasted to deceit;
[6] (Let me be weighed in an even balance,
That God may know mine integrity);
[7] If my step hath turned out of the way,
And my heart walked after mine eyes,
And if any spot hath cleaved to my hands:
[8] Then let me sow, and let another eat;
Yea, let the[2] produce of my field be rooted out.

[9] If my heart hath been enticed unto a woman,
And I have laid wait at my neighbor's door;
[10] Then let my wife grind unto another,
And let others bow down upon her.
[11] For that were a heinous crime;
Yea, it were an iniquity to be punished by the judges:
[12] For it is a fire that consumeth unto Destruction,[3]
And would root out all mine increase.
[13] If I have despised the cause of my man-servant or of my maid-servant,
When they contended with me;
[14] What then shall I do when God riseth up?
And when he visiteth, what shall I answer him?
[15] Did not he that made me in the womb make him?
And did not one fashion us in the womb?

[16] If I have withheld the[4] poor from *their* desire,
Or have caused the eyes of the widow to fail,
[17] Or have eaten my morsel alone,
And the fatherless hath not eaten thereof;

[2] Or, *my offspring*. Heb. *my produce*. [3] Heb. *Abaddon*. See ch. 26. 6.
[4] Or, *aught that the poor desired*.

[18] (Nay, from my youth he grew up with me as with a father,
And her have I guided from my mother's womb;)
[19] If I have seen any perish for want of clothing,
Or that the needy had no covering;
[20] If his loins have not blessed me,
And if he hath not been warmed with the fleece of my sheep;
[21] If I have lifted up my hand against the fatherless,
Because I saw my help in the gate:
[22] Then let my shoulder fall from the shoulder-blade,
And mine arm be broken from the bone.
[23] For calamity from God is a terror to me,
And by reason of his majesty I can do nothing.

[24] If I have made gold my hope,
And have said to the fine gold, *Thou art* my confidence;
[25] If I have rejoiced because my wealth was great,
And because my hand had gotten much;
[26] If I have beheld the[5] sun when it shined,
Or the moon walking in brightness,
[27] And my heart hath been secretly enticed,
And my[6] mouth hath kissed my hand:
[28] This also were an iniquity to be punished by the judges;
For I should have denied the God that is above.
[29] If I have rejoiced at the destruction of him that hated me,
Or lifted up myself when evil found him;
[30] (Yea, I have not suffered my mouth[7] to sin
By asking his life with a curse);
[31] If the men of my tent have not said,
Who can find one that hath not been filled with his meat?
[32] (The sojourner hath not lodged in the street;
But I have opened my doors to the[8] traveller);
[33] If like[9] Adam I have covered my transgressions,
By hiding mine iniquity in my bosom;
[34] Because I feared the great multitude,
And the contempt of families terrified me,
So that I kept silence, and went not out of the door—

[5] Heb. *the light.* [6] Heb. *my hand hath kissed my mouth.* [7] Heb. *palate.*
[8] Heb. *the way.* [9] Or, *after the manner of men.*

[35] Oh that I had one to hear me!
(Lo, here is my signature,[10] let the Almighty answer me);
And *that I had* the indictment[11] which mine adversary hath written!
[36] Surely I would carry it upon my shoulder;
I would bind it unto me as a crown:
[37] I would declare unto him the number of my steps;
As a prince would I go[12] near unto him.
[38] If my land crieth out against me,
And the furrows thereof weep together;
[39] If I have eaten the fruits[13] thereof without money,
Or have caused the owners thereof to lose their life:
[40] Let thistles[14] grow instead of wheat,
And cockle[15] instead of barley.

The words of Job are ended.

XXXII

[1] So these three men ceased to answer Job, because he was
righteous in his own eyes. [2] Then was kindled the wrath of
Elihu the son of Barachel the Buzite, of the family of Ram: against
Job was his wrath kindled, because he justified himself rather
than God. [3] Also against his three friends was his wrath kindled,
because they had found no answer, and yet had condemned Job.
[4] Now Elihu had waited[1] to speak unto Job because they were
elder than he. [5] And when Elihu saw that there was no answer
in the mouth of these three men, his wrath was kindled.

[6] And Elihu the son of Barachel the Buzite answered and said,
I am young, and ye are very old;
Wherefore I held back, and durst not show you mine opinion.
[7] I said, Days should speak,
And multitude of years should teach wisdom.
[8] But there is a spirit in man,
And the breath of the Almighty giveth them understanding.

[10] Heb. *mark.* [11] Heb. *book.* [12] Or, *present it* to him. [13] Heb. *strength.*
[14] Or, *thorns.* [15] Or, *noisome weeds.*
[1] Heb. *waited for Job with words.*

[9] It is not the great that are wise,
Nor the aged that understand justice.
[10] Therefore I said,[2] Hearken to me;
I also will show mine opinion.

[11] Behold, I waited for your words,
I listened for your reasonings,
Whilst ye searched out what to say.
[12] Yea, I attended unto you,
And, behold, there was none that convinced Job,
Or that answered his words, among you.
[13] Beware[3] lest ye say, We have found wisdom;
God may vanquish him, not man:
[14] For he hath not directed his words against me;
Neither will I answer him with your speeches.
[15] They are amazed, they answer no more:
They have not a word to say.
[16] And shall I wait, because they speak not,
Because they stand still, and answer no more?
[17] I also will answer my part,
I also will show mine opinion.
[18] For I am full of words;
The spirit within me constraineth me.
[19] Behold, my breast is as wine which hath no vent;
Like new wine-skins it[4] is ready to burst.
[20] I will speak, that I may be[5] refreshed;
I will open my lips and answer.
[21] Let me not, I pray you, respect any man's person;
Neither will I give flattering titles unto any man.
[22] For I know not to give flattering titles;
Else would my Maker soon take me away.

XXXIII

[1] HOWBEIT, Job, I pray thee, hear my speech,
And hearken to all my words.

[2] Or, *say.* [3] Or, *Lest ye should say, We have found out wisdom; God thrusteth him down, not man: now he &c.*
[4] Or, *which are ready.* [5] Or, *find relief.*

[2] Behold now, I have opened my mouth;
My tongue hath spoken in my mouth.[1]
[3] My words *shall utter* the uprightness of my heart;
And that which my lips know they shall speak sincerely.
[4] The Spirit of God hath made me,
And the breath of the Almighty giveth me life.
[5] If thou canst, answer thou me;
Set *thy words* in order before me, stand forth.
[6] Behold, I[2] am toward God even as thou art:
I also am formed out of the clay.
[7] Behold, my terror shall not make thee afraid,
Neither shall my pressure be heavy upon thee.

[8] Surely thou hast spoken in my hearing,
And I have heard the voice of *thy* words, *saying,*
[9] I am clean, without transgression;
I am innocent, neither is there iniquity in me:
[10] Behold, he findeth occasions[3] against me,
He counteth me for his enemy;
[11] He putteth my feet in the stocks,
He marketh all my paths.
[12] Behold, I[4] will answer thee, in this thou art not just;
For God is greater than man.

[13] Why dost thou strive against him,
For that he giveth not account of any of his matters?
[14] For God speaketh once,[5]
Yea twice, *though man* regardeth it not.
[15] In a dream, in a vision of the night,
When deep sleep falleth upon men,
In slumberings upon the bed;
[16] Then he openeth[6] the ears of men,
And sealeth their instruction,

[1] Heb. *palate.*
[2] Or, *I am according to thy wish in God's stead.* [3] Or, *causes of alienation.*
[4] Or, *in this thou art not just: I will answer thee; for &c.* [5] Or, *in one way, yea, in two.* [6] Heb. *uncovereth.*

[17] That[7] he may withdraw man *from his* purpose,
And hide pride from man;
[18] He[8] keepeth back his soul from the pit,
And his life from perishing by the sword.[9]

[19] He is chastened also with pain upon his bed,
And[10] with continual strife in his bones;
[20] So that his life abhorreth bread,
And his soul dainty food.
[21] His flesh is consumed away, that it cannot be seen;
And his bones that were not seen stick out.
[22] Yea, his soul draweth near unto the pit,
And his life to the destroyers.

[23] If there be with him an[11] angel,
An interpreter, one among[12] a thousand,
To show unto man what[13] is right for him;
[24] Then[14] *God* is gracious unto him, and saith,
Deliver him from going down to the pit,
I have found a ransom.
[25] His flesh shall be fresher than a child's;
He returneth to the days of his youth:
[26] He prayeth unto God, and he is favorable unto him;
So that he seeth his face with joy:
And he restoreth unto man his righteousness.
[27] He singeth[15] before men, and saith,
I have sinned, and perverted that which was right,
And it[16] profited me not:
[28] He hath redeemed my soul from going into the pit,
And my life shall behold the light.

[29] Lo, all these things doth God work,
Twice, *yea* thrice, with a man,

[7] Or, *That man may put away* his *purpose, and that he may hide.*
[8] Or, *That he may keep back.* [9] Or, *weapons.*
[10] Another reading is, *While all his bones are firm.*
[11] Or, *a messenger.* [12] Or, *of the thousand.* [13] Or, *his uprightness.*
[14] Or, *And he be gracious . . . and say . . . ransom: his flesh &c.*
[15] Or, *looketh upon men.* [16] Or, *it was not requited unto me.* Or, *it was not meet for me.*

[30] To bring back his soul from the pit,
That he may be enlightened with the light of the[17] living.
[31] Mark well, O Job, hearken unto me:
Hold thy peace, and I will speak.
[32] If thou hast any thing to say, answer me:
Speak, for I desire to justify thee.
[33] If not, hearken thou unto me:
Hold thy peace, and I will teach thee wisdom.

XXXIV

[1] MOREOVER Elihu answered and said,
[2] Hear my words, ye wise men;
And give ear unto me, ye that have knowledge.
[3] For the ear trieth words,
As the palate tasteth food.
[4] Let us choose for us that which is right:
Let us know among ourselves what is good.
[5] For Job hath said, I am righteous,
And God hath taken away my right:
[6] Notwithstanding[1] my right I am *accounted* a liar;
My[2] wound is incurable, *though I am* without transgression.
[7] What man is like Job,
Who drinketh up scoffing like water,
[8] Who goeth in company with the workers of iniquity,
And walketh with wicked men?
[9] For he hath said, It profiteth a man nothing
That he should delight[3] himself with God.

[10] Therefore hearken unto me, ye men of understanding:
Far be it from God, that he should do wickedness,
And from the Almighty, that he should commit iniquity.
[11] For the work of a man will he render unto him,
And cause every man to find according to his ways.
[12] Yea, of a surety, God will not do wickedly,
Neither will the Almighty pervert justice.

[17] Or, *life.* [1] Or, *Should I lie against my right?* [2] Heb. *Mine arrow.* [3] Or, *consent with.* See Ps. 50. 18.

[13] Who gave him a charge over the earth?
Or who hath disposed[4] the whole world?
[14] If[5] he set his heart upon himself,[6]
If he gather unto himself his spirit and his breath;
[15] All flesh shall perish together,
And man shall turn again unto dust.
[16] If[7] now *thou hast* understanding, hear this:
Hearken to the voice of my words.
[17] Shall even one that hateth justice govern?
And wilt thou condemn him that is righteous *and* mighty?—
[18] *Him*[8] that saith to a king, *Thou art* vile,
Or to nobles, *Ye are* wicked;
[19] That respecteth not the persons of princes,
Nor regardeth the rich more than the poor;
For they all are the work of his hands.
[20] In a moment they die, even[9] at midnight;
The people are shaken and pass away,
And the mighty are taken away without hand.

[21] For his eyes are upon the ways of a man,
And he seeth all his goings.
[22] There is no darkness, nor thick gloom,
Where the workers of iniquity may hide themselves.
[23] For he needeth not further to consider a man,
That he should go before God in judgment.
[24] He breaketh in pieces mighty men *in*[10] *ways* past finding out,
And setteth others in their stead.
[25] Therefore he taketh knowledge of their works;
And he overturneth them in the night, so that they are destroyed.[11]
[26] He striketh them as wicked men
In[12] the open sight of others;

[4] Or, *laid* upon him. [5] According to another reading, *If he cause his heart to return unto himself.* [6] Or, *man.* Heb. *him.* [7] Or, *Only understand.*
[8] The Heb. as pointed reads, *Is it* fit *to say to a king,* Thou *art vile?* Or, *to nobles,* Ye are *wicked?* [9] Or, *and at midnight the people &c.* [10] Or, *without inquisition.*
[11] Heb. *crushed.* [12] Heb. *In the place of beholders.*

[27] Because they turned aside from following him,
And would not have regard to any of his ways:
[28] So[13] that they caused the cry of the poor to come unto him,
And he heard the cry of the afflicted.
[29] When he giveth quietness, who then can condemn?
And when he hideth his face, who then can behold him?
Alike whether *it be done* unto a nation, or unto a man:
[30] That the godless man reign not,
That there be none to ensnare the people.

[31] For hath any said unto God, I have borne *chastisement,*
I[14] will not offend *any more:*
[32] That which I see not teach thou me:
If I have done iniquity, I will do it no more?
[33] Shall his recompense be as thou wilt, that thou refusest it?
For thou must choose, and not I:
Therefore speak what thou knowest.
[34] Men of understanding will say unto me,
Yea, every wise man that heareth me:
[35] Job speaketh without knowledge,
And his words are without wisdom.
[36] Would that Job were tried unto the end,
Because of his answering like wicked men.
[37] For he addeth rebellion unto his sin;
He clappeth his hands among us,
And multiplieth his words against God.

XXXV

[1] MOREOVER Elihu answered and said,
[2] Thinkest thou this to be *thy* right,
Or sayest thou, My righteousness is more than God's,
[3] That thou sayest, What advantage will it be unto thee?
And, What profit shall I have, more than if I had sinned?
[4] I will answer thee,
And thy companions with thee.

[13] Or, *That they might cause . . . And that he might hear.*
[14] Or, *though I offend not.*

[5] Look unto the heavens, and see;
And behold the skies, which are higher than thou.
[6] If thou hast sinned, what effectest thou against him?
And if thy transgressions be multiplied, what doest thou unto him?
[7] If thou be righteous, what givest thou him?
Or what receiveth he of thy hand?
[8] Thy wickedness *may hurt* a man as thou art;
And thy righteousness *may profit* a son of man.

[9] By reason of the multitude of oppressions they cry out;
They cry for help by reason of the arm of the mighty.
[10] But none saith, Where is God my Maker,
Who giveth songs in the night;
[11] Who teacheth us more than the beasts of the earth,
And maketh us wiser than the birds of the heavens?
[12] There they cry, but[1] none giveth answer,
Because of the pride of evil men.
[13] Surely God will not hear an empty *cry,*
Neither will the Almighty regard it.
[14] How much less when thou sayest thou[2] beholdest him not,
The cause is before him, and thou waitest for him!
[15] But now, because he hath not visited in his anger,
Neither[3] doth he greatly regard arrogance;
[16] Therefore doth Job open his mouth in vanity;
He multiplieth words without knowledge.

XXXVI

[1] Elihu also proceeded, and said,
[2] Suffer[4] me a little, and I will show thee;
For I[5] have yet somewhat to say on God's behalf.
[3] I will fetch my knowledge from afar,
And will ascribe righteousness to my Maker.
[4] For truly my words are not false:
One that is perfect in knowledge is with thee.

[1] Or, *but he answereth not.* [2] Or, *thou beholdest him not! The cause is before him; therefore wait thou for him.*
[3] Or, Thou sayest, *He doth not greatly regard arrogance. Thus doth &c.*
[4] Heb. *Wait for.* [5] Heb. there are *yet words for God.*

[5] Behold, God is mighty, and despiseth not any:
He is mighty in strength of understanding.[6]
[6] He preserveth not the life of the wicked,
But giveth to the afflicted *their* right.
[7] He withdraweth not his eyes from the righteous:
But with kings upon the throne
He setteth them for ever, and they are exalted.
[8] And if they be bound in fetters,
And be taken in the cords of affliction;
[9] Then he showeth them their work,
And their transgressions, that they have behaved themselves proudly.
[10] He openeth also their ear to instruction,
And commandeth that they return from iniquity.
[11] If they hearken and serve *him,*
They shall spend their days in prosperity,
And their years in pleasures.[7]
[12] But if they hearken not, they shall perish by the[8] sword,
And they shall die without knowledge.
[13] But they that are godless in heart lay up anger:
They cry not for help when he bindeth them.
[14] They[9] die in youth.
And their life *perisheth* among[10] the unclean.[11]
[15] He delivereth the afflicted by[12] their affliction,
And openeth their ear in[13] oppression.
[16] Yea, he would have allured thee out[14] of distress
Into a broad place, where there is no straitness;
And that which is set on thy table would be full of fatness.

[17] But thou art[15] full of the judgment of the wicked:
Judgment and justice take hold *on thee.*
[18] For[16] let not wrath stir thee up against chastisements;
Neither let the greatness of the ransom turn thee aside.
[19] Will thy cry avail, *that thou be* not in distress,
Or all the forces of *thy* strength?

[6] Heb. *heart.* [7] Or, *pleasantness.* [8] Or, *weapons.* [9] Heb. *Their soul dieth.* [10] Or, *like.* [11] Or, *sodomites.* See Deut. 23. 17. [12] Or, *in.* [13] Or, *by adversity.* [14] Heb. *out of the mouth of.* [15] Or, *hast filled up.* [16] Or, *Because there is wrath, beware lest thou be led away by thy sufficiency.*

[20] Desire not the night,
When peoples are[17] cut off in their place.
[21] Take heed, regard not iniquity:
For this hast thou chosen rather than affliction.
[22] Behold, God doeth loftily in his power:
Who is a teacher like unto him?
[23] Who hath enjoined him his way?
Or who can say, Thou hast wrought unrighteousness?

[24] Remember that thou magnify his work,
Whereof men have sung.
[25] All men have looked thereon;
Man beholdeth it afar off.
[26] Behold, God is great, and we know him not;
The number of his years is unsearchable.
[27] For he draweth up the drops of water,
Which distil in rain from[18] his[19] vapor,
[28] Which the skies pour down
And drop upon man abundantly.
[29] Yea, can any understand the spreadings of the clouds,
The thunderings of his pavilion?
[30] Behold, he spreadeth his light around[20] him;
And he covereth[21] the bottom of the sea.
[31] For by these he judgeth the peoples;
He giveth food in abundance.
[32] He covereth his hands with the lightning,[22]
And giveth it a charge that[23] it strike the mark.
[33] The noise thereof telleth concerning him,[24]
The cattle also concerning *the*[25] *storm* that cometh up.

XXXVII

[1] Yea, at this my heart trembleth,
And is moved out of its place.
[2] Hear, oh, hear the noise of his voice,
And the sound[1] that goeth out of his mouth.

[17] Heb. *go up*. [18] Heb. *belonging to*. [19] Or, *the vapor thereof*. [20] Or, *thereon*.
[21] Or, *covereth* it *with the depths of the sea*. [22] Heb. *light*.
[23] Or, *against the assailant*. [24] Or, *it*. [25] Or, *him*. [1] Or, *muttering*.

[3] He sendeth it forth under the whole heaven,
And his lightning[2] unto the ends[3] of the earth.
[4] After it a voice roareth;
He thundereth with the voice of his majesty;
And he restraineth not *the*[4] *lightnings* when his voice is heard.
[5] God thundereth marvellously with his voice;
Great things doeth he, which we cannot comprehend.
[6] For he saith to the snow,
Fall thou on the earth;
Likewise to the shower of rain,
And to the showers of his mighty rain.
[7] He sealeth up the hand of every man,
That all men whom he hath made may know *it.*
[8] Then the beasts go into coverts,
And remain in their dens.
[9] Out of the chamber *of the south* cometh the storm,
And cold out of the north.[5]
[10] By the breath of God ice is given;
And the breadth of the waters is straitened.[6]
[11] Yea, he ladeth the thick cloud with moisture;
He spreadeth abroad the cloud of his lightning:[2]
[12] And it is turned round about by his guidance,
That they may do whatsoever he commandeth them
Upon the face of the habitable world;
[13] Whether it be for correction, or for his land,[7]
Or for lovingkindness, that he cause it to come.

[14] Hearken unto this, O Job:
Stand still, and consider the wondrous works of God.
[15] Dost thou know how God layeth *his charge* upon them,
And causeth the lightning[2] of his cloud to shine?
[16] Dost thou know the balancings of the clouds,
The wondrous works of him who is perfect in knowledge?
[17] How[8] thy garments are warm,
When[9] the earth is still by reason of the south *wind?*

[2] Heb. *light.* [3] Heb. *skirts.* [4] Heb. *them.* [5] Heb. *scattering* winds.
[6] Or, *congealed.* [7] Or, *earth.* [8] Or, *Thou whose garments are &c.*
[9] Or, *When he quieteth the earth by the south* wind.

[18] Canst thou with him spread out the sky,
Which is strong as a molten mirror?
[19] Teach us what we shall say unto him;
For we cannot set *our speech* in order by reason of darkness.
[20] Shall it be told him that I would speak?
Or[10] should a man wish that he were swallowed up?

[21] And now men see[11] not the light which is bright in the skies;
But the wind passeth, and cleareth them.
[22] Out of the north cometh golden[12] splendor:
God hath upon him terrible majesty.
[23] *Touching* the Almighty, we cannot find him out:
He is excellent in power;
And in[13] justice and plenteous righteousness he will not afflict.
[24] Men do therefore fear him:
He regardeth not any that are wise of heart.

XXXVIII

[1] THEN Jehovah answered Job out of the whirlwind, and said,
[2] Who is this that darkeneth counsel
By words without knowledge?
[3] Gird up now thy loins like a man;
For I will demand of thee, and declare thou unto me.
[4] Where wast thou when I laid the foundations of the earth?
Declare, if[1] thou hast understanding.
[5] Who determined the measures thereof, if[2] thou knowest?
Or who stretched the line upon it?
[6] Whereupon were the foundations[3] thereof fastened?[4]
Or who laid the corner-stone thereof,
[7] When the morning stars sang together,
And all the sons of God shouted for joy?
[8] Or *who* shut up the sea with doors,
When it brake forth, *as*[5] *if* it had issued out of the womb;

[10] Or, *If a man speak, surely he shall be swallowed up.*
[11] Or, *cannot look on the light when it is bright in the skies, when the wind hath passed, and cleared them.* [12] Heb. *gold.* [13] Or, *to justice . . . he doeth no violence.*
[1] Heb. *if thou knowest understanding.* [2] Or, *seeing.* [3] Heb. *sockets.*
[4] Heb. *made to sink.* [5] Or, and *issued.*

[9] When I made clouds the garment thereof,
And thick darkness a swaddling-band for it,
[10] And marked[6] out for it my bound,
And set bars and doors,
[11] And said, Hitherto shalt thou come, but no further;
And here shall thy proud waves be stayed?

[12] Hast thou commanded the morning since thy days *began,*
And caused the dayspring to know its place;
[13] That it might take hold of the ends of the earth,
And the wicked be shaken out of it?
[14] It is changed as clay under the seal;
And *all things* stand forth as[7] a garment:
[15] And from the wicked their light is withholden,
And the high arm is broken.

[16] Hast thou entered into the springs of the sea?
Or hast thou walked in the recesses[8] of the deep?
[17] Have the gates of death been revealed unto thee?
Or hast thou seen the gates of the shadow of death?
[18] Hast thou comprehended the earth in its breadth?
Declare, if thou knowest it all.

[19] Where is the way to the dwelling of light?
And as for darkness, where is the place thereof,
[20] That thou shouldest take it to the bound thereof,
And that thou shouldest discern the paths to the house thereof?
[21] *Doubtless,* thou knowest, for thou wast then born,
And the number of thy days is great!
[22] Hast thou entered the treasuries of the snow,
Or hast thou seen the treasuries of the hail,
[23] Which I have reserved against the time of trouble,
Against the day of battle and war?
[24] By[9] what way is the light parted,
Or the east wind scattered upon the earth?

[6] Heb. *brake.* [7] Or, *as* in *a garment.* [8] Or, *search.*
[9] Or, *Which is the way* to the place where *the light is &c.*

[25] Who hath cleft a channel for the waterflood,
Or a way for the lightning of the thunder;
[26] To cause it to rain on a land where no man is;
On the wilderness, wherein there is no man;
[27] To satisfy the waste and desolate *ground,*
And to cause the tender[10] grass to spring forth?
[28] Hath the rain a father?
Or who hath begotten the drops of dew?
[29] Out of whose womb came the ice?
And the hoary frost of heaven, who hath gendered[11] it?
[30] The waters hide[12] themselves *and become* like stone,
And the face of the deep is[13] frozen.

[31] Canst thou bind the cluster[14] of the Pleiades,
Or loose the bands of Orion?
[32] Canst thou lead forth the[15] Mazzaroth in their season?
Or canst thou guide the Bear with her train?[16]
[33] Knowest thou the ordinances of the heavens?
Canst thou establish the dominion thereof in the earth?

[34] Canst thou lift up thy voice to the clouds,
That abundance of waters may cover thee?
[35] Canst thou send forth lightnings, that they may go,
And say unto thee, Here we are?
[36] Who hath put wisdom in the inward[17] parts?
Or who hath given understanding to the mind?[18]
[37] Who can number the clouds by wisdom?
Or who can pour[19] out the bottles of heaven,
[38] When the dust runneth into a mass,
And the clods cleave fast together?

[39] Canst thou hunt the prey for the lioness,
Or satisfy the appetite of the young lions,
[40] When they couch in their dens,
And abide in the covert to lie in wait?

[10] Or, *greensward.* [11] Or, *given it birth.* [12] Or, *are congealed like stone.* [13] Heb. *cohereth.* [14] Or, *chain.* Or, *sweet influences.* [15] Or, *the signs of the Zodiac.* [16] Heb. *sons.* [17] Or, *dark clouds.* [18] Or, *meteor.* [19] Heb. *cause to lie down.*

[41] Who provideth for the raven his prey,
When his young ones cry unto God,
And wander for lack of food?

XXXIX

[1] KNOWEST thou the time when the wild goats of the rock bring forth?
Or canst thou mark when the hinds do calve?
[2] Canst thou number the months that they fulfil?
Or knowest thou the time when they bring forth?
[3] They bow themselves, they bring forth their young,
They cast out their pains.
[4] Their young ones become strong, they grow up in the open field;
They go forth, and return[1] not again.

[5] Who hath sent out the wild ass free?
Or who hath loosed the bonds of the swift ass,
[6] Whose home I have made the wilderness
And the salt land his dwelling-place?
[7] He scorneth the tumult of the city,
Neither heareth he the shoutings of the driver.[2]
[8] The range of the mountains is his pasture,
And he searcheth after every green thing.
[9] Will the wild-ox be content to serve thee?
Or will he abide by thy crib?
[10] Canst thou bind the wild-ox with his band in the furrow?
Or will he harrow the valleys after thee?
[11] Wilt thou trust him, because his strength is great?
Or wilt thou leave to him thy labor?
[12] Wilt thou confide in him, that he will bring home thy seed,
And gather *the grain of* thy threshing-floor?

[13] The wings of the ostrich wave proudly;
But are they the pinions and plumage of love?[3]

[1] Or, *return not unto them.* [2] Or, *taskmaster.* [3] Or, *a stork.*

[14] For she leaveth her eggs on the earth,
And warmeth them in the dust,
[15] And forgetteth that the foot may crush them,
Or that the wild beast may trample them.
[16] She dealeth[4] hardly with her young ones, as if they were not hers:
Though her labor be in vain, *she is* without fear;
[17] Because God hath deprived[5] her of wisdom,
Neither hath he imparted to her understanding.
[18] What time she lifteth[6] up herself on high,
She scorneth the horse and his rider.

[19] Hast thou given the horse *his* might?
Hast thou clothed his neck with the quivering[7] mane?
[20] Hast thou made him to leap as a locust?
The glory of his snorting is terrible.
[21] He[8] paweth in the valley, and rejoiceth in his strength:
He goeth out to meet the[9] armed men.
[22] He mocketh at fear, and is not dismayed;
Neither turneth he back from the sword.
[23] The quiver rattleth against[10] him,
The flashing spear and the javelin.
[24] He swalloweth the ground with fierceness and rage;
Neither believeth[11] he that it is the voice of the trumpet.
[25] As oft as the trumpet *soundeth* he saith, Aha!
And he smelleth the battle afar off,
The thunder of the captains, and the shouting.

[26] Is it by thy wisdom that the hawk soareth,
And stretcheth her wings toward the south?
[27] Is it at thy command that the eagle mounteth up,
And maketh her nest on high?
[28] On the cliff she dwelleth, and maketh her home,
Upon the point of the cliff, and the stronghold.
[29] From thence she spieth out the prey;
Her eyes behold it afar off.

[4] Or, *is hardened against.* [5] Heb. *made her to forget wisdom.*
[6] Or, *rouseth herself up to flight.* [7] Heb. *shaking.* [8] Heb. *They paw.*
[9] Or, *the weapons.* [10] Or, *upon.* [11] Or, *standeth he still at &c.*

[30] Her young ones also suck up blood:
And where the slain are, there is she.

XL

[1] MOREOVER Jehovah answered Job, and said,
[2] Shall he that cavilleth contend with the Almighty?
He that argueth with God, let him answer it.

[3] Then Job answered Jehovah, and said,
[4] Behold, I am of small account; what shall I answer thee?
I lay my hand upon my mouth.
[5] Once have I spoken, and I will not answer;
Yea, twice, but I will proceed no further.

[6] Then Jehovah answered Job out of the whirlwind, and said,
[7] Gird up thy loins now like a man:
I will demand of thee, and declare thou unto me.
[8] Wilt thou even annul my judgment?
Wilt thou condemn me, that thou mayest be justified?
[9] Or hast thou an arm like God?
And canst thou thunder with a voice like him?

[10] Deck thyself now with excellency and dignity;
And array thyself with honor and majesty.
[11] Pour forth the overflowings of thine anger;
And look upon every one that is proud, and abase him.
[12] Look on every one that is proud, *and* bring him low;
And tread down the wicked where they stand.
[13] Hide them in the dust together;
Bind their faces in the hidden *place*.
[14] Then will I also confess of thee
That thine own right hand can save thee.

[15] Behold now, behemoth,[1] which I made as[2] well as thee;
He eateth grass as an ox.

[1] That is, *the hippopotamus*. [2] Heb. *with*.

[16] Lo now, his strength is in his loins,
And his force is in the muscles of his belly.
[17] He moveth his tail like a cedar:
The sinews of his thighs are knit together.
[18] His bones are *as* tubes of brass;
His limbs[3] are like bars of iron.

[19] He is the chief of the ways of God:
He *only* that made him giveth him his sword.
[20] Surely the mountains bring him forth food,
Where all the beasts of the field do play.
[21] He lieth under the lotus-trees,
In the covert of the reed, and the fen.
[22] The lotus-trees cover him with their shade;
The willows of the brook compass him about.
[23] Behold, if a river overflow,[4] he trembleth not;
He is confident, though a Jordan swell even to his mouth.
[24] Shall any take him when he is on the watch,
Or pierce through his nose with a snare?

XLI

[1] CANST thou draw out leviathan[5] with a fishhook?
Or press down his tongue with a cord?
[2] Canst thou put a[6] rope into his nose?
Or pierce his jaw through with a hook?[7]
[3] Will he make many supplications unto thee?
Or will he speak soft words unto thee?
[4] Will he make a covenant with thee,
That thou shouldest take him for a servant for ever?
[5] Wilt thou play with him as with a bird?
Or wilt thou bind him for thy maidens?
[6] Will the bands *of fishermen* make traffic of him?
Will they part him among the merchants?
[7] Canst thou fill his skin with barbed irons,
Or his head with fish-spears?

[3] Or, *ribs*. [4] Or, *be violent*.
[5] That is, *the crocodile*. [6] Heb. *a rope of rushes*. [7] Or, *spike*.

[8] Lay thy hand upon him;
Remember the battle, and do so no more.
[9] Behold, the hope of him is in vain:
Will not one be cast down even at the sight of him?
[10] None is so fierce that he dare stir him up;
Who then is he that can stand before me?
[11] Who hath first given unto me, that I should repay him?
Whatsoever is under the whole heaven is mine.

[12] I will not keep silence concerning his limbs,
Nor his mighty strength, nor his goodly frame.
[13] Who can strip[8] off his outer garment?
Who shall come within his jaws?
[14] Who can open the doors of his face?
Round[9] about his teeth is terror.
[15] *His* strong[10] scales are *his* pride,
Shut up together *as with* a close seal.
[16] One is so near to another,
That no air can come between them.
[17] They are joined one to another;
They stick together, so that they cannot be sundered.
[18] His sneezings flash forth light,
And his eyes are like the eyelids of the morning.
[19] Out of his mouth go burning torches,
And sparks of fire leap forth.
[20] Out of his nostrils a smoke goeth,
As of a boiling pot and *burning* rushes.
[21] His breath kindleth coals,
And a flame goeth forth from his mouth.
[22] In his neck abideth strength,
And terror danceth before him.
[23] The flakes of his flesh are joined together:
They are firm upon him; they cannot be moved.
[24] His heart is as firm as a stone;
Yea, firm as the nether millstone.

[8] Heb. *uncover the face of his garment.* [9] Or, *His teeth are terrible round about.*
[10] Or, *courses of scales.* Heb. *channels of shields.*

[25] When he raiseth himself up, the mighty are afraid:
By reason of consternation they are beside themselves.
[26] If one lay at him with the sword, it cannot avail;
Nor the spear, the dart, nor the pointed[11] shaft.
[27] He counteth iron as straw,
And brass as rotten wood.
[28] The arrow[12] cannot make him flee:
Sling-stones are turned with him into stubble.
[29] Clubs are counted as stubble:
He laugheth at the rushing of the javelin.
[30] His underparts are *like* sharp potsherds:
He spreadeth *as it were* a threshing-wain upon the mire.
[31] He maketh the deep to boil like a pot:
He maketh the sea like a pot of ointment.
[32] He maketh a path to shine after him;
One would think the deep to be hoary.
[33] Upon earth there is not his like,
That is made without fear.
[34] He beholdeth every thing that is high:
He is king over all the sons of pride.

XLII

[1] Then Job answered Jehovah, and said,
[2] I know that thou canst do all things,
And that no purpose of thine can be restrained.
[3] Who is this that hideth counsel without knowledge?
Therefore have I uttered that which I understood not,
Things too wonderful for me, which I knew not.
[4] Hear, I beseech thee, and I will speak;
I will demand of thee, and declare thou unto me.
[5] I had heard of thee by the hearing of the ear;
But now mine eye seeth thee:
[6] Wherefore I abhor[1] *myself,*
And repent in dust and ashes.

11 Or, *coat of mail.* 12 Heb. *son of the bow.* 1 Or, *loathe* my words.

[7] And it was so, that, after Jehovah had spoken these words unto Job, Jehovah said to Eliphaz the Temanite, My wrath is kindled against thee, and against thy two friends; for ye have not spoken of me the thing that is right, as my servant Job hath. [8] Now therefore, take unto you seven bullocks and seven rams, and go to my servant Job, and offer up for yourselves a burnt-offering; and my servant Job shall pray for you; for him will I accept, that I deal not with you after your folly; for ye have not spoken of me the thing that is right, as my servant Job hath. [9] So Eliphaz the Temanite and Bildad the Shuhite and Zophar the Naamathite went, and did according as Jehovah commanded them: and Jehovah accepted Job.

[10] And Jehovah turned the captivity of Job, when he prayed for his friends: and Jehovah gave Job twice as much as he had before. [11] Then came there unto him all his brethren, and all his sisters, and all they that had been of his acquaintance before, and did eat bread with him in his house: and they bemoaned him, and comforted him concerning all the evil that Jehovah had brought upon him: every man also gave him a piece[2] of money, and every one a ring of gold. [12] So Jehovah blessed the latter end of Job more than his beginning: and he had fourteen thousand sheep, and six thousand camels, and a thousand yoke of oxen, and a thousand she-asses. [13] He had also seven sons and three daughters. [14] And he called the name of the first, Jemimah; and the name of the second, Keziah; and the name of the third, Keren-happuch. [15] And in all the land were no women found so fair as the daughters of Job: and their father gave them inheritance among their brethren. [16] And after this Job lived a hundred and forty years, and saw his sons, and his sons' sons, *even* four generations. [17] So Job died, being old and full of days.

[2] Heb. *ḳesitah.*

(HEBREW)

THE BOOK OF PSALMS

INTRODUCTORY NOTE

THE Book of Psalms is a great collection of the religious lyrics of the Hebrew people. Of unknown authorship, and of uncertain dates, these hymns were gathered and arranged, in part at least, for use in the services of the Temple at Jerusalem; but their profundity of feeling, their simplicity of expression, and the variety of the religious experiences with which they deal have found them a welcome in the hearts of devout people far beyond the limits of Judaism.

The Psalms as they have come down to us are divided into five Books, each ending with a doxology; but it is probable that these divisions are of a later date than the actual collecting of the poems. One hundred of them are attached to individual names; and these names were long supposed to indicate the authors. Thus to David are attributed seventy-three, to Asaph twelve, to Moses one, to Solomon two, to the sons of Korah eleven. These ascriptions are, however, later than the Psalms themselves, and are by no means to be relied on, many of them being demonstrably false. The only poems which are now universally ascribed to David are those in 2 Samuel, I and III; it is doubtful whether he wrote any of the Psalms.

The question of the dates of the Psalms is almost as difficult as that of the authorship. Some have been supposed to be as old as 900 B. C.; none is likely to be later than the beginning of the second century B. C.; and their composition probably extended over more than five hundred years.

The religious moods to which they give utterance are manifold. Adoration and thanksgiving, prayer and penitence and imprecation, history and prophecy, the general worship of a whole people and the intimate impulses of an individual soul—all these and many more are represented in this supreme collection of sacred song.

THE BOOK OF PSALMS

BOOK I

I

[1] THE RIGHTEOUS AND THE WICKED CONTRASTED

BLESSED[1] is the man that walketh not in the counsel of the wicked,
Nor standeth in the way of sinners,
Nor sitteth in the seat of scoffers:
[2] But his delight is in the law of Jehovah;
And on his law doth he meditate day and night.
[3] And he shall be like a tree planted by the streams of water,
That bringeth forth its fruit in its season,
Whose leaf also doth not wither;
And whatsoever[2] he doeth shall prosper.
[4] The wicked are not so,
But are like the chaff which the wind driveth away.
[5] Therefore the wicked shall not stand in the judgment,
Nor sinners in the congregation of the righteous.
[6] For Jehovah knoweth the way of the righteous;
But the way of the wicked shall perish.

II

THE REIGN OF JEHOVAH'S ANOINTED

[1] WHY do the nations rage,[3]
And the peoples meditate a vain thing?
[2] The kings of the earth set themselves,
And the rulers take counsel together,
Against Jehovah, and against his anointed, *saying,*

[1] Or, *Happy.* [2] Or, *in whatsoever he doeth he shall prosper.*
[3] Or, *tumultuously assemble.*

[3] Let us break their bonds asunder,
And cast away their cords from us.
[4] He that sitteth in the heavens will laugh:
The Lord will have them in derision.
[5] Then will he speak unto them in his wrath,
And vex[4] them in his sore displeasure:
[6] Yet I have set my king
Upon my holy hill of Zion.

[7] I will tell of the decree:
Jehovah said unto me, Thou art my son;
This day have I begotten thee.
[8] Ask of me, and I will give *thee* the nations for thine inheritance,
And the uttermost parts of the earth for thy possession.
[9] Thou shalt break them with a rod of iron;
Thou shalt dash them in pieces like a potter's vessel.

[10] Now therefore be wise, O ye kings:
Be instructed, ye judges of the earth.
[11] Serve Jehovah with fear,
And rejoice with trembling.
[12] Kiss the son, lest he be angry, and ye perish in the way,
For his wrath will[5] soon be kindled.
Blessed[6] are all they that take refuge in him.

III

Morning Prayer of Trust in God

A Psalm of David, when he fled from Absalom his son.

[1] Jehovah, how are mine adversaries increased!
Many are they that rise up against me.
[2] Many there are that say of[1] my soul,
There is no help[2] for him in God. [Selah
[3] But thou, O Jehovah, art a shield about me;
My glory, and the lifter up of my head.
[4] I cry unto Jehovah with my voice,
And he answereth me out of his holy hill. [Selah

[4] Or, *trouble.* [5] Or, *may.* [6] Or, *Happy.* [1] Or, *to.* [2] Or, *salvation.*

[5] I laid me down and slept;
I awaked; for Jehovah sustaineth me.
[6] I will not be afraid of ten thousands of the people
That have set themselves against me round about.
[7] Arise, O Jehovah; save me, O my God:
For thou hast smitten all mine enemies upon the cheek bone;
Thou hast broken the teeth of the wicked.
[8] Salvation[3] belongeth unto Jehovah:
Thy blessing be upon thy people. [Selah

IV

Evening Prayer of Trust in God

For the Chief Musician; on stringed instruments. A Psalm of David.

[1] Answer me when I call, O God of my righteousness;
Thou hast set me at large *when I was* in distress:
Have[4] mercy upon me, and hear my prayer.
[2] O ye sons of men, how long shall my glory be turned into dishonor?
How long will ye love vanity, and seek after falsehood? [Selah
[3] But know that Jehovah hath set apart for himself him[5] that is godly:
Jehovah will hear when I call unto him.
[4] Stand[6] in awe, and sin not:
Commune with your own heart upon your bed, and be still. [Selah
[5] Offer the sacrifices of righteousness,
And put your trust in Jehovah.
[6] Many there are that say, Who will show us *any* good?
Jehovah, lift thou up the light of thy countenance upon us.
[7] Thou hast put gladness in my heart,
More than *they have* when their grain and their new wine are increased.

[3] Or, *Victory*. [4] Or, *Be gracious unto me*. [5] Or, *one that he favoreth*.
[6] Or, *Be ye angry*.

[8] In peace will I both lay me down and sleep;
For thou, Jehovah, alone[7] makest me dwell in safety.

V

Prayer for Protection from the Wicked

For the Chief Musician; with the Nehiloth.[8] A Psalm of David.

[1] Give ear to my words, O Jehovah,
Consider my meditation.
[2] Hearken unto the voice of my cry, my King, and my God;
For unto thee do I pray.
[3] O Jehovah, in the morning shalt thou hear my voice;
In the morning will I order *my prayer* unto thee, and will keep watch.
[4] For thou art not a God that hath pleasure in wickedness:
Evil[9] shall not sojourn with thee.
[5] The[10] arrogant shall not stand in thy sight:
Thou hatest all workers of iniquity.
[6] Thou wilt destroy them that speak lies:
Jehovah abhorreth the bloodthirsty and deceitful man.
[7] But as for me, in the abundance of thy lovingkindness will I come into thy house:
In thy fear will I worship toward thy holy temple.
[8] Lead me, O Jehovah, in thy righteousness because of mine[11] enemies:
Make thy way straight[12] before my face.
[9] For there is no faithfulness[13] in their mouth;
Their inward part is very[14] wickedness;
Their throat is an open sepulchre;
They flatter[15] with their tongue.
[10] Hold them guilty, O God;
Let them fall by[16] their own counsels;
Thrust them out in the multitude of their transgressions;
For they have rebelled against thee.

[7] Or, *in solitude.*
[8] Or, *wind instruments.* [9] Or, *The evil man.* [10] Or, *Fools.* [11] Or, *them that lie in wait for me.* [12] Or, *level.* [13] Or, *stedfastness.* [14] Or, *a yawning gulf.*
[15] Heb. *make smooth their tongue.* [16] Or, *from their counsels.*

[11] But[17] let all those that take refuge in thee rejoice,
Let them ever shout for joy, because thou defendest them:
Let them also that love thy name be joyful in thee.
[12] For thou wilt bless the righteous;
O Jehovah, thou wilt compass him with favor as with a shield.

VI

Prayer for Mercy in Time of Trouble

For the Chief Musician; on stringed instruments, set to the[1] Sheminith. A Psalm of David.

[1] O Jehovah, rebuke me not in thine anger,
Neither chasten me in thy hot displeasure.
[2] Have mercy upon me, O Jehovah; for I am withered away:
O Jehovah, heal me; for my bones are troubled.
[3] My soul also is sore troubled:
And thou, O Jehovah, how long?
[4] Return, O Jehovah, deliver my soul:
Save me for thy lovingkindness' sake.
[5] For in death there is no remembrance of thee:
In Sheol who shall give thee thanks?
[6] I am weary with my groaning;
Every night make I my bed to swim;
I water my couch with my tears.
[7] Mine eye wasteth away because of grief;
It waxeth old because of all mine adversaries.
[8] Depart from me, all ye workers of iniquity;
For Jehovah hath heard the voice of my weeping.
[9] Jehovah hath heard my supplication;
Jehovah will receive my prayer.
[10] All mine enemies shall be put to shame and sore troubled:
They shall turn back, they shall be put to shame suddenly.

[17] Or, *So shall all those . . . rejoice, They shall ever shout . . . and thou shalt defend them: They also . . . shall be joyful in thee.*
[1] Or, *the eighth.*

VII

Jehovah Implored to Defend the Psalmist Against the Wicked

Shiggaion of David, which he sang unto Jehovah, concerning the words of Cush a Benjamite.

[1] O Jehovah my God, in thee do I take refuge:
Save me from all them that pursue me, and deliver me,
[2] Lest they tear my soul like a lion,
Rending it in pieces, while there is none to deliver.
[3] O Jehovah my God, if I have done this;
If there be iniquity in my hands;
[4] If I have rewarded evil unto him that was at peace with me;
(Yea, I have delivered him that without cause was mine adversary);
[5] Let the enemy pursue my soul, and overtake it;
Yea, let him tread my life down to the earth,
And lay my glory in the dust. [Selah
[6] Arise, O Jehovah, in thine anger;
Lift up thyself against the rage of mine adversaries,
And awake for me; thou hast commanded judgment.
[7] And[1] let the congregation of the peoples compass thee about;
And over them return thou on high.
[8] Jehovah ministereth judgment to the peoples:
Judge me, O Jehovah, according to my righteousness, and to mine integrity that[2] is in me.
[9] Oh let the wickedness of the wicked come to an end, but establish thou the righteous:
For the righteous God trieth the minds and hearts.[3]
[10] My shield is with God,
Who saveth the upright in heart.
[11] God is a righteous judge,
Yea, a God that hath indignation every day.
[12] If[4] a man turn not, he will whet his sword;
He hath bent his bow, and made it ready.

[1] Or, *So shall.* [2] Or, *be it unto me.* [3] Heb. *reins.*
[4] Or, *Surely he will again whet.*

[13] He hath also prepared for him the instruments of death;
He maketh his arrows fiery *shafts.*
[14] Behold, he travaileth with iniquity;
Yea, he hath conceived mischief, and brought forth falsehood.
[15] He hath made a pit, and digged it,
And is fallen into the ditch which he made.
[16] His mischief shall return upon his own head,
And his violence shall come down upon his own pate.
[17] I will give thanks unto Jehovah according to his righteousness,
And will sing praise to the name of Jehovah Most High.

VIII

Jehovah's Glory and Man's Dignity

For the Chief Musician; set to the Gittith. A Psalm of David.

[1] O Jehovah, our Lord,
How excellent is thy name in all the earth,
Who hast set thy glory upon[1] the heavens!
[2] Out of the mouth of babes and sucklings hast thou established strength,
Because of thine adversaries,
That thou mightest still the enemy and the avenger.
[3] When I consider thy heavens, the work of thy fingers,
The moon and the stars, which thou hast ordained;
[4] What is man, that thou art mindful of him?
And the son of man, that thou visitest him?
[5] For thou hast made him but little lower than God,[2]
And crownest him with glory and honor.
[6] Thou makest him to have dominion over the works of thy hands;
Thou hast put all things under his feet:
[7] All sheep and oxen,
Yea, and the beasts of the field,
[8] The birds of the heavens, and the fish of the sea,
Whatsoever passeth through the paths of the seas.

[1] Or, *above.* [2] Or, *the angels.* Heb. *Elohim.*

[9] O Jehovah, our Lord,
How excellent is thy name in all the earth!

IX

A Psalm of Thanksgiving for God's Justice

For the Chief Musician; set to Muth-labben. A Psalm of David.

[1] I WILL give thanks unto Jehovah with my whole heart;
I will show forth all thy marvellous works.
[2] I will be glad and exult in thee;
I will sing praise to thy name, O thou Most[1] High.
[3] When mine enemies turn back,
They stumble and perish at thy presence.
[4] For thou hast maintained my right and my cause;
Thou sittest in the throne judging righteously.
[5] Thou hast rebuked the nations,[2] thou hast destroyed the wicked;
Thou hast blotted out their name for ever and ever.
[6] The[3] enemy are come to an end, they are desolate for ever;
And[4] the cities which thou hast overthrown,[5]
The very remembrance of them is perished.
[7] But Jehovah sitteth *as king* for ever:
He hath prepared his throne for judgment;
[8] And he will judge the world in righteousness,
He will minister judgment to the peoples[6] in uprightness.
[9] Jehovah also will be a high tower for the oppressed,
A high tower in times of trouble;
[10] And they that know thy name will put their trust in thee;
For thou, Jehovah, hast not forsaken them that seek thee.
[11] Sing praises to Jehovah, who dwelleth in Zion:
Declare among the people[7] his doings.
[12] For[8] he that maketh inquisition for blood remembereth them;
He forgetteth not the cry of the poor.[9]

[1] Or, *Most High; because mine &c.* [2] Or, *heathen.*
[3] Or, *O thou enemy, desolations are come to a perpetual end.*
[4] Or, *And* their *cities thou hast overthrown.*
[5] Heb. *plucked up.* [6] Or, *people.*
[7] Or, *peoples.* [8] Or, *For when he maketh . . . he remembereth.* [9] Or, *meek.*

[13] Have mercy upon me, O Jehovah;
Behold my affliction *which I suffer* of them that hate me,
Thou that liftest me up from the gates of death;
[14] That I may show forth all thy praise:
In the gates of the daughter of Zion
I will rejoice in thy salvation.[10]
[15] The nations are sunk down in the pit that they made:
In the net which they hid is their own foot taken.
[16] Jehovah hath made himself known, he hath executed judgment:
The[11] wicked is snared in the work of his own hands.
[Higgaion. Selah
[17] The wicked shall be turned back unto Sheol,
Even all the nations that forget God.
[18] For the needy shall not alway be forgotten,
Nor the expectation of the poor[12] perish for ever.
[19] Arise, O Jehovah; let not man prevail:
Let the nations be judged in thy sight.
[20] Put them in fear, O Jehovah:
Let the nations know themselves to be but men. [Selah

X

A Prayer for the Overthrow of the Wicked

[1] Why standest thou afar off, O Jehovah?
Why hidest thou thyself in times of trouble?
[2] In the pride of the wicked the[1] poor is[2] hotly pursued;
Let[3] them be taken in the devices that they have conceived.
[3] For the wicked boasteth of his heart's desire,
And[4] the covetous renounceth, *yea,* contemneth[5] Jehovah.
[4] The wicked, in the pride of his countenance, *saith,* He will not require *it.*
All his thoughts are, There is no God.
[5] His ways are firm[6] at all times;
Thy judgments are far above out of his sight:
As for all his adversaries, he puffeth at them.

[10] Or, *saving help.* [11] Or, *He snareth the wicked.* [12] Or, *meek.*
[1] Or, *he doth hotly pursue the poor.* [2] Heb. *is set on fire.* [3] Or, *They are taken.*
[4] Or, *blesseth the covetous,* but *contemneth &c.* [5] Or, *revileth.* [6] Or, *grievous.*

[6] He saith in his heart, I shall not be moved;
To all generations I shall not be in adversity.
[7] His mouth is full of cursing and deceit and oppression:[7]
Under his tongue is mischief and iniquity.
[8] He sitteth in the lurking-places of the villages;
In the secret places doth he murder the innocent;
His eyes are privily set against the helpless.[8]
[9] He lurketh in secret as a lion in his covert;
He lieth in wait to catch the poor:
He doth catch the poor, when he draweth him in his net.
[10] He[9] croucheth, he boweth down,
And the helpless[8] fall by his strong ones.
[11] He saith in his heart, God hath forgotten;
He hideth his face; he will never see it.
[12] Arise, O Jehovah; O God, lift up thy hand:
Forget not the poor.[10]
[13] Wherefore doth the wicked contemn God,
And say in his heart, Thou wilt not require *it?*
[14] Thou hast seen *it;* for thou beholdest mischief[11] and spite to[12] requite it with thy hand:
The helpless[8] committeth *himself* unto thee;
Thou hast been the helper of the fatherless.
[15] Break thou the arm of the wicked;
And as for the evil man, seek out his wickedness till thou find none.
[16] Jehovah is King for ever and ever:
The nations[13] are perished out of his land.
[17] Jehovah, thou hast heard the desire of the meek:
Thou wilt prepare[14] their heart, thou wilt cause thine ear to hear;
[18] To judge the fatherless and the oppressed,
That man who is of the earth may be terrible no more.

[7] Or, *fraud.* [8] Or, *hapless.* [9] Another reading is, *And being crushed.* [10] Or, *meek.* [11] Or, *travail and grief.* [12] Or, *to take it into thy hand.* [13] Or, *heathen.* [14] Or, *establish.*

XI

Jehovah a Refuge and Defence

For the Chief Musician. A Psalm of David.

[1] In Jehovah do I take refuge:
How say ye to my soul,
Flee *as*[1] a bird to your mountain;
[2] For, lo, the wicked bend the bow,
They make ready their arrow upon the string,
That they may shoot in darkness at the upright in heart;
[3] If[2] the foundations be destroyed,
What can the righteous do?
[4] Jehovah is in his holy temple;
Jehovah, his throne is in heaven;
His eyes behold, his eyelids try, the children of men.
[5] Jehovah trieth the righteous;
But the wicked and him that loveth violence his soul hateth.
[6] Upon the wicked he will rain snares;
Fire and brimstone and burning wind shall be the portion of their cup.
[7] For Jehovah is righteous; he loveth righteousness:[3]
The[4] upright shall behold his face.

XII

God a Helper Against the Treacherous

For the Chief Musician; set to the Sheminith.[5] A Psalm of David.

[1] Help, Jehovah; for the godly man ceaseth;
For the[6] faithful fail from among the children of men.
[2] They speak falsehood every one with his neighbor:
With flattering lip, and with a double heart, do they speak.
[3] Jehovah will cut off all flattering lips,
The tongue that speaketh great things;
[4] Who have said, With our tongue will we prevail;
Our lips are our[7] own: who is lord over us?

[1] Or, *ye birds.* [2] Or, *For the foundations are destroyed; What hath the righteous wrought?* [3] Or, *righteous deeds.* [4] Or, *His countenance doth behold the upright.* [5] Or, *the eighth.* [6] Or, *faithfulness faileth.* [7] Heb. *with us.*

[5] Because of the oppression of the poor, because of the sighing of the needy,
Now will I arise, saith Jehovah;
I will set him in the safety he panteth for.
[6] The words of Jehovah are pure words;
As silver tried in a furnace on the earth,
Purified seven times.
[7] Thou wilt keep them, O Jehovah,
Thou wilt preserve them from this generation for ever.
[8] The wicked walk on every side,
When vileness is exalted among the sons of men.

XIII

Prayer for Help in Affliction

For the Chief Musician. A Psalm of David.

[1] How long, O Jehovah? wilt thou forget me for ever?
How long wilt thou hide thy face from me?
[2] How long shall I take counsel in my soul,
Having sorrow in my heart all the day?
How long shall mine enemy be exalted over me?
[3] Consider *and* answer me, O Jehovah my God:
Lighten mine eyes, lest I sleep the *sleep of* death;
[4] Lest mine enemy say, I have prevailed against him;
Lest mine adversaries rejoice when I am moved.
[5] But I have trusted in thy lovingkindness;
My heart shall rejoice in thy salvation:
[6] I will sing unto Jehovah,
Because he hath dealt bountifully with me.

XIV

Folly and Wickedness of Men

For the Chief Musician. A Psalm of David.

[1] The fool hath said in his heart, There is no God.
They are corrupt, they have done abominable works;
There is none that doeth good.

[2] Jehovah looked down from heaven upon the children of men,
To see if there were any that did understand,[1]
That did seek after God.
[3] They are all gone aside; they are together become filthy;
There is none that doeth good, no, not one.
[4] Have all the workers of iniquity no knowledge,
Who eat up my people *as* they eat bread,
And call not upon Jehovah?
[5] There were they in great fear;
For God is in the generation of the righteous.
[6] Ye put to shame the counsel of the poor,
Because[2] Jehovah is his refuge.
[7] Oh that the salvation of Israel were come out of Zion!
When Jehovah bringeth[3] back the captivity of his people,
Then shall Jacob rejoice, *and* Israel shall be glad.

XV

Description of a Citizen of Zion

A Psalm of David.

[1] Jehovah, who shall sojourn in thy tabernacle?[4]
Who shall dwell in thy holy hill?
[2] He that walketh uprightly, and worketh righteousness,
And speaketh truth in his heart;
[3] He[5] that slandereth not with his tongue,
Nor doeth evil to his friend,
Nor taketh up a reproach against his neighbor;
[4] In whose[6] eyes a reprobate is despised,
But who honoreth them that fear Jehovah;
He[7] that sweareth to his own hurt, and changeth not;
[5] He[8] that putteth not out his money to interest,
Nor taketh reward against the innocent.
He that doeth these things shall never be moved.

[1] Or, *deal wisely.* [2] Or, *But.* [3] Or, *returneth to.*
[4] Heb. *tent.* [5] Or, *He slandereth.* [6] Or, *his.* [7] Or, *He sweareth.* [8] Or, *He putteth.*

XVI

Jehovah the Psalmist's Portion in Life and Deliverer in Death

Michtam of David.

[1] Preserve me, O God; for in thee do I take refuge.
[2] *O my soul,* thou hast said unto Jehovah, Thou art my[1] Lord:
I have no good beyond thee.
[3] As[2] for the saints that are in the earth,
They[3] are the excellent in whom is all my delight.
[4] Their sorrows shall be multiplied that give gifts for another *god:*
Their drink-offerings of blood will I not offer,
Nor take their names upon my lips.
[5] Jehovah is the portion of mine inheritance and of my cup:
Thou maintainest my lot.
[6] The lines are fallen unto me in pleasant places;
Yea, I have a goodly heritage.
[7] I will bless Jehovah, who hath given me counsel;
Yea, my heart[4] instructeth me in the night seasons.
[8] I have set Jehovah always before me:
Because he is at my right hand, I shall not be moved.
[9] Therefore my heart is glad, and my glory rejoiceth:
My flesh also shall dwell in[5] safety.
[10] For thou wilt not leave my soul to Sheol;
Neither wilt thou suffer thy holy[6] one to see corruption.[7]
[11] Thou wilt show me the path of life:
In thy presence is fulness of joy;
In thy right hand there are pleasures for evermore.

XVII

Prayer for Protection Against Oppressors

A Prayer of David.

[1] Hear the right, O Jehovah, attend unto my cry;
Give ear unto my prayer, that goeth not out of feigned lips.

[1] Or, *the Lord.* [2] Or, *Unto.* [3] Or, *And the excellent . . . delight: Their &c.* [4] Heb. *reins.* [5] Or, *confidently.* [6] Or, *godly.* Or, *beloved.* Another reading is, *holy ones.* [7] Or, *the pit.*

[2] Let my sentence come forth from thy presence;
Let[1] thine eyes look upon equity.
[3] Thou hast proved my heart; thou hast visited me in the night;
Thou hast tried me, and findest[2] nothing;
I am purposed that my mouth shall not transgress.
[4] As for the works of men, by the word of thy lips
I have kept me from the ways of the violent.
[5] My steps have held fast to thy paths,
My feet have not slipped.
[6] I have called upon thee, for thou wilt answer me, O God:
Incline thine ear unto me, *and* hear my speech.
[7] Show thy marvellous lovingkindness,
O thou that savest by[3] thy right hand them that take refuge *in thee*
From those that rise up *against them*.
[8] Keep me as the apple of the eye;
Hide me under the shadow of thy wings,
[9] From the wicked that oppress me,
My deadly enemies, that compass me about.
[10] They[4] are inclosed in their own fat:
With their mouth they speak proudly.
[11] They have now compassed us in our steps;
They set their eyes to cast *us* down to the earth.
[12] He is like a lion that is greedy of his prey,
And as it were a young lion lurking in secret places.
[13] Arise, O Jehovah,
Confront[5] him, cast him down:
Deliver my soul from the[6] wicked by thy sword;
[14] From men[7] by thy hand, O Jehovah,
From men of[8] the world, whose portion is in *this* life,
And whose belly thou fillest with thy treasure:
They are satisfied with children,
And leave the rest of their substance to their babes.

[1] Or, *Thine eyes behold with equity.*
[2] Or, *findest no evil purpose in me; My mouth &c.*
[3] Or, *them that take refuge . . . rise up against thy right hand.*
[4] Or, *They have shut up their heart.* [5] Or, *Forestall.* [6] Or, *the wicked, who is thy sword.* [7] Or, *men who are thy hand.* [8] Or, *whose portion in life is of the world.*

[15] As for me, I[9] shall behold thy face in righteousness;
I[9] shall be satisfied, when I awake, with *beholding* thy form.

XVIII

Jehovah Praised for Giving Victory and Dominion

For the Chief Musician. A Psalm of David the servant of Jehovah, who[1] spake unto Jehovah the words of this song in the day that Jehovah delivered him from the hand of all his enemies, and from the hand of Saul: and he said,

[1] I love thee, O Jehovah, my strength.
[2] Jehovah is my rock, and my fortress, and my deliverer;
My God, my rock, in whom I will take refuge;
My shield, and the horn of my salvation, my high tower.
[3] I will call upon Jehovah, who is worthy to be praised:
So shall I be saved from mine enemies.
[4] The cords of death compassed me,
And the floods of ungodliness[2] made me afraid.
[5] The cords of Sheol were round about me;
The snares of death came upon me.
[6] In my distress I called upon Jehovah,
And cried unto my God:
He heard my voice out of his temple,
And my cry before him came into his ears.
[7] Then the earth shook and trembled;
The foundations also of the mountains quaked
And were shaken, because he was wroth.
[8] There went up a smoke out[3] of his nostrils,
And fire out of his mouth devoured:
Coals were kindled by it.
[9] He bowed the heavens also, and came down;
And thick darkness was under his feet.
[10] And he rode upon a cherub, and did fly;
Yea, he soared upon the wings of the wind.
[11] He made darkness his hiding-place, his pavilion round about him,
Darkness of waters, thick clouds of the skies.

[9] Or, *let me.* [1] See 2 S. 22. 1–51. [2] Heb. *Belial.* [3] Or, *in his wrath.*

[12] At the brightness before him his thick clouds passed,
Hailstones and coals of fire.
[13] Jehovah also thundered in the heavens,
And the Most High uttered his voice,
Hailstones and coals of fire.
[14] And he sent out his arrows, and scattered them;
Yea,[4] lightnings manifold, and discomfited them.
[15] Then the channels of waters appeared,
And the foundations of the world were laid bare,
At thy rebuke, O Jehovah,
At the blast of the breath of thy nostrils.
[16] He sent from on high, he took me;
He drew me out of many[5] waters.
[17] He delivered me from my strong enemy,
And from them that hated me; for they were too mightv for me.
[18] They came upon me in the day of my calamity;
But Jehovah was my stay.
[19] He brought me forth also into a large place;
He delivered me, because he delighted in me.
[20] Jehovah hath rewarded me according to my righteousness;
According to the cleanness of my hands, hath he recompensed me.
[21] For I have kept the ways of Jehovah,
And have not wickedly departed from my God.
[22] For all his ordinances were before me,
And I put not away his statutes from me.
[23] I was also perfect with him,
And I kept myself from mine iniquity.
[24] Therefore hath Jehovah recompensed me according to my righteousness,
According to the cleanness of my hands in his eyesight.
[25] With the merciful thou wilt show thyself merciful;
With the perfect man thou wilt show thyself perfect;
[26] With the pure thou wilt show thyself pure;
And with the perverse thou wilt show thyself froward.

[4]Or, *And he shot out lightnings.* [5]Or, *great.*

[27] For thou wilt save the afflicted people;
But the haughty eyes thou wilt bring down.
[28] For thou wilt light my lamp:
Jehovah my God will lighten my darkness.
[29] For by thee I run upon[6] a troop;
And by my God do I leap over a wall.
[30] As for God, his way is perfect:
The word of Jehovah is tried;
He is a shield unto all them that take refuge in him.
[31] For who is God, save Jehovah?
And who is a rock, besides our God,
[32] The God that girdeth me with strength,
And maketh my way perfect?
[33] He maketh my feet like hinds' *feet:*
And setteth me upon my high places.
[34] He teacheth my hands to war;
So that mine arms do bend a bow of brass.
[35] Thou hast also given me the shield of thy salvation;
And thy right hand hath holden me up,
And thy gentleness[7] hath made me great.
[36] Thou hast enlarged my steps under me,
And my feet[8] have not slipped.
[37] I will pursue mine enemies, and overtake them;
Neither will I turn again till they are consumed.
[38] I will smite them through, so that they shall not be able to rise:
They shall fall under my feet.
[39] For thou hast girded me with strength unto the battle:
Thou hast subdued[9] under me those that rose up against me.
[40] Thou hast also made mine enemies turn their backs unto me,
That I might cut off them that hate me.
[41] They cried, but there was none to save;
Even unto Jehovah, but he answered them not.
[42] Then did I beat them small as the dust before the wind;
I did cast[10] them out as the mire of the streets.

[6] Or, *through*.
[7] Or, *condescension*. [8] Heb. *ankles*. [9] Heb. *caused to bow*.
[10] Heb. *empty*.

[43] Thou hast delivered me from the strivings of the people;
Thou hast[11] made me the head of the nations:
A people whom I have not known shall serve me.
[44] As soon as they hear of me they shall obey me;
The foreigners shall submit[12] themselves unto me.
[45] The foreigners shall fade away,
And shall come trembling out of their close places.
[46] Jehovah liveth; and blessed be my rock;
And exalted be the God of my salvation,
[47] Even the God that executeth vengeance for me,
And subdueth peoples under me.
[48] He rescueth me from mine enemies;
Yea, thou liftiest me up above them that rise up against me;
Thou deliverest me from the violent man.
[49] Therefore I will give thanks unto thee, O Jehovah, among the nations,
And will sing praises unto thy name.
[50] Great deliverance[13] giveth he to his king,
And showeth lovingkindness to his anointed,
To David and to his seed, for evermore.

XIX

The Works and the Word of God

For the Chief Musician. A Psalm of David.

[1] The heavens declare the glory of God:
And the firmament showeth his handiwork.
[2] Day unto day uttereth speech,
And night unto night showeth knowledge.
[3] There is no speech nor language;
Their voice is not heard.
[4] Their line is gone out through all the earth,
And their words to the end of the world.
In them hath he set a tabernacle[1] for the sun,

[11]Or, *wilt make.* [12]Or, *yield feigned obedience.* Heb. *lie.*
[13]Heb. *salvation.* [1]Heb. *tent.*

[5] Which is as a bridegroom coming out of his chamber,
And rejoiceth as a strong man to run his course.
[6] His going forth is from the end of the heavens,
And his circuit unto the ends of it;
And there is nothing hid from the heat thereof.

[7] The law of Jehovah is perfect, restoring the soul:
The testimony of Jehovah is sure, making wise the simple.
[8] The precepts of Jehovah are right, rejoicing the heart:
The commandment of Jehovah is pure, enlightening the eyes.
[9] The fear of Jehovah is clean, enduring for ever:
The ordinances of Jehovah are true, *and* righteous altogether.
[10] More to be desired are they than gold, yea, than much fine gold;
Sweeter also than honey and the droppings of the honeycomb.
[11] Moreover by them is thy servant warned:
In keeping them there is great reward.
[12] Who can discern *his* errors?
Clear thou me from hidden *faults.*
[13] Keep back thy servant also from[2] presumptuous *sins;*
Let them not have dominion over me:
Then shall I be upright,
And I shall be clear from great transgression.
[14] Let the words of my mouth and the meditation of my heart
Be acceptable in thy sight,
O Jehovah, my rock, and my redeemer.

XX

Prayer for Victory over Enemies

For the Chief Musician. A Psalm of David.

[1] Jehovah answer thee in the day of trouble;
The name of the God of Jacob set thee up on high;
[2] Send thee help from the sanctuary,
And strengthen[3] thee out of Zion;
[3] Remember all thy offerings,[4]
And accept[5] thy burnt sacrifice; [Selah

[2]Or, *from the proud.* [3]Or, *support.* [4]Or, *meal-offerings.* [5]Heb. *accept as fat.*

[4] Grant thee thy heart's desire,
And fulfil all thy counsel.
[5] We will triumph in thy salvation,[6]
And in the name of our God we will set up our banners:
Jehovah fulfil all thy petitions.
[6] Now know I that Jehovah saveth his anointed;
He will answer him from his holy heaven
With the saving strength of his right hand.
[7] Some *trust* in chariots, and some in horses;
But we will make mention of the name of Jehovah our God.
[8] They are bowed down and fallen;
But we are risen, and stand upright.
[9] Save, Jehovah:
Let the King answer us when we call.

XXI

Praise for Deliverance

For the Chief Musician. A Psalm of David.

[1] The King shall joy in thy strength, O Jehovah;
And in thy salvation how greatly shall he rejoice!
[2] Thou hast given him his heart's desire,
And hast not withholden the request of his lips. [Selah
[3] For thou meetest him with the blessings of goodness:[1]
Thou settest a crown of fine gold on his head.
[4] He asked life of thee, thou gavest it him,
Even length of days for ever and ever.
[5] His glory is great in thy salvation:
Honor and majesty dost thou lay upon him.
[6] For thou makest[2] him most blessed for ever:
Thou makest him glad with joy in thy presence.
[7] For the king trusteth in Jehovah;
And through the lovingkindness of the Most High he shall not be moved.

[6] Or, *victory*. [1] Or, *good things*.
[2] Heb. *settest him to be blessings*. See Gen. 12. 2.

[8] Thy hand will find out all thine enemies;
Thy right hand will find out those that hate thee.
[9] Thou wilt make them as a fiery furnace in the time of thine anger:[3]
Jehovah will swallow them up in his wrath,
And the fire shall devour them.
[10] Their fruit wilt thou destroy from the earth,
And their seed from among the children of men.
[11] For they intended evil against thee;
They conceived a device which they are not able to perform.
[12] For thou wilt make them turn their back;
Thou wilt make ready with thy bowstrings against their face.
[13] Be thou exalted, O Jehovah, in thy strength:
So will we sing and praise thy power.

XXII

A Cry of Anguish and a Song of Praise

For the Chief Musician; set to Aijeleth[4] hash-Shahar. A Psalm of David.

[1] My God, my God, why hast thou forsaken me?
Why[5] *art thou so* far from helping me, *and from* the words of my groaning?
[2] O my God, I cry in the daytime, but thou answerest not;
And in the night season, and[6] am not silent.
[3] But thou art holy,
O thou that inhabitest[7] the praises of Israel.
[4] Our fathers trusted in thee:
They trusted, and thou didst deliver them.
[5] They cried unto thee, and were delivered:
They trusted in thee, and were not put to shame.
[6] But I am a worm, and no man;
A reproach of men, and despised of the people.
[7] All they that see me laugh me to scorn:
They shoot out the lip, they shake the head, *saying,*

[3] Or, *presence.* Heb. *countenance.*

[4] That is, *The hind of the morning.* [5] Or, *Far from my help* are *the words of my groaning.* Heb. *roaring.* [6] Or, *but find no rest.* [7] Or, *art enthroned upon.*

[8] Commit[8] *thyself* unto Jehovah; let him deliver him:
Let him rescue him, seeing he delighteth in him.
[9] But thou art he that took me out of the womb;
Thou didst make me trust *when I was* upon my mother's breasts.
[10] I was cast upon thee from the womb;
Thou art my God since my mother bare me.
[11] Be not far from me; for trouble is near;
For there is none to help.
[12] Many bulls have compassed me;
Strong bulls of Bashan have beset me round.
[13] They gape upon me with their mouth,
As a ravening and a roaring lion.
[14] I am poured out like water,
And all my bones are out of joint:
My heart is like wax;
It is melted within me.
[15] My strength is dried up like a potsherd;
And my tongue cleaveth to my jaws;
And thou hast brought me into the dust of death.
[16] For dogs have compassed me:
A company of evil-doers have inclosed me;
They[9] pierced my hands and my feet.
[17] I may count all my bones;
They look and stare upon me.
[18] They part my garments among them,
And upon my vesture do they cast lots.
[19] But be not thou far off, O Jehovah:
O thou my succor, haste thee to help me.
[20] Deliver my soul from the sword,
My darling[10] from the power of the dog.
[21] Save me from the lion's mouth;
Yea, from the horns of the wild-oxen thou hast answered me.

[8] Or, *He trusted on Jehovah, that he would deliver him.*
[9] So the Sept., Vulg., and Syr. The Hebrew text as printed reads, *Like a lion, my &c.*
[10] Or, *dear* life. Heb. *only one.*

[22] I will declare thy name unto my brethren:
In the midst of the assembly will I praise thee.
[23] Ye that fear Jehovah, praise him;
All ye the seed of Jacob, glorify him;
And stand in awe of him, all ye the seed of Israel.
[24] For he hath not despised nor abhorred the affliction of the afflicted;
Neither hath he hid his face from him;
But when he cried unto him, he heard.
[25] Of thee cometh my praise in the great assembly:
I will pay my vows before them that fear him.
[26] The meek shall eat and be satisfied;
They shall praise Jehovah that seek after him:
Let your heart live for ever.
[27] All the ends of the earth shall remember and turn unto Jehovah;
And all the kindreds of the nations shall worship before thee.
[28] For the kingdom is Jehovah's;
And he is the ruler over the nations.
[29] All the fat ones of the earth shall eat and worship:
All they that go down to the dust shall bow before him,
Even he that cannot keep his soul alive.
[30] A seed shall serve him;
It shall be told[11] of the Lord unto the *next* generation.
[31] They shall come and shall declare his righteousness
Unto a people that shall be born, that he hath done it.

XXIII

JEHOVAH THE PSALMIST'S SHEPHERD

A Psalm of David.

[1] JEHOVAH is my shepherd;
I shall not want.
[2] He maketh me to lie down in green pastures;
He leadeth me beside still[1] waters.

[11] Or. *counted unto the Lord for* his *generations.* [1] Heb. *waters of rest.*

[3] He restoreth my soul:
He guideth me in the paths of righteousness for his name's sake.
[4] Yea, though I walk through the valley of the[2] shadow of death,
I will fear no evil; for thou art with me;
Thy rod and thy staff, they comfort me.
[5] Thou preparest a table before me in the presence of mine enemies:
Thou hast anointed my head with oil;
My cup runneth over.
[6] Surely[3] goodness and lovingkindness shall follow me all the days of my life;
And I shall dwell in the house of Jehovah for[4] ever.

XXIV

The King of Glory Entering Zion

A Psalm of David.

[1] The earth is Jehovah's and the fulness thereof;
The world, and they that dwell therein.
[2] For he hath founded it upon the seas,
And established it upon the floods.
[3] Who shall ascend into the hill of Jehovah?
And who shall stand in his holy place?
[4] He that hath clean hands, and a pure heart;
Who hath not lifted up his soul unto falsehood,
And hath not sworn deceitfully.
[5] He shall receive a blessing from Jehovah,
And righteousness from the God of his salvation.
[6] This is the generation of them that seek after him,
That seek thy face, *even* Jacob. [Selah

[7] Lift up your heads, O ye gates;
And be ye lifted up, ye everlasting[1] doors:
And the King of glory will come in.

[2] Or, *deep darkness* (and so elsewhere). [3] Or, *Only*.
[4] Heb. *for length of days*. [1] Or, *ancient*.

[8] Who is the King of glory?
Jehovah strong and mighty,
Jehovah mighty in battle.
[9] Lift up your heads, O ye gates;
Yea, lift them up, ye everlasting[1] doors:
And the King of glory will come in.
[10] Who is this King of glory?
Jehovah of hosts,
He is the King of glory. [Selah

XXV

PRAYER FOR PROTECTION, GUIDANCE, AND PARDON

A Psalm of David.

[1] UNTO thee, O Jehovah, do I lift up my soul.
[2] O my God, in thee have I trusted,
Let me not be put to shame;
Let not mine enemies triumph over me.
[3] Yea, none that wait for thee shall be put to shame:
They shall be put to shame that deal treacherously without cause.
[4] Show me thy ways, O Jehovah;
Teach me thy paths.
[5] Guide me in thy truth, and teach me;
For thou art the God of my salvation;
For thee do I wait all the day.
[6] Remember, O Jehovah, thy tender mercies and thy lovingkindnesses;
For they have been ever of old.
[7] Remember not the sins of my youth, nor my transgressions:
According to thy lovingkindness remember thou me,
For thy goodness' sake, O Jehovah.
[8] Good and upright is Jehovah:
Therefore will he instruct sinners in the way.
[9] The meek will he guide in justice;
And the meek will he teach his way.

[1] Or, *ancient*.

[10] All the paths of Jehovah are lovingkindness and truth
Unto such as keep his covenant and his testimonies.
[11] For thy name's sake, O Jehovah,
Pardon mine iniquity, for it is great.
[12] What man is he that feareth Jehovah?
Him shall he instruct in the way that he shall choose.
[13] His soul shall dwell at ease;
And his seed shall inherit the land.
[14] The friendship[1] of Jehovah is with them that fear him;
And[2] he will show them his covenant.
[15] Mine eyes are ever toward Jehovah;
For he will pluck my feet out of the net.
[16] Turn thee unto me, and have mercy upon me;
For I am desolate and afflicted.
[17] The troubles of my heart are[3] enlarged:
Oh bring thou me out of my distresses.
[18] Consider mine affliction and my travail;
And forgive all my sins.
[19] Consider mine enemies, for they are many;
And they hate me with cruel hatred.
[20] Oh keep my soul, and deliver me:
Let me not be put to shame, for I take refuge in thee.
[21] Let integrity and uprightness preserve me,
For I wait for thee.
[22] Redeem Israel, O God,
Out of all his troubles.

XXVI

Protestation of Integrity, and Prayer for Protection

A Psalm of David.

[1] Judge me, O Jehovah, for I have walked in mine integrity:
I have trusted also in Jehovah without[4] wavering.
[2] Examine me, O Jehovah, and prove me;
Try my heart[5] and my mind.

[1] Or, *counsel.* Or, *secret.* [2] Or, *And his covenant, to make them know it.*
[3] Or, as otherwise read, *relieve thou, And bring me &c.*
[4] Or, *I shall not slide.* [5] Heb. *reins.*

[3] For thy lovingkindness is before mine eyes;
And I have walked in thy truth.
[4] I have not sat with men of falsehood;
Neither will I go in with dissemblers.
[5] I hate the assembly of evil-doers,
And will not sit with the wicked.
[6] I will wash my hands in innocency:
So will I compass thine altar, O Jehovah;
[7] That I may make[6] the voice of thanksgiving to be heard,
And tell of all thy wondrous works.
[8] Jehovah, I love the habitation of thy house,
And the place where[7] thy glory dwelleth.
[9] Gather[8] not my soul with sinners,
Nor my life with men of blood;
[10] In whose hands is wickedness,
And their right hand is full of bribes.
[11] But as for me, I will walk in mine integrity:
Redeem me, and be merciful unto me.
[12] My foot standeth in an even place:
In the congregations will I bless Jehovah.

XXVII

A Psalm of Fearless Trust in God

A Psalm of David.

[1] Jehovah is my light and my salvation;
Whom shall I fear?
Jehovah is the strength[1] of my life;
Of whom shall I be afraid?
[2] When evil-doers came upon me to eat up my flesh,
Even mine adversaries and my foes, they stumbled and fell.
[3] Though a host should encamp against me,
My heart shall not fear:
Though war should rise against me,
Even[2] then will I be confident.

[6] Or, *publish with the voice of thanksgiving.*
[7] Heb. *of the tabernacle of thy glory.* [8] Or, *Take not away.*
[1] Or, *stronghold.* [2] Or, *In this.*

[4] One thing have I asked of Jehovah, that will I seek after;
That I may dwell in the house of Jehovah all the days of my life,
To behold the[3] beauty of Jehovah,
And to inquire[4] in his temple.
[5] For in the day of trouble he will keep me secretly in his pavilion:
In the covert of his tabernacle[5] will he hide me;
He will lift me up upon a rock.
[6] And now shall my head be lifted up above mine enemies round about me;
And I will offer in his tabernacle[5] sacrifices of joy,[6]
I will sing, yea, I will sing praises unto Jehovah.

[7] Hear, O Jehovah, when I cry with my voice:
Have mercy also upon me, and answer me.
[8] *When thou saidst,* Seek ye my face; my heart said unto thee,
Thy face, Jehovah, will I seek.
[9] Hide not thy face from me;
Put not thy servant away in anger:
Thou hast been my help;
Cast me not off, neither forsake me, O God of my salvation.
[10] When[7] my father and my mother forsake me,
Then Jehovah will take me up.
[11] Teach me thy way, O Jehovah;
And lead me in a plain path,
Because of mine[8] enemies.
[12] Deliver me not over unto the will of mine adversaries:
For false witnesses are risen up against me,
And such as breathe out cruelty.
[13] *I had fainted,* unless I had believed to see the goodness of Jehovah
In the land of the living.
[14] Wait for Jehovah:
Be strong, and let thy heart take courage;
Yea, wait thou for Jehovah.

[3] Or, *the pleasantness.* [4] Or, *consider his temple.* [5] Heb. *tent.*
[6] Or, *shouting.* Or, *trumpet-sound.*
[7] Or, *For my father and my mother have forsaken me, But Jehovah &c.*
[8] Or, *them that lie in wait for me.*

XXVIII

A Prayer for Help, and Praise for its Answer

A Psalm of David.

[1] Unto thee, O Jehovah, will I call:
My rock, be not thou deaf unto me;
Lest, if thou be silent unto me,
I become like them that go down into the pit.
[2] Hear the voice of my supplications, when I cry unto thee,
When I lift up my hands toward[1] thy holy oracle.
[3] Draw me not away with the wicked,
And with the workers of iniquity;
That speak peace with their neighbors,
But mischief is in their hearts.
[4] Give them according to their work, and according to the wickedness of their doings:
Give them after the operation of their hands;
Render to them their desert.
[5] Because they regard not the works of Jehovah,
Nor the operation of his hands,
He will break them down and not build them up.

[6] Blessed be Jehovah,
Because he hath heard the voice of my supplications.
[7] Jehovah is my strength and my shield;
My heart hath trusted in him, and I am helped:
Therefore my heart greatly rejoiceth;
And with my song will I praise him.
[8] Jehovah is their strength,
And he is a stronghold of salvation to his anointed.
[9] Save thy people, and bless thine inheritance:
Be their shepherd also, and bear them up for ever.

[1] Or, *toward the innermost place of thy sanctuary.*

XXIX

The Voice of Jehovah in the Storm

A Psalm of David.

[1] Ascribe unto Jehovah, O ye sons[1] of the mighty,[2]
Ascribe unto Jehovah glory and strength.
[2] Ascribe unto Jehovah the glory due unto his name;
Worship Jehovah in[3] holy array.

[3] The voice of Jehovah is upon the waters:
The God of glory thundereth,
Even Jehovah upon many[4] waters.
[4] The voice of Jehovah is powerful;
The voice of Jehovah is full of majesty.
[5] The voice of Jehovah breaketh the cedars;
Yea, Jehovah breaketh in pieces the cedars of Lebanon.
[6] He maketh them also to skip like a calf;
Lebanon and Sirion like a young wild-ox.
[7] The voice of Jehovah cleaveth[5] the flames of fire.
[8] The voice of Jehovah shaketh the wilderness;
Jehovah shaketh the wilderness of Kadesh.
[9] The voice of Jehovah maketh the hinds to calve,
And strippeth the forests bare:
And in his temple every thing saith, Glory.

[10] Jehovah sat *as King* at the Flood;
Yea, Jehovah sitteth as King for ever.
[11] Jehovah will give strength unto his people;
Jehovah will bless his people with peace.

[1] Or, *sons of God.* [2] Or, *gods.* See Ex. 15. 11.
[3] Or, *in the beauty of holiness.* [4] Or, *great.*
[5] Or, *heweth out flames of fire.*

XXX

Thanksgiving for Deliverance from Death

A Psalm; a Song at the Dedication of the House. A Psalm of David.

[1] I will extol thee, O Jehovah; for thou hast raised[1] me up,
And hast not made my foes to rejoice over me.
[2] O Jehovah my God,
I cried unto thee, and thou hast healed me.
[3] O Jehovah, thou hast brought up my soul from Sheol;
Thou hast kept me alive, that[2] I should not go down to the pit.
[4] Sing praise unto Jehovah, O ye saints of his,
And give thanks to his holy memorial *name*.
[5] For his anger is but for a moment;
His[3] favor is for a life-time:
Weeping may[4] tarry for the night,
But joy *cometh* in the morning.
[6] As for me, I said in my prosperity,
I shall never be moved.
[7] Thou, Jehovah, of thy favor hadst made my mountain to stand strong:
Thou didst hide thy face; I was troubled.
[8] I cried to thee, O Jehovah;
And unto Jehovah I made supplication:
[9] What profit is there in my blood, when I go down to the pit?
Shall the dust praise thee? shall it declare thy truth?
[10] Hear, O Jehovah, and have mercy upon me:
Jehovah, be thou my helper.
[11] Thou hast turned for me my mourning into dancing;
Thou hast loosed my sackcloth, and girded me with gladness;
[12] To the end that *my* glory may sing praise to thee, and not be silent.
O Jehovah my God, I will give thanks unto thee for ever.

[1] Or, *drawn*. [2] Another reading is, *from among them that go down to the pit.*
[3] Or, *In his favor is life*. [4] Heb. *may come in to lodge at even.*

XXXI

A Psalm of Complaint and of Praise

For the Chief Musician. A Psalm of David.

[1] In thee, O Jehovah, do I take refuge;
Let me never be put to shame:
Deliver me in thy righteousness.
[2] Bow down thine ear unto me; deliver me speedily:
Be thou to me a strong rock,
A house of defence[1] to save me.
[3] For thou art my rock and my fortress;
Therefore for thy name's sake lead me and guide me.
[4] Pluck me out of the net that they have laid privily for me;
For thou art my stronghold.
[5] Into thy hand I commend my spirit:
Thou hast redeemed me, O Jehovah, thou God of truth.
[6] I hate them that regard lying vanities;
But I trust in Jehovah.
[7] I will be glad and rejoice in thy lovingkindness;
For thou hast seen my affliction:
Thou hast known my[2] soul in adversities;
[8] And thou hast not shut me up into the hand of the enemy;
Thou hast set my feet in a large place.
[9] Have mercy upon me, O Jehovah, for I am in distress:
Mine eye wasteth away with grief, *yea,* my soul and my body.
[10] For my life is spent with sorrow,
And my years with sighing:
My strength faileth because of mine iniquity,
And my bones are wasted away.
[11] Because of all mine adversaries I am become a reproach,
Yea, unto my neighbors exceedingly,
And a fear to mine acquaintance:
They that did see me without fled from me.
[12] I am forgotten as a dead man out of mind:
I am like a broken vessel.

[1] Heb. *fortresses.* [2] Or, *the adversities of my soul.*

[13] For I have heard the defaming of many,
Terror on every side:
While they took counsel together against me,
They devised to take away my life.
[14] But I trusted in thee, O Jehovah:
I said, Thou art my God.
[15] My times are in thy hand:
Deliver me from the hand of mine enemies, and from them that persecute me.
[16] Make thy face to shine upon thy servant:
Save me in thy lovingkindness.
[17] Let me not be put to shame, O Jehovah; for I have called upon thee:
Let the wicked be put to shame, let them be silent in Sheol.
[18] Let the lying lips be dumb,
Which speak against the righteous insolently,
With pride and contempt.
[19] Oh how great is thy goodness,
Which thou hast laid up for them that fear thee,
Which thou hast wrought for them that take refuge in thee,
Before the sons of men!
[20] In the covert of thy presence wilt thou hide them from the plottings of man:
Thou wilt keep them secretly in a pavilion from the strife of tongues.
[21] Blessed be Jehovah;
For he hath showed me his marvellous lovingkindness in a strong city.
[22] As for me, I said in my haste,[3]
I am cut off from before thine eyes:
Nevertheless thou heardest the voice of my supplications
When I cried unto thee.
[23] Oh love Jehovah, all ye his saints:
Jehovah preserveth the[4] faithful,
And plentifully rewardeth him that dealeth proudly.
[24] Be strong, and let your heart take courage,
All ye that hope[5] in Jehovah.

[3] Or, *alarm.* [4] Or, *faithfulness.* [5] Or, *wait for.*

XXXII

Blessedness of Forgiveness and of Trust in God

A Psalm of David. Maschil.

[1] Blessed is he whose transgression is forgiven,
Whose sin is covered.
[2] Blessed is the man unto whom Jehovah imputeth not iniquity,
And in whose spirit there is no guile.
[3] When I kept silence, my bones wasted away
Through my groaning[1] all the day long.
[4] For day and night thy hand was heavy upon me:
My moisture was changed *as*[2] with the drought of summer. [Selah

[5] I acknowledged my sin unto thee,
And mine iniquity did I not hide:
I said, I will confess my transgressions unto Jehovah;
And thou forgavest the iniquity of my sin. [Selah
[6] For this let every one that is godly pray unto thee in[3] a time when thou mayest be found:
Surely when the great waters overflow they shall not reach unto him.
[7] Thou art my hiding-place; thou wilt preserve me from trouble;
Thou wilt compass me about with songs of deliverance. [Selah
[8] I will instruct thee and teach thee in the way which thou shalt go:
I will counsel thee with mine eye upon thee.
[9] Be ye not as the horse, or as the mule, which have no understanding;
Whose trappings must be bit and bridle to hold them in,
Else[4] they will not come near unto thee.
[10] Many sorrows shall be to the wicked;
But he that trusteth in Jehovah, lovingkindness shall compass him about.
[11] Be glad in Jehovah, and rejoice, ye righteous;
And shout for joy, all ye that are upright in heart.

[1] Heb *roaring.* [2] Or, *into the.* [3] Or, *in the time of finding out* sin.
[4] Or, *That they come not near.*

XXXIII

Praise to the Creator and Preserver

[1] Rejoice in Jehovah, O ye righteous:
Praise is comely for the upright.
[2] Give thanks unto Jehovah with the harp:
Sing praises unto him with the psaltery of ten strings.
[3] Sing unto him a new song;
Play skilfully with a loud noise.
[4] For the word of Jehovah is right;
And all his work is *done* in faithfulness.
[5] He loveth righteousness and justice:
The earth is full of the lovingkindness of Jehovah.
[6] By the word of Jehovah were the heavens made,
And all the host of them by the breath of his mouth.
[7] He gathereth the waters of the sea together as a heap:
He layeth up the deeps in store-houses.
[8] Let all the earth fear Jehovah:
Let all the inhabitants of the world stand in awe of him.
[9] For he spake, and it was done;
He commanded, and it stood fast.
[10] Jehovah bringeth the counsel of the nations to nought;
He maketh the thoughts of the peoples to be of no effect.
[11] The counsel of Jehovah standeth fast for ever,
The thoughts of his heart to all generations.
[12] Blessed is the nation whose God is Jehovah,
The people whom he hath chosen for his own inheritance.
[13] Jehovah looketh from heaven;
He beholdeth all the sons of men;
[14] From the place of his habitation he looketh forth
Upon all the inhabitants of the earth,
[15] He that fashioneth the hearts of them all,
That considereth all their works.
[16] There is no king saved by the[1] multitude of a host:
A mighty man is not delivered by great strength.

[1] Or, *a great power*.

[17] A horse is a vain thing for safety;
Neither doth he deliver any by his great power.
[18] Behold, the eye of Jehovah is upon them that fear him,
Upon them that hope[2] in his lovingkindness;
[19] To deliver their soul from death,
And to keep them alive in famine.
[20] Our soul hath waited for Jehovah:
He is our help and our shield.
[21] For our heart shall rejoice in him,
Because we have trusted in his holy name.
[22] Let thy lovingkindness, O Jehovah, be upon us,
According as we have[2] hoped in thee.

XXXIV

Jehovah a Provider and Deliverer

A Psalm of David; when[3] he changed[4] his behavior before Abimelech, who drove him away, and he departed.

[1] I will bless Jehovah at all times:
His praise shall continually be in my mouth.
[2] My soul shall make her boast in Jehovah:
The meek shall hear thereof, and be glad.
[3] Oh magnify Jehovah with me,
And let us exalt his name together.
[4] I sought Jehovah, and he answered me,
And delivered me from all my fears.
[5] They looked unto him, and were radiant:
And their faces shall never be confounded.
[6] This poor man cried, and Jehovah heard him,
And saved him out of all his troubles.
[7] The angel of Jehovah encampeth round about them that fear him,
And delivereth them.
[8] Oh taste and see that Jehovah is good:
Blessed is the man that taketh refuge in him.

[2] Or, *wait for*. [3] See 1 S. 21. 10–15. [4] Or, *feigned madness*.

[9] Oh fear Jehovah, ye his saints;
For there is no want to them that fear him.
[10] The young lions do lack, and suffer hunger;
But they that seek Jehovah shall not want any good thing.
[11] Come, ye children, hearken unto me:
I will teach you the fear of Jehovah.
[12] What man is he that desireth life,
And loveth *many* days, that he may see good?
[13] Keep thy tongue from evil,
And thy lips from speaking guile.
[14] Depart from evil, and do good;
Seek peace, and pursue it.
[15] The eyes of Jehovah are toward the righteous,
And his ears are *open* unto their cry.
[16] The face of Jehovah is against them that do evil,
To cut off the remembrance of them from the earth.
[17] *The righteous* cried, and Jehovah heard,
And delivered them out of all their troubles.
[18] Jehovah is nigh unto them that are of a broken heart,
And saveth such as are of a contrite spirit.
[19] Many are the afflictions of the righteous;
But Jehovah delivereth him out of them all.
[20] He keepeth all his bones:
Not one of them is broken.
[21] Evil shall slay the wicked;
And they that hate the righteous shall be condemned.[5]
[22] Jehovah redeemeth the soul of his servants;
And none of them that take refuge in him shall be condemned.[5]

XXXV

Prayer for Rescue from Enemies

A Psalm of David.

[1] Strive thou, O Jehovah, with them that strive with me:
Fight thou against them that fight against me.
[2] Take hold of shield and buckler,
And stand up for my help.

[5] Or, *held guilty.*

[3] Draw out also the spear, and[1] stop the way against them that pursue me:
Say unto my soul, I am thy salvation.
[4] Let them be put to shame and brought to dishonor that seek after my soul:
Let them be turned back and confounded that devise my hurt.
[5] Let them be as chaff before the wind,
And the angel of Jehovah driving *them* on.
[6] Let their way be dark[2] and slippery,
And the angel of Jehovah pursuing them.
[7] For without cause have they hid for me their[3] net *in* a pit;
Without cause have they digged *a pit* for my soul.
[8] Let destruction come upon him unawares;
And let his net that he hath hid catch himself:
With[4] destruction let him fall therein.
[9] And my soul shall be joyful in Jehovah:
It shall rejoice in his salvation.
[10] All my bones shall say, Jehovah, who is like unto thee,
Who deliverest the poor from him that is too strong for him,
Yea, the poor and the needy from him that robbeth him?
[11] Unrighteous[5] witnesses rise up;
They ask me of things that I know not.
[12] They reward me evil for good,
To the bereaving of my soul.
[13] But as for me, when they were sick, my clothing was sackcloth:
I afflicted my soul with fasting;
And my prayer returned[6] into mine own bosom.
[14] I behaved myself as though it had been my friend or my brother:
I bowed down mourning, as one that bewaileth his mother.
[15] But in mine[7] adversity they rejoiced, and gathered themselves together:
The abjects[8] gathered themselves together against me, and I knew[9] *it* not;
They did tear me, and ceased not:

[1] Or, *and the battle axe against &c.* [2] Heb. *darkness and slippery places.*
[3] Or, *the pit of their net.* [4] Or, *Into that very destruction let him fall.*
[5] Or, *Malicious.* See Ex. 23. 1. [6] Or, *shall return.*
[7] Heb. *my limping.* [8] Or, *smiters.* [9] Or, those whom *I knew not.*

[16] Like[10] the profane mockers in feasts,
They gnashed upon me with their teeth.
[17] Lord, how long wilt thou look on?
Rescue my soul from their destructions,
My darling[11] from the lions.
[18] I will give thee thanks in the great assembly:
I will praise thee among much[12] people.
[19] Let not them that are mine enemies wrongfully[13] rejoice over me;
Neither let them wink with the eye that hate me without a cause.
[20] For they speak not peace;
But they devise deceitful words against them that are quiet in the land.
[21] Yea, they opened their mouth wide against me;
They said, Aha, aha, our eye hath seen it.
[22] Thou hast seen it, O Jehovah; keep not silence:
O Lord, be not far from me.
[23] Stir up thyself, and awake to the justice *due* unto me,
Even unto my cause, my God and my Lord.
[24] Judge me, O Jehovah my God, according to thy righteousness;
And let them not rejoice over me.
[25] Let them not say in their heart, Aha,[14] so would we have it:
Let them not say, We have swallowed him up.
[26] Let them be put to shame and confounded together that rejoice at my hurt:
Let them be clothed with shame and dishonor that magnify themselves against me.
[27] Let them shout for joy, and be glad, that favor[15] my righteous cause:
Yea, let them say continually, Jehovah be magnified,
Who hath pleasure in the prosperity of his servant.
[28] And my tongue shall talk of thy righteousness
And of thy praise all the day long.

[10] Or, *Among*. [11] Or, *dear* life. Heb. *only one*.
[12] Or, *a mighty people*. [13] Heb. *falsely*.
[14] Heb. *Aha, our desire*. [15] Heb. *have pleasure in my righteousness*.

XXXVI

Wickedness of Men and Lovingkindness of God

For the Chief Musician. A Psalm of David the servant of Jehovah.

[1] The[1] transgression of the wicked saith[2] within my heart,
There is no fear of God before his eyes.
[2] For he[3] flattereth himself in his own eyes,
That[4] his iniquity will not be found out and be hated.
[3] The words of his mouth are iniquity and deceit:
He hath ceased to be wise *and* to do good.
[4] He deviseth iniquity upon his bed;
He setteth himself in a way that is not good;
He abhorreth not evil.

[5] Thy lovingkindness, O Jehovah, is in the heavens;
Thy faithfulness *reacheth* unto the skies.
[6] Thy righteousness is like the mountains of God;
Thy judgments are a great deep:
O Jehovah, thou preservest man and beast.
[7] How precious is thy lovingkindness, O God!
And the children of men take refuge under the shadow of thy wings.
[8] They shall be abundantly[5] satisfied with the fatness of thy house;
And thou wilt make them drink of the river of thy pleasures.
[9] For with thee is the fountain of life:
In thy light shall we see light.
[10] Oh continue thy lovingkindness unto them that know thee,
And thy righteousness to the upright in heart.
[11] Let not the foot of pride come against me,
And let not the hand of the wicked drive me away.
[12] There are the workers of iniquity fallen:
They are thrust down, and shall not be able to rise.

[1] Or, *Transgression saith to the wicked.* [2] Or, *uttereth its oracle.* [3] Or, *it* (or *he*) *flattereth him in his eyes.* [4] Or, *Until his iniquity be found and be hated.* Heb. *Concerning the finding out of his iniquity and hating it.* [5] Heb. *watered.*

XXXVII

Security of those who Trust in Jehovah, and Insecurity of the Wicked

A Psalm of David.

[1] Fret not thyself because of evil-doers,
Neither be thou envious against them that work unrighteousness.
[2] For they shall soon be cut down like the grass,
And wither as the green herb.
[3] Trust in Jehovah, and do good;
Dwell[1] in the land, and feed[2] on *his* faithfulness.
[4] Delight[3] thyself also in Jehovah;
And he will give thee the desires[4] of thy heart.
[5] Commit[5] thy way unto Jehovah;
Trust also in him, and he will bring it to pass.
[6] And he will make thy righteousness to go forth as the light,
And thy justice as the noonday.
[7] Rest[6] in Jehovah, and wait patiently for him:
Fret not thyself because of him who prospereth in his way,
Because of the man who bringeth wicked devices to pass.
[8] Cease from anger, and forsake wrath:
Fret not thyself, *it tendeth* only to evil-doing.
[9] For evil-doers shall be cut off;
But those that wait for Jehovah, they shall inherit the[7] land.
[10] For yet a little while, and the wicked shall not be:
Yea, thou shalt diligently consider his place, and he[8] shall not be.
[11] But the meek shall inherit the land,
And shall delight themselves in the abundance of peace.
[12] The wicked plotteth against the just,
And gnasheth upon him with his teeth.
[13] The Lord will laugh at him;
For he seeth that his day is coming.

[1]Or, *So shalt thou dwell in the land and feed securely.*
[2]Or, verily *thou shalt be fed.* [3]Or, *So shalt thou have thy delight in &c.*
[4]Heb. *petitions.* [5]Heb. *Roll thy way upon Jehovah.*
[6]Or, *Be still before* (Heb. *silent to*) *Jehovah.*
[7]Or, *the earth* (and so in ver. 11, 22, 29, 34). [8]Or, *it.*

[14] The wicked have drawn out the sword, and have bent their bow,
To cast down the poor and needy,
To slay such as are upright in the way.
[15] Their sword shall enter into their own heart,
And their bows shall be broken.
[16] Better is a little that the righteous hath
Than the abundance of many wicked.
[17] For the arms of the wicked shall be broken;
But Jehovah upholdeth the righteous.
[18] Jehovah knoweth the days of the perfect;
And their inheritance shall be for ever.
[19] They shall not be put to shame in the time of evil;
And in the days of famine they shall be satisfied.
[20] But the wicked shall perish,
And the enemies of Jehovah shall be as the[9] fat of lambs:
They shall consume; in[10] smoke shall they consume away.
[21] The wicked borroweth, and payeth not again;
But the righteous dealeth graciously, and giveth.
[22] For such as are blessed of him shall inherit the land;
And they that are cursed of him shall be cut off.
[23] A man's goings are established of Jehovah;
And he delighteth in his way.
[24] Though he fall, he shall not be utterly cast down;
For Jehovah upholdeth[11] him with his hand.
[25] I have been young, and now am old;
Yet have I not seen the righteous forsaken,
Nor his seed begging bread.
[26] All the day long he dealeth graciously, and lendeth;
And his seed is blessed.
[27] Depart from evil, and do good;
And dwell for evermore.
[28] For Jehovah loveth justice,
And forsaketh not his saints;
They are preserved for ever:
But the seed of the wicked shall be cut off.

[9] Or, *the excellency of the pastures.* [10] Or, *like smoke.*
[11] Or, *upholdeth his hand.*

[29] The righteous shall inherit the land,
And dwell therein for ever.
[30] The mouth of the righteous talketh of wisdom,
And his tongue speaketh justice.
[31] The law of his God is in his heart;
None of his steps shall slide.
[32] The wicked watcheth the righteous,
And seeketh to slay him.
[33] Jehovah will not leave him in his hand,
Nor condemn him when he is judged.
[34] Wait for Jehovah, and keep his way,
And he will exalt thee to inherit the land:
When the wicked are cut off, thou shalt see it.
[35] I have seen the wicked in great power,
And spreading himself like a green tree in its native soil.
[36] But[12] one passed by, and, lo, he was not:
Yea, I sought him, but he could not be found.
[37] Mark the perfect man, and behold the upright;
For there is a *happy* end to the man of peace.
[38] As for transgressors, they shall be destroyed together:
The end of the wicked shall be cut off.
[39] But the salvation of the righteous is of Jehovah:
He is their stronghold in the time of trouble.
[40] And Jehovah helpeth them, and rescueth them:
He rescueth them from the wicked, and saveth them,
Because they have taken refuge in him.

XXXVIII

Prayer of a Suffering Penitent

A Psalm of David, to[1] bring to remembrance.

[1] O Jehovah, rebuke me not in thy wrath;
Neither chasten me in thy hot displeasure.
[2] For thine arrows stick[2] fast in me,
And thy hand presseth[2] me sore.

[12] Or, *Yet he passed away.* [1] Or, *to make memorial.* [2] Heb. *lighted on me.*

[3] There is no soundness in my flesh because of thine indignation;
Neither is there any health[3] in my bones because of my sin.
[4] For mine iniquities are gone over my head:
As a heavy burden they are too heavy for me.
[5] My wounds are loathsome and corrupt,
Because of my foolishness.
[6] I am pained[4] and bowed down greatly;
I go mourning all the day long.
[7] For my loins are filled with burning;
And there is no soundness in my flesh.
[8] I am faint and sore bruised:
I have groaned[5] by reason of the disquietness of my heart.
[9] Lord, all my desire is before thee;
And my groaning is not hid from thee.
[10] My heart throbbeth, my strength faileth me:
As for the light of mine eyes, it also is gone from me.
[11] My lovers and my friends stand aloof from my plague;
And my kinsmen stand afar off.
[12] They also that seek after my life lay snares *for me;*
And they that seek my hurt speak mischievous things,
And meditate deceits all the day long.
[13] But I, as a deaf man, hear not;
And I am as a dumb man that openeth not his mouth.
[14] Yea, I am as a man that heareth not,
And in whose mouth are no reproofs.[6]
[15] For in thee, O Jehovah, do I hope:
Thou wilt answer, O Lord my God.
[16] For I said, Lest they rejoice over me:
When my foot slippeth, they magnify themselves against me.
[17] For I am ready to fall,
And my sorrow is continually before me.
[18] For I will declare mine iniquity;
I will be sorry for my sin.
[19] But mine enemies are lively, *and* are strong;
And they that hate me wrongfully[7] are multiplied.

[3] Or, *rest.* [4] Heb. *bent.* [5] Heb. *roared.*
[6] Or, *arguments.* [7] Heb. *falsely.*

[20] They also that render evil for good
Are adversaries unto me, because I follow the thing that is good.
[21] Forsake me not, O Jehovah:
O my God, be not far from me.
[22] Make haste to help me,
O Lord, my salvation.

XXXIX

The Vanity of Life

For the Chief Musician, for Jeduthun.[1] A Psalm of David.

[1] I said, I will take heed to my ways,
That I sin not with my tongue:
I will keep my[2] mouth with a bridle,
While the wicked is before me.
[2] I was dumb with silence, I held my peace, even[3] from good;
And my sorrow was stirred.
[3] My heart was hot within me;
While I was musing the fire burned:
Then spake I with my tongue:
[4] Jehovah, make me to know mine end,
And the measure of my days, what it is;
Let me know how frail I am.
[5] Behold, thou hast made my days *as* handbreadths;
And my life-time is as nothing before thee:
Surely every man at[4] his best estate is altogether vanity.[5] [Selah
[6] Surely every man walketh in[6] a vain show;
Surely they are disquieted in[7] vain:
He heapeth up *riches,* and knoweth not who shall gather them.
[7] And now, Lord, what wait I for?
My hope is in thee.
[8] Deliver me from all my transgressions:
Make me not the reproach of the foolish.

[1] Ps. 62. title; 77. title; 1 Chr. 16. 41; 25. 1.
[2] Heb. *a bridle* (or, *muzzle*) *for my mouth.*
[3] Or, *and had no comfort.* Heb. *away from good.*
[4] Heb. *standing firm.* [5] Heb. *a breath.* [6] Or, *as a shadow.* [7] Or, *for vanity.*

[9] I was dumb, I opened not my mouth;
Because thou didst it.
[10] Remove thy stroke away from me:
I am consumed by the blow[8] of thy hand.
[11] When thou with rebukes dost correct man for iniquity,
Thou makest[9] his beauty to consume away like a moth:
Surely every man is vanity.[5] [Selah
[12] Hear my prayer, O Jehovah, and give ear unto my cry;
Hold not thy peace at my tears:
For I am a stranger with thee,
A sojourner, as all my fathers were.
[13] Oh spare[10] me, that I may recover[11] strength,
Before I go hence, and be no more.

XL

A Sacrifice of Praise, and Prayer for Help

For the Chief Musician. A Psalm of David.

[1] I WAITED patiently for Jehovah;
And he inclined unto me, and heard my cry.
[2] He brought me up also out of a[1] horrible pit, out of the miry clay;
And he set my feet upon a rock, and established my goings.
[3] And he hath put a new song in my mouth, even praise unto our God:
Many shall see it, and fear,
And shall trust in Jehovah.
[4] Blessed is the man that maketh Jehovah his trust,
And respecteth not the proud, nor such as turn[2] aside to lies.
[5] Many, O Jehovah my God, are the wonderful works which thou hast done,
And thy thoughts which are to us-ward:
They[3] cannot be set in order unto thee;
If I would declare and speak of them,
They are more than can be numbered.

[8] Heb. *conflict.* [9] Or, *consumest like a moth his delights.* [10] Or, *look away from me.*
[11] Heb. *brighten up.* [1] Heb. *a pit of tumult* (or, *destruction*).
[2] Or, *fall away treacherously.* [3] Or, *There is none to be compared unto thee.*

[6] Sacrifice and offering[4] thou hast no delight in;
Mine[5] ears hast thou opened:
Burnt-offering and sin-offering hast thou not required.
[7] Then said I, Lo, I am come;
In the roll of the book it is written[6] of me:
[8] I delight to do thy will, O my God;
Yea, thy law is within my heart.
[9] I have proclaimed glad tidings of righteousness in the great assembly;
Lo, I will not refrain my lips,
O Jehovah, thou knowest.
[10] I have not hid thy righteousness within my heart;
I have declared thy faithfulness and thy salvation;
I have not concealed thy lovingkindness and thy truth from the great assembly.
[11] Withhold not thou thy tender mercies from me, O Jehovah;
Let thy lovingkindness and thy truth continually preserve me.
[12] For innumerable evils have compassed me about;
Mine iniquities have overtaken me, so that I am not able to look up;
They are more than the hairs of my head;
And my heart hath failed[7] me.
[13] Be pleased, O Jehovah, to deliver me:
Make haste to help me, O Jehovah.
[14] Let them be put to shame and confounded together that seek after my soul to destroy it:
Let them be turned backward and brought to dishonor
That delight in my hurt.
[15] Let them be desolate[8] by[9] reason of their shame
That say unto me, Aha, aha.
[16] Let all those that seek thee rejoice and be glad in thee:
Let such as love thy salvation say continually,
Jehovah be magnified.

[4] Or, *meal-offering.* [5] Heb. *Ears hast thou digged* (or, *pierced*) *for me.*
[6] Or, *prescribed to.* [7] Heb. *forsaken.* [8] Or, *astonished.* [9] Or, *for a reward of.*

[17] But I am poor and needy;
Yet the Lord thinketh upon me:
Thou art my help and my deliverer;
Make no tarrying, O my God.

XLI

The Psalmist in Sickness Complains of Enemies and False Friends

For the Chief Musician. A Psalm of David.

[1] Blessed is he that considereth the[1] poor:
Jehovah will deliver him in the day of evil.
[2] Jehovah will preserve him, and keep him alive,
And he shall be blessed upon[2] the earth;
And deliver not thou him unto the will of his enemies.
[3] Jehovah will support him upon the couch of languishing:
Thou makest[3] all his bed in his sickness.
[4] I said, O Jehovah, have mercy upon me:
Heal my soul; for I have sinned against thee.
[5] Mine enemies speak evil against me, *saying,*
When will he die, and his name perish?
[6] And if he come to see *me,* he speaketh falsehood;
His heart gathereth iniquity to itself:
When he goeth abroad, he telleth it.
[7] All that hate me whisper together against me;
Against me do they devise my hurt.
[8] An[4] evil disease, *say they,* cleaveth[5] fast unto him;
And now that he lieth he shall rise up no more.
[9] Yea, mine own familiar friend, in whom I trusted,
Who did eat of my bread,
Hath lifted up his heel against me.
[10] But thou, O Jehovah, have mercy upon me, and raise me up,
That I may requite them.
[11] By this I know that thou delightest in me,
Because mine enemy doth not triumph over me.

[1] Or, *the weak.*
[2] Or, *in the land.* [3] Heb. *turnest,* or, *changest.*
[4] Or, *some wicked thing.* [5] Or, *is poured out upon him.*

[12] And as for me, thou upholdest me in mine integrity,
And settest me before thy face for ever.

[13] Blessed be Jehovah, the God of Israel,
From everlasting and to everlasting.
Amen, and Amen.

BOOK II

XLII

Thirsting for God in Trouble and Exile

For the Chief Musician. Maschil of the sons of Korah.

[1] As the hart panteth after the water brooks,
So panteth my soul after thee, O God.
[2] My soul thirsteth for God, for the living God:
When shall I come and appear before God?
[3] My tears have been my food day and night,
While they continually[1] say unto me, Where is thy God?
[4] These things I remember, and pour out my soul within[2] me,
How I went with the throng, and led[3] them to the house of God,
With the voice of joy and praise, a multitude keeping holyday.
[5] Why art thou cast[4] down, O my soul?
And *why* art thou disquieted within me?
Hope thou in God; for I shall yet praise him
For the help of his countenance.

[6] O my God, my soul is cast down within me:
Therefore do I remember thee from the land of the Jordan,
And the Hermons, from the[5] hill Mizar.
[7] Deep calleth unto deep at the noise of thy waterfalls:
All thy waves and thy billows are gone over me.
[8] *Yet* Jehovah will command his lovingkindness in the day-time;
And in the night his song shall be with me,
Even a prayer unto the God of my life.

[1] Heb. *all the day.* [2] Heb. *upon.* [3] Or, *went in procession with them.*
[4] Heb. *bowed down.* [5] Or, *the little mountain.*

[9] I will say unto God my rock,
Why hast thou forgotten me?
Why go I mourning because[6] of the oppression of the enemy?
[10] As with a[7] sword in my bones, mine adversaries reproach me,
While they continually say unto me, Where is thy God?
[11] Why art thou cast down, O my soul?
And why art thou disquieted within me?
Hope thou in God; for I shall yet praise him,
Who is the help of my countenance, and my God.

XLIII

Prayer for Deliverance

[1] Judge me, O God, and plead my cause against an ungodly nation:
Oh deliver me from the deceitful and unjust man.
[2] For thou art the God of my strength; why hast thou cast me off?
Why go I mourning because[6] of the oppression of the enemy?
[3] Oh send out thy light and thy truth; let them lead me:
Let them bring me unto thy holy hill,
And to thy tabernacles
[4] Then will I go unto the altar of God,
Unto God my[1] exceeding joy;
And upon the harp will I praise thee, O God, my God.
[5] Why art thou cast down, O my soul?
And why art thou disquieted within me?
Hope thou in God; for I shall yet praise him,
Who is the help of my countenance, and my God.

XLIV

Former Deliverances and Present Troubles

For the Chief Musician. A Psalm of the sons of Korah. Maschil.

[1] We have heard with our ears, O God,
Our fathers have told us,
What work thou didst in their days,
In the days of old.

[6] Or, *while the enemy oppresseth.* [7] Or, *crushing.* [1] Heb. *the gladness of my joy.*

[2] Thou didst drive out the nations with thy hand;
But them thou didst plant:
Thou didst afflict the peoples;
But them thou didst spread abroad.
[3] For they gat not the land in possession by their own sword,
Neither did their own arm save them;
But thy right hand, and thine arm, and the light of thy countenance,
Because thou wast favorable unto them.
[4] Thou art my King, O God:
Command deliverance[1] for Jacob.
[5] Through thee will we push down our adversaries:
Through thy name will we tread them under that rise up against us.
[6] For I will not trust in my bow,
Neither shall my sword save me.
[7] But thou hast saved us from our adversaries,
And hast put them to shame that hate us.
[8] In God have we made our boast all the day long,
And we will give thanks unto thy name for ever. [Selah

[9] But now thou hast cast *us* off, and brought us to dishonor,
And goest not forth with our hosts.
[10] Thou makest us to turn back from the adversary;
And they that hate us take spoil for themselves.
[11] Thou hast made us like sheep *appointed* for food,
And hast scattered us among the nations.
[12] Thou sellest thy people for nought,
And hast not increased *thy wealth* by their price.
[13] Thou makest us a reproach to our neighbors,
A scoffing and a derision to them that are round about us.
[14] Thou makest us a byword among the nations,
A shaking of the head among the peoples.
[15] All the day long is my dishonor before me,
And the shame of my face hath covered me,

[1] Or, *victories*.

[16] For the voice of him that reproacheth and blasphemeth,
By reason of the enemy and the avenger.
[17] All this is come upon us; yet have we not forgotten thee,
Neither have we dealt falsely in thy covenant.
[18] Our heart is not turned back,
Neither have our steps declined from thy way,
[19] That[2] thou hast sore broken us in the place of jackals,
And covered us with the shadow of death.
[20] If we have forgotten the name of our God,
Or spread forth our hands to a strange god;
[21] Will not God search this out?
For he knoweth the secrets of the heart.
[22] Yea, for thy sake are we killed all the day long;
We are accounted as sheep for the slaughter.
[23] Awake, why sleepest thou, O Lord?
Arise, cast *us* not off for ever.
[24] Wherefore hidest thou thy face,
And forgettest our affliction and our oppression?
[25] For our soul is bowed down to the dust:
Our body cleaveth unto the earth.
[26] Rise up for our help,
And redeem us for thy lovingkindness' sake.

XLV

A Song Celebrating the King's Marriage

For the Chief Musician; set to Shoshannim.[3] A Psalm of the sons of Korah. Maschil. A Song of loves.

[1] My heart overfloweth with a goodly matter;
I[4] speak the things which I have made touching the king:
My tongue is the pen of a ready writer.
[2] Thou art fairer than the children of men;
Grace is poured into[5] thy lips:
Therefore God hath blessed thee for ever.

[2] Or, *Though.* [3] That is, *Lilies.* [4] Or, *I speak: my work is for a king.* [5] Or, *upon.*

[3] Gird thy sword upon thy thigh, O mighty one,
Thy glory and thy majesty.
[4] And in thy majesty ride on prosperously,
Because[6] of truth and meekness *and* righteousness:
And thy[7] right hand shall teach thee terrible things.
[5] Thine arrows are sharp;
The peoples fall under thee;
They are in the heart of the king's enemies.
[6] Thy[8] throne, O God, is for ever and ever:
A sceptre of equity is the sceptre of thy kingdom.
[7] Thou hast loved righteousness, and hated wickedness:
Therefore God, thy God, hath anointed thee
With the oil of gladness above thy fellows.
[8] All thy garments *smell of* myrrh, and aloes, *and* cassia;
Out of ivory palaces stringed instruments have made thee glad.
[9] Kings' daughters are among thy honorable women:
At thy right hand doth stand the queen in gold of Ophir.
[10] Hearken, O daughter, and consider, and incline thine ear;
Forget also thine own people, and thy father's house:
[11] So will the king desire thy beauty;
For he is thy lord; and reverence thou him.
[12] And the daughter of Tyre *shall be there* with a gift;
The rich among the people shall entreat thy favor.
[13] The king's daughter within[9] *the palace* is all glorious:
Her clothing is inwrought with gold.
[14] She shall be led unto the king in[10] broidered work:
The virgins her companions that follow her
Shall be brought unto thee.
[15] With gladness and rejoicing shall they be led:
They shall enter into the king's palace.
[16] Instead of thy fathers shall be thy children,
Whom thou shalt make princes in all the earth.
[17] I will make thy name to be remembered in all generations:
Therefore shall the peoples give thee thanks for ever and ever.

[6] Or, *In behalf of.* [7] Or, *let thy right hand teach.*
[8] Or, *Thy throne is* the throne of *God &c.*
[9] Or, *in the inner part* of the palace. [10] Or, *upon.*

XLVI

God the Refuge of His People

For the Chief Musician. A Psalm of the sons of Korah; set to Alamoth. A Song.

[1] God is our refuge and strength,
A very present help in trouble.
[2] Therefore will we not fear, though the earth do change,
And though the mountains be shaken into the heart of the seas;
[3] Though the waters thereof roar and be troubled,
Though the mountains tremble with the swelling[1] thereof.
[Selah

[4] There is a river, the streams whereof make glad the city of God,
The holy place of the tabernacles of the Most High.
[5] God is in the midst of her; she shall not be moved:
God will help her, and[2] that right early.
[6] The nations raged, the kingdoms were moved:
He uttered his voice, the earth melted.
[7] Jehovah of hosts is with us;
The God of Jacob is our refuge.[3] [Selah
[8] Come, behold the works of Jehovah,
What[4] desolations he hath made in the earth.
[9] He maketh wars to cease unto the end of the earth;
He breaketh the bow, and cutteth the spear in sunder;
He burneth the chariots in the fire.
[10] Be[5] still, and know that I am God:
I will be exalted among the nations, I will be exalted in the earth.
[11] Jehovah of hosts is with us;
The God of Jacob is our refuge.[6] [Selah

[1] Or, *pride.* [2] Heb. *at the dawn of morning.* [3] Or, *high tower.*
[4] Or, *Who hath made desolations &c.* [5] Or, *Let be.* [6] Or, *high tower.*

XLVII

God the King of the Earth

For the Chief Musician. A Psalm of the sons of Korah.

[1] Oh clap your hands, all ye peoples;
Shout unto God with the voice of triumph.
[2] For Jehovah[1] Most High is terrible;
He is a great King over all the earth.
[3] He subdueth peoples under us,
And nations under our feet.
[4] He chooseth our inheritance for us,
The glory of Jacob whom he loved.[2] [Selah
[5] God is gone up with a shout,
Jehovah with the sound of a trumpet.
[6] Sing praises to God, sing praises:
Sing praises unto our King, sing praises.
[7] For God is the King of all the earth:
Sing ye praises with[3] understanding.
[8] God reigneth over the nations:
God sitteth upon his holy throne.
[9] The princes of the peoples are gathered together
To[4] *be* the people of the God of Abraham:
For the shields of the earth belong unto God;
He is greatly exalted.

XLVIII

The Beauty and Glory of Zion

A Song; a Psalm of the sons of Korah.

[1] Great is Jehovah, and greatly to be praised,
In the city of our God, in his holy mountain.
[2] Beautiful in elevation, the joy of the whole earth,
Is mount Zion, *on* the sides of the north,
The city of the great King.
[3] God hath made himself known in her palaces for a refuge.[5]

[1] Or, *Jehovah is most high* and *terrible.* [2] Or, *loveth.* [3] Or, *in a skilful psalm.* Heb. *Maschil.* [4] Or, Unto *the people.* [5] Or, *high tower.*

[4] For, lo, the kings assembled themselves,
They passed[6] by together.
[5] They saw it, then were they amazed;
They were dismayed, they hasted[7] away.
[6] Trembling took hold of them there,
Pain, as of a woman in travail.
[7] With[8] the east wind
Thou breakest the ships of Tarshish.
[8] As we have heard, so have we seen
In the city of Jehovah of hosts, in the city of our God:
God will establish it for ever. [Selah
[9] We have thought on thy lovingkindness, O God,
In the midst of thy temple.
[10] As is thy name, O God,
So is thy praise unto the ends of the earth:
Thy right hand is full of righteousness.
[11] Let mount Zion be glad,
Let the daughters of Judah rejoice,
Because of thy judgments.
[12] Walk about Zion, and go round about her;
Number the towers thereof;
[13] Mark ye well her bulwarks;
Consider[9] her palaces:
That ye may tell it to the generation following.
[14] For this God is our God for ever and ever:
He will be our guide *even* unto death.

XLIX

The Folly of Trusting in Riches

For the Chief Musician. A Psalm of the sons of Korah.

[1] Hear this, all ye peoples;
Give ear, all ye inhabitants of the world,
[2] Both low and high,
Rich and poor together.

[6] Or, *passed away.* [7] Or, *were stricken with terror.*
[8] Or, As *with the east wind that breaketh.* [9] Or, *Traverse.*

[3] My mouth shall speak wisdom;
And the meditation of my heart shall be of understanding.
[4] I will incline mine ear to a parable:
I will open my dark saying upon the harp.
[5] Wherefore should I fear in the days of evil,
When iniquity[1] at my heels compasseth me about?
[6] They that trust in their wealth,
And boast themselves in the multitude of their riches;
[7] None *of them* can by any means redeem his brother,
Nor give to God a ransom for him;
[8] (For the redemption of their life is costly,
And it faileth for ever);
[9] That he should still live alway,
That he should not see corruption.[2]
[10] For he[3] shall see it. Wise men die;
The fool and the brutish alike perish,
And leave their wealth to others.
[11] Their inward thought is, *that* their houses *shall continue* for ever,
And their dwelling places to all generations;
They call their lands after their own names.
[12] But man *being* in honor abideth not:
He is like the beasts that perish.
[13] This their[4] way is their[5] folly:
Yet after them men approve their sayings. [Selah
[14] They are appointed as a flock for Sheol;
Death shall be their shepherd:
And the upright shall have dominion over them in the morning;
And their beauty[6] shall be for Sheol to consume,
That there be no habitation for it.
[15] But God will redeem my soul from the power[7] of Sheol;
For he will receive me. [Selah

[1] Or, *the iniquity of them that would supplant me compasseth me about? Even of them that trust . . . riches?*
[2] Or, *the pit.* [3] Or, *he seeth that wise men &c.*
[4] Or, *is the way of them that are foolish.* [5] Or, *their confidence: and after &c.*
[6] Or, *form.* [7] Heb. *hand.*

[16] Be not thou afraid when one is made rich,
When the glory[8] of his house is increased:
[17] For when he dieth he shall carry nothing away;
His glory shall not descend after him.
[18] Though while he lived he blessed his soul,
(And men praise thee, when thou doest well to thyself),
[19] He[9] shall go to the generation of his fathers;
They[10] shall never see the light.
[20] Man that is in honor, and understandeth not,
Is like the beasts that perish.

L

God the Judge of the Righteous and the Wicked

A Psalm of Asaph.

[1] The Mighty One, God, Jehovah, hath spoken,
And called the earth from the rising of the sun unto the going down thereof.
[2] Out of Zion, the perfection of beauty,
God hath shined forth.
[3] Our God cometh, and doth not keep silence:
A fire devoureth before him,
And it is very tempestuous round about him.
[4] He calleth to the heavens above,
And to the earth, that he may judge his people:
[5] Gather my saints together unto me,
Those that have made a covenant with me by sacrifice.
[6] And the heavens shall[1] declare his righteousness;
For God is judge himself. [Selah
[7] Hear, O my people, and I will speak;
O Israel, and I will testify unto[2] thee:
I am God, *even* thy God.
[8] I will not reprove thee for thy sacrifices:
And[3] thy burnt-offerings are continually before me.

[8] Or, *wealth.* [9] Heb. *Thou shalt go,* or, *It shall go.* [10] Or, *Who never more see*
[1] Or, *declare.* [2] Or, *against* [3] Or, *Nor for thy burnt-offerings, which are &c*

[9] I will take no bullock out of thy house,
Nor he-goats out of thy folds.
[10] For every beast of the forest is mine,
And the cattle upon[4] a thousand hills.
[11] I know all the birds of the mountains;
And the wild beasts of the field are mine.[5]
[12] If I were hungry, I would not tell thee;
For the world is mine, and the fulness thereof.
[13] Will I eat the flesh of bulls,
Or drink the blood of goats?
[14] Offer unto God the sacrifice of thanksgiving;
And pay thy vows unto the Most High:
[15] And call upon me in the day of trouble;
I will deliver thee, and thou shalt glorify me.

[16] But unto the wicked God saith,
What hast thou to do to declare my statutes,
And that thou hast taken my covenant in thy mouth?
[17] Seeing thou hatest instruction,[6]
And castest my words behind thee.
[18] When thou sawest a thief, thou consentedst with him,
And hast[7] been partaker with adulterers.
[19] Thou givest thy mouth to evil,
And thy tongue frameth deceit.
[20] Thou sittest and speakest against thy brother;
Thou slanderest[8] thine own mother's son.
[21] These things hast thou done, and I kept silence;
Thou thoughtest that I was altogether such a one as thyself:
But I will reprove thee, and set *them* in order before thine eyes.

[22] Now consider this, ye that forget God,
Lest I tear you in pieces, and there be none to deliver:
[23] Whoso offereth the sacrifice of thanksgiving glorifieth me;
And to[9] him that ordereth his way *aright*
Will I show the salvation of God.

[4] Or, *upon the mountains where thousands are.* [5] Or, *in my mind.* Heb. *with me.*
[6] Or, *correction* [7] Heb. *thy portion was with adulterers.* [8] Or, *givest a thrust against.*
[9] Or, *prepareth a way that I may show him.*

LI

A Contrite Sinner's Prayer for Pardon

For the Chief Musician. A Psalm of David; when Nathan the prophet came unto him, after he had gone in to Bath-sheba.

[1] Have mercy upon me, O God, according to thy lovingkindness:
According to the multitude of thy tender mercies blot out my transgressions.
[2] Wash me thoroughly from mine iniquity,
And cleanse me from my sin.
[3] For I know my transgressions;
And my sin is ever before me.
[4] Against thee, thee only, have I sinned,
And done that which is evil in thy sight;
That thou mayest be justified when thou speakest,
And be clear when thou judgest.
[5] Behold, I was brought forth in iniquity;
And in sin did my mother conceive me.
[6] Behold, thou desirest truth in the inward parts;
And in the hidden part thou wilt make me to know wisdom.
[7] Purify me with hyssop, and I shall be clean:
Wash me, and I shall be whiter than snow.
[8] Make me to hear joy and gladness,
That the bones which thou hast broken may rejoice.
[9] Hide thy face from my sins,
And blot out all mine iniquities.
[10] Create in[1] me a clean heart, O God;
And renew a right[2] spirit within me.
[11] Cast me not away from thy presence;
And take not thy holy Spirit from me.
[12] Restore unto me the joy of thy salvation;
And uphold me with a willing spirit.
[13] Then will I teach transgressors thy ways;
And sinners shall be[3] converted unto thee.

[1] Or, *for me*. [2] Or, *stedfast*. [3] Or, *return*.

[14] Deliver me from bloodguiltiness, O God, thou God of my salvation;
And my tongue shall sing aloud of thy righteousness.
[15] O Lord, open thou my lips;
And my mouth shall show forth thy praise.
[16] For thou delightest not in sacrifice; else[4] would I give it:
Thou hast no pleasure in burnt-offering.
[17] The sacrifices of God are a broken spirit:
A broken and a contrite heart, O God, thou wilt not despise.

[18] Do good in thy good pleasure unto Zion:
Build thou the walls of Jerusalem.
[19] Then wilt thou delight in the sacrifices of righteousness,
In burnt-offering and whole burnt-offering:
Then will they offer bullocks upon thine altar.

LII

Futility of Boastful Wickedness

For the Chief Musician. Maschil of David; when Doeg the Edomite came and told Saul, and said unto him, David is come to the house of Ahimelech.

[1] Why boastest thou thyself in mischief, O mighty man?
The lovingkindness of God *endureth* continually.
[2] Thy tongue deviseth very wickedness,
Like a sharp razor, working deceitfully.
[3] Thou lovest evil more than good,
And lying rather than to speak righteousness. [Selah
[4] Thou lovest all devouring words,
O[1] thou deceitful tongue.
[5] God will likewise destroy[2] thee for ever;
He will take thee up, and pluck thee out of thy tent,
And root thee out of the land of the living. [Selah
[6] The righteous also shall see *it,* and fear,
And shall laugh at him, *saying,*

[4] Or, *that I should give it.* [1] Or, And *the deceitful tongue.*
[2] Or, *break thee down.*

[7] Lo, this is the man that made not God his strength,[3]
But trusted in the abundance of his riches,
And strengthened himself in his wickedness.
[8] But as for me, I am like a green olive-tree in the house of God:
I trust in the lovingkindness of God for ever and ever.
[9] I will give thee thanks for ever, because thou hast done it;
And I will hope in thy name for it is good, in the presence of thy saints.

LIII

Folly and Wickedness of Men

For the Chief Musician; set to Mahalath. Maschil of David.

[1] The fool hath said in his heart, There is no God.
Corrupt are they, and have done abominable iniquity;
There is none that doeth good.
[2] God looked down from heaven upon the children of men,
To see if there were any that did understand,[1]
That did seek after God.
[3] Every one of them is gone back; they are together become filthy;
There is none that doeth good, no, not one.
[4] Have the workers of iniquity no knowledge,
Who eat up my people *as* they eat bread,
And call not upon God?
[5] There were they in great fear, where no fear was;
For God hath scattered the bones of him that encampeth against thee:
Thou hast put them to shame, because God hath rejected them.
[6] Oh that the salvation of Israel were come out of Zion!
When God bringeth[2] back the captivity of his people,
Then shall Jacob rejoice, *and* Israel shall be glad.

[3] Or, *stronghold*. [1] Or, *deal wisely*. [2] Or, *returneth to*.

LIV

Prayer for Defence Against Enemies

For the Chief Musician; on stringed instruments. Maschil of David; when the Ziphites came and said to Saul, Doth not David hide himself with us?

[1] Save me, O God, by thy name,
And judge me in thy might.
[2] Hear my prayer, O God;
Give ear to the words of my mouth.
[3] For strangers are risen up against me,
And violent men have sought after my soul:
They have not set God before them. [Selah
[4] Behold, God is my helper:
The Lord is of[1] them that uphold my soul.
[5] He[2] will requite the evil unto mine[3] enemies:
Destroy thou them in thy truth.
[6] With a freewill-offering will I sacrifice unto thee:
I will give thanks unto thy name, O Jehovah, for it is good.
[7] For he hath delivered me out of all trouble;
And mine eye hath seen *my desire* upon mine enemies.

LV

Prayer for the Destruction of the Treacherous

For the Chief Musician; on stringed instruments. Maschil of David.

[1] Give ear to my prayer, O God;
And hide not thyself from my supplication.
[2] Attend unto me, and answer me:
I am restless in my complaint, and moan,
[3] Because of the voice of the enemy,
Because of the oppression of the wicked;
For they cast iniquity upon me,
And in anger they persecute me.
[4] My heart is sore pained within me:
And the terrors of death are fallen upon me.

[1] Or, *with*. [2] Another reading is, *The evil shall return.*
[3] Or, *them that lie in wait for me.*

[5] Fearfulness and trembling are come upon me,
And horror hath overwhelmed me.
[6] And I said, Oh that I had wings like a dove!
Then would I fly away, and be at rest.
[7] Lo, then would I wander far off,
I would lodge in the wilderness. [Selah
[8] I would haste[1] me to a shelter
From the stormy wind and tempest.
[9] Destroy,[2] O Lord, *and* divide their tongue;
For I have seen violence and strife in the city.
[10] Day and night they go about it upon the walls thereof:
Iniquity also and mischief are in the midst of it.
[11] Wickedness is in the midst thereof:
Oppression[3] and guile depart not from its streets.
[12] For it was not an enemy that reproached me;
Then I could have borne it:
Neither was it he that hated me that did magnify himself against me;
Then I would have hid myself from him:
[13] But it was thou, a man mine equal,
My companion, and my familiar friend.
[14] We took sweet counsel together;
We walked in the house of God with the throng.
[15] Let[4] death come suddenly upon them,
Let them go down alive into Sheol;
For wickedness is in their dwelling, in the[5] midst of them.
[16] As for me, I will call upon God;
And Jehovah will save me.
[17] Evening, and morning, and at noonday, will I complain, and moan;
And he will hear my voice.
[18] He hath redeemed my soul in peace from[6] the battle that was against me;
For they were many *that strove* with me.

[1] Or, *hasten my escape.* [2] Heb. *Swallow up.* [3] Or, *Fraud.*
[4] Or, as otherwise read, *Desolations be upon them!*
[5] Or, *their inward part.*
[6] Or. *so that none came nigh me.*

[19] God will hear, and answer[7] them,
Even he that abideth of old, [Selah
The men who have no changes,
And who fear not God.
[20] He hath put forth his hands against such as were at peace with him:
He hath profaned his covenant.
[21] His mouth was smooth as butter,
But his heart was war:
His words were softer than oil,
Yet were they drawn swords.
[22] Cast thy[8] burden upon Jehovah, and he will sustain thee:
He will never suffer the righteous to be moved.
[23] But thou, O God, wilt bring them down into the pit of destruction:
Bloodthirsty and deceitful men shall not live out half their days;
But I will trust in thee.

LVI

Supplication for Deliverance, and Grateful Trust in God

For the Chief Musician; set to Jonath[1] elem rehokim. A Psalm of David. Michtam; when the Philistines took him in Gath.

[1] Be merciful unto me, O God; for man would swallow me up:
All the day long he fighting oppresseth me.
[2] Mine[2] enemies would swallow me up all the day long;
For they are many that fight proudly against me.
[3] What time I am afraid,
I will put my trust in thee.
[4] In God (I will praise his word),
In God have I put my trust, I will not be afraid;
What can flesh do unto me?

[7] Or, *afflict.* [8] Or, *what he hath given thee.*

[1] That is, *The silent dove of them that are afar off.* Or, as otherwise read, *The dove of the distant terebinths.*

[2] Or, *They that lie in wait for me.*

[5] All the day long they wrest my words:
All their thoughts are against me for evil.
[6] They gather themselves together, they hide themselves,
They mark my steps,
Even[3] as they have waited for my soul.
[7] Shall[4] they escape by iniquity?
In anger cast down the people, O God.
[8] Thou numberest my wanderings:
Put thou my tears into thy bottle;
Are they not in thy book[5]?
[9] Then shall mine enemies turn back in the day that I call:
This I know, that[6] God is for me.
[10] In God (I will praise *his* word),
In Jehovah (I will praise *his* word),
[11] In God have I put my trust, I will not be afraid;
What can man do unto me?
[12] Thy vows are upon me, O God:
I will render thank-offerings unto thee.
[13] For thou hast delivered my soul from death:
Hast thou not *delivered* my feet from falling,
That I may walk before God
In the light of the[7] living?

LVII

Prayer for Rescue from Persecutors

For the Chief Musician; set to Al-tashheth. A Psalm of David. Michtam; when he fled from Saul, in the cave.

[1] Be merciful unto me, O God, be merciful unto me;
For my soul taketh refuge in thee:
Yea, in the shadow of thy wings will I take refuge,
Until *these* calamities[1] be overpast.
[2] I will cry unto God Most High,
Unto God that performeth *all things* for me.

[3] Or, *Inasmuch as.* [4] Or, *They think to escape.*
[5] Or, *record.* [6] Or, *for.* [7] Or, *life.*
[1] Or, *wickednesses.*

[3] He will send from heaven, and save me,
When he that would swallow me up reproacheth; [Selah
God will send forth his lovingkindness and his truth.
[4] My soul is among lions;
I lie[2] among them that are set on fire,
Even the sons of men, whose teeth are spears and arrows,
And their tongue a sharp sword.
[5] Be thou exalted, O God, above the heavens;
Let thy glory *be* above all the earth.

[6] They have prepared a net for my steps;
My soul is bowed down:
They have digged a pit before me;
They are fallen into the midst thereof themselves. [Selah
[7] My heart is fixed, O God, my heart is fixed:
I will sing, yea, I will sing praises.
[8] Awake up, my glory; awake, psaltery and harp:
I myself will[3] awake right early.
[9] I will give thanks unto thee, O Lord, among the peoples:
I will sing praises unto thee among the nations.
[10] For thy lovingkindness is great unto the heavens,
And thy truth unto the skies.
[11] Be thou exalted, O God, above the heavens;
Let thy glory *be* above all the earth.

LVIII

Prayer for the Punishment of the Wicked

For the Chief Musician; set to Al-tashheth. A Psalm of David. Michtam.

[1] Do[4] ye indeed in[5] silence speak righteousness?
Do ye judge[6] uprightly, O ye sons of men?
[2] Nay, in heart ye work wickedness;
Ye weigh out the violence of your hands in the earth.

[2] Or, *must lie* [3] Or, *will awake the dawn.*
[4] Or, *Is the righteousness ye should speak dumb?*
[5] Or, as otherwise read, *O ye gods.* Or, *O ye mighty ones.*
[6] Or, *judge uprightly the sons of men.*

[3] The wicked are estranged from the womb:
They go astray as soon as they are born, speaking lies.
[4] Their poison is like the poison of a serpent:
They are like the deaf adder that stoppeth her ear,
[5] Which hearkeneth not to the voice of charmers,[7]
Charming never so wisely.
[6] Break their teeth, O God, in their mouth:
Break out the great teeth of the young lions, O Jehovah.
[7] Let them melt away as water that runneth apace:
When he aimeth his arrows, let them be as though they were cut off.
[8] *Let them be* as a snail which melteth and passeth away,
Like the untimely birth of a woman, that[8] hath not seen the sun.
[9] Before your pots can feel the thorns,
He[9] will take them away with a whirlwind, the green and the burning alike.
[10] The righteous shall rejoice when he seeth the vengeance:
He shall wash his feet in the blood of the wicked:
[11] So that men shall say, Verily there is a[10] reward for the righteous:
Verily there is a God that judgeth in the earth.

LIX

Prayer for Deliverance from Enemies

For the Chief Musician; set to Al-tashheth. A Psalm of David. Michtam; when Saul sent, and they watched the house to kill him.

[1] Deliver me from mine enemies, O my God:
Set me on high from them that rise up against me.
[2] Deliver me from the workers of iniquity.
And save me from the bloodthirsty men.
[3] For, lo, they lie in wait for my soul;
The mighty gather themselves together against me:
Not for my transgression, nor for my sin, O Jehovah.

[7] Or, *enchanters*. [8] Or, like them *that have not seen the sun*.
[9] Or, *Wrath shall take them away whiie living as with a whirlwind*.
[10] Heb. *fruit*.

[4] They run and prepare themselves without *my* fault:
Awake thou to help[1] me, and behold.
[5] Even thou, O Jehovah God of hosts, the God of Israel,
Arise to visit all the nations:
Be not merciful to any wicked transgressors. [Selah
[6] They return at evening, they howl like a dog,
And go round about the city.
[7] Behold, they belch out with their mouth;
Swords are in their lips:
For who, *say they,* doth hear?
[8] But thou, O Jehovah, wilt laugh at them;
Thou wilt have all the nations in derision.
[9] *Because*[2] *of* his strength I will give heed unto thee;
For God is my high tower.
[10] My God with his lovingkindness will meet me:
God will let me see *my desire* upon mine[3] enemies,
[11] Slay them not, lest my people forget:
Scatter[4] them by thy power, and bring them down,
O Lord our shield.
[12] *For* the sin of their mouth, *and* the words of their lips,
Let them even be taken in their pride,
And for cursing and lying which they speak.
[13] Consume them in wrath, consume them, so that they shall be no more:
And let them know that God ruleth in Jacob,
Unto the ends of the earth. [Selah
[14] And at evening let them return, let them howl like a dog,
And go round about the city.
[15] They shall wander up and down for food,
And tarry all night if they be not satisfied.
[16] But I will sing of thy strength;
Yea, I will sing aloud of thy lovingkindness in the morning:
For thou hast been my high tower,
And a refuge in the day of my distress.

1 Heb. *meet.*
2 Acc. to Sept. and Vulg., *My strength.*
3 Or, *them that lie in wait for me.*
4 Or, *Make them wander to and fro.*

[17] Unto thee, O my strength, will I sing praises:
For God is my high tower, the God of my mercy.

LX

Lament Over Defeat in Battle, and Prayer for Help

For the Chief Musician; set to Shushan[1] Eduth. Michtam of David, to teach; when he strove with Aram-naharaim and with Aram-zobah, and Joab returned, and smote of Edom in the Valley of Salt twelve thousand.

[1] O God, thou hast cast us off, thou hast broken us down;
Thou hast been angry; oh restore us again.
[2] Thou hast made the land to tremble; thou hast rent it:
Heal the breaches thereof; for it shaketh.
[3] Thou hast showed thy people hard things:
Thou hast made us to drink the wine of staggering.
[4] Thou hast given a banner to them that fear thee,
That it may be displayed because of the truth. [Selah
[5] That thy beloved may be delivered,
Save with thy right hand, and answer us.[2]
[6] God hath spoken in his holiness: I will exult;
I will divide Shechem, and mete out the valley of Succoth.
[7] Gilead is mine, and Manasseh is mine;
Ephraim also is the defence of my head;
Judah is my sceptre.[3]
[8] Moab is my washpot;
Upon[4] Edom will I cast my shoe:
Philistia, shout thou because of me.
[9] Who will bring me into the strong city?
Who[5] hath led me unto Edom?
[10] Hast[6] not thou, O God, cast us off?
And thou goest not forth, O God, with our hosts.
[11] Give us help against the adversary;
For vain is the help[7] of man.

[1] That is, *The lily of testimony.*
[2] Another reading is, *me.* [3] Or, *lawgiver.* [4] Or, *Unto.* [5] Or, *Who will lead me &c.*
[6] Or, *Wilt not thou, O God, who hast cast us off, and goest . . . hosts?*
[7] Heb. *salvation.*

[12] Through God we shall do valiantly;
For he it is that will tread down our adversaries.

LXI

Confidence in God's Protection

For the Chief Musician; on a stringed instrument. A Psalm of David.

[1] Hear my cry, O God;
Attend unto my prayer.
[2] From the end of the earth will I call unto thee, when my heart is[1] overwhelmed:
Lead me to the[2] rock that is higher than I.
[3] For thou hast been a refuge for me,
A strong tower from the enemy.
[4] I will dwell in thy tabernacle[3] for ever:
I will take refuge in the covert of thy wings. [Selah
[5] For thou, O God, hast heard my vows:
Thou hast given[4] *me* the heritage of those that fear thy name.
[6] Thou wilt prolong the king's life;
His years shall be as many generations.
[7] He shall abide before God for ever:
Oh prepare lovingkindness and truth, that they may preserve him.
[8] So will I sing praise unto thy name for ever,
That I may daily perform my vows.

LXII

God Alone a Refuge from Treachery and Oppression

For the Chief Musician; after the manner of Jeduthun
A Psalm of David.

[1] My soul waiteth[5] in silence for God only:
From him *cometh* my salvation.
[2] He only is my rock and my salvation:
He is my high tower; I shall not be greatly moved.

[1] Or, *fainteth.* [2] Or, *a rock that is too high for me.* [3] Heb. *tent.*
[4] Or, *given a heritage unto those &c.* [5] Heb. *is silent unto God.*

[3] How long will ye set upon a man,
That[6] ye may slay *him,* all of you,
Like a leaning wall, like a tottering fence?
[4] They only consult to thrust him down from his dignity;
They delight in lies;
They bless with their mouth, but they curse inwardly. [Selah
[5] My soul, wait[7] thou in silence for God only;
For my expectation is from him.
[6] He only is my rock and my salvation:
He is my high tower; I shall not be moved.
[7] With God is my salvation and my glory:
The rock of my strength, and my refuge, is in God.
[8] Trust in him at all times, ye people;
Pour out your heart before him:
God is a refuge for us. [Selah
[9] Surely men of low degree are vanity,[8] and men of high degree are a lie:
In the balances they will go up;
They are together lighter than vanity.[8]
[10] Trust not in oppression,
And become not vain in robbery:
If riches increase, set not your heart *thereon.*
[11] God hath spoken once,
Twice have I heard this;
That power belongeth unto God:
[12] Also unto thee, O Lord, belongeth lovingkindness;
For thou renderest to every man according to his work.

LXIII

The Thirsting Soul Satisfied in God

A Psalm of David, when he was in the wilderness of Judah.

[1] O God, thou art my God; earnestly will I seek thee:
My soul thirsteth for thee, my flesh longeth for thee,
In a dry and weary land, where no water is.

[6] Or, as otherwise read, *Ye shall be slain &c.* [7] Heb. *be thou silent unto God.*
[8] Heb. *a breath.*

[2] So have I looked upon thee in the sanctuary,
To see thy power and thy glory.
[3] Because thy lovingkindness is better than life,
My lips shall praise thee.
[4] So will I bless thee while I live:
I will lift up my hands in thy name.
[5] My soul shall be satisfied as with marrow[1] and fatness;
And my mouth shall praise thee with joyful lips;
[6] When I remember thee upon my bed,
And[2] meditate on thee in the night-watches.
[7] For thou hast been my help,
And in the shadow of thy wings will I rejoice.
[8] My soul followeth hard after thee:
Thy right hand upholdeth me.
[9] But those that seek my soul, to[3] destroy it,
Shall go into the lower parts of the earth.
[10] They shall be given[4] over to the power of the sword:
They shall be a portion for foxes.[5]
[11] But the king shall rejoice in God:
Every one that sweareth by him shall glory;
For the mouth of them that speak lies shall be stopped.

LXIV

Prayer for Deliverance from Secret Enemies

For the Chief Musician. A Psalm of David.

[1] Hear my voice, O God, in my complaint:
Preserve my life from fear of the enemy.
[2] Hide me from the secret counsel of evil-doers,
From the tumult[6] of the workers of iniquity;
[3] Who have whet their tongue like a sword,
And have aimed their arrows, even bitter words;
[4] That they may shoot in secret places at the perfect:
Suddenly do they shoot at him, and fear not.

[1] Heb. *fat*. [2] Or, *I meditate*. [3] Or, *shall be destroyed; They shall &c.*
[4] Or, *poured out by*. [5] Or, *jackals*.
[6] Or, *throng*.

[5] They encourage themselves in an evil purpose;
They commune of laying snares privily;
They say, Who will see them?
[6] They search out iniquities;
We[7] have accomplished, *say they,* a diligent search:
And the inward thought and the heart of every one is deep.
[7] But God will shoot at them;
With an arrow suddenly shall they be wounded.
[8] So they[8] shall be made to stumble, their own tongue being against them:
All that see them shall wag[9] the head.
[9] And all men shall fear;
And they shall declare the work of God,
And shall wisely consider of his doing.
[10] The righteous shall be glad in Jehovah, and shall take refuge in him;
And all the upright in heart shall glory.

LXV

God's Abundant Favor to Earth and Man

For the Chief Musician. A Psalm. A Song of David.

[1] Praise[1] waiteth for thee, O God, in Zion;
And unto thee shall the vow be performed.
[2] O thou that hearest prayer,
Unto thee shall all flesh come.
[3] Iniquities[2] prevail against me:
As for our transgressions, thou wilt forgive[3] them.
[4] Blessed is the man whom thou choosest, and causest to approach *unto thee,*
That he may dwell in thy courts:
We shall be satisfied with the goodness of thy house,
Thy holy temple.

[7] Or, as otherwise read, *They have accomplished* (or, *have hidden*).
[8] Or, *shall they against whom their tongue was make them to stumble.*
[9] Or, *flee away.*
[1] Or, *There shall be silence before thee,* and *praise, O God &c.*
[2] Heb. *Words* (or, *Matters*) *of iniquities.* [3] Or, *expiate.*

[5] By terrible things thou wilt answer us in righteousness,
O God of our salvation,
Thou that art the confidence of all the ends of the earth,
And of[4] them that are afar off upon the sea:
[6] Who by his strength setteth fast the mountains,
Being girded about with might;
[7] Who stilleth the roaring of the seas,
The roaring of their waves,
And the tumult of the peoples.
[8] They also that dwell in the uttermost parts are afraid at thy tokens:
Thou makest the outgoings of the morning and evening to rejoice.
[9] Thou visitest the earth, and waterest it,
Thou greatly enrichest it;
The river of God is full of water:
Thou providest them grain, when[5] thou hast so prepared the[6] earth.
[10] Thou waterest its furrows abundantly;
Thou settlest[7] the ridges thereof:
Thou makest it soft with showers;
Thou blessest the springing thereof.
[11] Thou crownest the[8] year with thy goodness;
And thy paths drop fatness.
[12] They[9] drop upon the pastures of the wilderness;
And the hills are girded with joy.
[13] The pastures are clothed with flocks;
The valleys also are covered over with grain;
They shout for joy, they also sing.

[4] Or, *of the sea, afar off.* [5] Or, *for so preparest thou.* [6] Heb. *it.*
[7] Heb. *lowerest.* [8] Heb. *the year of thy goodness.*
[9] Or, *The pastures . . . do drop.*

LXVI

Praise for God's Mighty Deeds and for His Answer to Prayer

For the Chief Musician. A Song, a Psalm.

[1] Make a joyful noise unto God, all the earth:
[2] Sing forth the glory of his name:
Make his praise glorious.
[3] Say unto God, How terrible are thy works!
Through the greatness of thy power shall thine enemies submit[1] themselves unto thee.
[4] All the earth shall worship thee,
And shall sing unto thee;
They shall sing to thy name. [Selah
[5] Come, and see the works of God;
He is terrible in his doing toward the children of men.
[6] He turned the sea into dry land;
They went through the river on foot:
There did[2] we rejoice in him.
[7] He ruleth by his might for ever;
His eyes observe the nations:
Let not the rebellious exalt themselves. [Selah
[8] Oh bless our God, ye peoples,
And make the voice of his praise to be heard;
[9] Who holdeth[3] our soul in life,
And suffereth not our feet to be moved.
[10] For thou, O God, hast proved us:
Thou hast tried us, as silver is tried.
[11] Thou broughtest us into the net;
Thou layedst a sore burden upon our loins.
[12] Thou didst cause men to ride over our heads;
We went through fire and through water;
But thou broughtest us out into a[4] wealthy place.
[13] I will come into thy house with burnt-offerings;
I will pay thee my vows,

[1] Or, *yield feigned obedience.* Heb. *lie.* [2] Or, *let us rejoice.*
[3] Heb. *putteth.* [4] Heb. *abundance.*

[14] Which my lips uttered,
And my mouth spake, when I was in distress.
[15] I will offer unto thee burnt-offerings of fatlings,
With the incense of rams;
I will offer bullocks with goats. [Selah
[16] Come, and hear, all ye that fear God,
And I will declare what he hath done for my soul.
[17] I cried unto him with my mouth,
And he[5] was extolled with my tongue.
[18] If I regard[6] iniquity in my heart,
The Lord will[7] not hear:
[19] But verily God hath heard;
He hath attended to the voice of my prayer.
[20] Blessed be God,
Who hath not turned away my prayer,
Nor his lovingkindness from me.

LXVII

The Nations Exhorted to Praise God

For the Chief Musician; on stringed instruments. A Psalm, a Song.

[1] God be merciful unto us, and bless us,
And cause his face to shine upon[1] us; [Selah
[2] That thy way may be known upon earth,
Thy salvation among all nations.
[3] Let the peoples praise[2] thee, O God;
Let all the peoples praise thee.
[4] Oh let the nations be glad and sing for joy;
For thou wilt judge the peoples with equity,
And govern[3] the nations upon earth. [Selah
[5] Let the peoples praise thee, O God;
Let all the peoples praise thee.
[6] The earth hath yielded its increase:
God, even our own God, will bless us.

[5] Or, as otherwise read, *high praise was under my tongue.* [6] Or, *had regarded.*
[7] Or, *would.*
[1] Heb. *with us.* [2] Or, *give thanks unto.* [3] Heb. *lead.*

[7] God will bless us;
And all the ends of the earth shall fear him.

LXVIII

JEHOVAH THE GOD OF SINAI AND OF THE SANCTUARY

For the Chief Musician. A Psalm of David, a Song.

[1] LET[1] God arise, let his enemies be scattered;
Let them also that hate him flee before him.
[2] As smoke is driven away, so drive them away:
As wax melteth before the fire,
So let the wicked perish at the presence of God.
[3] But let the righteous be glad; let them exult before God:
Yea, let them rejoice with gladness.
[4] Sing unto God, sing praises to his name:
Cast up a highway for him that rideth through the deserts;
His name is Jehovah[2]; and exult ye before him.
[5] A father of the fatherless, and a judge of the widows,
Is God in his holy habitation.
[6] God setteth[3] the solitary in families:
He bringeth out the prisoners into prosperity;
But the rebellious dwell in a parched land.

[7] O God, when thou wentest forth before thy people,
When thou didst march through the wilderness; [Selah
[8] The earth trembled,
The heavens also dropped *rain* at the presence of God:
Yon Sinai *trembled* at the presence of God, the God of Israel.
[9] Thou, O God, didst send a plentiful rain,
Thou didst confirm thine inheritance, when it was weary.
[10] Thy congregation[4] dwelt therein:
Thou, O God, didst prepare of thy goodness for the poor.
[11] The Lord giveth the word:
The women that publish the tidings are a great host.

[1] Or, *God ariseth;* and so throughout ver. 1, 2, 3. [2] Heb. *Jah.*
[3] Heb. *maketh the solitary to dwell in a house.* [4] Or, *troop.*

[12] Kings of armies flee, they flee;
And she that tarrieth at home divideth the spoil.
[13] When[5] ye lie among the sheepfolds,
It is as the wings of a dove covered with silver,
And her pinions with yellow gold.
[14] When the Almighty scattered kings therein,
It was[6] *as when* it snoweth in Zalmon.
[15] A mountain of God is the mountain of Bashan;
A high[7] mountain is the mountain of Bashan.
[16] Why look ye askance, ye high mountains,
At the mountain which God hath desired for his abode?
Yea, Jehovah will dwell *in it* for ever.
[17] The chariots of God are twenty thousand, even thousands upon thousands:
The Lord is among them, *as*[8] *in* Sinai, in the sanctuary.
[18] Thou hast ascended on high, thou hast led away captives;
Thou hast received gifts among men,
Yea, *among* the rebellious also, that Jehovah[9] God might dwell[10] *with them.*

[19] Blessed be the[11] Lord, who daily beareth our burden,
Even the God who is our salvation. [Selah
[20] God is unto us a God of deliverances;
And unto Jehovah the Lord belongeth escape from death.
[21] But God will smite through the head of his enemies,
The hairy scalp of such a one as goeth on still in his guiltiness.
[22] The Lord said, I will bring again from Bashan,
I will bring *them* again from the depths of the sea;
[23] That thou mayest crush *them, dipping* thy foot in blood,
That the tongue of thy dogs may have its portion from *thine* enemies.
[24] They have seen thy goings, O God,
Even the goings of my God, my King, into[12] the sanctuary.

[5] Or, *Will ye lie among the sheepfolds,* as *the wings . . . gold?*
[6] Or, *snowed.* [7] Heb. *mountain of summits.* [8] Or, *Sinai* is *in the sanctuary.*
[9] Heb. *Jah.* See ver. 4. [10] Or, *dwell* there. [11] Or, *the Lord day by day: if one oppresseth us, God is our salvation.*
[12] Or, *in the sanctuary.* Or, *in holiness.*

[25] The singers went before, the minstrels followed after,
In the midst of the damsels playing with timbrels.
[26] Bless ye God in the congregations,
Even the Lord, *ye that are* of the fountain of Israel.
[27] There is little Benjamin their ruler,
The princes of Judah *and* their council,[13]
The princes of Zebulun, the princes of Naphtali.

[28] Thy God hath commanded thy strength:
Strengthen,[14] O God, that which thou hast[15] wrought for us.
[29] Because of thy temple at Jerusalem
Kings shall bring presents unto thee.
[30] Rebuke the wild beast of the reeds,
The multitude of the bulls, with the calves of the peoples,
Trampling[16] under foot the pieces of silver:
He[17] hath scattered the peoples that delight in war.
[31] Princes shall come out of Egypt;
Ethiopia[18] shall haste to stretch out her hands unto God.
[32] Sing unto God, ye kingdoms of the earth;
Oh sing praises unto the Lord; [Selah
[33] To him that rideth upon the heaven of heavens, which are of old;
Lo, he uttereth his voice, a mighty voice.
[34] Ascribe ye strength unto God:
His excellency is over Israel,
And his strength is in the skies.
[35] O[19] God, *thou art* terrible out of thy holy places:
The God of Israel, he giveth strength and power unto *his* people.
Blessed be God.

13 Or, *company.*
14 Or, *Be strong, O God, thou that hast &c.*
15 Or, *hast wrought for us out of thy temple. Unto Jerusalem &c.*
16 Or, Every one *submitting himself with pieces of silver.*
17 Or, as otherwise read, *Scatter thou.* 18 Heb. *Cush.*
19 Or, *Terrible is God.*

LXIX

A Cry of Distress, and Imprecation on Adversaries

For the Chief Musician; set to Shoshannim.[1] A Psalm of David.

[1] Save me, O God;
For the waters are come in unto my soul.
[2] I sink in deep mire, where there is no standing:
I am come into deep waters, where the floods overflow me.
[3] I am weary with my crying; my throat is dried:
Mine eyes fail while I wait for my God.
[4] They that hate me without a cause are more than the hairs of my head:
They that would cut me off, being mine enemies wrongfully,[2] are mighty:
That which I took not away I have to restore.
[5] O God, thou knowest my foolishness;
And my sins[3] are not hid from thee.
[6] Let not them that wait for thee be put to shame through me, O Lord Jehovah of hosts:
Let not those that seek thee be brought to dishonor through me, O God of Israel:
[7] Because for thy sake I have borne reproach;
Shame hath covered my face.
[8] I am become a stranger unto my brethren,
And an alien unto my mother's children.
[9] For the zeal of thy house hath eaten me up;
And the reproaches of them that reproach thee are fallen upon me.
[10] When I wept, *and chastened* my soul with fasting,
That was to my reproach.
[11] When I made sackcloth my clothing,
I became a byword unto them.
[12] They that sit in the gate talk of me;
And *I am* the song of the drunkards.

[1] That is, *Lilies*. [2] Heb. *falsely*. [3] Heb. *guiltinesses*.

[13] But as for me, my prayer is unto thee, O Jehovah, in an acceptable time:
O God, in the abundance of thy lovingkindness,
Answer me in the truth of thy salvation.
[14] Deliver me out of the mire, and let me not sink:
Let me be delivered from them that hate me, and out of the deep waters.
[15] Let not the waterflood overwhelm me,
Neither let the deep swallow me up;
And let not the pit shut its mouth upon me.
[16] Answer me, O Jehovah; for thy lovingkindness is good:
According to the multitude of thy tender mercies turn thou unto me.
[17] And hide not thy face from thy servant;
For I am in distress; answer me speedily.
[18] Draw nigh unto my soul, and redeem it:
Ransom me because of mine enemies.
[19] Thou knowest my reproach, and my shame, and my dishonor:
Mine adversaries are all before thee.
[20] Reproach hath broken my heart; and I am full[4] of heaviness:
And I looked for some to take pity, but there was none;
And for comforters, but I found none.
[21] They gave me also gall for my food;
And in my thirst they gave me vinegar to drink.
[22] Let their table before them become a snare;
And when they are in peace, *let it become* a trap.
[23] Let their eyes be darkened, so that they cannot see;
And make their loins continually to shake.
[24] Pour out thine indignation upon them,
And let the fierceness of thine anger overtake them.
[25] Let their habitation[5] be desolate;
Let none dwell in their tents.
[26] For they persecute him whom thou hast smitten;
And they tell of the sorrow[6] of those whom thou hast wounded.

[4] Or, *sore sick*. [5] Or, *encampment*. [6] Or, *pain*.

[27] Add iniquity unto their iniquity;
And let them not come into thy righteousness.
[28] Let them be blotted out of the book of life,[7]
And not be written with the righteous.
[29] But I am poor and sorrowful:[8]
Let thy salvation, O God, set me up on high.
[30] I will praise the name of God with a song,
And will magnify him with thanksgiving.
[31] And it will please Jehovah better than an ox,
Or a bullock that hath horns and hoofs.
[32] The meek have seen it, and are glad:
Ye that seek after God, let your heart live.
[33] For Jehovah heareth the needy,
And despiseth not his prisoners.
[34] Let heaven and earth praise him,
The seas, and every thing that moveth therein.
[35] For God will save Zion, and build the cities of Judah;
And they shall abide there, and have it in possession.
[36] The seed also of his servants shall inherit it;
And they that love his name shall dwell therein.

LXX

Prayer for Help Against Persecutors

For the Chief Musician. A Psalm of David; to[1] bring to remembrance.

[1] *Make haste,* O God, to deliver me;
Make haste to help me, O Jehovah.
[2] Let them be put to shame and confounded
That seek after my soul:
Let them be turned backward and brought to dishonor
That delight in my hurt.
[3] Let them be turned back by[2] reason of their shame
That say, Aha, aha.

[7] Or, *the living.* [8] Or, *in pain.*
[1] Or, *to make memorial.* [2] Or, *for a reward of.*

[4] Let all those that seek thee rejoice and be glad in thee;
And let such as love thy salvation say continually,
Let God be magnified.
[5] But I am poor and needy;
Make haste unto me, O God:
Thou art my help and my deliverer;
O Jehovah, make no tarrying.

LXXI

Prayer of an Old Man for Deliverance

[1] In thee, O Jehovah, do I take refuge:
Let me never be put to shame.
[2] Deliver me in thy righteousness, and rescue me:
Bow down thine ear unto me, and save me.
[3] Be thou to me a rock of habitation, whereunto I may continually resort:
Thou hast given commandment to save me;
For thou art my rock and my fortress.
[4] Rescue me, O my God, out of the hand of the wicked,
Out of the hand of the unrighteous and cruel man.
[5] For thou art my hope, O Lord Jehovah:
Thou art my trust from my youth.
[6] By thee have I been holden up from the womb;
Thou art[1] he that took me out of my mother's bowels:
My praise shall be continually of thee.
[7] I am as a wonder unto many;
But thou art my strong refuge.
[8] My mouth shall be filled with thy praise,
And with thy honor all the day.
[9] Cast me not off in the time of old age;
Forsake me not when my strength faileth.
[10] For mine enemies speak concerning me;
And they that watch for my soul take counsel together,
[11] Saying, God hath forsaken him:
Pursue and take him; for there is none to deliver.

[1] Or, *hast been my benefactor from &c.*

[12] O God, be not far from me;
O my God, make haste to help me.
[13] Let them be put to shame *and* consumed that are adversaries to my soul;
Let them be covered with reproach and dishonor that seek my hurt.
[14] But I will hope continually,
And will praise thee yet more and more.
[15] My mouth shall tell of thy righteousness,
And of thy salvation all the day;
For I know not the numbers *thereof*.
[16] I will come with[2] the mighty acts of the Lord Jehovah:
I will make mention of thy righteousness, even of thine only.
[17] O God, thou hast taught me from my youth;
And hitherto have I declared thy wondrous works.
[18] Yea, even when[3] I am old and grayheaded, O God, forsake me not,
Until I have declared thy[4] strength unto *the next* generation,
Thy might to every one that is to come.
[19] Thy righteousness also, O God, is very high;
Thou who hast done great things,
O God, who is like unto thee?
[20] Thou, who hast showed us[5] many and sore troubles,
Wilt quicken us[5] again,
And wilt bring us[5] up again from the depths of the earth.
[21] Increase thou my greatness,
And turn again and comfort me.
[22] I will also praise thee with the psaltery,
Even thy truth, O my God:
Unto thee will I sing praises with the harp,
O thou Holy One of Israel.
[23] My lips shall shout for joy when I sing praises unto thee;
And my soul, which thou hast redeemed.
[24] My tongue also shall talk of thy righteousness all the day long;
For they are put to shame, for they are confounded, that seek my hurt.

[2] Or, *in the strength.* [3] Heb. *unto old age and gray hairs.*
[4] Heb. *thine arm.* [5] Another reading is, *me.*

LXXII

The Reign of the Righteous King

A Psalm of Solomon.

[1] Give the king thy judgments, O God,
And thy righteousness unto the king's son.
[2] He[1] will judge thy people with righteousness,
And thy poor with justice.
[3] The mountains shall bring peace to the people,
And the hills, in righteousness.
[4] He will judge the poor of the people,
He will save the children of the needy,
And will break in pieces the oppressor.
[5] They shall fear thee while the sun endureth,
And so[2] long as the moon, throughout all generations.
[6] He will come down like rain upon the mown grass,
As showers that water the earth.
[7] In his days shall the righteous flourish,
And abundance of peace, till the moon be no more.
[8] He shall have dominion also from sea to sea,
And from the River unto the ends of the earth.
[9] They that dwell in the wilderness shall bow before him;
And his enemies shall lick the dust.
[10] The kings of Tarshish and of the isles shall render tribute:
The kings of Sheba and Seba shall offer gifts.
[11] Yea, all kings shall fall down before him;
All nations shall serve him.
[12] For he will deliver the needy when he crieth,
And the poor, that[3] hath no helper.
[13] He will have pity on the poor[4] and needy,
And the souls of the needy he will save.
[14] He will redeem their soul from oppression[5] and violence;
And precious will their blood be in his sight:

[1] Or, *Let him* (and so throughout the Psalm).
[2] Heb. *before the moon.*
[3] Or, *and him that hath.*
[4] Or, *weak.* [5] Or, *fraud.*

[15] And they[6] shall live; and to him shall be given of the gold of Sheba:
And men shall pray for him continually;
They[6] shall bless him all the day long.
[16] There shall be abundance[7] of grain in the earth[8] upon the top of the mountains;
The fruit thereof shall shake like Lebanon:
And they of the city shall flourish like grass of the earth.
[17] His name shall endure for ever;
His name shall be[9] continued as[10] long as the sun:
And men shall be[11] blessed in him;
All nations shall call him happy.

[18] Blessed be Jehovah God, the God of Israel,
Who only doeth wondrous things:
[19] And blessed be his glorious name for ever;
And let the whole earth be filled with his glory.
Amen, and Amen.

[20] The prayers of David the son of Jesse are ended.

BOOK III

LXXIII

The End of the Wicked Contrasted with that of the Righteous

A Psalm of Asaph.

[1] Surely[1] God is good to Israel,
Even to such as are pure in heart.
[2] But as for me, my feet were almost gone;
My steps had well nigh slipped.
[3] For I was envious at the arrogant,[2]
When I saw the prosperity of the wicked.

[6] Or, *he.* [7] Or, *a handful.* [8] Or, *land.* [9] Or, *have issue.*
[10] Heb. *before the sun.* [11] Or, *bless themselves.*
[1] Or, *Only good is God.* [2] Or, *fools.*

[4] For there are no pangs in their death;
But their strength is firm.
[5] They are not in[3] trouble as *other* men;
Neither are they plagued like *other* men.
[6] Therefore pride is as a chain about their neck;
Violence covereth them as a garment.
[7] Their eyes stand out with fatness:
They[4] have more than heart could wish.
[8] They scoff, and in wickedness utter oppression:
They speak loftily.[5]
[9] They have set their mouth in[6] the heavens,
And their tongue walketh through the earth.
[10] Therefore his[7] people return hither:
And waters of a full *cup* are drained by them.
[11] And they say, How doth God know?
And is there knowledge in the Most High?
[12] Behold, these are the wicked;
And, being alway at ease, they increase in riches.
[13] Surely in vain have I cleansed my heart,
And washed my hands in innocency;
[14] For all the day long have I been plagued,
And chastened[8] every morning.
[15] If I had said, I will speak thus;
Behold, I had dealt treacherously with the generation of thy children.
[16] When I thought how I might know this,
It was too[9] painful for me;
[17] Until I went into the sanctuary of God,
And considered their latter end.
[18] Surely thou settest them in slippery places:
Thou castest them down to destruction.[10]
[19] How are they become a desolation in a moment!
They are utterly consumed with terrors.

[3] Heb. *in the trouble of men.*
[4] Or, *The imaginations of their heart overflow.* [5] Or, *from on high.*
[6] Or, *against.* [7] Another reading is, *he will bring back his people.*
[8] Heb. *my chastisement* was. [9] Heb. *labor in mine eyes.* [10] Heb. *ruins.*

[20] As a dream when one awaketh,
So, O Lord, when[11] thou awakest, thou wilt despise their image.
[21] For my soul was[12] grieved,
And I was pricked in my heart:[13]
[22] So brutish was[14] I, and ignorant;
I was *as* a beast before[15] thee.
[23] Nevertheless I am continually with thee:
Thou hast holden my right hand.
[24] Thou wilt guide me with thy counsel,
And afterward receive me to[16] glory.
[25] Whom have I in heaven *but thee?*
And there is none upon earth that I desire besides[17] thee.
[26] My flesh and my heart faileth;
But God is the strength[18] of my heart and my portion for ever.
[27] For, lo, they that are far from thee shall perish:
Thou hast destroyed all them that play the harlot, *departing* from thee.
[28] But it is good for me to draw near unto God:
I have made the Lord Jehovah my refuge,
That I may tell of all thy works.

LXXIV

A Complaint over the Devastation of the Land by the Enemy

Maschil of Asaph.

[1] O God, why hast thou cast *us* off for ever?
Why doth thine anger smoke against the sheep of thy pasture?
[2] Remember thy congregation, which thou hast gotten of old,
Which thou hast redeemed to be the tribe of thine inheritance;
And mount Zion, wherein thou hast dwelt.
[3] Lift up thy feet unto the perpetual ruins,
All[1] the evil that the enemy hath done in the sanctuary.
[4] Thine adversaries have roared in the midst of thine assembly;
They have set up their ensigns for signs.

[11] Or, *in the city.* [12] Heb. *was in a ferment.* [13] Heb. *reins.* [14] Or, *am.*
[15] Heb. *with thee.* [16] Or, *with.* [17] Or, *with thee.* [18] Heb. *rock.*
[1] Or, *The enemy hath wrought all evil.*

[5] They seemed[2] as men that lifted up
Axes upon a thicket of trees.
[6] And now all the carved work thereof
They break down with hatchet and hammers.
[7] They have set thy sanctuary on fire;
They have profaned the dwelling-place of thy name *by casting it* to the ground.
[8] They said in their heart, Let us make havoc of them altogether:
They have burned up all the synagogues[3] of God in the land.
[9] We see not our signs:
There is no more any prophet;
Neither is there among us any that knoweth how long.
[10] How long, O God, shall the adversary reproach?
Shall the enemy blaspheme thy name for ever?
[11] Why drawest thou back thy hand, even thy right hand?
Pluck it out of thy bosom *and* consume *them*.

[12] Yet God is my King of old,
Working salvation in the midst of the earth.
[13] Thou didst divide[4] the sea by thy strength:
Thou brakest the heads of the sea-monsters in the waters.
[14] Thou brakest the heads of leviathan in pieces;
Thou gavest him to be food to the people inhabiting the wilderness.
[15] Thou didst cleave fountain and flood:
Thou driest up mighty[5] rivers.
[16] The day is thine, the night also is thine:
Thou hast prepared the light[6] and the sun.
[17] Thou hast set all the borders of the earth:
Thou hast made summer and winter.
[18] Remember this, that the enemy hath[7] reproached, O Jehovah,
And that a foolish people hath blasphemed thy name.
[19] Oh deliver not the[8] soul of thy turtle-dove unto the wild beast:
Forget not the life[9] of thy poor for ever.

[2] Or, *made themselves known.* [3] Or, *places of assembly.*
[4] Heb. *break up.* [5] Or, *ever-flowing.* [6] Heb. *luminary.*
[7] Or, *hath reproached Jehovah.* [8] Or, *thy turtle-dove unto the greedy multitude.*
[9] Or, *multitude.*

[20] Have respect unto the covenant;
For the dark places of the earth[10] are full of the habitations of violence.
[21] Oh let not the oppressed return ashamed:
Let the poor and needy praise thy name.
[22] Arise, O God, plead thine own cause:
Remember how the foolish man reproacheth thee all the day.
[23] Forget not the voice of thine adversaries:
The tumult of those that rise up against thee ascendeth[11] continually.

LXXV

God Abases the Proud, but Exalts the Righteous

For the Chief Musician; set to Al-tashheth. A Psalm of Asaph, a Song.

[1] We give thanks unto thee, O God;
We give thanks, for[1] thy name is near:
Men tell of thy wondrous works.
[2] When I shall find[2] the set time,
I will judge uprightly.
[3] The[3] earth and all the inhabitants thereof are dissolved:
I have set[4] up the pillars of it. [Selah
[4] I said unto the arrogant,[5] Deal not arrogantly;
And to the wicked, Lift not up the horn:
[5] Lift not up your horn on high;
Speak not with[6] a stiff neck.
[6] For neither from the east, nor from the west,
Nor yet from[7] the south,[8] *cometh* lifting up.
[7] But God is the judge:
He putteth down one, and lifteth up another.
[8] For in the hand of Jehovah there is a cup, and the wine foameth;[9]
It is full of mixture, and he poureth out of the same:
Surely the dregs thereof, all the wicked of the earth shall drain them, and drink them.

10 Or, *land*. 11 Or, *which ascendeth*. 1 Or, *for* that *thy name is near Thy wondrous works declare*. 2 Heb. *take*. 3 Or, *When the earth . . . I set up*.
4 Heb. *proportioned*. 5 Or, *fools*. 6 Or, *insolently with a* haughty *neck*. 7 Or, *from the wilderness of mountains* cometh judgment. 8 Heb. *wilderness*. 9 Or, *is red*.

[9] But I will declare for ever,
I will sing praises to the God of Jacob.
[10] All the horns of the wicked also will I cut off;
But the horns of the righteous shall be lifted up.

LXXVI

The Victorious Power of the God of Jacob

For the Chief Musician; on stringed instruments. A Psalm of Asaph, a Song.

[1] In Judah is God known:
His name is great in Israel.
[2] In Salem also is his tabernacle,[1]
And his dwelling-place[2] in Zion.
[3] There he brake the arrows[3] of the bow;
The shield, and the sword, and the battle. [Selah
[4] Glorious art thou *and* excellent,
From[4] the mountains of prey.
[5] The stouthearted are made a spoil,
They have slept their sleep;
And none of the men of might have found their hands.
[6] At thy rebuke, O God of Jacob,
Both chariot and horse are cast into a dead sleep.
[7] Thou, even thou, art to be feared;
And who may stand in thy sight when once thou art angry?
[8] Thou didst cause sentence to be heard from heaven;
The earth feared, and was still,
[9] When God arose to judgment,
To save all the meek of the earth. [Selah
[10] Surely the wrath of man shall praise thee:
The residue of wrath shalt thou gird[5] upon thee.
[11] Vow, and pay unto Jehovah your God:
Let all that are round about him bring presents unto him that ought to be feared.
[12] He will cut off the spirit of princes:
He is terrible to the kings of the earth.

[1] Or, *covert.* [2] Or, *lair.* [3] Or, *fiery shafts.* Or, *lightnings.* [4] Or, *More than.*
[5] Or, *restrain.*

LXXVII

Comfort in Trouble from Recalling God's Mighty Deeds

For the Chief Musician; after the manner of Jeduthun.
A Psalm of Asaph.

[1] I WILL cry unto God with my voice,
Even unto God with my voice; and he will give ear unto me.
[2] In the day of my trouble I sought the Lord:
My hand was stretched out in the night, and slacked not;
My soul refused to be comforted.
[3] I remember God, and am disquieted:
I complain, and my spirit is[1] overwhelmed. [Selah
[4] Thou holdest mine eyes watching:
I am so troubled that I cannot speak.
[5] I have considered the days of old,
The years of ancient times.
[6] I call to remembrance my song in the night:
I commune with mine own heart;
And my spirit maketh diligent search.
[7] Will the Lord cast off for ever?
And will he be favorable no more?
[8] Is his lovingkindness clean gone for ever?
Doth his promise fail for evermore?
[9] Hath God forgotten to be gracious?
Hath he in anger shut up his tender mercies? [Selah
[10] And I said, This[2] is my infirmity;
But I will remember the years of the right hand of the Most High.
[11] I will make mention of the deeds of Jehovah;[3]
For I will remember thy wonders of old.
[12] I will meditate also upon all thy work,
And muse on thy doings.
[13] Thy way, O God, is in[4] the sanctuary:
Who is a great god like unto God?

[1] Or, *fainteth.*
[2] Or, *This is my grief, That the right hand of the Most High doth change.*
[3] Heb. *Jah.* [4] Or, *in holiness.*

[14] Thou art the God that doest wonders:
Thou hast made known thy strength among the peoples.
[15] Thou hast with thine arm redeemed thy people,
The sons of Jacob and Joseph. [Selah
[16] The waters saw thee, O God;
The waters saw thee, they were[5] afraid:
The depths also trembled.
[17] The clouds poured out water;
The skies sent out a sound:
Thine arrows also went abroad.
[18] The voice of thy thunder was in the whirlwind;
The lightnings lightened the world:
The earth trembled and shook.
[19] Thy way was in the sea,
And thy paths in the great waters,
And thy footsteps were not known.
[20] Thou leddest thy people like a flock,
By the hand of Moses and Aaron.

LXXVIII

God's Guidance of His People in spite of their Unfaithfulness

Maschil of Asaph.

[1] Give ear, O my people, to my law:[1]
Incline your ears to the words of my mouth.
[2] I will open my mouth in a parable;
I will utter dark sayings of old,
[3] Which we have heard and known,
And our fathers have told us.
[4] We will not hide them from their children,
Telling to the generation to come the praises of Jehovah,
And his strength, and his wondrous works that he hath done.
[5] For he established a testimony in Jacob,
And appointed a law in Israel,
Which he commanded our fathers,
That they should make them known to their children;

[5] Or, *were in pain*. [1] Or, *teaching*.

[6] That the generation to come might know *them,* even the children that should be born;
Who should arise and tell *them* to their children,
[7] That they might set their hope in God,
And not forget the works of God,
But keep his commandments,
[8] And might not be as their fathers,
A stubborn and rebellious generation,
A generation that[2] set not their heart aright,
And whose spirit was not stedfast with God.
[9] The children of Ephraim, being armed and carrying bows,
Turned back in the day of battle.
[10] They kept not the covenant of God,
And refused to walk in his law;
[11] And they forgat his doings,
And his wondrous works that he had showed them.
[12] Marvellous things did he in the sight of their fathers,
In the land of Egypt, in the field of Zoan.
[13] He clave the sea, and caused them to pass through;
And he made the waters to stand as a heap.
[14] In the day-time also he led them with a cloud,
And all the night with a light of fire.
[15] He clave rocks in the wilderness,
And gave them drink abundantly as out of the depths.
[16] He brought streams also out of the rock,
And caused waters to run down like rivers.
[17] Yet went they on still to sin against him,
To rebel against the Most High in the[3] desert.
[18] And they tempted God in their heart
By asking food according[4] to their desire.
[19] Yea, they spake against God;
They said, Can God prepare a table in the wilderness?
[20] Behold, he smote the rock, so that waters gushed out,
And streams overflowed;
Can he give bread also?
Will he provide flesh for his people?

[2] Or, *that prepared not their heart.* [3] Or, *a dry land.* [4] Or, *for themselves.*

[21] Therefore Jehovah heard, and was wroth;
And a fire was kindled against Jacob,
And anger also went up against Israel;
[22] Because they believed not in God,
And trusted not in his salvation.
[23] Yet he commanded the skies above,
And opened the doors of heaven;
[24] And he rained down manna upon them to eat,
And gave them food[5] from heaven.
[25] Man[6] did eat the bread of the mighty:
He sent them food to the full.
[26] He caused[7] the east wind to blow in the heavens;
And by his power he guided the south wind.
[27] He rained flesh also upon them as the dust,
And winged birds as the sand of the seas:
[28] And he let it fall in the midst of their camp,
Round about their habitations.
[29] So they did eat, and were well filled;
And he gave them their own desire.
[30] They were not estranged from that which they desired,
Their food was yet in their mouths,
[31] When the anger of God went up against them,
And slew of the fattest of them,
And smote down the young men of Israel.
[32] For all this they sinned still,
And believed not in his wondrous works.
[33] Therefore their days did he consume in vanity,
And their years in terror.
[34] When he slew them, then they inquired after him;
And they returned and sought God earnestly.
[35] And they remembered that God was their rock,
And the Most High God their redeemer.
[36] But they flattered him with their mouth,
And lied unto him with their tongue.
[37] For their heart was not right[8] with him,
Neither were they faithful in his covenant.

[5] Heb. *grain.* [6] Or, *Every one.* [7] Heb. *led forth the east wind.*
[8] Or, *stedfast.*

[38] But he, being merciful, forgave *their* iniquity, and destroyed *them* not:
Yea, many a time turned he his anger away,
And did not stir up all his wrath.
[39] And he remembered that they were but flesh,
A wind that passeth away, and cometh not again.
[40] How oft did they rebel against him in the wilderness,
And grieve him in the desert!
[41] And they turned again and tempted God,
And provoked[9] the Holy One of Israel.
[42] They remembered not his hand,
Nor the day when he redeemed them from the adversary;
[43] How he set his signs in Egypt,
And his wonders in the field of Zoan,
[44] And turned their rivers into blood,
And their streams, so that they could not drink.
[45] He sent among them swarms of flies, which devoured them;
And frogs, which destroyed them.
[46] He gave also their increase unto the caterpillar,
And their labor unto the locust.
[47] He destroyed[10] their vines with hail,
And their sycomore-trees with frost.[11]
[48] He gave over their cattle also to the hail,
And their flocks to hot thunderbolts.
[49] He cast upon them the fierceness of his anger,
Wrath, and indignation, and trouble,
A[12] band of angels of evil.
[50] He made[13] a path for his anger;
He spared not their soul from death,
But gave their[14] life over to the pestilence,
[51] And smote all the first-born in Egypt,
The chief[15] of their strength in the tents of Ham.
[52] But he led forth his own people like sheep,
And guided them in the wilderness like a flock.

[9] Or, *limited.* [10] Heb. *killed.* [11] Or, *great hailstones.*
[12] Heb. *A sending.* [13] Heb. *levelled.* [14] Or, *their beasts to the murrain.*
[15] Heb. *beginning.* See Deut. 21. 17.

[53] And he led them safely, so that they feared not;
But the sea overwhelmed their enemies.
[54] And he brought them to the[16] border of his sanctuary,
To this mountain,[17] which his right hand had gotten.
[55] He drove out the nations also before them,
And allotted them for an inheritance by line,
And made the tribes of Israel to dwell in their tents.
[56] Yet they tempted and rebelled against the Most High God,
And kept not his testimonies;
[57] But turned back, and dealt treacherously like their fathers:
They were turned aside like a deceitful bow.
[58] For they provoked him to anger with their high places,
And moved him to jealousy with their graven images.
[59] When God heard *this,* he was wroth,
And greatly abhorred Israel;
[60] So that he forsook the tabernacle of Shiloh,
The tent which he placed among men;
[61] And delivered his strength into captivity,
And his glory into the adversary's hand.
[62] He gave his people over also unto the sword,
And was wroth with his inheritance.
[63] Fire devoured their young men;
And their virgins had no marriage-song.
[64] Their priests fell by the sword;
And their widows made no lamentation.
[65] Then the Lord awaked as one out of sleep,
Like a mighty man that shouteth by reason of wine.
[66] And he smote his adversaries backward:
He put them to a perpetual reproach.
[67] Moreover he refused the tent of Joseph,
And chose not the tribe of Ephraim,
[68] But chose the tribe of Judah,
The mount Zion which he loved.
[69] And he built his sanctuary like the heights,
Like the earth which he hath established for ever.

[16] Or, *his holy border.*
[17] Or, *mountain land.*

[70] He chose David also his servant,
And took him from the sheepfolds:
[71] From following the ewes that have their young he brought him,
To be the shepherd of Jacob his people, and Israel his inheritance.
[72] So he was their shepherd according to the integrity of his heart,
And guided them by the skilfulness of his hands.

LXXIX

A Lament over the Destruction of Jerusalem, and Prayer for Help

A Psalm of Asaph.

[1] O God, the nations are come into thine inheritance;
Thy holy temple have they defiled;
They have laid Jerusalem in heaps.
[2] The dead bodies of thy servants have they given to be food unto the birds of the heavens,
The flesh of thy saints unto the beasts of the earth.
[3] Their blood have they shed like water round about Jerusalem;
And there was none to bury them.
[4] We are become a reproach to our neighbors,
A scoffing and derision to them that are round about us.
[5] How long, O Jehovah? wilt thou be angry for ever?
Shall thy jealousy burn like fire?
[6] Pour out thy wrath upon the nations that know thee not,
And upon the kingdoms that call not upon thy name.
[7] For they have devoured Jacob,
And laid waste his habitation.[1]
[8] Remember not against us the iniquities of our forefathers:
Let thy tender mercies speedily meet us;
For we are brought very low.
[9] Help us, O God of our salvation, for the glory of thy name;
And deliver us, and forgive[2] our sins, for thy name's sake.
[10] Wherefore should the nations say, Where is their God?
Let the avenging of the blood of thy servants which is shed
Be known among the nations in our sight.

[1] Or, *pasture*. [2] Or, *expiate*.

[11] Let the sighing of the prisoner come before thee:
According to the greatness of thy[3] power preserve thou those that are appointed to death;
[12] And render unto our neighbors sevenfold into their bosom
Their reproach, wherewith they have reproached thee, O Lord.
[13] So we thy people and sheep of thy pasture
Will give thee thanks for ever:
We will show forth thy praise to all generations.

LXXX

God Implored to Rescue His People from their Calamities

For the Chief Musician; set to Shoshannim[5] Eduth. A Psalm of Asaph.

[1] Give ear, O Shepherd of Israel,
Thou that leadest Joseph like a flock;
Thou that sittest[6] *above* the cherubim, shine forth.
[2] Before Ephraim and Benjamin and Manasseh, stir up thy might,
And come to save us.
[3] Turn[7] us again, O God;
And cause thy face to shine, and we shall be saved.

[4] O Jehovah God of hosts,
How long wilt[8] thou be angry against the prayer of thy people?
[5] Thou hast fed them with the bread of tears,
And given them tears to drink in large measure.
[6] Thou makest us a strife unto our neighbors;
And our enemies laugh among themselves.
[7] Turn[7] us again, O God of hosts;
And cause thy face to shine, and we shall be saved.

[8] Thou broughtest a vine out of Egypt.
Thou didst drive out the nations, and plantedst it.
[9] Thou preparedst *room* before it,
And it took deep root, and filled the land.
[10] The mountains were covered with the shadow of it,
And the[9] boughs thereof were *like* cedars[10] of God.

[3] Heb. *thine arm.* [4] Heb. *the children of death.* [5] That is, *Lilies, a testimony.*
[6] Or, *art enthroned.* [7] Or, *Restore.* [8] Heb. *wilt thou smoke.* See Ps. 74. 1.
[9] Or, *the cedars of God with the boughs thereof.* [10] Or, *goodly cedars.*

[11] It sent out its branches unto the sea,
And its shoots unto the River.
[12] Why hast thou broken down its walls,
So that all they that pass by the way do pluck it?
[13] The boar out of the wood doth ravage it,
And the wild beasts of the field feed on it.
[14] Turn again, we beseech thee, O God of hosts:
Look down from heaven, and behold, and visit this vine,
[15] And the[11] stock which thy right hand planted,
And the branch[12] that thou madest strong for thyself.
[16] It is burned with fire, it is cut down:
They perish at the rebuke of thy countenance.
[17] Let thy hand be upon the man of thy right hand,
Upon the son of man whom thou madest strong for thyself.
[18] So shall we not go back from thee:
Quicken thou us, and we will call upon thy name.
[19] Turn[7] us again, O Jehovah God of hosts;
Cause thy face to shine, and we shall be saved.

LXXXI

God's Goodness and Israel's Waywardness

For the Chief Musician; set to the Gittith. A Psalm of Asaph.

[1] Sing aloud unto God our strength:
Make a joyful noise unto the God of Jacob.
[2] Raise a song, and bring[1] hither the timbrel,
The pleasant harp with the psaltery.
[3] Blow the trumpet at the new moon,
At the full moon, on our feast-day.
[4] For it is a statute for Israel,
An ordinance of the God of Jacob.
[5] He appointed it in Joseph for a testimony,
When he went out over[2] the land of Egypt,
Where I heard a[3] language that I knew not.

[11] Or, *protect* (or, *maintain*) *that which &c.* [12] Heb. *son*.
[1] Or, *strike the timbrel.* [2] Or, *against.*
[3] Or, *the speech of one that &c.*

[6] I removed his shoulder from the burden:
His hands were freed from the basket.
[7] Thou calledst in trouble, and I delivered thee;
I answered thee in the secret place of thunder;
I proved thee at the waters of Meribah. [Selah
[8] Hear, O my people, and I will testify unto thee:
O Israel, if thou wouldest hearken unto me!
[9] There shall no strange god be in thee;
Neither shalt thou worship any foreign god.
[10] I am Jehovah thy God,
Who brought thee up out of the land of Egypt:
Open thy mouth wide, and I will fill it.
[11] But my people hearkened not to my voice;
And Israel would none of me.
[12] So I let them go after the stubbornness of their heart,
That they might walk in their own counsels.
[13] Oh that my people would hearken unto me,
That Israel would walk in my ways!
[14] I would soon subdue their enemies,
And turn my hand against their adversaries.
[15] The haters of Jehovah should submit[4] themselves unto him:
But their time should endure for ever.
[16] He would feed them also with the finest[5] of the wheat;
And with honey out of the rock would I satisfy thee.

LXXXII

Unjust Judgments Rebuked

A Psalm of Asaph.

[1] God standeth in the congregation of God;
He judgeth among the gods.
[2] How long will ye judge unjustly,
And respect the persons of the wicked? [Selah
[3] Judge the poor[1] and fatherless:
Do justice to the afflicted and destitute.

[4] Or, *yield feigned obedience.* Heb. *lie.* [5] Heb. *fat of wheat.*
[1] Or, *weak.*

[4] Rescue the poor[1] and needy:
Deliver them out of the hand of the wicked.
[5] They know not, neither do they understand;
They walk to and fro in darkness:
All the foundations of the earth are shaken.
[6] I said, Ye are gods,
And all of you sons of the Most High.
[7] Nevertheless ye shall die like men,
And fall like one of the princes.
[8] Arise, O God, judge the earth;
For thou shalt inherit all the nations.

LXXXIII

God Implored to Confound His Enemies

A Song, a Psalm of Asaph.

[1] O God, keep not thou silence:
Hold not thy peace, and be not still, O God.
[2] For, lo, thine enemies make a tumult:
And they that hate thee have lifted up the head.
[3] They take crafty counsel against thy people,
And consult together against thy hidden ones.
[4] They have said, Come, and let us cut them off from being a nation;
That the name of Israel may be no more in remembrance.
[5] For they have consulted together with one consent;
Against thee do they make a covenant:
[6] The tents of Edom and the Ishmaelites;
Moab, and the Hagarenes;[2]
[7] Gebal, and Ammon, and Amalek;
Philistia with the inhabitants of Tyre:
[8] Assyria also is joined with them;
They have helped[3] the children of Lot. [Selah
[9] Do thou unto them as unto Midian,
As to Sisera, as to Jabin, at the river Kishon;

[2] Or, *Hagrites*. See 1 Chr. 5. 10.
[3] Heb. *been an arm to the children of Lot.*

[10] Who perished at En-dor,
Who became as dung for the earth.
[11] Make their nobles like Oreb and Zeeb;
Yea, all their princes like Zebah and Zalmunna;
[12] Who said, Let us take to ourselves in possession
The habitations[4] of God.
[13] O my God, make them like the whirling dust;
As stubble before the wind.
[14] As the fire that burneth the forest,
And as the flame that setteth the mountains on fire;
[15] So pursue them with thy tempest,
And terrify them with thy storm.
[16] Fill their faces with confusion,
That they may seek thy name, O Jehovah.
[17] Let them be put to shame and dismayed for ever;
Yea, let them be confounded and perish;
[18] That they may know that thou[5] alone, whose name is Jehovah,
Art the Most High over all the earth.

LXXXIV

Longing for the Temple Worship

For the Chief Musician; set to the Gittith. A Psalm of the sons of Korah.

[1] How amiable[1] are thy tabernacles,
O Jehovah of hosts!
[2] My soul longeth, yea, even fainteth for the courts of Jehovah;
My heart and my flesh cry[2] out unto the living God.
[3] Yea, the sparrow hath found her a house,
And the swallow a nest for herself, where she may lay her young,
Even thine altars, O Jehovah of hosts,
My King, and my God.
[4] Blessed are they that dwell in thy house:
They will be still praising thee. [Selah

[4] Or, *pastures.* [5] Or, *thou, whose name alone is Jehovah, art &c.*
[1] Or, *lovely.* [2] Or, *sing for joy.*

[5] Blessed is the man whose strength is in thee;
In whose heart are the highways *to Zion*.
[6] Passing through the valley of Weeping[3] they make it a place of springs;
Yea, the early rain covereth it with blessings.
[7] They go from strength to strength;
Every one of them appeareth before God in Zion.
[8] O Jehovah God of hosts, hear my prayer;
Give ear, O God of Jacob. [Selah
[9] Behold,[4] O God our shield,
And look upon the face of thine anointed.
[10] For a day in thy courts is better than a thousand.
I had rather be[5] a doorkeeper in the house of my God,
Than to dwell in the tents of wickedness.
[11] For Jehovah God is a sun and a shield:
Jehovah will give grace and glory;
No good thing will he withhold from them that walk uprightly.
[12] O Jehovah of hosts,
Blessed is the man that trusteth in thee.

LXXXV

Prayer for God's Mercy upon the Nation

For the Chief Musician. A Psalm of the sons of Korah.

[1] Jehovah, thou hast been favorable unto thy land;
Thou hast brought[1] back the captivity of Jacob.
[2] Thou hast forgiven the iniquity of thy people;
Thou hast covered all their sin. [Selah
[3] Thou hast taken away all thy wrath;
Thou hast turned *thyself* from the fierceness of thine anger.
[4] Turn[2] us, O God of our salvation,
And cause thine indignation toward us to cease.
[5] Wilt thou be angry with us for ever?
Wilt thou draw out thine anger to all generations?

[3] Or, *balsam trees.* Heb. *Baca* See 2 S. 5. 23.
[4] Or, *Behold our shield, O God.* [5] Or, *stand at the threshold of &c.*
[1] Or, *returned to.* [2] Or, *Turn to us.*

[6] Wilt thou not quicken us again,
That thy people may rejoice in thee?
[7] Show us thy lovingkindness, O Jehovah,
And grant us thy salvation.
[8] I will hear what God Jehovah will speak;
For he will speak peace unto his people, and to his saints:
But let them not turn again to folly.
[9] Surely his salvation is nigh them that fear him,
That glory may dwell in our land.
[10] Mercy and truth are met together;
Righteousness and peace have kissed each other.
[11] Truth springeth out of the earth;
And righteousness hath looked down from heaven.
[12] Yea, Jehovah will give that which is good;
And our land shall yield its increase.
[13] Righteousness shall go before him,
And shall make[3] his footsteps a way *to walk in.*

LXXXVI

A Psalm of Supplication and Trust

A Prayer of David.

[1] Bow down thine ear, O Jehovah, and answer me;
For I am poor and needy.
[2] Preserve my soul; for I am godly:
O thou my God, save thy servant that trusteth in thee.
[3] Be merciful unto me, O Lord;
For unto thee do I cry all the day long.
[4] Rejoice the soul of thy servant;
For unto thee, O Lord, do I lift up my soul.
[5] For thou, Lord, art good, and ready to forgive,
And abundant in lovingkindness unto all them that call upon thee.
[6] Give ear, O Jehovah, unto my prayer;
And hearken unto the voice of my supplications.

[3] Or, *set* us *in the way of his steps.*

[7] In the day of my trouble I will call upon thee;
For thou wilt answer me.
[8] There is none like unto thee among the gods, O Lord;
Neither *are there any works* like unto thy works.
[9] All nations whom thou hast made shall come and worship before thee, O Lord;
And they shall glorify thy name.
[10] For thou art great, and doest wondrous things:
Thou are God alone.
[11] Teach me thy way, O Jehovah; I will walk in thy truth:
Unite my heart to fear thy name.
[12] I will praise thee, O Lord my God, with my whole heart;
And I will glorify thy name for evermore.
[13] For great is thy lovingkindness toward me;
And thou hast delivered my soul from the lowest Sheol.
[14] O God, the proud are risen up against me,
And a company of violent men have sought after my soul,
And have not set thee before them.
[15] But thou, O Lord, art a God merciful and gracious,
Slow to anger, and abundant in lovingkindness and truth.
[16] Oh turn unto me, and have[1] mercy upon me;
Give thy strength unto thy servant,
And save the son of thy handmaid.
[17] Show me a token for good,
That they who hate me may see it, and be put to shame,
Because thou, Jehovah, hast helped me, and comforted me.

LXXXVII

The Privileges of Citizenship in Zion

A Psalm of the sons of Korah; a Song.

[1] His[2] foundation is in the holy mountains.
[2] Jehovah loveth the gates of Zion
More than all the dwellings of Jacob.

[1] Or, *be gracious unto.*
[2] Or, *His foundation in the holy mountains Jehovah loveth, even the gates &c.*

[3] Glorious things are spoken of thee,
O city of God. [Selah
[4] I will make mention of Rahab[3] and Babylon as among them that know me:
Behold, Philistia, and Tyre, with Ethiopia:[4]
This one was born there.
[5] Yea, of Zion it shall be said, This one and that one was born in her;
And the Most High himself will establish her.
[6] Jehovah will count, when he writeth up the peoples,
This one was born there. [Selah
[7] They that sing as well as they[5] that dance *shall say,*
All my foundations are in thee.

LXXXVIII

A Petition to be Saved from Death

A Song, a Psalm of the sons of Korah; for the Chief Musician; set to Mahalath Leannoth.[1] Maschil of Heman the Ezrahite.

[1] O Jehovah, the God of my salvation,
I have cried day and night before thee.
[2] Let my prayer enter into thy presence;
Incline thine ear unto my cry:
[3] For my soul is full of troubles,
And my life draweth nigh unto Sheol.
[4] I am reckoned with them that go down into the pit;
I am as a man that hath no help,
[5] Cast off[2] among the dead,
Like the slain that lie in the grave,
Whom thou rememberest no more,
And they are cut off from thy hand.
[6] Thou hast laid me in the lowest pit,
In dark places, in the deeps.
[7] Thy wrath lieth hard upon me,
And thou hast afflicted me with all thy waves. [Selah

[3] Or, *Egypt.* [4] Heb. *Cush.*
[5] Or, *the players on instruments* shall be there.
[1] Or, *for singing.* [2] Or, *away.*

[8] Thou hast put mine acquaintance far from me;
Thou hast made me an abomination unto them:
I am shut up, and I cannot come forth.
[9] Mine eye wasteth away by reason of affliction:
I have called daily upon thee, O Jehovah;
I have spread forth my hands unto thee.
[10] Wilt thou show wonders to the dead?
Shall they[3] that are deceased arise and praise thee? [Selah
[11] Shall thy lovingkindness be declared in the grave?
Or thy faithfulness in Destruction[4]?
[12] Shall thy wonders be known in the dark?
And thy righteousness in the land of forgetfulness?
[13] But unto thee, O Jehovah, have I cried;
And in the morning shall my prayer come before thee.
[14] Jehovah, why castest thou off my soul?
Why hidest thou thy face from me?
[15] I am afflicted and ready to die from my youth up:
While I suffer thy terrors I am distracted.
[16] Thy fierce wrath is gone over me;
Thy terrors have cut me off.
[17] They came round about me like water all the day long;
They compassed me about together.
[18] Lover and friend hast thou put far from me,
And mine acquaintance into[5] darkness.

LXXXIX

Jehovah's Covenant with David, and Israel's Afflictions

Maschil of Ethan the Ezrahite.

[1] I will sing of the lovingkindness of Jehovah for ever:
With my mouth will I make known thy faithfulness to all generations.
[2] For I have said, Mercy shall be built up for ever;
Thy faithfulness wilt thou establish in the very heavens.

[3] I have made a covenant with my chosen,
I have sworn unto David my servant:

[3] Or, *the shades.* Heb. *Rephaim.* [4] Heb. *Abaddon.* See Job 26. 6. [5] Or, *are darkness.*

[4] Thy seed will I establish for ever,
And build up thy throne to all generations. [Selah

[5] And the heavens shall praise thy wonders, O Jehovah;
Thy faithfulness also in the assembly of the holy ones.
[6] For who in the skies can be compared unto Jehovah?
Who among the sons[1] of the mighty[2] is like unto Jehovah,
[7] A God very terrible in the council of the holy ones,
And to be feared above all them that are round about him?
[8] O Jehovah God of hosts,
Who is a mighty one, like unto thee, O Jehovah?[3]
And thy faithfulness is round about thee.
[9] Thou rulest the pride of the sea:
When the waves thereof arise, thou stillest them.
[10] Thou hast broken Rahab[4] in pieces, as one that is slain;
Thou hast scattered thine enemies with the arm of thy strength.
[11] The heavens are thine, the earth also is thine:
The world and the fulness thereof, thou hast founded them.
[12] The north and the south, thou hast created them:
Tabor and Hermon rejoice in thy name.
[13] Thou hast a[5] mighty arm;
Strong is thy hand, and high is thy right hand.
[14] Righteousness and justice are the foundation of thy throne:
Lovingkindness and truth go before thy face.
[15] Blessed is the people that know the joyful[6] sound:
They walk, O Jehovah, in the light of thy countenance.
[16] In thy name do they rejoice all the day;
And in thy righteousness are they exalted.
[17] For thou art the glory of their strength;
And in thy favor our[7] horn shall be exalted.
[18] For our shield belongeth unto Jehovah;
And[8] our king to the Holy One of Israel.

[19] Then thou spakest in vision to thy saints,[9]
And saidst, I have laid help upon one that is mighty;
I have exalted one chosen out of the people.

[1] Or, *sons of God*. [2] Or, *gods*. See Ps. 29. 1.
[3] Heb. *Jah*. [4] Or, *Egypt*. [5] Heb. *an arm with might*.
[6] Or, *trumpet sound*. [7] Another reading is, *thou shalt exalt our horn*.
[8] Or, *Even to the Holy One of Israel our King*. [9] Or, as otherwise read, *saint*.

[20] I have found David my servant;
With my holy oil have I anointed him:
[21] With whom my hand shall be established;
Mine arm also shall strengthen him.
[22] The enemy shall not exact[10] from him,
Nor the son of wickedness afflict him.
[23] And I will beat down his adversaries before him,
And smite them that hate him.
[24] But my faithfulness and my lovingkindness shall be with him;
And in my name shall his horn be exalted.
[25] I will set his hand also on the sea,
And his right hand on the rivers.
[26] He shall cry unto me, Thou art my Father,
My God, and the rock of my salvation.
[27] I also will make him *my* first-born,
The highest of the kings of the earth.
[28] My lovingkindness will I keep for him for evermore;
And my covenant shall stand[11] fast with him.
[29] His seed also will I make to endure for ever,
And his throne as the days of heaven.
[30] If his children forsake my law,
And walk not in mine ordinances;
[31] If they break[12] my statutes,
And keep not my commandments;
[32] Then will I visit their transgression with the rod,
And their iniquity with stripes.
[33] But my lovingkindness will I not utterly take from him,
Nor suffer my faithfulness to fail.
[34] My covenant will I not break,[12]
Nor alter the thing that is gone out of my lips.
[35] Once[13] have I sworn by my holiness:
I will not lie unto David:
[36] His seed shall endure for ever,
And his throne as the sun before me.
[37] It[14] shall be established for ever as the moon,
And[15] *as* the faithful witness in the sky. [Selah

[10] Or, *do him violence.* [11] Or, *be faithful.* [12] Heb. *profane.* [13] Or, *One thing.*
[14] Or, *As the moon which is established for ever.*
[15] Or, *And the witness in the sky is faithful.*

[38] But thou hast cast off and rejected,
Thou hast been wroth with thine anointed.
[39] Thou hast abhorred the covenant of thy servant:
Thou hast profaned his crown *by casting it* to the ground.
[40] Thou hast broken down all his hedges;
Thou hast brought his strongholds to ruin.
[41] All that pass by the way rob him:
He is become a reproach to his neighbors.
[42] Thou hast exalted the right hand of his adversaries;
Thou hast made all his enemies to rejoice.
[43] Yea, thou turnest back the edge of his sword,
And hast not made him to stand in the battle.
[44] Thou hast made his brightness to cease,
And cast his throne down to the ground.
[45] The days of his youth hast thou shortened:
Thou hast covered him with shame. [Selah
[46] How long, O Jehovah? wilt thou hide thyself for ever?
How long shall thy wrath burn like fire?
[47] Oh remember how short my time is:
For what vanity hast thou created all the children of men!
[48] What man is he that shall live and not see death,
That shall deliver his soul from the power[16] of Sheol? [Selah
[49] Lord, where are thy former lovingkindnesses,
Which thou swarest unto David in thy faithfulness?
[50] Remember, Lord, the reproach of thy servants;
How I do bear in my bosom *the reproach of* all the mighty[17] peoples,
[51] Wherewith thine enemies have reproached, O Jehovah,
Wherewith they have reproached the footsteps of thine anointed.

[52] Blessed be Jehovah for evermore.
Amen, and Amen.

[16] Heb. *hand.* [17] Or, *many.*

BOOK IV

XC

God's Eternity and Man's Transitoriness

A Prayer of Moses the man of God.

[1] Lord, thou hast been our dwelling-place
In all generations.
[2] Before the mountains were brought forth,
Or ever thou hadst[1] formed the earth and the world,
Even from everlasting to everlasting, thou art God.
[3] Thou turnest man to destruction,[2]
And sayest, Return, ye children of men.
[4] For a thousand years in thy sight
Are but as yesterday when[3] it is past,
And as a watch in the night.
[5] Thou carriest them away as with a flood; they are as a sleep:
In the morning they are like grass which groweth up.
[6] In the morning it flourisheth, and groweth up;
In the evening it is cut down, and withereth.
[7] For we are consumed in thine anger,
And in thy wrath are we troubled.
[8] Thou hast set our iniquities before thee,
Our secret sins in the light of thy countenance.
[9] For all our days are passed away in thy wrath:
We bring our years to an end as a[4] sigh.
[10] The days of our years are threescore years and ten,
Or even by reason of strength fourscore years;
Yet is their pride but labor and sorrow;
For it is soon gone, and we fly away.
[11] Who knoweth the power of thine anger,
And thy wrath according to the fear that is due unto thee?
[12] So teach us to number our days,
That we may get us a heart of wisdom.

[1] Heb. *gavest birth to.* [2] Or, *dust.* Heb, *crushing.*
[3] Or, *when it passeth.* [4] Or, *a sound.*

[13] Return, O Jehovah; how long?
And let it repent thee concerning thy servants.
[14] Oh satisfy us in the morning with thy lovingkindness,
That we may rejoice and be glad all our days.
[15] Make us glad according to the days wherein thou hast afflicted us,
And the years wherein we have seen evil.
[16] Let thy work appear unto thy servants,
And thy glory upon their children.
[17] And let the favor[5] of the Lord our God be upon us;
And establish thou the work of our hands upon us;
Yea, the work of our hands establish thou it.

XCI

Security of Him Who Trusts in Jehovah

[1] He that dwelleth in the secret place of the Most High
Shall[1] abide under the shadow of the Almighty.
[2] I will say of Jehovah, He is my refuge and my fortress;
My God, in whom I trust.
[3] For he will deliver thee from the snare of the fowler,
And from the deadly pestilence.
[4] He will cover thee with his pinions,
And under his wings shalt thou take refuge:
His truth is a shield and a buckler.
[5] Thou shalt not be afraid for the terror by night,
Nor for the arrow that flieth by day;
[6] For the pestilence that walketh in darkness,
Nor for the destruction that wasteth at noonday.
[7] A thousand shall fall at thy side,
And ten thousand at thy right hand;
But it shall not come nigh thee.
[8] Only with thine eyes shalt thou behold,
And see the reward of the wicked.
[9] For[2] thou, O Jehovah, art my refuge!
Thou hast made the Most High thy habitation;

[5] Or, *beauty.*
[1] Or, *That abideth . . . Almighty; Even I &c.*
[2] Or, *Because thou* hast said, *Jehovah is my refuge.*

[10] There shall no evil befall thee,
Neither shall any plague come nigh thy tent.
[11] For he will give his angels charge over thee,
To keep thee in all thy ways.
[12] They shall bear thee up in their hands,
Lest thou dash thy foot against a stone.
[13] Thou shalt tread upon the lion and adder:
The young lion and the serpent shalt thou trample under foot.
[14] Because he hath set his love upon me, therefore will I deliver him:
I will set him on high, because he hath known my name.
[15] He shall call upon me, and I will answer him;
I will be with him in trouble:
I will deliver him, and honor him.
[16] With long life will I satisfy him,
And show him my salvation.

XCII

Praise for Jehovah's Goodness

A Psalm, a Song for the sabbath day.

[1] It is a good thing to give thanks unto Jehovah,
And to sing praises unto thy name, O Most High;
[2] To show forth thy lovingkindness in the morning,
And thy faithfulness every night,
[3] With an instrument of ten strings, and with the psaltery;
With a solemn sound upon the harp.
[4] For thou, Jehovah, hast made me glad through thy work:
I will triumph in the works of thy hands.
[5] How great are thy works, O Jehovah!
Thy thoughts are very deep.
[6] A brutish man knoweth not;
Neither doth a fool understand this:
[7] When the wicked spring as the grass,
And when all the workers of iniquity do flourish;
It is that they shall be destroyed for ever:
[8] But thou, O Jehovah, art on high for evermore.

[9] For, lo, thine enemies, O Jehovah,
For, lo, thine enemies shall perish;
All the workers of iniquity shall be scattered.
[10] But my horn hast thou exalted like *the horn of* the wild-ox:
I am anointed with fresh oil.
[11] Mine eye also hath seen *my desire* on mine[1] enemies,
Mine ears have heard *my desire* of the evil-doers that rise up against me.
[12] The righteous shall flourish like the palm-tree:
He shall grow like a cedar in Lebanon.
[13] They are planted in the house of Jehovah;
They shall flourish in the courts of our God.
[14] They shall still bring forth fruit in old age;
They shall be full of sap and green:
[15] To show that Jehovah is upright;
He is my rock, and there is no unrighteousness in him.

XCIII

The Majesty of Jehovah

[1] Jehovah reigneth; he is clothed with majesty;
Jehovah is clothed with strength; he hath girded himself therewith:
The world also is established, that it cannot be moved.
[2] Thy throne is established of old:
Thou art from everlasting.
[3] The floods have lifted up, O Jehovah,
The floods have lifted up their voice;
The floods lift up their waves.[2]
[4] Above the voices of many waters,
The mighty breakers of the sea,
Jehovah on high is mighty.
[5] Thy testimonies are very sure:
Holiness becometh thy house,
O Jehovah, for evermore.

[1] Or, *them that lie in wait for me.*
[2] Or, *roaring.*

XCIV

Jehovah Implored to Avenge His People

[1] O Jehovah, thou God to whom vengeance belongeth,
Thou God to whom vengeance belongeth, shine forth.
[2] Lift up thyself, thou judge of the earth:
Render to the proud *their* desert.
[3] Jehovah, how long shall the wicked,
How long shall the wicked triumph?
[4] They prate, they speak arrogantly:
All the workers of iniquity boast themselves.
[5] They break in pieces thy people, O Jehovah,
And afflict thy heritage.
[6] They slay the widow and the sojourner,
And murder the fatherless.
[7] And they say, Jehovah[1] will not see,
Neither will the God of Jacob consider.
[8] Consider, ye brutish among the people;
And ye fools, when will ye be wise?
[9] He that planted the ear, shall he not hear?
He that formed the eye, shall he not see?
[10] He that chastiseth[2] the nations, shall not he correct,
Even he that teacheth man knowledge?
[11] Jehovah knoweth the thoughts of man,
That[3] they are vanity.[4]
[12] Blessed is the man whom thou chastenest, O Jehovah,[5]
And teachest out of thy law;
[13] That thou mayest give him rest from the days of adversity,
Until the pit be digged for the wicked.
[14] For Jehovah will not cast off his people,
Neither will he forsake his inheritance.
[15] For judgment shall return unto righteousness;
And all the upright in heart shall follow it.
[16] Who will rise up for me against the evil-doers?
Who will stand up for me against the workers of iniquity?

[1] Heb. *Jah.* [2] Or, *instructeth.* [3] Or, *For.* [4] Heb. *a breath.* [5] Heb. *Jah.*

[17] Unless Jehovah had been my help,
My soul had soon dwelt in silence.
[18] When I said, My foot slippeth;
Thy lovingkindness, O Jehovah, held me up.
[19] In the multitude of my thoughts[6] within me
Thy comforts delight my soul.
[20] Shall the throne[7] of wickedness have fellowship with thee,
Which frameth mischief by statute?
[21] They gather themselves together against the soul of the righteous,
And condemn the innocent blood.
[22] But Jehovah hath been my high tower,
And my God the rock of my refuge.
[23] And he hath brought upon them their own iniquity,
And will cut them off in their own wickedness;
Jehovah our God will cut them off.

XCV

Praise to Jehovah, and Warning against Unbelief

[1] Oh come, let us sing unto Jehovah;
Let us make a joyful noise to the rock of our salvation.
[2] Let us come before his presence with thanksgiving;
Let us make a joyful noise unto him with psalms.
[3] For Jehovah is a great God,
And a great King above all gods.
[4] In his hand are the deep places of the earth;
The heights[1] of the mountains are his also.
[5] The sea is his, and he made it;
And his hands formed the dry land.
[6] Oh come, let us worship and bow down;
Let us kneel before Jehovah our Maker:
[7] For he is our God,
And we are the people of his pasture, and the sheep of his hand.
To-day, oh[2] that ye would hear his voice!

[6] Or, *doubts.* [7] Or, *seat.*
[1] Or, *strength* [2] Or, *if ye will hear his voice, Harden &c.*

[8] Harden not your heart, as at Meribah,[3]
As in the day of Massah[4] in the wilderness;
[9] When your fathers tempted me,
Proved me, and saw my work.
[10] Forty years long was I grieved with *that* generation,
And said, It is a people that do err in their heart,
And they have not known my ways:
[11] Wherefore I sware in my wrath,
That they should not enter into my rest.

XCVI

A Call to Worship Jehovah the Righteous Judge

[1] Oh sing unto Jehovah a new song:
Sing unto Jehovah, all the earth.
[2] Sing unto Jehovah, bless his name;
Show forth his salvation from day to day.
[3] Declare his glory among the nations,
His marvellous works among all the peoples.
[4] For great is Jehovah, and greatly to be praised:
He is to be feared above all gods.
[5] For all the gods of the peoples are idols;[1]
But Jehovah made the heavens.
[6] Honor and majesty are before him:
Strength and beauty are in his sanctuary.
[7] Ascribe unto Jehovah, ye kindreds of the peoples,
Ascribe unto Jehovah glory and strength.
[8] Ascribe unto Jehovah the glory due unto his name:
Bring an offering, and come into his courts.
[9] Oh worship Jehovah in[2] holy array:
Tremble before him, all the earth.
[10] Say among the nations, Jehovah reigneth:
The world also is established that it cannot be moved:
He will judge the peoples with equity.

[3] That is, *strife*. [4] That is, *temptation*.
[1] Or, *things of nought*. [2] Or, *in the beauty of holiness*.

[11] Let the heavens be glad, and let the earth rejoice;
Let the sea roar, and the fulness thereof;
[12] Let the field exult, and all that is therein;
Then shall all the trees of the wood sing for joy
[13] Before Jehovah; for he cometh,
For he cometh to judge the earth:
He will judge the world with righteousness,
And the peoples with[3] his truth.

XCVII

Jehovah's Power and Dominion

[1] Jehovah reigneth; let the earth rejoice;
Let the multitude of isles be glad.
[2] Clouds and darkness are round about him:
Righteousness and justice are the foundation of his throne.
[3] A fire goeth before him,
And burneth up his adversaries round about.
[4] His lightnings lightened the world:
The earth saw, and trembled.
[5] The mountains melted like wax at the presence of Jehovah,
At the presence of the Lord of the whole earth.
[6] The heavens declare his righteousness,
And all the peoples have seen his glory.
[7] Let all them be put to shame that serve graven images,
That boast themselves of idols:
Worship him, all ye gods.
[8] Zion heard and was glad,
And the daughters of Judah rejoiced,
Because of thy judgments, O Jehovah.
[9] For thou, Jehovah, art most high above all the earth:
Thou art exalted far above all gods.
[10] O ye that love Jehovah, hate evil:
He preserveth the souls of his saints;
He delivereth them out of the hand of the wicked.

[3] Or, *in his faithfulness.*

[11] Light is sown for the righteous,
And gladness for the upright in heart.
[12] Be glad in Jehovah, ye righteous;
And give thanks to his holy memorial *name*.

XCVIII

A Call to Praise Jehovah for His Righteousness

A Psalm.

[1] Oh sing unto Jehovah a new song;
For he hath done marvellous things:
His right hand, and his holy arm, hath wrought salvation for him.
[2] Jehovah hath made known his salvation:
His righteousness hath he openly showed in the sight of the nations.
[3] He hath remembered his lovingkindness and his faithfulness toward the house of Israel:
All the ends of the earth have seen the salvation of our God.
[4] Make a joyful noise unto Jehovah, all the earth:
Break forth and sing for joy, yea, sing praises.
[5] Sing praises unto Jehovah with the harp;
With the harp and the voice of melody.
[6] With trumpets and sound of cornet
Make a joyful noise before the King, Jehovah.
[7] Let the sea roar, and the fulness thereof;
The world, and they that dwell therein;
[8] Let the floods clap their hands;
Let the hills sing for joy together
[9] Before Jehovah; for he cometh to judge the earth:
He will judge the world with righteousness,
And the peoples with equity.

XCIX

Praise to Jehovah for His Fidelity to Israel

[1] Jehovah reigneth; let the peoples tremble:
He sitteth[1] *above* the cherubim; let the earth be moved

[1] Or, *is enthroned*.

[2] Jehovah is great in Zion;
And he is high above all the peoples.
[3] Let them praise thy great and terrible name:
Holy is he.

[4] The king's strength also loveth justice;
Thou dost establish equity;
Thou executest justice and righteousness in Jacob.
[5] Exalt ye Jehovah our God,
And worship at his footstool:
Holy is he.

[6] Moses and Aaron among his priests,
And Samuel among them that call upon his name;
They called upon Jehovah, and he answered them.
[7] He spake unto them in the pillar of cloud:
They kept his testimonies,
And the statute that he gave them.
[8] Thou answeredst them, O Jehovah our God:
Thou wast a God that forgavest them,
Though thou tookest vengeance of their doings.
[9] Exalt ye Jehovah our God,
And worship at his holy hill;
For Jehovah our God is holy.

C

All Men Exhorted to Praise God

A Psalm of [1] thanksgiving.

[1] Make a joyful noise unto Jehovah, all[2] ye lands.
[2] Serve Jehovah with gladness:
Come before his presence with singing.
[3] Know ye that Jehovah, he is God:
It is he that hath made us, and[3] we are his;
We are his people, and the sheep of his pasture.

[1] Or, *for the thank-offering.* [2] Heb. *all the earth.*
[3] Another reading is, *and not we ourselves.*

[4] Enter into his gates with thanksgiving,[4]
And into his courts with praise:
Give thanks unto him, and bless his name.
[5] For Jehovah is good; his lovingkindness *endureth* for ever,
And his faithfulness unto all generations.

CI

The Psalmist's Profession of Uprightness

A Psalm of David.

[1] I WILL sing of lovingkindness and justice:
Unto thee, O Jehovah, will I sing praises.
[2] I will behave[5] myself wisely in a perfect way:
Oh when wilt thou come unto me?
I will walk within my house with[6] a perfect heart.
[3] I will set no base thing before mine eyes:
I hate the[7] work of them that turn aside;
It shall not cleave unto me.
[4] A perverse heart shall depart from me:
I will know no evil[8] thing.
[5] Whoso privily slandereth his neighbor, him will I destroy:
Him that hath a high look and a proud heart will I not suffer.
[6] Mine eyes shall be upon the faithful of the land, that they may dwell with me:
He that walketh in a perfect way, he shall minister unto me.
[7] He that worketh deceit shall not dwell within my house:
He that speaketh falsehood shall not be established before mine eyes.
[8] Morning by morning will I destroy all the wicked of the land;
To cut off all the workers of iniquity from the city of Jehovah.

[4] Or, *a thank-offering.*
[5] Or, *give heed unto the perfect way.* [6] Or, *in the integrity of my heart.*
[7] Or, *the doing of unfaithfulness.* [8] Or, *evil person.*

CII

Prayer of an Afflicted One for Mercy on Himself and on Zion

A Prayer of the afflicted, when he is[1] overwhelmed, and poureth out his complaint before Jehovah.

[1] Hear my prayer, O Jehovah,
And let my cry come unto thee.
[2] Hide not thy face from me in the day of my distress:
Incline thine ear unto me;
In the day when I call answer me speedily.
[3] For my days consume away like[2] smoke,
And my bones are burned as[3] a firebrand.
[4] My heart is smitten like grass, and withered;
For I forget to eat my bread.
[5] By reason of the voice of my groaning
My bones cleave to my flesh.
[6] I am like a pelican of the wilderness;
I am become as an owl of the waste places.
[7] I watch, and am become like a sparrow
That is alone upon the housetop.
[8] Mine enemies reproach me all the day;
They that are mad against me do curse by me.
[9] For I have eaten ashes like bread,
And mingled my drink with weeping,
[10] Because of thine indignation and thy wrath:
For thou hast taken me up, and cast me away.
[11] My days are like a shadow that declineth;[4]
And I am withered like grass.

[12] But thou, O Jehovah, wilt[5] abide for ever;
And thy memorial *name* unto all generations.
[13] Thou wilt arise, and have mercy upon Zion;
For it is time to have pity upon her,
Yea, the set time is come.

[1] Or, *fainteth.* [2] Or, *in smoke.* [3] Or, *as a hearth.* [4] Or, *is stretched out.*
[5] Or, *sittest* as King.

[14] For thy servants take pleasure in her stones,
And have pity upon her dust.
[15] So the nations shall fear the name of Jehovah,
And all the kings of the earth thy glory:
[16] For Jehovah hath built up Zion;
He hath appeared in his glory;
[17] He hath regarded the prayer of the destitute,
And hath not despised their prayer.
[18] This shall be written for the generation to come;
And a people which shall be created shall praise Jehovah.[6]
[19] For he hath looked down from the height of his sanctuary;
From heaven did Jehovah behold the earth;
[20] To hear the sighing of the prisoner;
To loose those[7] that are appointed to death;
[21] That men may declare the name of Jehovah in Zion,
And his praise in Jerusalem;
[22] When the peoples are gathered together,
And the kingdoms, to serve Jehovah.

[23] He weakened[8] my strength in the way;
He shortened my days.
[24] I said, O my God, take me not away in the midst of my days:
Thy years are throughout all generations.
[25] Of old didst thou lay the foundation of the earth;
And the heavens are the work of thy hands.
[26] They shall perish, but thou shalt endure;
Yea, all of them shall wax old like a garment;
As a vesture shalt thou change them, and they shall be changed:
[27] But thou art the same,
And thy years shall have no end.
[28] The children of thy servants shall continue,
And their seed shall be established before thee.

[6] Heb. *Jah.* [7] Heb, *the children of death.*
[8] Another reading is, *afflicted* me with *his strength.*

CIII

Praise for Jehovah's Mercies

A Psalm of David.

[1] Bless Jehovah, O my soul;
And all that is within me, *bless* his holy name.
[2] Bless Jehovah, O my soul,
And forget not all his benefits:
[3] Who forgiveth all thine iniquities;
Who healeth all thy diseases;
[4] Who redeemeth thy life from destruction;[1]
Who crowneth thee with lovingkindness and tender mercies;
[5] Who satisfieth thy[2] desire with good things,
So that thy youth is renewed like the eagle.
[6] Jehovah executeth righteous acts,
And judgments for all that are oppressed.
[7] He made known his ways unto Moses,
His doings unto the children of Israel.
[8] Jehovah is merciful and gracious,
Slow to anger, and abundant in lovingkindness.
[9] He will not always chide;
Neither will he keep *his anger* for ever.
[10] He hath not dealt with us after our sins,
Nor rewarded us after our iniquities.
[11] For as the heavens are high above the earth,
So great is his lovingkindness toward them that fear him.
[12] As far as the east is from the west,
So far hath he removed our transgressions from us.
[13] Like as a father pitieth his children,
So Jehovah pitieth them that fear him.
[14] For he knoweth our frame;
He remembereth that we are dust.
[15] As for man, his days are as grass;
As a flower of the field, so he flourisheth.

[1] Or, *the pit.* [2] Or, *thy years.* Or, *thy prime.* Heb. *thine ornament.*

[16] For the wind passeth over it, and it is gone;
And the place thereof shall know it no more.
[17] But the lovingkindness of Jehovah is from everlasting to everlasting upon them that fear him,
And his righteousness unto children's children;
[18] To such as keep his covenant,
And to those that remember his precepts to do them.
[19] Jehovah hath established his throne in the heavens;
And his kingdom ruleth over all.
[20] Bless Jehovah, ye his angels,
That are mighty in strength, that fulfil his word,
Hearkening unto the voice of his word.
[21] Bless Jehovah, all ye his hosts,
Ye ministers of his, that do his pleasure.
[22] Bless Jehovah, all ye his works,
In all places of his dominion:
Bless Jehovah, O my soul.

CIV

Jehovah's Care over all His Works

[1] Bless Jehovah, O my soul.
O Jehovah my God, thou art very great;
Thou art clothed with honor and majesty:
[2] Who coverest thyself with light as with a garment;
Who stretchest out the heavens like a curtain;
[3] Who layeth the beams of his chambers in the waters;
Who maketh the clouds his chariot;
Who walketh upon the wings of the wind;
[4] Who maketh winds[1] his messengers;
Flames of fire his ministers;
[5] Who[2] laid the foundations of the earth,
That it should not be moved for ever.
[6] Thou coveredst it with the deep as with a vesture;
The waters stood above the mountains.

[1] Or, *his angels winds.* [2] Heb. *He founded the earth upon its bases.*

[7] At thy rebuke they fled;
At the voice of thy thunder they hasted away.
[8] (The[3] mountains rose, the valleys sank down)
Unto the place which thou hadst founded for them.
[9] Thou hast set a bound that they may not pass over;
That they turn not again to cover the earth.
[10] He sendeth forth springs into the valleys;
They run among the mountains;
[11] They give drink to every beast of the field;
The wild asses quench their thirst.
[12] By them the birds of the heavens have their habitation;
They sing[4] among the branches.
[13] He watereth the mountains from his chambers:
The earth is filled with the fruit of thy works.
[14] He causeth the grass to grow for the cattle,
And herb for the service[5] of man;
That he may bring forth food[6] out of the earth,
[15] And wine that maketh glad the heart of man,
And[7] oil to make his face to shine,
And bread that strengtheneth man's heart.
[16] The trees of Jehovah are filled *with moisture;*
The cedars of Lebanon, which he hath planted;
[17] Where the birds make their nests:
As for the stork, the fir-trees are her house.
[18] The high mountains are for the wild goats;
The rocks are a refuge for the conies.
[19] He appointed the moon for seasons:
The sun knoweth his going down.
[20] Thou makest darkness, and it is night,
Wherein all the beasts of the forest creep forth.
[21] The young lions roar after their prey,
And seek their food from God.
[22] The sun ariseth, they get them away,
And lay them down in their dens.

[3] Or, *They went up by the mountains, they went down by the valleys.*
[4] Heb. *utter their voice.* [5] Or, *labor.* [6] Heb. *bread.*
[7] Heb. *To make his face to shine with oil.*

[23] Man goeth forth unto his work
And to his labor until the evening.
[24] O Jehovah, how manifold are thy works!
In wisdom hast thou made them all:
The earth is full of thy riches.[8]
[25] Yonder is the sea, great and wide,
Wherein are things creeping innumerable,
Both small and great beasts.
[26] There go the ships;
There is leviathan, whom thou hast formed to play therein.[9]
[27] These wait all for thee,
That thou mayest give them their food in due season.
[28] Thou givest unto them, they gather;
Thou openest thy hand, they are satisfied with good.
[29] Thou hidest thy face, they are troubled;
Thou takest[10] away their breath, they die,
And return to their dust.
[30] Thou sendest forth thy Spirit, they are created;
And thou renewest the face of the ground.
[31] Let the glory of Jehovah endure for ever;
Let Jehovah rejoice in his works:
[32] Who looketh on the earth, and it trembleth;
He toucheth the mountains, and they smoke.
[33] I will sing unto Jehovah as long as I live:
I will sing praise to my God while I have any being.
[34] Let my meditation be sweet unto him:
I will rejoice in Jehovah.
[35] Let sinners be consumed out of the earth,
And let the wicked be no more.
Bless Jehovah, O my soul.
Praise[11] ye Jehovah.

[8] Or, *creatures*. [9] Or, *with him*. See Job 41. 5.
[10] Or, *gatherest in*. [11] Heb. *Hallelujah*.

CV

Jehovah's Wonderful Works in Behalf of Israel

[1] Oh give thanks unto Jehovah, call upon his name;
Make known among the peoples his doings.
[2] Sing unto him, sing praises unto him;
Talk[1] ye of all his marvellous works.
[3] Glory ye in his holy name:
Let the heart of them rejoice that seek Jehovah.
[4] Seek ye Jehovah and his strength;
Seek his face evermore.
[5] Remember his marvellous works that he hath done,
His wonders, and the judgments of his mouth,
[6] O ye seed of Abraham his servant,
Ye children of Jacob, his chosen ones.
[7] He is Jehovah our God:
His judgments are in all the earth.
[8] He hath remembered his covenant for ever,
The word which he commanded to a thousand generations,
[9] *The covenant* which he made with Abraham,
And his oath unto Isaac,
[10] And confirmed the same unto Jacob for a statute,
To Israel for an everlasting covenant,
[11] Saying, Unto thee will I give the land of Canaan,
The lot[2] of your inheritance;
[12] When they were but a few men in number,
Yea, very few, and sojourners in it.
[13] And they went about from nation to nation,
From one kingdom to another people.
[14] He suffered no man to do them wrong;
Yea, he reproved kings for their sakes,
[15] *Saying,* Touch not mine anointed ones,
And do my prophets no harm.
[16] And he called for a famine upon the land;
He brake the whole staff of bread.

[1] Or, *Meditate.* [2] Heb. *cord,* or, *line.*

[17] He sent a man before them;
Joseph was sold for a servant:
[18] His feet they hurt with fetters:
He[3] was laid in *chains of* iron,
[19] Until the time that his word came to pass,
The word of Jehovah tried him.
[20] The king sent and loosed him;
Even the ruler of peoples, and let him go free.
[21] He made him lord of his house,
And ruler of all his substance;
[22] To bind his princes at his pleasure,
And teach his elders wisdom.
[23] Israel also came into Egypt;
And Jacob sojourned in the land of Ham.
[24] And he increased his people greatly,
And made them stronger than their adversaries.
[25] He turned their heart to hate his people,
To deal subtly with his servants.
[26] He sent Moses his servant,
And Aaron whom he had chosen.
[27] They set among them his[4] signs,
And wonders in the land of Ham.
[28] He sent darkness, and made it dark;
And they rebelled not against his words.
[29] He turned their waters into blood,
And slew their fish.
[30] Their land swarmed with frogs
In the chambers of their kings.
[31] He spake, and there came swarms of flies,
And lice in all their borders.
[32] He gave them hail for rain,
And flaming fire in their land.
[33] He smote their vines also and their fig-trees,
And brake the trees of their borders.
[34] He spake, and the locust came,
And the grasshopper, and that without number,

[3] Heb. *His soul entered into the iron.* [4] Heb. *the words of his signs.*

[35] And did eat up every herb in their land,
And did eat up the fruit of their ground.
[36] He smote also all the first-born in their land,
The chief[5] of all their strength.
[37] And he brought them forth with silver and gold;
And there was not[6] one feeble person among his tribes.
[38] Egypt was glad when they departed;
For the fear of them had fallen upon them.
[39] He spread a cloud for a covering,
And fire to give light in the night.
[40] They asked, and he brought quails,
And satisfied them with the bread of heaven.
[41] He opened the rock, and waters gushed out;
They ran in the dry places *like* a river.
[42] For he remembered his holy word,
And Abraham his servant.
[43] And he brought forth his people with joy,
And his chosen with singing.
[44] And he gave them the lands of the nations;
And they took the labor of the peoples in possession:
[45] That they might keep his statutes,
And observe his laws.
Praise[7] ye Jehovah.

CVI

Israel's Rebelliousness and Jehovah's Deliverances

[1] Praise[7] ye Jehovah.
Oh give thanks unto Jehovah; for he is good;
For his lovingkindness *endureth* for ever.
[2] Who can utter the mighty acts of Jehovah,
Or show forth all his praise?
[3] Blessed are they that keep justice,
And he that doeth righteousness at all times.

[5] Heb. *beginning*. See Deut. 21. 17. [6] Or, *none that stumbled*.
[7] Heb. *Hallelujah*.

[4] Remember me, O Jehovah, with the favor that thou bearest
unto thy people;
Oh visit me with thy salvation,
[5] That I may see the prosperity of thy chosen,
That I may rejoice in the gladness of thy nation,
That I may glory with thine inheritance.

[6] We have sinned with our fathers,
We have committed iniquity, we have done wickedly.
[7] Our fathers understood not thy wonders in Egypt;
They remembered not the multitude of thy lovingkindnesses,
But were rebellious at the sea, even at the Red Sea.
[8] Nevertheless he saved them for his name's sake,
That he might make his mighty power to be known.
[9] He rebuked the Red Sea also, and it was dried up:
So he led them through the depths, as through a wilderness.[1]
[10] And he saved them from the hand of him that hated them,
And redeemed them from the hand of the enemy.
[11] And the waters covered their adversaries;
There was not one of them left.
[12] Then believed they his words;
They sang his praise.
[13] They soon forgat his works;
They waited not for his counsel,
[14] But lusted exceedingly in the wilderness,
And tempted God in the desert.
[15] And he gave them their request,
But sent leanness into their soul.
[16] They envied Moses also in the camp,
And Aaron the saint[2] of Jehovah.
[17] The earth opened and swallowed up Dathan,
And covered the company of Abiram.
[18] And a fire was kindled in their company;
Their flame burned up the wicked.
[19] They made a calf in Horeb,
And worshipped a molten image.

[1] Or, *pasture land.* [2] Or, *holy one.*

[20] Thus they changed their glory
For the likeness of an ox that eateth grass.
[21] They forgat God their Saviour,
Who had done great things in Egypt,
[22] Wondrous works in the land of Ham,
And terrible things by the Red Sea.
[23] Therefore he said that he would destroy them,
Had not Moses his chosen stood before him in the breach,
To turn away his wrath, lest he should destroy *them*.
[24] Yea, they despised the pleasant land
They believed not his word,
[25] But murmured in their tents,
And hearkened not unto the voice of Jehovah.
[26] Therefore he sware[3] unto them,
That he would overthrow[4] them in the wilderness,
[27] And that he would overthrow their seed among the nations,
And scatter them in the lands.
[28] They joined themselves also unto Baal-peor,
And ate the sacrifices of the dead.
[29] Thus they provoked him to anger with their doings;
And the plague brake in upon them.
[30] Then stood up Phinehas, and executed judgment;
And so the plague was stayed.
[31] And that was reckoned unto him for righteousness,
Unto all generations for evermore.
[32] They angered him also at the waters of Meribah,[5]
So that it went ill with Moses for their sakes;
[33] Because they were rebellious against his spirit,
And he spake unadvisedly with his lips.
[34] They did not destroy the peoples,
As Jehovah commanded them,
[35] But mingled themselves with the nations,
And learned their works,
[36] And served their idols,
Which became a snare unto them.
[37] Yea, they sacrificed their sons and their daughters unto demons,

[3] Heb. *lifted up his hand.* [4] Heb. *make them fall.* [5] Or, *strife.*

[38] And shed innocent blood,
Even the blood of their sons and of their daughters,
Whom they sacrificed unto the idols of Canaan;
And the land was polluted with blood.
[39] Thus were they defiled with their works,
And played the harlot in their doings.
[40] Therefore was the wrath of Jehovah kindled against his people,
And he abhorred his inheritance.
[41] And he gave them into the hand of the nations;
And they that hated them ruled over them.
[42] Their enemies also oppressed them,
And they were brought into subjection under their hand.
[43] Many times did he deliver them;
But they were rebellious in their counsel,
And were brought low in their iniquity.
[44] Nevertheless he regarded their distress,
When he heard their cry:
[45] And he remembered for them his covenant,
And repented according to the multitude of his lovingkindnesses.
[46] He made them also to be pitied
Of all those that carried them captive.

[47] Save us, O Jehovah our God,
And gather us from among the nations,
To give thanks unto thy holy name,
And to triumph in thy praise.

[48] Blessed be Jehovah, the God of Israel,
From everlasting even to everlasting.
And let all the people say, Amen.
Praise[6] ye Jehovah.

[6] Heb. *Hallelujah.*

BOOK V

CVII

Jehovah Delivers Men from Manifold Troubles

[1] O give thanks unto Jehovah; for he is good;
For his lovingkindness *endureth* for ever.
[2] Let the redeemed of Jehovah say *so,*
Whom he hath redeemed from the hand of the adversary,
[3] And gathered out of the lands,
From the east and from the west,
From the north and from[1] the south.

[4] They wandered in the wilderness in a desert way;
They found no city of habitation.
[5] Hungry and thirsty,
Their soul fainted in them.
[6] Then they cried unto Jehovah in their trouble,
And he delivered them out of their distresses.
[7] He led them also by a straight way,
That they might go to a city of habitation.
[8] Oh that men would praise Jehovah for his lovingkindness,
And for his wonderful works to the children of men!
[9] For he satisfieth the longing soul,
And the hungry soul he filleth with good.

[10] Such as sat in darkness and in the shadow of death,
Being bound in affliction and iron,
[11] Because they rebelled against the words of God,
And contemned the counsel of the Most High:
[12] Therefore he brought down their heart with labor;
They fell down, and there was none to help.
[13] Then they cried unto Jehovah in their trouble,
And he saved them out of their distresses.
[14] He brought them out of darkness and the shadow of death,
And brake their bonds in sunder.

[1] Heb. *from the sea.*

[15] Oh that men would praise Jehovah for his lovingkindness,
And for his wonderful works to the children of men!
[16] For he hath broken the gates of brass,
And cut the bars of iron in sunder.

[17] Fools because of their[2] transgression,
And because of their iniquities, are afflicted.
[18] Their soul abhorreth all manner of food;
And they draw near unto the gates of death.
[19] Then they cry unto Jehovah in their trouble,
And he saveth them out of their distresses.
[20] He sendeth his word, and healeth them,
And delivereth *them* from their destructions.[3]
[21] Oh that men would praise Jehovah for his lovingkindness,
And for his wonderful works to the children of men!
[22] And let them offer the sacrifices of thanksgiving,
And declare his works with singing.

[23] They that go down to the sea in ships,
That do business in great waters;
[24] These see the works of Jehovah,
And his wonders in the deep.
[25] For he commandeth, and raiseth the stormy wind,
Which lifteth up the waves thereof.
[26] They mount up to the heavens, they go down again to the depths:
Their soul melteth away because of trouble.
[27] They reel to and fro, and stagger like a drunken man,
And are[4] at their wits' end.
[28] Then they cry unto Jehovah in their trouble,
And he bringeth them out of their distresses.
[29] He maketh the storm a calm,
So that the waves thereof are still.
[30] Then are they glad because they are quiet;
So he bringeth them unto their desired haven.

[2] Heb. *the way of their transgression.* [3] Heb. *pits.*
[4] Heb. *all their wisdom is swallowed up.*

[31] Oh that men would praise Jehovah for his lovingkindness,
And for his wonderful works to the children of men!
[32] Let them exalt him also in the assembly of the people,
And praise him in the seat of the elders.

[33] He turneth rivers into a wilderness,
And watersprings into a thirsty ground;
[34] A fruitful land into a salt desert,
For the wickedness of them that dwell therein.
[35] He turneth a wilderness into a pool of water,
And a dry land into watersprings.
[36] And there he maketh the hungry to dwell,
That they may prepare a city of habitation,
[37] And sow fields, and plant vineyards,
And get them fruits of increase.
[38] He blesseth them also, so that they are multiplied greatly;
And he suffereth not their cattle to decrease.
[39] Again, they are diminished and bowed down
Through oppression, trouble, and sorrow.
[40] He poureth contempt upon princes,
And causeth them to wander in the waste, where there is no way.
[41] Yet setteth he the needy on high from affliction,
And maketh *him* families like a flock.
[42] The upright shall see it, and be glad;
And all iniquity shall stop her mouth.
[43] Whoso is wise will give heed to these things;
And they will consider the lovingkindnesses of Jehovah.

CVIII

God Praised, and Supplicated to Give Victory

A Song, a Psalm of David.

[1] My heart is fixed, O God;
I will sing, yea, I will sing praises, even with my glory.
[2] Awake, psaltery and harp:
I myself will[1] awake right early.

[1] Or, *awake the dawn.*

[3] I will give thanks unto thee, O Jehovah, among the peoples;
And I will sing praises unto thee among the nations.
[4] For thy lovingkindness is great above the heavens;
And thy truth *reacheth* unto the skies.
[5] Be thou exalted, O God, above the heavens,
And thy glory above all the earth.
[6] That thy beloved may be delivered,
Save with thy right hand, and answer us.[2]
[7] God hath spoken in his holiness: I will exult;
I will divide Shechem, and mete out the valley of Succoth.
[8] Gilead is mine; Manasseh is mine;
Ephraim also is the defence of my head;
Judah is my sceptre.[3]
[9] Moab is my washpot;
Upon[4] Edom will I cast my shoe;
Over Philistia will I shout.
[10] Who will bring me into the fortified city?
Who hath[5] led me unto Edom?
[11] Hast[6] not thou cast us off, O God?
And thou goest not forth, O God, with our hosts.
[12] Give us help against the adversary;
For vain is the help[7] of man.
[13] Through God we shall do valiantly:
For he it is that will tread down our adversaries.

CIX

Vengeance Invoked Upon Adversaries

For the Chief Musician. A Psalm of David.

[1] Hold not thy peace, O God of my praise;
[2] For the mouth of the wicked and the mouth of deceit have they opened against me:
They have spoken unto[1] me with a lying tongue.
[3] They have compassed me about also with words of hatred,
And fought against me without a cause.

[2] Another reading is *me*. [3] Or, *lawgiver*. [4] Or, *Unto*. [5] Or, *will lead me &c.*
[6] Or, *Wilt not thou, O God, who hast cast us off, And goest . . . hosts?*
[7] Heb. *salvation*. [1] Or, *against*.

[4] For my love they are my adversaries:
But I *give myself unto* prayer.
[5] And they have rewarded[2] me evil for good,
And hatred for my love.
[6] Set thou a wicked man over him;
And let an[3] adversary stand at his right hand.
[7] When he is judged, let him come forth guilty;
And let his prayer be[4] turned into sin.
[8] Let his days be few;
And let another take his office.
[9] Let his children be fatherless,
And his wife a widow.
[10] Let his children be vagabonds, and beg;
And let them seek *their bread* out[5] of their desolate places.
[11] Let the extortioner catch[6] all that he hath;
And let strangers make spoil of his labor.
[12] Let there be none to extend[7] kindness unto him;
Neither let there be any to have pity on his fatherless children.
[13] Let his posterity be cut off;
In the generation following let their name be blotted out.
[14] Let the iniquity of his fathers be remembered with Jehovah;
And let not the sin of his mother be blotted out.
[15] Let them be before Jehovah continually,
That he may cut off the memory of them from the earth;
[16] Because he remembered not to show kindness,
But persecuted the poor and needy man,
And the broken in heart, to slay *them*.
[17] Yea, he loved cursing, and it came unto him;
And he delighted not in blessing, and it was far from him.
[18] He clothed himself also with cursing as with his garment,
And it came into his inward parts like water,
And like oil into his bones.
[19] Let it be unto him as the raiment wherewith he covereth himself,
And for the girdle wherewith he is girded continually.

[2] Heb. *laid upon me.* [3] Or, *Satan.* Or, *an accuser.*
[4] Or, *become.* [5] Or, *far from.* [6] Heb. *snare.* [7] Or, *continue.*

[20] This is the reward of mine adversaries from Jehovah,
And of them that speak evil against my soul.
[21] But deal thou with me, O Jehovah the Lord, for thy name's sake:
Because thy lovingkindness is good, deliver thou me;
[22] For I am poor and needy,
And my heart is wounded within me.
[23] I am gone like the shadow when it declineth:[8]
I am tossed up and down as the locust.
[24] My knees are[9] weak through fasting;
And my flesh faileth of fatness.
[25] I am become also a reproach unto them:
When they see me, they shake their head.
[26] Help me, O Jehovah my God;
Oh save me according to thy lovingkindness:
[27] That they may know that this is thy hand;
That thou, Jehovah, hast done it.
[28] Let them curse, but bless thou:
When they arise, they shall be put to shame,
But thy servant shall rejoice.
[29] Let[10] mine adversaries be clothed with dishonor,
And let them cover themselves with their own shame as with a robe.
[30] I will give great thanks unto Jehovah with my mouth;
Yea, I will praise him among the multitude.
[31] For he will stand at the right hand of the needy,
To save him from them that judge his soul.

CX

Jehovah Gives Dominion to the King

A Psalm of David.

[1] Jehovah saith unto my lord, Sit thou at my right hand,
Until I make thine enemies thy footstool.
[2] Jehovah will send[1] forth the rod[2] of thy strength out of Zion:
Rule thou in the midst of thine enemies.

[8] Or, *is stretched out.* [9] Or, *totter.* [10] Or, *Mine adversaries shall be clothed . . . And they shall cover &c.* [1] Or, *stretch.* [2] Or, *sceptre.*

[3] Thy people offer[3] themselves willingly
In the day of thy power,[4] in[5] holy array:
Out of the womb of the morning
Thou[6] hast the dew of thy youth.
[4] Jehovah hath sworn, and will not repent:
Thou art a priest for ever
After the order[7] of Melchizedek.
[5] The Lord at thy right hand
Will[8] strike through kings in the day of his wrath.
[6] He will judge among the nations,
He[9] will[10] fill *the places* with dead bodies;
He will[11] strike through the head in[12] many countries.
[7] He will drink of the brook in the way:
Therefore will he lift up the head.

CXI

Jehovah Praised for His Goodness

[1] Praise[1] ye Jehovah.
I will give thanks unto Jehovah with my whole heart,
In the council of the upright, and in the congregation.
[2] The works of Jehovah are great,
Sought out of all them that have pleasure therein.
[3] His work is honor and majesty;
And his righteousness endureth for ever.
[4] He hath made his wonderful works to be remembered:
Jehovah is gracious and merciful.
[5] He hath given food[2] unto them that fear him:
He will ever be mindful of his covenant.
[6] He hath showed his people the power of his works,
In giving them the heritage of the nations.
[7] The works of his hands are truth and justice;
All his precepts are sure.

[3] Heb. *are freewill-offerings.*
[4] Or, *army.* [5] Or, *in the beauty of holiness.*
[6] Or, *Thy youth are to thee* as *the dew.*
[7] Or, *manner.* [8] Or, *Hath stricken.*
[9] Or, The places *are full of &c.* [10] Or, *hath filled.* [11] Or, *Hath stricken.* [12] Or, *over a wide land.* [1] Heb. *Hallelujah.* [2] Heb. *prey.*

[8] They are established for ever and ever;
They are done[3] in truth and uprightness.
[9] He hath sent redemption unto his people;
He hath commanded his covenant for ever:
Holy and reverend is his name.
[10] The fear of Jehovah is the beginning of wisdom;
A[4] good understanding have all they that do *his*[5] *commandments:*
His praise endureth for ever.

CXII

Prosperity of Him that Fears Jehovah

[1] Praise[1] ye Jehovah.
Blessed is the man that feareth Jehovah,
That delighteth greatly in his commandments.
[2] His seed shall be mighty upon earth:
The generation of the upright shall be blessed.
[3] Wealth and riches are in his house;
And his righteousness endureth for ever.
[4] Unto the upright there ariseth light in the darkness:
He is gracious, and merciful, and righteous.
[5] Well is it with the man that dealeth graciously and lendeth;
He shall maintain his cause in judgment.
[6] For he shall never be moved;
The righteous shall be had in everlasting remembrance.
[7] He shall not be afraid of evil tidings:
His heart is fixed, trusting in Jehovah.
[8] His heart is established, he shall not be afraid,
Until he see *his desire* upon his adversaries.
[9] He hath dispersed, he hath given to the needy;
His righteousness endureth for ever:
His horn shall be exalted with honor.
[10] The wicked shall see it, and be grieved;
He shall gnash with his teeth, and melt away:
The desire of the wicked shall perish.

[3] Or. *made.* [4] Or. *Good repute.* [5] Heb. *them.* [1] Heb. *Hallelujah.*

CXIII

Jehovah Praised for Exalting the Humble

[1] Praise[1] ye Jehovah.
Praise, O ye servants of Jehovah,
Praise the name of Jehovah.
[2] Blessed be the name of Jehovah
From this time forth and for evermore.
[3] From the rising of the sun unto the going down of the same
Jehovah's name is to be praised.
[4] Jehovah is high above all nations,
And his glory above the heavens.
[5] Who is like unto Jehovah our God,
That hath his seat on high,
[6] That humbleth himself to[2] behold
The things that are in heaven and in the earth?
[7] He raiseth up the poor out of the dust,
And lifteth up the needy from the dunghill;
[8] That he may set him with princes,
Even with the princes of his people.
[9] He maketh the barren woman to keep house,
And to be a joyful mother of children.
Praise[1] ye Jehovah.

CXIV

God's Deliverance of Israel from Egypt

[1] When Israel went forth out of Egypt,
The house of Jacob from a people of strange language;
[2] Judah became his sanctuary,
Israel his dominion.
[3] The sea saw it, and fled;
The Jordan was driven back.
[4] The mountains skipped like rams,
The little hills like lambs.

[1] Heb. *Hallelujah.* [2] Or, *to regard the heavens and the earth.*

[5] What aileth thee, O thou sea, that thou fleest?
Thou Jordan, that thou turnest back?
[6] Ye mountains, that ye skip like rams;
Ye little hills, like lambs?
[7] Tremble, thou earth, at the presence of the Lord,
At the presence of the God of Jacob,
[8] Who turned the rock into a pool of water,
The flint into a fountain of waters.

CXV

Heathen Idols Contrasted with Jehovah

[1] Not unto us, O Jehovah, not unto us,
But unto thy name give glory,
For thy lovingkindness, and for thy truth's sake.
[2] Wherefore should the nations say,
Where is now their God?
[3] But our God is in the heavens:
He hath done whatsoever he pleased.
[4] Their idols are silver and gold,
The work of men's hands.
[5] They have mouths, but they speak not;
Eyes have they, but they see not;
[6] They have ears, but they hear not;
Noses have they, but they smell not;
[7] They have hands, but they handle not;
Feet have they, but they walk not;
Neither speak they through their throat.
[8] They that make them shall be like unto them;
Yea, every one that trusteth in them.
[9] O Israel, trust thou in Jehovah:
He is their help and their shield.
[10] O house of Aaron, trust ye in Jehovah:
He is their help and their shield.
[11] Ye that fear Jehovah, trust in Jehovah:
He is their help and their shield.

[12] Jehovah hath been mindful of us; he will bless *us:*
He will bless the house of Israel;
He will bless the house of Aaron.
[13] He will bless them that fear Jehovah,
Both small and great.
[14] Jehovah increase you more and more,
You and your children.
[15] Blessed are ye of Jehovah,
Who made heaven and earth.
[16] The heavens are the heavens of Jehovah;
But the earth hath he given to the children of men.
[17] The dead praise not Jehovah,[1]
Neither any that go down into silence;
[18] But we will bless Jehovah[1]
From this time forth and for evermore.
Praise[2] ye Jehovah.

CXVI

THANKSGIVING FOR DELIVERANCE FROM DEATH

[1] I LOVE Jehovah, because he heareth
My voice and my supplications.
[2] Because he hath inclined his ear unto me,
Therefore will I call *upon him* as long as I live.
[3] The cords of death compassed me,
And the pains of Sheol gat[3] hold upon me:
I found trouble and sorrow.
[4] Then called I upon the name of Jehovah:
O Jehovah, I beseech thee, deliver my soul.
[5] Gracious is Jehovah, and righteous;
Yea, our God is merciful.
[6] Jehovah preserveth the simple:
I was brought low, and he saved me.
[7] Return unto thy rest, O my soul;
For Jehovah hath dealt bountifully with thee.

[1] Heb. *Jah.* [2] Heb. *Hallelujah.*
[3] Or, *found me.*

[8] For thou hast delivered my soul from death,
Mine eyes from tears,
And my feet from falling.
[9] I will walk before Jehovah
In the land[4] of the living.
[10] I believe,[5] for I will speak:
I was greatly afflicted:
[11] I said in my haste,[6]
All men are liars.
[12] What shall I render unto Jehovah
For all his benefits toward me?
[13] I will take the cup of salvation,
And call upon the name of Jehovah.
[14] I will pay my vows unto Jehovah,
Yea, in the presence of all his people.
[15] Precious in the sight of Jehovah
Is the death of his saints.
[16] O Jehovah, truly I am thy servant:
I am thy servant, the son of thy handmaid;
Thou hast loosed my bonds.
[17] I will offer to thee the sacrifice of thanksgiving,
And will call upon the name of Jehovah.
[18] I will pay my vows unto Jehovah,
Yea, in the presence of all his people,
[19] In the courts of Jehovah's house,
In the midst of thee, O Jerusalem.
Praise[7] ye Jehovah.

CXVII

A Psalm of Praise

[1] O PRAISE Jehovah, all ye nations;
Laud him, all ye peoples.
[2] For his lovingkindness is great toward us;
And the truth of Jehovah *endureth* for ever.
Praise[7] ye Jehovah.

[4] Heb. *lands.* [5] Or, *believed, when I spake* thus. [6] Or, *alarm.* [7] Hallelujah.

CXVIII

Thanksgiving for Jehovah's Saving Goodness

[1] Oh give thanks unto Jehovah; for he is good;
For his lovingkindness *endureth* for ever.
[2] Let Israel now say,
That his lovingkindness *endureth* for ever.
[3] Let the house of Aaron now say,
That his lovingkindness *endureth* for ever.
[4] Let them now that fear Jehovah say,
That his lovingkindness *endureth* for ever.
[5] Out of my distress I called upon Jehovah:[1]
Jehovah[1] answered me *and set me* in a large place.
[6] Jehovah is on my side; I will not fear:
What can man do unto me?
[7] Jehovah is on my side among them that help me:
Therefore shall I see *my desire* upon them that hate me.
[8] It is better to take refuge in Jehovah
Than to put confidence in man.
[9] It is better to take refuge in Jehovah
Than to put confidence in princes.
[10] All nations compassed me about:
In the name of Jehovah I will cut them off.
[11] They compassed me about; yea, they compassed me about:
In the name of Jehovah I will cut them off.
[12] They compassed me about like bees; they are quenched as the fire of thorns:
In the name of Jehovah I will cut them off.
[13] Thou didst thrust sore at me that I might fall;
But Jehovah helped me.
[14] Jehovah[1] is my strength and song;
And he is become my salvation.
[15] The voice of rejoicing and salvation is in the tents of the righteous:
The right hand of Jehovah doeth valiantly.

[1] Heb. *Jah.*

[16] The right hand of Jehovah is exalted:
The right hand of Jehovah doeth valiantly.
[17] I shall not die, but live,
And declare the works of Jehovah.[1]
[18] Jehovah[1] hath chastened me sore;
But he hath not given me over unto death.
[19] Open to me the gates of righteousness:
I will enter into them, I will give thanks unto Jehovah.[1]
[20] This is the gate of Jehovah;
The righteous shall enter into it.
[21] I will give thanks unto thee; for thou hast answered me,
And art become my salvation.
[22] The stone which the builders rejected
Is become the head of the corner.
[23] This is Jehovah's[2] doing;
It is marvellous in our eyes.
[24] This is the day which Jehovah hath made;
We will rejoice and be glad in it.
[25] Save now, we beseech thee, O Jehovah:
O Jehovah, we beseech thee, send now prosperity.
[26] Blessed be he that cometh[3] in the name of Jehovah:
We have blessed you out of the house of Jehovah.
[27] Jehovah is God, and he hath given us light:
Bind the sacrifice with cords, even unto the horns of the altar.
[28] Thou art my God, and I will give thanks unto thee:
Thou art my God, I will exalt thee.
[29] Oh give thanks unto Jehovah; for he is good;
For his lovingkindness *endureth* for ever.

CXIX

Meditations and Prayers Relating to the Law of God

א ALEPH

[1] Blessed are they that are perfect[4] in the way,
Who walk in the law of Jehovah.

[1] Heb. *Jah.* [2] Heb. *from Jehovah.*
[3] Or, *entereth.* [4] Or, *upright in way.*

[2] Blessed are they that keep his testimonies,
That seek him with the whole heart.
[3] Yea, they do no unrighteousness;
They walk in his ways.
[4] Thou hast commanded *us* thy precepts,
That we should observe them diligently.
[5] Oh that my ways were established
To observe thy statutes!
[6] Then shall I not be put to shame,
When I have respect unto all thy commandments.
[7] I will give thanks unto thee with uprightness of heart,
When I learn thy righteous judgments.
[8] I will observe thy statutes:
Oh forsake me not utterly.

ב BETH

[9] Wherewith shall a young man cleanse his way?
By taking heed *thereto* according to thy word.
[10] With my whole heart have I sought thee:
Oh let me not wander from thy commandments.
[11] Thy word have I laid up in my heart,
That I might not sin against thee.
[12] Blessed art thou, O Jehovah:
Teach me thy statutes.
[13] With my lips have I declared
All the ordinances of thy mouth.
[14] I have rejoiced in the way of thy testimonies,
As much as in all riches.
[15] I will meditate on thy precepts,
And have respect unto thy ways.
[16] I will delight myself in thy statutes:
I will not forget thy word.

ג GIMEL

[17] Deal bountifully with thy servant, that I may live;
So will I observe thy word.

[18] Open thou mine eyes, that I may behold
Wondrous things out of thy law.
[19] I am a sojourner in the earth:
Hide not thy commandments from me.
[20] My soul breaketh for the longing
That it hath unto thine ordinances at all times.
[21] Thou hast rebuked the proud that[5] are cursed,
That do wander from thy commandments.
[22] Take away from me reproach and contempt;
For I have kept thy testimonies.
[23] Princes also sat and talked against me;
But thy servant did meditate on thy statutes.
[24] Thy testimonies also are my delight
And my[6] counsellors.

ד DALETH

[25] My soul cleaveth unto the dust:
Quicken thou me according to thy word.
[26] I declared my ways, and thou answeredst me:
Teach me thy statutes.
[27] Make me understand the way of thy precepts:
So shall I meditate on thy wondrous works.
[28] My soul melteth[7] for heaviness:
Strengthen thou me according unto thy word.
[29] Remove from me the way of falsehood;
And grant me thy law graciously.
[30] I have chosen the way of faithfulness:
Thine ordinances have I set *before me.*
[31] I cleave unto thy testimonies:
O Jehovah, put me not to shame.
[32] I will run the way of thy commandments,
When thou shalt enlarge my heart.

ה HE

[33] Teach me, O Jehovah, the way of thy statutes;
And I shall keep it unto the end.

[5] Or, *Cursed are they that &c.* [6] Heb. *the men of my counsel.* [7] Heb. *droppeth.*

[34] Give me understanding, and I shall keep thy law;
Yea, I shall observe it with my whole heart.
[35] Make me to go in the path of thy commandments;
For therein do I delight.
[36] Incline my heart unto thy testimonies,
And not to covetousness.
[37] Turn away mine eyes from beholding vanity,
And quicken me in thy ways.
[38] Confirm unto thy servant thy word,
Which[8] *is in order* unto the fear of thee.
[39] Turn away my reproach whereof I am afraid;
For thine ordinances are good.
[40] Behold, I have longed after thy precepts:
Quicken me in thy righteousness.

ו VAV

[41] Let thy lovingkindnesses also come unto me, O Jehovah,
Even thy salvation, according to thy word.
[42] So shall I have an answer for him that reproacheth me;
For I trust in thy word.
[43] And take not the word of truth utterly out of my mouth;
For I have hoped in thine ordinances.
[44] So shall I observe thy law continually
For ever and ever.
[45] And I shall walk at liberty;
For I have sought thy precepts.
[46] I will also speak of thy testimonies before kings,
And shall not be put to shame.
[47] And I will delight myself in thy commandments,
Which I have loved.
[48] I will lift up my hands also unto thy commandments which I have loved;
And I will meditate on thy statutes.

[8] Or, *Who* is devoted *to.*

ז ZAYIN

[49] Remember the word unto thy servant,
Because[9] thou hast made me to hope.
[50] This is my comfort in my affliction;
For[10] thy word hath quickened me.
[51] The proud have had me greatly in derision:
Yet have I not swerved from thy law.
[52] I have remembered thine ordinances of old, O Jehovah,
And have comforted myself.
[53] Hot[11] indignation hath taken hold upon me,
Because of the wicked that forsake thy law.
[54] Thy statutes have been my songs
In the house of my pilgrimage.
[55] I have remembered thy name, O Jehovah, in the night,
And have observed thy law.
[56] This I have had,
Because[12] I have kept thy precepts.

ח HHETH

[57] Jehovah[13] is my portion:
I have said that I would observe thy words.
[58] I entreated thy favor with my whole heart:
Be merciful unto me according to thy word.
[59] I thought on my ways,
And turned my feet unto thy testimonies.
[60] I made haste, and delayed not,
To observe thy commandments.
[61] The cords of the wicked have wrapped me round;
But I have not forgotten thy law.
[62] At midnight I will rise to give thanks unto thee
Because of thy righteous ordinances.
[63] I am a companion of all them that fear thee,
And of them that observe thy precepts.

[9] Or, *Wherein.* [10] Or, *That.* [11] Or, *Horror.* [12] Or, *That.*
[13] Or, *Jehovah is my portion, have I said: That I may observe &c.*

[64] The earth, O Jehovah, is full of thy lovingkindness:
Teach me thy statutes.

ט TETH

[65] Thou hast dealt well with thy servant,
O Jehovah, according unto thy word.
[66] Teach me good judgment and knowledge;
For I have believed in thy commandments.
[67] Before I was afflicted I went astray;
But now I observe thy word.
[68] Thou art good, and doest good;
Teach me thy statutes.
[69] The proud have forged a lie against me:
With my whole heart will I keep thy precepts.
[70] Their heart is as fat as grease;
But I delight in thy law.
[71] It is good for me that I have been afflicted;
That I may learn thy statutes.
[72] The law of thy mouth is better unto me
Than thousands of gold and silver.

י YODH

[73] Thy hands have made me and fashioned[14] me:
Give me understanding, that I may learn thy commandments.
[74] They that fear thee shall see me and be glad,
Because I have hoped in thy word.
[75] I know, O Jehovah, that thy judgments are righteous,
And that in faithfulness thou hast afflicted me.
[76] Let, I pray thee, thy lovingkindness be for my comfort,
According to thy word unto thy servant.
[77] Let thy tender mercies come unto me, that I may live;
For thy law is my delight.
[78] Let the proud be put to shame; for they have overthrown me wrongfully:[15]
But I will meditate on thy precepts.

[14] Or, *established*. [15] Or, *with falsehood*.

[79] Let those that fear thee turn unto me;
And[16] they shall know thy testimonies.
[80] Let my heart be perfect in thy statutes,
That I be not put to shame.

כ KAPH

[81] My soul fainteth for thy salvation;
But I hope in thy word.
[82] Mine eyes fail for thy word,
While I say, When wilt thou comfort me?
[83] For I am become like a wine-skin in the smoke;
Yet do I not forget thy statutes.
[84] How many are the days of thy servant?
When wilt thou execute judgment on them that persecute me?
[85] The proud have digged pits for me,
Who are not according to thy law.
[86] All thy commandments are faithful:
They persecute me wrongfully;[15] help thou me.
[87] They had almost consumed me upon earth;
But I forsook not thy precepts.
[88] Quicken me after thy lovingkindness;
So shall I observe the testimony of thy mouth.

ל LAMEDH

[89] For ever, O Jehovah,
Thy word is settled in heaven.
[90] Thy faithfulness is unto all generations:
Thou hast established the earth, and it abideth.
[91] They[17] abide this day according to thine ordinances;
For all things are thy servants.
[92] Unless thy law had been my delight,
I should then have perished in mine affliction.
[93] I will never forget thy precepts;
For with them thou hast quickened me.

[16] Another reading is, *Even they that know.*
[17] Or, *As for thine ordinances, they abide this day.*

[94] I am thine, save me;
For I have sought thy precepts.
[95] The wicked have waited for me, to destroy me;
But I will consider thy testimonies.
[96] I have seen an end of all perfection;
But thy commandment is exceeding broad.

מ MEM

[97] Oh how love I thy law!
It is my meditation all the day.
[98] Thy[18] commandments make me wiser than mine enemies;
For they are ever with me.
[99] I have more understanding than all my teachers;
For thy testimonies are my meditation.
[100] I understand more than the aged,
Because I have kept thy precepts.
[101] I have refrained my feet from every evil way,
That I might observe thy word.
[102] I have not turned aside from thine ordinances;
For thou hast taught me.
[103] How sweet are thy words unto my taste![19]
Yea, sweeter than honey to my mouth!
[104] Through thy precepts I get understanding:
Therefore I hate every false way.

נ NUN

[105] Thy word is a lamp unto my feet,
And light unto my path.
[106] I have sworn, and have confirmed it,
That I will observe thy righteous ordinances.
[107] I am afflicted very much:
Quicken me, O Jehovah, according unto thy word.
[108] Accept, I beseech thee, the freewill-offerings of my mouth, O Jehovah,
And teach me thine ordinances.

[18] Or, *Thou through thy commandments makest.* [19] Heb. *palate.*

[109] My soul is continually in my hand;
Yet do I not forget thy law.
[110] The wicked have laid a snare for me;
Yet have I not gone astray from thy precepts.
[111] Thy testimonies have I taken as a heritage for ever;
For they are the rejoicing of my heart.
[112] I have inclined my heart to perform thy statutes
For ever, even unto the end.

ס SAMEKH

[113] I hate them that are of a double mind;
But thy law do I love.
[114] Thou art my hiding-place and my shield:
I hope in thy word.
[115] Depart from me, ye evil-doers,
That I may keep the commandments of my God.
[116] Uphold me according unto thy word, that I may live;
And let me not be ashamed of my hope.
[117] Hold thou me up, and I shall be safe,
And shall have respect unto thy statutes continually.
[118] Thou hast set at nought all them that err from thy statutes;
For their deceit is falsehood.[20]
[119] Thou puttest[21] away all the wicked of the earth like dross:
Therefore I love thy testimonies.
[120] My flesh trembleth for fear of thee;
And I am afraid of thy judgments.

ע AYIN

[121] I have done justice and righteousness:
Leave me not to mine oppressors.
[122] Be surety for thy servant for good:
Let not the proud oppress me.
[123] Mine eyes fail for thy salvation,
And for thy righteous word.
[124] Deal with thy servant according unto thy lovingkindness,
And teach me thy statutes.

[20] Or, *vain*. [21] Heb. *causest to cease*.

[125] I am thy servant; give me understanding,
That I may know thy testimonies.
[126] It is time for Jehovah to work;
For they have made void thy law.
[127] Therefore I love thy commandments
Above gold, yea, above fine gold.
[128] Therefore I esteem all *thy* precepts concerning all *things* to be right;
And I hate every false way.

פ PE

[129] Thy testimonies are wonderful;
Therefore doth my soul keep them.
[130] The opening of thy words giveth light;
It giveth understanding unto the simple.
[131] I opened wide my mouth, and panted;
For I longed for thy commandments.
[132] Turn thee unto me, and have mercy upon me,
As thou usest to do unto those that love thy name.
[133] Establish my footsteps in thy word;
And let not any iniquity have dominion over me.
[134] Redeem me from the oppression of man:
So will I observe thy precepts.
[135] Make thy face to shine upon thy servant;
And teach me thy statutes.
[136] Streams of water run down mine eyes,
Because they observe not thy law.

צ TSADHE

[137] Righteous art thou, O Jehovah,
And upright are[22] thy judgments.
[138] Thou hast commanded thy testimonies in righteousness
And very faithfulness.
[139] My zeal hath consumed[23] me,
Because mine adversaries have forgotten thy words.

[22] Or, *in thy judgments.* [23] Heb. *cut me off.*

[140] Thy word is very pure;[24]
Therefore thy servant loveth it.
[141] I am small and despised;
Yet do I not forget thy precepts.
[142] Thy righteousness is an everlasting righteousness,
And thy law is truth.
[143] Trouble and anguish have taken[25] hold on me;
Yet thy commandments are my delight.
[144] Thy testimonies are righteous for ever:
Give me understanding, and I shall live.

ק QOPH

[145] I have called with my whole heart; answer me, O Jehovah
I will keep thy statutes.
[146] I have called unto thee; save me,
And I shall observe thy testimonies.
[147] I anticipated the dawning of the morning, and cried:
I hoped in thy words.
[148] Mine eyes anticipated the night-watches,
That I might meditate on thy word.
[149] Hear my voice according unto thy lovingkindness:
Quicken me, O Jehovah, according[26] to thine ordinances.
[150] They draw nigh that[27] follow after wickedness;
They are far from thy law.
[151] Thou art nigh, O Jehovah;
And all thy commandments are truth.
[152] Of old have I known from thy testimonies,
That thou hast founded them for ever.

ר RESH

[153] Consider mine affliction, and deliver me;
For I do not forget thy law.
[154] Plead thou my cause, and redeem me:
Quicken me according to thy word.

[24] Heb. *tried,* or, *refined.* [25] Or, *found me.*
[26] Or, *as thou art wont.* [27] Or, *that persecute* me *with wickedness.*

[155] Salvation is far from the wicked;
For they seek not thy statutes.
[156] Great are thy tender mercies, O Jehovah:
Quicken me according to thine ordinances.
[157] Many are my persecutors and mine adversaries;
Yet have I not swerved from thy testimonies.
[158] I beheld the treacherous, and was[28] grieved,
Because they observe not thy word.
[159] Consider how I love thy precepts:
Quicken me, O Jehovah, according to thy lovingkindness.
[160] The sum of thy word is truth;
And every one of thy righteous ordinances *endureth* for ever.

ש SHIN

[161] Princes have persecuted me without a cause;
But my heart standeth in awe of thy words.
[162] I rejoice at thy word,
As one that findeth great spoil.
[163] I hate and abhor falsehood;
But thy law do I love.
[164] Seven times a day do I praise thee,
Because of thy righteous ordinances.
[165] Great peace have they that love thy law;
And they have no occasion of stumbling.
[166] I have hoped for thy salvation, O Jehovah,
And have done thy commandments.
[167] My soul hath observed thy testimonies;
And I love them exceedingly.
[168] I have observed thy precepts and thy testimonies;
For all my ways are before thee.

ת TAV

[169] Let my cry come near before thee, O Jehovah:
Give me understanding according to thy word.
[170] Let my supplication come before thee:
Deliver me according to thy word.

[28] Or, *loathed* them.

[171] Let my lips utter praise;
For thou teachest me thy statutes.
[172] Let my tongue sing of thy word;
For all thy commandments are righteousness.
[173] Let thy hand be ready to help me;
For I have chosen thy precepts.
[174] I have longed for thy salvation, O Jehovah;
And thy law is my delight.
[175] Let my soul live, and it shall praise thee;
And let thine ordinances help me.
[176] I have gone astray like a lost sheep; seek thy servant;
For I do not forget thy commandments.

CXX

Prayer for Deliverance from the Treacherous

A Song of Ascents

[1] In my distress I cried unto Jehovah,
And he answered me.
[2] Deliver my soul, O Jehovah, from lying lips,
And from a deceitful tongue.
[3] What shall be given unto thee, and what shall be done more unto thee,
Thou deceitful tongue?
[4] Sharp[1] arrows of the mighty,
With coals of juniper.[2]
[5] Woe is me, that I sojourn in Meshech,
That I dwell among the tents of Kedar!
[6] My soul hath long had her dwelling
With him that hateth peace.
[7] I am *for* peace:
But when I speak, they are for war.

[1] Or, It is as *the sharp arrows of the mighty* man.
[2] Or, *broom.*

CXXI

Jehovah the Keeper of Israel

A Song of Ascents.

[1] I will lift up mine eyes unto the mountains:
From whence shall my help come?
[2] My help *cometh* from Jehovah,
Who made heaven and earth.

[3] He[1] will not suffer thy foot to be moved:
He that keepeth thee will not slumber.
[4] Behold, he that keepeth Israel
Will neither slumber nor sleep.
[5] Jehovah is thy keeper:
Jehovah is thy shade upon thy right hand.
[6] The sun shall not smite thee by day,
Nor the moon by night.
[7] Jehovah will keep thee from all evil;
He will keep thy soul.
[8] Jehovah will keep thy going out and thy coming in
From this time forth and for evermore.

CXXII

Prayer for the Peace of Jerusalem

A Song of Ascents; of David

[1] I was glad when they said unto me,
Let us go unto the house of Jehovah.
[2] Our feet are[2] standing
Within thy gates, O Jerusalem,
[3] Jerusalem, that art builded
As a city that is compact together;
[4] Whither the tribes go up, even the tribes of Jehovah,[3]
For an[4] ordinance for Israel,
To give thanks unto the name of Jehovah.

[1] Or, *Let him not suffer . . . Let him not slumber that &c.*
[2] Or, *have stood.* [3] Heb. *Jah.* [4] Heb. *a testimony.*

[5] For there are[5] set thrones for judgment,
The thrones of the house of David.
[6] Pray[6] for the peace of Jerusalem:
They[7] shall prosper that love thee.
[7] Peace be within thy walls,
And prosperity within thy palaces.
[8] For my brethren and companions' sakes,
I will now say,[8] Peace be within thee.
[9] For the sake of the house of Jehovah our God
I will seek thy good.

CXXIII

An Expectant Prayer for Jehovah's Help

A Song of Ascents.

[1] Unto thee do I lift up mine eyes,
O thou that sittest in the heavens.
[2] Behold, as the eyes of servants *look* unto the hand of their master,
As the eyes of a maid unto the hand of her mistress;
So our eyes *look* unto Jehovah our God,
Until he have mercy upon us.
[3] Have mercy upon us, O Jehovah, have mercy upon us;
For we are exceedingly filled with contempt.
[4] Our soul is exceedingly filled
With the scoffing of those that are at ease,
And with the contempt of the proud.

CXXIV

Praise for Rescue from Enemies

A Song of Ascents; of David.

[1] If it had not been Jehovah who was on our side,
Let Israel now say,

[5] Or, *were.* [6] Or, *Salute ye Jerusalem.* [7] Or, *May they.*
[8] Or, *speak peace concerning thee.*

[2] If it had not been Jehovah who was on our side,
When men rose up against us;
[3] Then they had swallowed us up alive,
When their wrath was kindled against us:
[4] Then the waters had overwhelmed us,
The stream had gone over our soul;
[5] Then the proud waters had gone over our soul.
[6] Blessed be Jehovah,
Who hath not given us as a prey to their teeth.
[7] Our soul is escaped as a bird out of the snare of the fowlers:
The snare is broken, and we are escaped.
[8] Our help is in the name of Jehovah,
Who made heaven and earth.

CXXV

Jehovah Round about His People

A Song of Ascents.

[1] They that trust in Jehovah
Are as mount Zion, which cannot be moved, but abideth for ever.
[2] As the mountains are round about Jerusalem,
So Jehovah is round about his people
From this time forth and for evermore.
[3] For the sceptre of wickedness shall not rest upon the lot of the righteous;
That the righteous put not forth their hands unto iniquity.
[4] Do good, O Jehovah, unto those that are good,
And to them that are upright in their hearts.
[5] But as for such as turn aside unto their crooked ways,
Jehovah will lead them forth with the workers of iniquity.
Peace be upon Israel.

CXXVI

Thanksgiving for Return from Captivity

A Song of Ascents.

[1] When Jehovah brought back those that returned to Zion,
We were like unto them that dream.
[2] Then was our mouth filled with laughter,
And our tongue with singing:
Then said they among the nations,
Jehovah hath done great things for them.
[3] Jehovah hath done great things for us;
Whereof we are glad.
[4] Turn again our captivity, O Jehovah,
As the streams in the South.
[5] They that sow in tears shall reap in joy.
[6] He that goeth forth and weepeth, bearing[1] seed for sowing,
Shall doubtless come again with joy, bringing his sheaves *with him.*

CXXVII

Prosperity Comes from Jehovah

A Song of Ascents; of Solomon.

[1] Except Jehovah build the house,
They labor in vain that build it:
Except Jehovah keep the city,
The watchman waketh but in vain.
[2] It is vain for you to rise up early,
To take rest late,
To eat the bread of toil;
For so he giveth unto his beloved sleep.[2]
[3] Lo, children are a heritage of Jehovah;
And the fruit of the womb is *his* reward.
[4] As arrows in the hand of a mighty man,
So are the children of youth.

[1] Or, *bearing the measure of seed.*
[2] Or, *in sleep.*

[5] Happy is the man that hath his quiver full of them:
They shall not be put to shame,
When they speak with their enemies in the gate.

CXXVIII

Blessedness of the Fear of Jehovah

A Song of Ascents.

[1] Blessed is every one that feareth Jehovah,
That walketh in his ways.
[2] For thou shalt eat the labor of thy hands:
Happy shalt thou be, and it shall be well with thee.
[3] Thy wife shall be as a fruitful vine,
In the innermost parts of thy house;
Thy children like olive plants,
Round about thy table.
[4] Behold, thus shall the man be blessed
That feareth Jehovah.
[5] Jehovah bless thee out of Zion:
And see thou the good of Jerusalem all the days of thy life.
[6] Yea, see thou thy children's children.
Peace[1] be upon Israel.

CXXIX

Prayer for the Overthrow of Zion's Enemies

A Song of Ascents.

[1] Many[2] a time have they afflicted me from my youth up,
Let Israel now say,
[2] Many[2] a time have they afflicted me from my youth up:
Yet they have not prevailed against me.
[3] The plowers plowed upon my back;
They made long their furrows.
[4] Jehovah is righteous:
He hath cut asunder the cords of the wicked.
[5] Let them be put to shame and turned backward,
All they that hate Zion.

[1] Or, And *peace upon Israel*. [2] Or, *Much*.

[6] Let them be as the grass upon the housetops,
Which withereth before it groweth[3] up;
[7] Wherewith the reaper filleth not his hand,
Nor he that bindeth sheaves his bosom:
[8] Neither do they that go by say,
The blessing of Jehovah be upon you;
We bless you in the name of Jehovah.

CXXX

Hope in the Lord's Forgiving Love

A Song of Ascents.

[1] Out of the depths have I cried unto thee, O Jehovah.
[2] Lord, hear my voice:
Let thine ears be attentive
To the voice of my supplications.
[3] If thou Jehovah,[1] shouldest mark iniquities,
O Lord, who could stand?
[4] But there is forgiveness with thee,
That thou mayest be feared.
[5] I wait for Jehovah, my soul doth wait,
And in his word do I hope.
[6] My soul *waiteth* for the Lord
More than watchmen *wait* for the morning;
Yea, more than watchmen for the morning.
[7] O Israel, hope in Jehovah;
For with Jehovah there is lovingkindness,
And with him is plenteous redemption.
[8] And he will redeem Israel
From all his iniquities.

CXXXI

Childlike Trust in Jehovah

A Song of Ascents; of David.

[1] Jehovah, my heart is not haughty, nor mine eyes lofty;
Neither do I exercise[2] myself in great matters,

[3] Or, *is plucked up.* [1] Heb. *Jah.* [2] Heb. *walk.*

Or in things too wonderful for me.
[2] Surely I have stilled and quieted my soul;
Like a weaned child with his mother,
Like a weaned child is my soul within me.
[3] O Israel, hope in Jehovah
From this time forth and for evermore.

CXXXII

Prayer for Jehovah's Blessing upon the Sanctuary

A Song of Ascents.

[1] Jehovah, remember for David
All his affliction;
[2] How he sware unto Jehovah,
And vowed unto the Mighty One of Jacob:
[3] Surely I will not come into the tabernacle[1] of my house,
Nor go up into my[2] bed;
[4] I will not give sleep to mine eyes,
Or slumber to mine eyelids;
[5] Until I find out a place for Jehovah,
A[3] tabernacle for the Mighty One of Jacob.
[6] Lo, we heard of it in Ephrathah:[4]
We found it in the field of the[5] wood.
[7] We will go into his tabernacles;
We will worship at his footstool.
[8] Arise, O Jehovah, into thy resting-place;
Thou, and the ark of thy strength.
[9] Let thy priests be clothed with righteousness;
And let thy saints shout for joy.
[10] For thy servant David's sake
Turn not away the face of thine anointed.
[11] Jehovah hath sworn unto David in truth;
He will not turn from it:
Of the fruit of thy body will I set upon thy throne.

[1] Heb. *tent.* [2] Heb. *the couch of my bed.* [3] Heb. *Tabernacles.*
[4] Or, *Ephraim.* [5] Or, *Jaar.* See 1 Chr. 13. 5.

[12] If thy children will keep my covenant
And my testimony that I shall teach them,
Their children also shall sit upon thy throne for evermore.
[13] For Jehovah hath chosen Zion;
He hath desired it for his habitation.
[14] This is my resting-place for ever:
Here will I dwell; for I have desired it.
[15] I will abundantly[6] bless her provision:
I will satisfy her poor with bread.
[16] Her priests also will I clothe with salvation;
And her saints shall shout aloud for joy.
[17] There will I make the[7] horn of David to bud:
I have ordained[8] a lamp for mine anointed.
[18] His enemies will I clothe with shame;
But upon himself shall his crown flourish.

CXXXIII

The Excellency of Brotherly Unity

A Song of Ascents; of David.

[1] Behold, how good and how pleasant it is
For brethren to dwell together in unity!
[2] It is like the precious oil upon the head,
That ran down upon the beard,
Even Aaron's beard;
That came down upon the skirt[1] of his garments;
[3] Like the dew of Hermon,
That cometh down upon the mountains of Zion:
For there Jehovah commanded the blessing,
Even life for evermore.

CXXXIV

Greetings of Night-Watchers

A Song of Ascents.

[1] Behold, bless ye Jehovah, all ye servants of Jehovah,
That by night stand in the house of Jehovah.

[6] Or, *surely*. [7] Or, *a horn to spring forth unto David*. [8] Or, *prepared*.
[1] Or, *collar*.

[2] Lift up your hands to[1] the sanctuary,
And bless ye Jehovah.
[3] Jehovah bless thee out of Zion;
Even he that made heaven and earth.

CXXXV

Praise for Jehovah's Wonderful Works. Vanity of Idols

[1] Praise[2] ye Jehovah.
Praise ye the name of Jehovah;
Praise *him,* O ye servants of Jehovah,
[2] Ye that stand in the house of Jehovah,
In the courts of the house of our God.
[3] Praise ye Jehovah; for Jehovah is good:
Sing praises unto his name; for it is pleasant.
[4] For Jehovah[3] hath chosen Jacob unto himself,
And Israel for his own possession.
[5] For I know that Jehovah is great,
And that our Lord is above all gods.
[6] Whatsoever Jehovah pleased, that hath he done,
In heaven and in earth, in the seas and in all deeps;
[7] Who causeth the vapors to ascend from the ends of the earth;
Who maketh lightnings for the rain;
Who bringeth forth the wind out of his treasuries;
[8] Who smote the first-born of Egypt,
Both of man and beast;
[9] Who sent signs and wonders into the midst of thee, O Egypt,
Upon Pharaoh, and upon all his servants;
[10] Who smote many[4] nations,
And slew mighty kings,
[11] Sihon king of the Amorites,
And Og king of Bashan,
And all the kingdoms of Canaan,
[12] And gave their land for a heritage,
A heritage unto Israel his people.

[1] Or, *in holiness.*
[2] Heb. *Hallelujah.* [3] Heb. *Jah.* [4] Or, *great.*

[13] Thy name, O Jehovah, *endureth* for ever;
Thy memorial *name,* O Jehovah, throughout all generations.
[14] For Jehovah will judge his people,
And repent himself concerning his servants.
[15] The idols of the nations are silver and gold,
The work of men's hands.
[16] They have mouths, but they speak not;
Eyes have they, but they see not;
[17] They have ears, but they hear not;
Neither is there any breath in their mouths.
[18] They that make them shall be like unto them;
Yea, every one that trusteth in them.
[19] O house of Israel, bless ye Jehovah:
O house of Aaron, bless ye Jehovah:
[20] O house of Levi, bless ye Jehovah:
Ye that fear Jehovah, bless ye Jehovah.
[21] Blessed be Jehovah out of Zion,
Who dwelleth at Jerusalem.
Praise[5] ye Jehovah.

CXXXVI

Thanks for Jehovah's Goodness to Israel

[1] Oh give thanks unto Jehovah; for he is good;
For his lovingkindness *endureth* for ever.
[2] Oh give thanks unto the God of gods;
For his lovingkindness *endureth* for ever.
[3] Oh give thanks unto the Lord of lords;
For his lovingkindness *endureth* for ever:
[4] To him who alone doeth great wonders;
For his lovingkindness *endureth* for ever:
[5] To him that by understanding made the heavens;
For his lovingkindness *endureth* for ever:
[6] To him that spread forth the earth above the waters;
For his lovingkindness *endureth* for ever:

[5] Heb. *Hallelujah.*

[7] To him that made great lights;
For his lovingkindness *endureth* for ever:
[8] The sun to rule by day;
For his lovingkindness *endureth* for ever;
[9] The moon and stars to rule by night;
For his lovingkindness *endureth* for ever:
[10] To him that smote Egypt in their first-born;
For his lovingkindness *endureth* for ever;
[11] And brought out Israel from among them;
For his lovingkindness *endureth* for ever;
[12] With a strong hand, and with an outstretched arm;
For his lovingkindness *endureth* for ever:
[13] To him that divided the Red Sea in sunder;
For his lovingkindness *endureth* for ever;
[14] And made Israel to pass through the midst of it;
For his lovingkindness *endureth* for ever;
[15] But overthrew[1] Pharaoh and his host in the Red Sea;
For his lovingkindness *endureth* for ever:
[16] To him that led his people through the wilderness;
For his lovingkindness *endureth* for ever:
[17] To him that smote great kings;
For his lovingkindness *endureth* for ever;
[18] And slew famous kings;
For his lovingkindness *endureth* for ever:
[19] Sihon king of the Amorites;
For his lovingkindness *endureth* for ever;
[20] And Og king of Bashan;
For his lovingkindness *endureth* for ever;
[21] And gave their land for a heritage;
For his lovingkindness *endureth* for ever;
[22] Even a heritage unto Israel his servant;
For his lovingkindness *endureth* for ever:
[23] Who remembered us in our low estate;
For his lovingkindness *endureth* for ever;
[24] And hath delivered us from our adversaries;
For his lovingkindness *endureth* for ever:

[1] Heb. *shook off*.

[25] Who giveth food to all flesh;
For his lovingkindness *endureth* for ever.
[26] Oh give thanks unto the God of heaven;
For his lovingkindness *endureth* for ever.

CXXXVII

An Experience of the Captivity

[1] By the rivers of Babylon,
There we sat down, yea, we wept,
When we remembered Zion.
[2] Upon the willows in the midst thereof
We hanged up our harps.
[3] For there they that led us captive required of us songs,[1]
And they[2] that wasted us *required of us* mirth, *saying,*
Sing us one of the songs of Zion.
[4] How shall we sing Jehovah's song
In a foreign land?
[5] If I forget thee, O Jerusalem,
Let my right hand forget *her skill.*
[6] Let my tongue cleave to the roof of my mouth,
If I remember thee not;
If I prefer not Jerusalem
Above my chief joy.
[7] Remember, O Jehovah, against the children of Edom
The day of Jerusalem;
Who said, Rase it, rase it,
Even to the foundation thereof.
[8] O daughter of Babylon, that[3] art to be destroyed,
Happy shall he be, that rewardeth thee
As thou hast served us.
[9] Happy shall he be, that taketh and dasheth thy little ones
Against the rock.

[1] Heb. *words of song.* [2] Or, *our tormentors.* [3] Or, *that art laid waste.*

CXXXVIII

THANKSGIVING FOR JEHOVAH'S FAVOR

A Psalm of David.

[1] I WILL give thee thanks with my whole heart:
Before the gods will I sing praises unto thee.
[2] I will worship toward thy holy temple,
And give thanks unto thy name for thy lovingkindness and for thy truth:
For thou hast magnified thy word above all thy name.
[3] In the day that I called thou answeredest me,
Thou didst encourage me with strength in my soul.
[4] All the kings of the earth shall give thee thanks, O Jehovah,
For they have heard the words of thy mouth.
[5] Yea, they shall sing of the ways of Jehovah;
For great is the glory of Jehovah.
[6] For though Jehovah is high, yet hath he respect unto the lowly;
But the haughty he knoweth from afar.
[7] Though I walk in the midst of trouble, thou wilt revive me;
Thou wilt stretch forth thy hand against the wrath of mine enemies,
And thy right hand will save me.
[8] Jehovah will perfect that which concerneth me:
Thy lovingkindness, O Jehovah, *endureth* for ever;
Forsake not the works of thine own hands.

CXXXIX

GOD'S OMNIPRESENCE AND OMNISCIENCE

For the Chief Musician. A Psalm of David.

[1] O JEHOVAH, thou hast searched me, and known *me*.
[2] Thou knowest my downsitting and mine uprising;
Thou understandest my thought afar off.
[3] Thou searchest[1] out my path and my lying down,
And art acquainted with all my ways.

[1] Or, *winnowest*.

[4] For there is not a word in my tongue,
But, lo, O Jehovah, thou knowest it altogether.
[5] Thou hast beset me behind and before,
And laid thy hand upon me.
[6] *Such* knowledge is too wonderful for me;
It is high, I cannot attain unto it.
[7] Whither shall I go from thy Spirit?
Or whither shall I flee from thy presence?
[8] If I ascend up into heaven, thou art there:
If I make my bed in Sheol, behold, thou art there.
[9] If I take the wings of the morning,
And dwell in the uttermost parts of the sea;
[10] Even there shall thy hand lead me,
And thy right hand shall hold me.
[11] If I say, Surely the darkness shall overwhelm[2] me,
And[3] the light about me shall be night;
[12] Even the darkness hideth not from thee,
But the night shineth as the day:
The darkness and the light are both alike *to thee.*
[13] For thou didst form my inward[4] parts:
Thou didst cover[5] me in my mother's womb.
[14] I will give thanks unto thee; for I am fearfully and wonderfully made:
Wonderful are thy works;
And that my soul knoweth right well.
[15] My frame was not hidden from thee,
When I was made in secret,
And curiously wrought in the lowest parts of the earth.
[16] Thine eyes did see mine unformed substance;
And in thy book they were all written,
Even the days that were ordained *for me,*
When as yet there was none of them.
[17] How precious also are thy thoughts unto me, O God!
How great is the sum of them!

[2] Or, *cover.* [3] Or, *Then the night shall be light about me.* [4] Heb. *reins.*
[5] Or, *knit me together.*

[18] If I should count them, they are more in number than the sand:
When I awake, I am still with thee.
[19] Surely[6] thou wilt slay the wicked, O God:
Depart from me therefore, ye bloodthirsty men.
[20] For they speak[7] against thee wickedly,
And thine enemies take[8] *thy name* in vain.
[21] Do not I hate them, O Jehovah, that hate thee?
And am[9] not I grieved with those that rise up against thee?
[22] I hate them with perfect hatred:
They are become mine enemies.
[23] Search me, O God, and know my heart:
Try me, and know my thoughts;
[24] And see if there be any wicked[10] way in me,
And lead me in the way everlasting.

CXL

Prayer for Protection against the Wicked

For the Chief Musician. A Psalm of David.

[1] Deliver me, O Jehovah, from the evil man;
Preserve me from the violent man:
[2] Who devise mischiefs in their heart;
Continually do they gather[1] themselves together for war.
[3] They have sharpened their tongue like a serpent;
Adders' poison is under their lips. [Selah
[4] Keep me, O Jehovah, from the hands of the wicked;
Preserve me from the violent man:
Who have purposed to thrust aside my steps.
[5] The proud have hid a snare for me, and cords;
They have spread a net by the wayside;
They have set gins for me. [Selah

[6] I said unto Jehovah, Thou art my God:
Give ear unto the voice of my supplications, O Jehovah.

[6] Or, *Oh that thou wouldest slay.* [7] Or, *utter thy name* (Heb. *thee*). Or, as otherwise read, *rebel against thee.* [8] Or, *lift themselves up* against thee *for vanity.*
[9] Or, *do not I loathe.* [10] Or, *way of pain.*
[1] Or, *stir up wars.*

[7] O Jehovah the Lord, the strength of my salvation,
Thou hast covered my head in the day of battle.
[8] Grant not, O Jehovah, the desires of the wicked;
Further not his evil device, *lest* they exalt themselves. [Selah
[9] As for the head of those that compass me about,
Let the mischief of their own lips cover them.
[10] Let burning coals fall upon them:
Let them be cast into the fire,
Into deep[2] pits, whence they shall not rise.
[11] An[3] evil speaker shall not be established in the earth:
Evil shall hunt the violent man to overthrow him.
[12] I know that Jehovah will maintain the cause of the afflicted,
And justice for the needy.
[13] Surely the righteous shall give thanks unto thy name:
The upright shall dwell in thy presence.

CXLI

An Evening Prayer for Sanctification and Protection

A Psalm of David.

[1] Jehovah, I have called upon thee; make haste unto me:
Give ear unto my voice, when I call unto thee.
[2] Let my prayer be set forth as incense before thee;
The lifting up of my hands as the evening sacrifice.[4]
[3] Set a watch, O Jehovah, before my mouth;
Keep the door of my lips.
[4] Incline not my heart to any evil thing,
To practise deeds of wickedness
With men that work iniquity:
And let me not eat of their dainties.
[5] Let the righteous smite me, *it shall be* a kindness;
And let him reprove me, *it shall be as* oil upon the head;
Let not my head refuse it:
For even[5] in their wickedness[6] shall my prayer continue.

[2] Or, *floods.* [3] Heb. *A man of tongue.*
[4] Or, *oblation* [5] Or, *still is my prayer against their wickedness.* [6] Or, *calamities.*

[6] Their judges are thrown down by the sides of the rock;
And they shall hear my words; for they are sweet.
[7] As when one ploweth and cleaveth the earth,
Our bones are scattered at the mouth of Sheol.
[8] For mine eyes are unto thee, O Jehovah the Lord:
In thee do I take refuge; leave[7] not my soul destitute.
[9] Keep me from the snare which they have laid for me,
And from the gins of the workers of iniquity.
[10] Let the wicked fall into their own nets,
Whilst that I withal escape.[8]

CXLII

Prayer for Help in Trouble

Maschil of David, when he was in the cave; a Prayer.

[1] I cry with my voice unto Jehovah;
With my voice unto Jehovah do I make supplication.
[2] I pour out my complaint before him;
I show before him my trouble.
[3] When my spirit was[1] overwhelmed within me,
Thou knewest my path.
In the way wherein I walk
Have they hidden a snare for me.
[4] Look on *my* right hand, and see;
For there is no man that knoweth me:
Refuge hath failed me;
No man careth for my soul.
[5] I cried unto thee, O Jehovah;
I said, thou art my refuge,
My portion in the land of the living.
[6] Attend unto my cry;
For I am brought very low:
Deliver me from any persecutors;
For they are stronger than I.

[7] Or, *pour thou not out my life.* [8] Heb. *pass over.*
[1] Or, *fainted.*

[7] Bring my soul out of prison,
That I may give thanks unto thy name:
The righteous shall compass[2] me about;
For thou wilt deal bountifully with me.

CXLIII

Prayer for Deliverance and Guidance

A Psalm of David.

[1] Hear my prayer, O Jehovah; give ear to my supplications:
In thy faithfulness answer me, *and* in thy righteousness.
[2] And enter not into judgment with thy servant;
For in thy sight no man living is righteous.
[3] For the enemy hath persecuted my soul;
He hath smitten my life down to the ground:
He hath made me to dwell in dark places, as those that have been long dead.
[4] Therefore is[3] my spirit overwhelmed within me;
My heart within me is desolate.
[5] I remember the days of old;
I meditate on all thy doings;
I muse on the work of thy hands.
[6] I spread forth my hands unto thee:
My soul *thirsteth* after thee, as a weary land. [Selah
[7] Make haste to answer me, O Jehovah; my spirit faileth:
Hide not thy face from me,
Lest I become like them that go down into the pit.
[8] Cause me to hear thy lovingkindness in the morning;
For in thee do I trust:
Cause me to know the way wherein I should walk;
For I lift up my soul unto thee.
[9] Deliver me, O Jehovah, from mine enemies:
I[4] flee unto thee to hide me.

[2] Or, *crown themselves because of me.*
[3] Or, *my spirit fainteth.*
[4] Heb. *Unto thee have I hidden.*

[10] Teach me to do thy will;
For thou art my God:
Thy[5] spirit is good;
Lead me in the[6] land of uprightness.
[11] Quicken me, O Jehovah, for thy name's sake:
In thy righteousness bring my soul out of trouble.
[12] And in thy lovingkindness cut off mine enemies,
And destroy all them that afflict my soul;
For I am thy servant.

CXLIV

Prayer for Rescue and Prosperity

A Psalm of David.

[1] Blessed be Jehovah my rock,
Who teacheth my hands to war,
And my fingers to fight:
[2] My lovingkindness, and my fortress,
My high tower, and my deliverer;
My shield, and he in whom I take refuge;
Who subdueth my people under me.
[3] Jehovah, what is man, that thou takest knowledge of him?
Or the son of man, that thou makest account of him?
[4] Man is like to vanity:[1]
His days are as a shadow that passeth away.
[5] Bow thy heavens, O Jehovah, and come down:
Touch the mountains, and they shall smoke.
[6] Cast forth lightning, and scatter them;
Send out thine arrows, and discomfit them.
[7] Stretch forth thy hand from above;
Rescue me, and deliver me out of great waters,
Out of the hand of aliens;
[8] Whose mouth speaketh deceit,
And whose right hand is a right hand of falsehood.

[5] Or, *Let thy good Spirit lead me.* [6] Or, *a plain country.*
[1] Heb. *a breath.*

[9] I will sing a new song unto thee, O God:
Upon a psaltery of ten strings will I sing praises unto thee.
[10] Thou art he that giveth salvation unto kings;
Who rescueth David his servant from the hurtful sword.
[11] Rescue me, and deliver me out of the hand of aliens,
Whose mouth speaketh deceit,
And whose right hand is a right hand of falsehood.

[12] When our sons shall be as plants grown up in their youth,
And our daughters as cornerstones hewn after the fashion of a palace;
[13] *When* our garners are full, affording all manner of store,
And our sheep bring forth thousands and ten thousands in our fields;
[14] *When* our oxen are well laden;
When there is no breaking in, and no going[2] forth,
And no outcry in our streets:
[15] Happy is the people that is in such a case;
Yea, happy is the people whose God is Jehovah.

CXLV

Jehovah Extolled for His Goodness and Power

A Psalm of praise; of David.

[1] I WILL extol thee, my God, O King;
And I will bless thy name for ever and ever.
[2] Every day will I bless thee;
And I will praise thy name for ever and ever.
[3] Great is Jehovah, and greatly to be praised;
And his greatness is unsearchable.
[4] One generation shall laud thy works to another,
And shall declare thy mighty acts.
[5] Of the glorious majesty of thine honor,
And of thy wondrous works, will I meditate.
[6] And men shall speak of the might of thy terrible acts;
And I will declare thy greatness.
[7] They shall utter the memory of thy great goodness,
And shall sing of thy righteousness.

[2] Or, *sallying*.

[8] Jehovah is gracious, and merciful;
Slow to anger, and of great lovingkindness.
[9] Jehovah is good to all;
And his tender mercies are over all his works.
[10] All thy works shall give thanks unto thee. O Jehovah;
And thy saints shall bless thee.
[11] They shall speak of the glory of thy kingdom,
And talk of thy power;
[12] To make known to the sons of men his mighty acts,
And the glory of the majesty of his kingdom.
[13] Thy kingdom is an everlasting kingdom,
And thy dominion *endureth* throughout all generations.
[14] Jehovah upholdeth all that fall,
And raiseth up all those that are bowed down.
[15] The eyes of all wait for thee;
And thou givest them their food in due season.
[16] Thou openest thy hand,
And satisfiest[1] the desire of every living thing.
[17] Jehovah is righteous in all his ways,
And gracious in all his works.
[18] Jehovah is nigh unto all them that call upon him,
To all that call upon him in truth.
[19] He will fulfil the desire of them that fear him;
He also will hear their cry, and will save them.
[20] Jehovah preserveth all them that love him;
But all the wicked will he destroy.
[21] My mouth shall speak the praise of Jehovah;
And let all flesh bless his holy name for ever and ever.

CXLVI

Praise to Jehovah the Abundant Helper

[1] Praise[2] ye Jehovah.
Praise Jehovah, O my soul.
[2] While I live will I praise Jehovah:
I will sing praises unto my God while I have any being.

[1] Or, *satisfiest every living thing with favor.*
[2] Heb. *Hallelujah.*

[3] Put not your trust in princes,
Nor in the son of man, in whom there is no help.
[4] His breath goeth forth, he returneth to his earth;
In that very day his thoughts[3] perish.
[5] Happy is he that hath the God of Jacob for his help,
Whose hope is in Jehovah his God:
[6] Who made heaven and earth,
The sea, and all that in them is;
Who keepeth truth for ever;
[7] Who executeth justice for the oppressed;
Who giveth food to the hungry.
Jehovah looseth the prisoners;
[8] Jehovah openeth *the eyes of* the blind;
Jehovah raiseth up them that are bowed down;
Jehovah loveth the righteous;
[9] Jehovah preserveth the sojourners;
He upholdeth the fatherless and widow;
But the way of the wicked he turneth[4] upside down.
[10] Jehovah will reign for ever,
Thy God, O Zion, unto all generations.
Praise[2] ye Jehovah.

CXLVII

Praise for Jehovah's Restoration and Prosperity

[1] Praise[2] ye Jehovah;
For[5] it is good to sing praises unto our God;
For it is pleasant, *and* praise is comely.
[2] Jehovah doth build up Jerusalem;
He gathereth together the outcasts of Israel.
[3] He healeth the broken in heart,
And bindeth up their wounds.[6]
[4] He counteth the number of the stars;
He calleth them all by *their* names.

[3] Or, *purposes.* [4] Or, *maketh crooked.*
[2] Heb. *Hallelujah.*
[5] Or, *For he is good: sing praises unto our God; For he is gracious.*
[6] Heb. *sorrows.*

[5] Great is our Lord, and mighty in power;
His understanding is infinite.
[6] Jehovah upholdeth the meek:
He bringeth the wicked down to the ground.
[7] Sing unto Jehovah with thanksgiving;
Sing praises upon the harp unto our God:
[8] Who covereth the heavens with clouds,
Who prepareth rain for the earth,
Who maketh grass to grow upon the mountains.
[9] He giveth to the beast his food,
And to the young ravens which cry.
[10] He delighteth not in the strength of the horse:
He taketh no pleasure in the legs of a man.
[11] Jehovah taketh pleasure in them that fear him,
In those that hope in his lovingkindness.
[12] Praise Jehovah, O Jerusalem;
Praise thy God, O Zion.
[13] For he hath strengthened the bars of thy gates;
He hath blessed thy children within thee.
[14] He maketh peace[7] in thy borders;
He filleth thee with the finest[8] of the wheat.
[15] He sendeth out his commandment upon earth;
His word runneth very swiftly.
[16] He giveth snow like wool;
He scattereth the hoar-frost like ashes.
[17] He casteth forth his ice like morsels:
Who can stand before his cold?
[18] He sendeth out his word, and melteth them:
He causeth his wind to blow, and the waters flow.
[19] He showeth his word unto Jacob,
His statutes and his ordinances unto Israel.
[20] He hath not dealt so with any nation:
And as for his ordinances, they have not known them.
Praise[2] ye Jehovah.

[7] Heb. *thy border peace.* [8] Heb. *fat of wheat.*
[2] Heb. *Hallelujah.*

CXLVIII

The Whole Creation Invoked to Praise Jehovah

[1] Praise[1] ye Jehovah.
Praise ye Jehovah from the heavens:
Praise him in the heights.
[2] Praise ye him, all his angels:
Praise ye him, all his host.
[3] Praise ye him, sun and moon:
Praise him, all ye stars of light.
[4] Praise him, ye heavens of heavens,
And ye waters that are above the heavens.
[5] Let them praise the name of Jehovah;
For he commandeth, and they were created.
[6] He hath also established them for ever and ever:
He hath made a decree which[2] shall not pass away.
[7] Praise Jehovah from the earth,
Ye sea-monsters, and all deeps;
[8] Fire and hail, snow and vapor;
Stormy wind, fulfilling his word;
[9] Mountains and all hills;
Fruitful trees and all cedars;
[10] Beasts and all cattle;
Creeping things and flying birds;
[11] Kings of the earth and all peoples;
Princes and all judges of the earth;
[12] Both young men and virgins;
Old men and children:
[13] Let them praise the name of Jehovah;
For his name alone is exalted;
His glory is above the earth and the heavens.
[14] And he hath lifted up the[3] horn of his people,
The praise of all his saints;
Even of the children of Israel, a people near unto him.
Praise[1] ye Jehovah.

[1] Heb. *Hallelujah.*
[2] Or, *which none shall transgress.* [3] Or, *a horn for his people, A praise for all his saints; Even for &c.*

CXLIX

Israel Invoked to Praise Jehovah

[1] Praise[1] ye Jehovah.
Sing unto Jehovah a new song,
And his praise in the assembly of the saints.
[2] Let Israel rejoice in him that made him:
Let the children of Zion be joyful in their King.
[3] Let them praise his name in the dance:
Let them sing praises unto him with timbrel and harp.
[4] For Jehovah taketh pleasure in his people:
He will beautify the meek with salvation.[2]
[5] Let the saints exult in glory:
Let them sing for joy upon their beds.
[6] *Let* the high praises of God *be* in their mouth,[3]
And a two-edged sword in their hand;
[7] To execute vengeance upon the nations,
And punishments upon the peoples;
[8] To bind their kings with chains,
And their nobles with fetters of iron;
[9] To execute upon them the judgment written:
This[4] honor have all his saints.
Praise[1] ye Jehovah.

CL

A Psalm of Praise

[1] Praise[1] ye Jehovah.
Praise God in his sanctuary:
Praise him in the firmament of his power.
[2] Praise him for his mighty acts:
Praise him according to his excellent greatness.
[3] Praise him with trumpet sound:
Praise him with psaltery and harp.

[2] Or, *victory.* [3] Heb. *throat.* [4] Or, *He is the honor of all his saints.*
[1] Heb. *Hallelujah.*

[4] Praise him with timbrel and dance:
Praise him with stringed instruments and pipe.
[5] Praise him with loud cymbals:
Praise him with high sounding cymbals.
[6] Let every thing that hath breath praise Jehovah.[5]
Praise[1] ye Jehovah.

[5] Heb. *Jah.*

(HEBREW)

ECCLESIASTES

OR, THE PREACHER

INTRODUCTORY NOTE

THE Book of Ecclesiastes, in Hebrew, "Koheleth," is now generally regarded by scholars as of late date, perhaps about the third century before Christ. The ascription of the authorship to Solomon in the opening sentence was probably meant merely as a literary device, Solomon being chosen as a pre-eminent type of the man who had had opportunity to test all that life has to offer. Of the actual author nothing is known.

The general spirit of the work is despondent, even pessimistic. The opening sentences strike the keynote; and though the book contains many contradictions, there is no question as to its prevailing tone. Nowhere else in the Old Testament is there such insistence on the futility of human endeavor, such cold-blooded proclaiming of the vanity of the attempts of man to dignify his existence. Yet the book has, as has been said, many inconsistencies; and it closes with an epilogue so different from the general tone and, in some respects, so contrary to it, that the hypothesis of a plurality of authors has naturally been proposed. Even those who interpret the contradictions in the body of the work as expressions of the varying moods of one author, grant, as a rule, that the epilogue (XII, 9–14) is a later addition; while others account for such opposite views as are found, for example in VIII, 12–13 and VIII, 14, as due to the insertion of protests by some more orthodox and pious writer.

However these things are to be explained, the book is one of the great utterances of that mood of despair which the perplexities of life, and the weariness of struggle or satiety, cause to descend at times upon the human spirit in all epochs and under all civilizations. Its religious value has often been debated; there is no question as to its standing as literature.

ECCLESIASTES

OR, THE PREACHER

[1] I

THE words of the[1] Preacher, the son of David, king in
Jerusalem.
[2] Vanity of vanities, saith the Preacher; vanity of vanities, all is vanity. [3] What profit hath man of all his labor wherein
he laboreth under the sun? [4] One generation goeth, and another
generation cometh; but the earth abideth for ever. [5] The sun also
ariseth, and the sun goeth down, and hasteth to its place where it
ariseth. [6] The wind goeth toward the south, and turneth about
unto the north; it turneth about continually in its course, and the
wind returneth again to its circuits. [7] All the rivers[2] run into the
sea, yet the sea is not full; unto the place whither the rivers go,
thither they go again. [8] All[3] things are full of weariness; man
cannot utter *it:* the eye is not satisfied with seeing, nor the ear filled
with hearing. [9] That which hath been is that which shall be; and
that which hath been done is that which shall be done: and there
is no new thing under the sun. [10] Is there a thing whereof it may
be said, See, this is new? it hath been long ago, in the ages which
were before us. [11] There is no remembrance of the former *generations;* neither shall there be any remembrance of the latter *generations* that are to come, among those that shall come after.

[12] I the Preacher was king over Israel in Jerusalem. [13] And
I applied my heart to seek and to search out by wisdom concerning
all that is done under heaven: it is a sore travail that God hath given
to the sons of men to be exercised therewith. [14] I have seen all
the works that are done under the sun; and, behold, all is vanity and
a[4] striving after wind. [15] That which is crooked cannot be made

[1] Heb. *Koheleth.* [2] Or, *torrents.* [3] Or, *All words are feeble.*
[4] Or, *a feeding on wind* (see Hos. 12. 1). Or, *vexation of spirit* (and so elsewhere).

straight; and that[5] which is wanting cannot be numbered. [16] I
communed with mine own heart, saying, Lo, I have gotten me great
wisdom above[6] all that were before me in[7] Jerusalem; yea, my heart
hath[8] had great experience of wisdom and knowledge. [17] And I
applied my heart to know wisdom, and to know madness and folly:
I perceived that this also was a striving after wind. [18] For in
much wisdom is much grief; and he that increaseth knowledge
increaseth sorrow.

II

[1] I SAID in my heart, Come now, I will prove thee with mirth;
therefore[9] enjoy pleasure:[10] and, behold, this also was vanity. [2] I
said of laughter, It is mad; and of mirth, What doeth it? [3]
I searched in my heart how to cheer my flesh with wine, my heart
yet guiding[11] *me* with wisdom, and how to lay hold on folly, till I
might see what it was good for the sons of men that they should
do under heaven all[12] the days of their life. [4] I made me great
works; I builded me houses; I planted me vineyards; [5] I made
me gardens and parks, and I planted trees in them of all kinds of
fruit; [6] I made me pools of water, to water therefrom the forest
where trees were reared; [7] I bought men-servants and maidservants, and had servants born in my house; also I had great possessions of herds and flocks, above all that were before me in Jerusalem;
[8] I gathered me also silver and gold, and the treasure of kings
and of the provinces; I gat me men-singers and women-singers, and
the delights of the sons of men, musical[13] instruments, and that of
all sorts. [9] So I was great, and increased more than all that were
before me in Jerusalem: also my wisdom remained[14] with me. [10]
And whatsoever mine eyes desired I kept not from them; I withheld not my heart from any joy; for my heart rejoiced because of
all my labor; and this was my portion from all my labor. [11] Then
I looked on all the works that my hands had wrought, and on the
labor that I had labored to do; and, behold, all was vanity and a
striving after wind, and there was no profit under the sun.

[5] Heb. *defect.* [6] Or, *yea, more than all.* [7] Heb. *over.* [8] Heb. *hath seen abundantly.*

[9] Or, *and thou shalt enjoy.* [10] Or, *good.* [11] Or, *holding its course.* [12] Heb. *the number of days of their life.* [13] Or, *concubines very many.* The meaning of the Hebrew is very uncertain. [14] Or, *stood by me.*

[12] And I turned myself to behold wisdom, and madness, and folly: for what *can* the man *do* that cometh after[15] the king? *even* that which hath been done long ago. [13] Then I saw that wisdom excelleth folly, as far as light excelleth darkness. [14] The wise man's eyes are in his head, and the fool walketh in darkness: and yet I perceived that one event happeneth to them all. [15] Then said I in my heart, As it happeneth to the fool, so will it happen even to me; and why was I then more wise? Then said I in my heart, that this also is vanity. [16] For of the wise man, even as of the fool, there is no remembrance for ever; seeing that in the days to come all will have been long forgotten. And how doth the wise man die even as the fool! [17] So I hated life, because the work that is wrought under the sun was grievous unto me; for all is vanity and a striving after wind.

[18] And I hated all my labor wherein I labored under the sun, seeing that I must leave it unto the man that shall be after me. [19] And who knoweth whether he will be a wise man or a fool? yet will he have rule over all my labor wherein I have labored, and wherein I have showed myself wise under the sun. This also is vanity. [20] Therefore I turned about to cause my heart to despair concerning all the labor wherein I had labored under the sun. [21] For there is a man whose labor is with wisdom, and with knowledge, and with skilfulness;[16] yet to a man that hath not labored therein shall he leave[17] it for his portion. This also is vanity and a great evil. [22] For what hath a man of all his labor, and of the striving[18] of his heart, wherein he laboreth under the sun? [23] For all his days are *but* sorrows, and his travail is grief; yea, even in the night his heart taketh no rest. This also is vanity.

[24] There is nothing better for a man *than* that he should eat and drink, and make his soul enjoy good in his labor. This also I saw, that it is from the hand of God. [25] For who can eat, or who can have[19] enjoyment, more[20] than I? [26] For to the man that pleaseth him *God* giveth wisdom, and knowledge, and joy; but to the sinner he giveth travail, to gather and to heap up, that he may

[15] Or, *after the king, even him whom they made king long ago?* Or, *after the king, in those things which have been already done?*

[16] Or, *success.* [17] Heb. *give.*

[18] Or, *vexation.* [19] Or, *hasten* thereto. [20] Acc. to Sept. and Syr. *apart from him.*

give to him that pleaseth God. This also is vanity and a striving after wind.

III

[1] For every thing there is a season, and a time for every purpose[1] under heaven: [2] a time to be born, and a time to die; a time to plant, and a time to pluck up that which is planted; [3] a time to kill, and a time to heal; a time to break down, and a time to build up; [4] a time to weep, and a time to laugh; a time to mourn, and a time to dance; [5] a time to cast away stones, and a time to gather stones together; a time to embrace, and a time to refrain from embracing; [6] a time to seek, and a time to lose; a time to keep, and a time to cast away; [7] a time to rend, and a time to sew; a time to keep silence, and a time to speak; [8] a time to love, and a time to hate; a time for war, and a time for peace. [9] What profit hath he that worketh in that wherein he laboreth? [10] I have seen the travail which God hath given to the sons of men to be exercised therewith. [11] He hath made every thing beautiful in its time: also he hath set eternity[2] in their heart, yet so that man cannot find out the work that God hath done from the beginning even to the end. [12] I know that there is nothing better for them, than to rejoice, and to[3] do good so long as they live. [13] And also that every man should eat and drink, and enjoy good in all his labor, is the gift of God. [14] I know that, whatsoever God doeth, it shall be for ever: nothing can be put to it, nor anything taken from it; and God hath done it, that men should fear before him. [15] That[4] which is hath been long ago; and that which is to be hath long ago been: and God seeketh again that which is passed[5] away.

[16] And moreover I saw under the sun, in the place of justice, that wickedness was there; and in the place of righteousness, that wickedness was there. [17] I said in my heart, God will judge the righteous and the wicked; for there is a time there for every purpose[6] and for every work. [18] I[7] said in my heart, *It is* because of the sons of men, that God may prove them, and that they may see that they themselves are *but as* beasts. [19] For that which befalleth

1 Or, *matter.* 2 Or, *the world.* 3 Or, *to get good.*
4 Or, *That which hath been is now.* 5 Heb. *driven away.* 6 Or, *matter.*
7 Or, *I said in my heart concerning the sons of men.* It is *that God &c.*

the sons of men befalleth beasts; even one thing befalleth them: as the one dieth, so dieth the other; yea, they have all one breath;[8] and man hath no preeminence above the beasts: for all is vanity. [20] All go unto one place; all are of the dust, and all turn to dust again. [21] Who knoweth the spirit of[9] man, whether[10] it goeth upward, and the spirit of the beast, whether[10] it goeth downward to the earth? [22] Wherefore I saw that there is nothing better, than that a man should rejoice in his works; for that is his portion: for who shall bring him *back* to see what shall be after him?

IV

[1] THEN I returned and saw all the oppressions that are done under the sun: and, behold, the tears of such as were oppressed, and they had no comforter; and on the side of their oppressors there was power; but they had no comforter. [2] Wherefore I praised the dead that have been long dead more than the living that are yet alive; [3] yea, better[1] than them both *did I esteem* him that hath not yet been, who hath not seen the evil work that is done under the sun.

[4] Then I saw all labor and every skilful[2] work, that for[3] this a man is envied of his neighbor. This also is vanity and a striving after wind. [5] The fool foldeth his hands together, and eateth his own flesh. [6] Better is a handful, with[4] quietness, than two handfuls with[4] labor and striving after wind.

[7] Then I returned and saw vanity under the sun. [8] There is one that is alone, and he hath not a second; yea, he hath neither son nor brother; yet is there no end of all his labor, neither are his eyes satisfied with riches. For whom then, *saith he,* do I labor, and deprive my soul of good? This also is vanity, yea, it is a sore travail. [9] Two are better than one; because they have a good reward for their labor. [10] For if they fall, the one will lift up his fellow; but woe to him that is alone when he falleth, and hath not another to lift him up. [11] Again, if two lie together, then they have warmth; but how can one be warm *alone?* [12] And if a man prevail against

[8] Or, spirit. [9] Heb. *of the sons of men.* [10] Or, *that goeth.*
[1] Or, *better than they both is he that &c.*
[2] Or, *successful.* [3] Or, *it cometh of a man's rivalry with his neighbor.* [4] Or, *of.*

him that is alone, two shall withstand him; and a threefold cord is not quickly broken.

[13] Better is a poor and wise youth than an old and foolish king, who knoweth not how to receive admonition any more. [14] For out of prison he came forth to be king; yea, even in his kingdom he was born poor. [15] I saw all the living that walk under the sun, that they were with the youth, the second, that stood up in his stead. [16] There[5] was no end of all the people, even of all them over whom he was: yet they that come after shall not rejoice in him. Surely this also is vanity and a striving after wind.

V

[1] KEEP thy foot when thou goest to the house of God; for to draw nigh to hear is better than to give the sacrifice of fools: for they know not that they do evil. [2] Be not rash with thy mouth, and let not thy heart be hasty to utter any[6] thing before God; for God is in heaven, and thou upon earth: therefore let thy words be few. [3] For a dream cometh with a multitude of business,[7] and a fool's voice with a multitude of words. [4] When thou vowest a vow unto God, defer not to pay it; for he hath no pleasure in fools: pay that which thou vowest. [5] Better is it that thou shouldest not vow, than that thou shouldest vow and not pay. [6] Suffer not thy mouth to cause thy flesh to sin; neither say thou before the angel,[8] that it was an error: wherefore should God be angry at thy voice, and destroy the work of thy hands? [7] For in the multitude of dreams there are vanities, and in many words: but fear thou God.

[8] If thou seest the oppression of the poor, and the violent taking away of justice and righteousness in a[9] province, marvel not at the matter: for one higher than the high regardeth; and there are higher than they. [9] Moreover[10] the profit of the earth is for all: the king *himself* is served by the field.

[10] He that loveth silver shall not be satisfied with silver; nor he that loveth abundance, with increase: this also is vanity. [11] When goods increase, they are increased that eat them; and what

[5] Or, *There is no end, in the mind of all the people, to all that hath been before them; they also &c.* [6] Or, *a word.* [7] Or, *travail.* [8] Or, *messenger* of God. See Mal. 2. 7. [9] Or, *the state.* [10] Or, *But the profit of a land every way is a king that maketh himself servant to the field* (or, *is a king over the cultivated field*).

advantage is there to the owner thereof, save the beholding *of them* with his eyes? [12] The sleep of a laboring man is sweet, whether he eat little or much; but the fulness of the rich will not suffer him to sleep.

[13] There is a grievous evil which I have seen under the sun, *namely,* riches kept by the owner thereof to his hurt: [14] and those riches perish by evil adventure;[2] and if he hath begotten a son, there is nothing in his hand. [15] As he came forth from his mother's womb, naked shall he go again as he came, and shall take nothing for his labor, which he may carry away in his hand. [16] And this also is a grievous evil, that in all points as he came, so shall he go: and what profit hath he that he laboreth for the wind? [17] All his days also he eateth in darkness, and he is sore vexed, and hath sickness and wrath.

[18] Behold, that[11] which I have seen to be good and to be comely is for one to eat and to drink, and to enjoy good in all his labor, wherein he laboreth under the sun, all[12] the days of his life which God hath given him: for this is his portion. [19] Every man also to whom God hath given riches and wealth, and hath given him power to eat thereof, and to take his portion, and to rejoice in his labor,—this is the gift of God. [20] For he shall not much remember the days of his life; because God answereth *him* in the joy of his heart.

VI

[1] THERE is an evil which I have seen under the sun, and it is heavy upon men: [2] a man to whom God giveth riches, wealth, and honor, so that he lacketh nothing for his soul of all that he desireth, yet God giveth him not power to eat thereof, but an alien eateth it; this is vanity, and it is an evil disease. [3] If a man beget a hundred children, and live many years, so that the days of his years are many, but his soul be not filled with good, and moreover he have no burial; I say, that an untimely birth is better than he: [4] for it cometh in vanity, and departeth in darkness, and the name thereof is covered with darkness; [5] moreover it hath not seen the

[2] Or, *travail.* [11] Or, *that which I have seen: it is good and comely for one &c.*
[12] Heb. *the number of the days.*

sun nor[1] known it; this[2] hath rest rather than the other: [6] yea, though he live a thousand years twice told, and yet enjoy no good, do not all go to one place?

[7] All the labor of man is for his mouth, and yet the appetite is not filled. [8] For what advantage hath the wise more than the fool? *or*[3] what hath the poor man, that knoweth how to walk before the living? [9] Better is the sight of the eyes than the wandering of the desire: this also is vanity and a striving after wind.

[10] Whatsoever[4] hath been, the name thereof was given long ago; and it is known what man[5] is; neither can he contend with him that is mightier than he. [11] Seeing there are many things[6] that increase vanity, what is man the better? [12] For who knoweth what is good for man in *his* life, all[7] the days of his vain life which he spendeth as a shadow? for who can tell a man what shall be after him under the sun?

VII

[1] A *good* name is better than precious oil; and the day of death, than the day of one's birth. [2] It is better to go to the house of mourning than to go to the house of feasting: for that is the end of all men; and the living will lay it to his heart. [3] Sorrow is better than laughter: for by the sadness of the countenance the heart is made glad.[8] [4] The heart of the wise is in the house of mourning; but the heart of fools is in the house of mirth.

[5] It is better to hear the rebuke of the wise, than for a man to hear the song of fools. [6] For as the crackling of thorns under a pot, so is the laughter of the fool: this also is vanity. [7] Surely[9] extortion maketh the wise man foolish; and a bribe destroyeth the understanding.

[8] Better is the end of a thing than the beginning thereof; *and* the patient in spirit is better than the proud in spirit. [9] Be not hasty in thy spirit to be angry;[10] for anger[11] resteth in the bosom of fools. [10] Say not thou, What is the cause that the former days

[1] Or, *neither had any knowledge.* [2] Or, *it is better with this than with the other.*
[3] Or, or *the poor man that hath understanding, in walking before the living.*
[4] Or, *Whatsoever he be, his name was given him long ago, and it is known that he is man.* [5] Heb. *Adam.* See Gen. 2. 7. [6] Or, *words.* [7] Heb. *the number of the days.*
[8] Or, *better.* [9] Or, *For.* [10] Or, *vexed.* [11] Or, *vexation.*

were better than these? for thou dost not inquire wisely[12] concerning this.

[11] Wisdom is[13] as good as an inheritance; yea, more excellent is it for them that see the sun. [12] For wisdom is a defence, even as money is a defence; but the excellency of knowledge is, that wisdom preserveth the life of him that hath it. [13] Consider the work of God: for who can make that straight, which he hath made crooked? [14] In the day of prosperity be joyful, and in the day of adversity consider; yea, God hath made the one side by side with the other, to the end that man should not find out any thing *that shall be* after him.

[15] All this have I seen in my days of vanity: there is a righteous man that perisheth in his righteousness, and there is a wicked man that prolongeth *his life* in his evil-doing. [16] Be not righteous overmuch; neither make thyself overwise: why shouldest thou destroy thyself? [17] Be not overmuch wicked, neither be thou foolish: why shouldest thou die before thy time? [18] It is good that thou shouldest take hold of this; yea, also from that withdraw not thy hand: for he that feareth God shall come forth from them all.

[19] Wisdom is a strength to the wise man more than ten rulers that are in a city. [20] Surely[2] there is not a righteous man upon earth, that doeth good, and sinneth not. [21] Also take[14] not heed unto all words that are spoken, lest thou hear thy servant curse thee; [22] for oftentimes also thine own heart knoweth that thou thyself likewise hast cursed others.

[23] All this have I proved[15] in wisdom: I said, I will be wise; but it was far from me. [24] That which is,[16] is far off and exceeding deep; who can find it out? [25] I turned about, and my heart *was set* to know and to search out, and to seek wisdom and the reason *of things,* and to know that[17] wickedness is folly, and that foolishness is madness. [26] And I find more bitter than death the woman whose[18] heart is snares and nets, *and* whose hands are bands: whoso pleaseth God shall escape from her; but the sinner shall be

[12] Heb. *out of wisdom.* [13] Or, *is good together with an inheritance, and profitable unto them &c.* [14] Heb. *give not thy heart.* [15] Or, *tried by.* [16] Or, *hath been.*

[17] Or, *the wickedness of folly, and foolishness* which is *madness.*

[18] Or, *who is a snare, and her heart is* as *nets.*

taken by her. [27] Behold, this have I found, saith the Preacher, *laying*[19] one thing to another, to find out the account; [28] which my soul still seeketh, but I have not found: one man among a thousand have I found; but a women among all those have I not found. [29] Behold, this only have I found: that God made man upright; but they have sought out many inventions.

VIII

[1] WHO is as the wise man? and who knoweth the interpretation of a thing? A man's wisdom maketh his face to shine, and the hardness[1] of his face is changed. [2] I *counsel thee,* Keep the king's command, and that in regard of the oath of God. [3] Be not hasty to go out of his presence; persist not in an evil thing: for he doeth whatsoever pleaseth him. [4] For the king's word *hath* power; and who may say unto him, What doest thou? [5] Whoso keepeth the commandment shall know no evil thing; and a wise man's heart discerneth time and judgment: [6] for to every purpose[2] there is a time and judgment; because the misery[3] of man is great upon him: [7] for he knoweth not that which shall be; for[4] who can tell him how it shall be? [8] There is no man that hath power over the spirit[5] to retain the spirit;[5] neither hath he power over the day of death; and there is no discharge in[6] war: neither shall wickedness deliver him that is given to it.

[9] All this have I seen, and applied my heart unto every work that is done under the sun: *there*[7] *is* a time wherein one man hath power over another to[8] his hurt. [10] So I saw the wicked buried, and[9] they came *to the grave;* and they that had done right went away from the holy place, and were forgotten in the city: this also is vanity. [11] Because sentence against an evil work is not executed speedily, therefore the heart of the sons of men is fully[10] set in them to do evil. [12] Though a sinner do evil a hundred times, and prolong his *days,* yet surely I know that it shall be well with them that

[19] Or, weighing *one thing after another, to find out the reason.*
[1] Heb. *strength.* [2] Or, *matter.* [3] Or, *evil.*
[4] Or, *for* even *when it cometh to pass, who shall declare it unto him?*
[5] Or, *wind.* [6] Or, *in battle.* [7] Or, *what time one man had &c.*
[8] Or, *to his own hurt.* [9] Or, *who had come and gone away from the holy place; and they were forgotten in the city where they had so done.* Or, *and men came and went &c.* [10] Or, *emboldened.*

fear God, that fear before him: [13] but it shall not be well with the wicked, neither shall he prolong *his* days, *which are* as a shadow; because he feareth not before God.

[14] There is a vanity which is done upon the earth, that there are righteous men unto whom it happeneth according to the work of the wicked; again, there are wicked men to whom it happeneth according to the work of the righteous: I said that this also is vanity. [15] Then I commended mirth, because a man hath no better thing under the sun, than to eat, and to drink, and to be joyful: for[11] that shall abide with him in his labor *all* the days of his life which God hath given him under the sun.

[16] When I applied my heart to know wisdom, and to see the business[12] that is done upon the earth, (for[13] also there is that neither day nor night seeth sleep with his eyes), [17] then I beheld all the work of God, that man cannot find out the work that is done under the sun: because however much a man labor to seek it out, yet he shall not find it; yea moreover, though a wise man think to know it, yet shall he not be able to find it.

IX

[1] For all this I laid to my heart, even to explore all this: that the righteous, and the wise, and their works, are in the hand of God; whether it be love or hatred, man knoweth it not; all is before them.

[2] All things come alike to all: there is one event to the righteous and to the wicked; to the good and to the clean and to the unclean; to him that sacrificeth and to him that sacrificeth not; as is the good, so is the sinner; *and* he that sweareth, as he that feareth an oath. [3] This is an evil in all that is done under the sun, that there is one even unto all: yea also, the heart of the sons of men is full of evil, and madness is in their heart while they live, and after that *they go* to the dead. [4] For[1] to him that is joined with all the living there is hope; for a living dog is better than a dead lion. [5] For the living know that they shall die: but the dead know not any thing, neither

[11] Or, *and that this should accompany him.* [12] Or, *travail.*

[13] Or, *how that neither by day nor by night do men see sleep with their eyes.*

[1] Another reading is, *For who is exempted? With all &c.*, or, *who can choose? With all &c.*

have they any more a reward; for the memory of them is forgotten. [6] As well their love, as their hatred and their envy, is perished long ago; neither have they any more a portion for ever in any thing that is done under the sun.

[7] Go thy way, eat thy bread with joy, and drink thy wine with a merry heart; for God hath already accepted thy works. [8] Let thy garments be always white; and let not thy head lack oil. [9] Live[2] joyfully with the wife whom thou lovest all the days of thy life of vanity, which he hath given thee under the sun, all thy days of vanity: for that is thy portion in life, and in thy labor wherein thou laborest under the sun. [10] Whatsoever thy hand findeth[3] to do, do *it* with thy might; for there is no work, nor device, nor knowledge, nor wisdom, in Sheol, whither thou goest.

[11] I returned, and saw under the sun, that the race is not to the swift, nor the battle to the strong, neither yet bread to the wise, nor yet riches to men of understanding, nor yet favor to men of skill; but time and chance happeneth to them all. [12] For man also knoweth not his time: as the fishes that are taken in an evil net, and as the birds that are caught in the snare, even so are the sons of men snared in an evil time, when it falleth suddenly upon them.

[13] I have also seen wisdom under the sun on this wise, and it seemed great unto me: [14] There was a little city, and few men within it; and there came a great king against it, and besieged it, and built great bulwarks against it: [15] Now there was found in it a poor wise man, and he by his wisdom delivered the city; yet no man remembered that same poor man. [16] Then said I, Wisdom is better than strength: nevertheless the poor man's wisdom is despised, and his words are not heard.

[17] The words of the wise heard in quiet are better than the cry of him that ruleth among fools. [18] Wisdom is better than weapons of war; but one sinner destroyeth much good.

X

[1] DEAD flies cause the oil of the perfumer to[4] send forth an evil odor; *so* doth a little folly outweigh[5] wisdom and honor. [2] A wise

[2] Or, *Enjoy* (Heb. *See*) *life*. [3] Or, *attaineth to do by thy strength,* that *do*.
[4] Or, *to stink and putrefy*. [5] Or, *him that is valued for wisdom*.

man's heart is at his right hand; but a fool's heart at his left. [3] Yea also, when the fool walketh by the way, his understanding[6] faileth him, and he saith to[7] every one *that* he is a fool. [4] If the spirit of the ruler rise up against thee, leave not thy place; for gentleness[8] allayeth great offences.

[5] There is an evil which I have seen under the sun, as it were an error which proceedeth from the ruler: [6] folly is set in great dignity,[9] and the rich sit in a low place. [7] I have seen servants upon horses, and princes walking like servants upon the earth.

[8] He that diggeth a pit shall fall into it; and whoso breaketh through a wall, a serpent shall bite him. [9] Whoso heweth[10] out stones shall be hurt therewith; *and* he that cleaveth wood is endangered thereby. [10] If the iron be blunt, and one do not whet the edge, then must he put to more strength: but wisdom is profitable to direct. [11] If[11] the serpent bite before[12] it is charmed, then is there no advantage in the[13] charmer.

[12] The words of a wise man's mouth are gracious; but the lips of a fool will swallow up himself. [13] The beginning of the words of his mouth is foolishness; and the end of his[14] talk is mischievous madness. [14] A fool also multiplieth words: *yet* man knoweth not what shall be; and that which shall be after him, who can tell him? [15] The labor of fools wearieth every one of them; for he knoweth not how to go to the city.

[16] Woe to thee, O land, when thy king is a child,[15] and thy princes eat in the morning! [17] Happy art thou, O land, when thy king is the[16] son of nobles, and thy princes eat in due season, for strength, and not for drunkenness! [18] By slothfulness the roof[17] sinketh in; and through idleness of the hands the house leaketh. [19] A feast is made for laughter, and wine maketh glad the life; and money answereth all things. [20] Revile not the king, no, not in thy thought; and revile not the rich in thy bed-chamber: for a bird of the heavens shall carry the voice, and that which hath wings shall tell the matter.

[6] Heb. *heart.* [7] Or, *of.* [8] Or, *calmness leaveth great sins undone.*
[9] Heb. *heights.* [10] Or, *moveth stones.* [11] Or, *Surely the serpent will bite where there is no enchantment; and the slanderer is no better.*
[12] Heb. *without enchantment.* [13] Heb. *the master of the tongue.* [14] Heb. *his mouth.* [15] Or, *servant.* [16] Or, *a free man.* [17] Or, *rafters sink.*

XI

[1] Cast[1] thy bread upon[2] the waters; for thou shalt find it after
many days. [2] Give[3] a portion to seven, yea, even unto eight; for
thou knowest not what evil shall be upon the earth. [3] If the
clouds be full of rain, they empty themselves upon the earth; and if
a tree fall toward[4] the south, or toward[4] the north, in the place where
the tree falleth, there shall it be. [4] He that observeth the wind
shall not sow; and he that regardeth the clouds shall not reap. [5]
As thou knowest not what is the way of the wind,[5] *nor* how the
bones *do grow* in the womb of her that is with child; even so thou
knowest not the work of God who doeth all. [6] In the morning
sow thy seed, and in the evening withhold not thy hand; for thou
knowest not which shall prosper, whether this or that, or whether
they both shall be alike good. [7] Truly the light is sweet, and a
pleasant thing it is for the eyes to behold the sun. [8] Yea,[6] if a
man live many years, let him rejoice in them all; but[7] let him
remember the days of darkness, for they shall be many. All that
cometh is vanity.

[9] Rejoice, O young man, in thy youth, and let thy heart cheer
thee in the days of thy youth, and walk in the ways of thy heart,
and in the sight of thine eyes; but know thou, that for all these
things God will bring thee into judgment. [10] Therefore remove
sorrow[8] from thy heart, and put away evil from thy flesh; for youth
and the dawn of life are vanity.

XII

[1] Remember also thy Creator in the days of thy youth, before
the evil days come, and the years draw nigh, when thou shalt say,
I have no pleasure in them; [2] before the sun, and the light, and
the moon, and the stars, are darkened, and the clouds return after
the rain; [3] in the day when the keepers of the house shall tremble,
and the strong men shall bow themselves, and the grinders[9] cease
because they are few, and those that look out of the windows shall

[1] Or, *Send forth.* [2] Heb. *upon the face of the waters.* [3] Or, *Divide a portion into seven, yea, even into eight.* [4] Or, *in.* [5] Or, *spirit.* [6] Or, *For.*
[7] Or, *and remember.* [8] Or, *vexation.* Or, *provocation.* [9] Or, *grinding women.*

be darkened, [4] and the doors shall be shut in the street; when the
sound of the grinding is low, and one shall rise up at the voice of
a bird, and all the daughters of music shall be brought low; [5] yea,
they shall be afraid of[10] *that which is* high, and terrors *shall be* in the
way; and the almond-tree shall blossom, and the grasshopper shall[11]
be a burden, and desire[12] shall fail;[13] because man goeth to his everlasting home, and the mourners go about the streets: [6] before the
silver cord is loosed,[14] or the golden bowl is broken, or the pitcher is
broken at the fountain, or the wheel broken at the cistern, [7] and
the dust returneth to the earth as it was, and the spirit returneth unto
God who gave it. [8] Vanity of vanities, saith the Preacher; all is
vanity.

[9] And further, because the Preacher was wise, he still taught the
people knowledge; yea, he pondered,[15] and sought out, *and* set in
order many proverbs. [10] The Preacher sought to find out acceptable[16] words, and that which was written uprightly, *even* words of
truth.

[11] The words of the wise are as goads; and as nails well fastened
are *the words of* the masters[17] of assemblies, *which* are given from one
shepherd. [12] And[18] furthermore, my son, be admonished: of
making many books there is no end; and much study is a weariness
of the flesh.

[13] *This*[19] *is* the end of the matter; all hath been heard: fear
God, and keep his commandments; for this[20] is the whole *duty* of
man. [14] For God will bring every work into judgment, with[21]
every hidden thing, whether it be good, or whether it be evil.

[10] Or, of danger *from on high.* [11] Or, *shall drag itself along.*
[12] Or, *the caperberry.* [13] Or, *burst.* [14] Or, *snapped asunder.* [15] Or, *gave ear.*
[16] Heb. *words of delight.* [17] Or, *collectors of sentences.* [18] Or, *And as for more than these, my son, be warned.* [19] Or, *Let us hear the conclusion of the whole matter.*
[20] Or, *this is* the duty of *all men.* [21] Or, *concerning.*

(CHRISTIAN)

THE GOSPEL ACCORDING TO LUKE

INTRODUCTORY NOTE

The "Gospel according to Luke" was probably written not far from the year 70 A. D. It is quoted in the first half of the second century, and in a fragment dated about 175 A. D. we find the earliest extant ascription of the authorship to Luke. The third Gospel, says the so-called "Canon of Muratori," "Luke compiled in his own name from report, the physician whom Paul took with him after the ascension of Christ, as it were, for a traveling companion; however he did not himself see the Lord in the flesh, and hence begins his account with the birth of John." Eusebius states that Luke was born at Antioch, and Paul seems to imply that he was a Gentile.

The sources from which the compilation was made are still a matter of dispute. Much of the narrative of events seems to be drawn from "Mark"; of the speeches, from that collection of the discourses of Christ which is supposed by scholars to lie behind the gospel of "Matthew." But the author of "Luke" had peculiar sources not used by the other evangelists; and from these come some of the most precious contents of this gospel.

There has been much discussion on the question as to the existence in "Luke" of a Jewish or of a Gentile bias. Those who find it markedly Jewish in tone incline to distrust the tradition ascribing its composition to the Gentile physician; those who regard it as the Pauline gospel naturally find it easier to associate it with the companion of the apostle to the Gentiles. The question is closely connected with the authorship of "The Acts of the Apostles," a continuation of "Luke" by the same hand, which is generally admitted to contain descriptions of Paul's travels recorded by his companion.

The author, whether Luke or another, opens by stating his purpose to be to trace accurately and in order "those matters which have been fulfilled among us." It would be an impertinence to comment on the importance to mankind of the carrying out of his purpose.

THE GOSPEL ACCORDING TO LUKE

[1] I

FORASMUCH as many have taken in hand to draw up a narrative concerning those matters which have been fulfilled[1] among us, [2] even as they delivered them unto us, who from the beginning were eyewitnesses and ministers of the word, [3] it seemed good to me also, having traced the course of all things accurately from the first, to write unto thee in order, most excellent Theophilus; [4] that thou mightest know the certainty concerning the things[2] wherein[3] thou wast instructed.

[5] There was in the days of Herod, king of Judæa, a certain priest named Zacharias, of the course of Abijah: and he had a wife of the daughters of Aaron, and her name was Elisabeth. [6] And they were both righteous before God, walking in all the commandments and ordinances of the Lord blameless. [7] And they had no child, because that Elisabeth was barren, and they both were *now* well[4] stricken in years.

[8] Now it came to pass, while he executed the priest's office before God in the order of his course, [9] according to the custom of the priest's office, his lot was to enter into the temple[5] of the Lord and burn incense. [10] And the whole multitude of the people were praying without at the hour of incense. [11] And there appeared unto him an angel of the Lord standing on the right side of the altar of incense. [12] And Zacharias was troubled when he saw *him,* and fear fell upon him. [13] But the angel said unto him, Fear not, Zacharias: because thy supplication is heard, and thy wife Elisabeth shall bear thee a son, and thou shalt call his name John. [14] And

[1] Or, *fully established.* [2] Gr. *words.*
[3] Or, *which thou wast taught by word of mouth.*
[4] Gr. *advanced in their days.* [5] Or, *sanctuary.*

thou shalt have joy and gladness; and many shall rejoice at his birth. [15] For he shall be great in the sight of the Lord, and he shall drink no wine nor strong[6] drink; and he shall be filled with the Holy Spirit, even from his mother's womb. [16] And many of the children of Israel shall he turn unto the Lord their God. [17] And he shall go[7] before his face in the spirit and power of Elijah, to turn the hearts of the fathers to the children, and the disobedient *to walk* in the wisdom of the just; to make ready for the Lord a people prepared *for him*. [18] And Zacharias said unto the angel, Whereby shall I know this? for I am an old man, and my wife well[8] stricken in years. [19] And the angel answering said unto him, I am Gabriel, that stand in the presence of God; and I was sent to speak unto thee, and to bring thee these good tidings. [20] And behold, thou shalt be silent and not able to speak, until the day that these things shall come to pass, because thou believedst not my words, which shall be fulfilled in their season. [21] And the people were waiting for Zacharias, and they marvelled while[9] he tarried in the temple.[5] [22] And when he came out, he could not speak unto them: and they perceived that he had seen a vision in the temple:[5] and he continued making signs unto them, and remained dumb. [23] And it came to pass, when the days of his ministration were fulfilled, he departed unto his house.

[24] And after these days Elisabeth his wife conceived; and she hid herself five months, saying, [25] Thus hath the Lord done unto me in the days wherein he looked upon *me,* to take away my reproach among men.

[26] Now in the sixth month the angel Gabriel was sent from God unto a city of Galilee, named Nazareth, [27] to a virgin betrothed to a man whose name was Joseph, of the house of David; and the virgin's name was Mary. [28] And he came in unto her, and said, Hail, thou that art highly[10] favored, the Lord *is* with thee.[11] [29] But she was greatly troubled at the saying, and cast in her mind what manner of salutation this might be. [30] And the angel said unto her, Fear not, Mary: for thou hast found favor[12] with God.

[6] Gr. *sikera.* [7] Some ancient authorities read, *come nigh before his face.*
[8] Gr. *advanced in her days.* [9] Or, *at his tarrying.* [10] Or, *endued with grace.*
[11] Many ancient authorities add *blessed* art *thou among women.* See ver. 42.
[12] Or, *grace.*

[31] And behold, thou shalt conceive in thy womb, and bring forth
a son, and shalt call his name JESUS. [32] He shall be great, and shall
be called the Son of the Most High: and the Lord God shall give
unto him the throne of his father David: [33] and he shall reign
over the house of Jacob for[13] ever; and of his kingdom there shall
be no end. [34] And Mary said unto the angel, How shall this be,
seeing I know not a man? [35] And the angel answered and said
unto her, The Holy Spirit shall come upon thee, and the power of
the Most High shall overshadow thee: wherefore also the[14] holy
thing which is begotten[15] shall be called the Son of God. [36] And
behold, Elisabeth thy kinswoman, she also hath conceived a son in
her old age; and this is the sixth month with her that was[16] called
barren. [37] For no word from God shall be void of power. [38]
And Mary said, Behold, the handmaid[17] of the Lord; be it unto me
according to thy word. And the angel departed from her.

[39] And Mary arose in these days and went into the hill country
with haste, into a city of Judah; [40] and entered into the house of
Zacharias and saluted Elisabeth. [41] And it came to pass, when
Elisabeth heard the salutation of Mary, the babe leaped in her
womb; and Elisabeth was filled with the Holy Spirit; [42] and she
lifted up her voice with a loud cry, and said, Blessed *art* thou among
women, and blessed *is* the fruit of thy womb. [43] And whence is
this to me, that the mother of my Lord should come unto me?
[44] For behold, when the voice of thy salutation came into mine
ears, the babe leaped in my womb for joy. [45] And blessed *is* she
that believed;[18] for there shall be a fulfilment of the things which
have been spoken to her from the Lord. [46] And Mary said,

My soul doth magnify the Lord,
[47] And my spirit hath rejoiced in God my Saviour.
[48] For he hath looked upon the low estate of his handmaid:[17]
For behold, from henceforth all generations shall call me
blessed.
[49] For he that is mighty hath done to me great things;
And holy is his name.

[13] Gr. *unto the ages.*
[14] Or, *that which is to be born shall be called holy, the Son of God.*
[15] Some ancient authorities insert *of thee.*
[16] Or, *is.* [17] Gr. *bondmaid.* [18] Or, *believed that there shall be.*

[50] And his mercy is unto generations and generations
On them that fear him.
[51] He hath showed strength with his arm;
He hath scattered the proud in[19] the imagination of their heart.
[52] He hath put down princes from *their* thrones,
And hath exalted them of low degree.
[53] The hungry he hath filled with good things;
And the rich he hath sent empty away.
[54] He hath given help to Israel his servant,
That he might remember mercy
[55] (As he spake unto our fathers)
Toward Abraham and his seed for ever.

[56] And Mary abode with her about three months, and returned
unto her house.

[57] Now Elisabeth's time was fulfilled that she should be
delivered; and she brought forth a son. [58] And her neighbors
and her kinsfolk heard that the Lord had magnified his mercy
towards her; and they rejoiced with her. [59] And it came to pass
on the eighth day, that they came to circumcise the child; and they
would have called him Zacharias, after the name of his father. [60]
And his mother answered and said, Not so; but he shall be called
John. [61] And they said unto her, There is none of thy kindred
that is called by this name. [62] And they made signs to his father,
what he would have him called. [63] And he asked for a writing
tablet, and wrote, saying, His name is John. And they marvelled all.
[64] And his mouth was opened immediately, and his tongue *loosed*,
and he spake, blessing God. [65] And fear came on all that dwelt
round about them: and all these sayings were noised abroad throughout all the hill country of Judæa. [66] And all that heard them laid
them up in their heart, saying, What then shall this child be? For
the hand of the Lord was with him.

[67] And his father Zacharias was filled with the Holy Spirit, and
prophesied, saying,
[68] Blessed *be* the Lord, the God of Israel;
For he hath visited and wrought redemption for his people,
[69] And hath raised up a horn of salvation for us

[19] Or, *by*.

In the house of his servant David
[70] (As he spake by the mouth of his holy prophets that have been from of old),
[71] Salvation from our enemies, and from the hand of all that hate us;
[72] To show mercy towards our fathers,
And to remember his holy covenant;
[73] The oath which he sware unto Abraham our father,
[74] To grant unto us that we being delivered out of the hand of our enemies
Should serve him without fear,
[75] In holiness and righteousness before him all our days.
[76] Yea and thou, child, shalt be called the prophet of the Most High:
For thou shalt go before the face of the Lord to make ready his ways;
[77] To give knowledge of salvation unto his people
In the remission of their sins,
[78] Because of the tender[20] mercy of our God,
Whereby[21] the dayspring from on high shall[22] visit us,
[79] To shine upon them that sit in darkness and the shadow of death;
To guide our feet into the way of peace.

[80] And the child grew, and waxed strong in spirit, and was in the deserts till the day of his showing unto Israel.

II

[1] Now it came to pass in those days, there went out a decree
from Cæsar Augustus, that all the[1] world should be enrolled. [2]
This was the first enrolment made when Quirinius was governor
of Syria. [3] And all went to enrol themselves, every one to his own
city. [4] And Joseph also went up from Galilee, out of the city of
Nazareth, into Judæa, to the city of David, which is called Bethlehem, because he was of the house and family of David; [5] to enrol
himself with Mary, who was betrothed to him, being great with

[20] Or, *heart of mercy*. [21] Or, *Wherein*.
[22] Many ancient authorities read *hath visited us*. [1] Gr. *the inhabited earth*.

child. [6] And it came to pass, while they were there, the days were fulfilled that she should be delivered. [7] And she brought forth her firstborn son; and she wrapped him in swaddling clothes, and laid him in a manger, because there was no room for them in the inn.

[8] And there were shepherds in the same country abiding in the field, and keeping watch[2] by night over their flock. [9] And an angel of the Lord stood by them, and the glory of the Lord shone round about them: and they were sore afraid. [10] And the angel said unto them, Be not afraid; for behold, I bring you good tidings of great joy which shall be to all the people: [11] for there is born to you this day in the city of David a Saviour, who is Christ[3] the Lord. [12] And this *is* the sign unto you: Ye shall find a babe wrapped in swaddling clothes, and lying in a manger. [13] And suddenly there was with the angel a multitude of the heavenly host praising God, and saying,

[14] Glory to God in the highest,
And on earth peace[4] among men[5] in whom he is well pleased.

[15] And it came to pass, when the angels went away from them into heaven, the shepherds said one to another, Let us now go even unto Bethlehem, and see this thing[6] that is come to pass, which the Lord hath made known unto us. [16] And they came with haste, and found both Mary and Joseph, and the babe lying in the manger. [17] And when they saw it, they made known concerning the saying which was spoken to them about this child. [18] And all that heard it wondered at the things which were spoken unto them by the shepherds. [19] But Mary kept all these sayings,[7] pondering them in her heart. [20] And the shepherds returned, glorifying and praising God for all the things that they had heard and seen, even as it was spoken unto them.

[21] And when eight days were fulfilled for circumcising him, his name was called Jesus, which was so called by the angel before he was conceived in the womb.

[22] And when the days of their purification according to the law of Moses were fulfilled they brought him up to Jerusalem, to present

[2] Or, *night-watches.* [3] Or, *Anointed Lord.* [4] Many ancient authorities read *peace, good pleasure among men.* [5] Gr. *men of good pleasure.* [6] Or, *saying.* [7] Or, *things.*

him to the Lord [23] (as it is written in the law of the Lord, Every
male that openeth the womb shall be called holy to the Lord), [24]
and to offer a sacrifice according to that which is said in the law of
the Lord, A pair of turtledoves, or two young pigeons. [25] And
behold, there was a man in Jerusalem, whose name was Simeon;
and this man was righteous and devout, looking for the consolation
of Israel: and the Holy Spirit was upon him. [26] And it had been
revealed unto him by the Holy Spirit, that he should not see death,
before he had seen the Lord's Christ. [27] And he came in the
Spirit into the temple: and when the parents brought in the child
Jesus, that they might do concerning him after the custom of the
law, [28] then he received him into his arms, and blessed God, and
said,

[29] Now lettest thou thy servant[8] depart, Lord,[9]
According to thy word, in peace;
[30] For mine eyes have seen thy salvation,
[31] Which thou hast prepared before the face of all peoples;
[32] A light for revelation[10] to the Gentiles,
And the glory of thy people Israel.

[33] And his father and his mother were marvelling at the things
which were spoken concerning him; [34] and Simeon blessed them,
and said unto Mary his mother, Behold, this *child* is set for the
falling and the rising of many in Israel; and for a sign which is
spoken against; [35] yea and a sword shall pierce through thine own
soul; that thoughts out of many hearts may be revealed. [36] And
there was one Anna, a prophetess, the daughter of Phanuel, of the
tribe of Asher (she was of[11] a great age, having lived with a husband
seven years from her virginity, [37] and she had been a widow even
unto fourscore and four years), who departed not from the temple,
worshipping with fastings and supplications night and day. [38]
And coming up at that very hour she gave thanks unto God, and
spake of him to all them that were looking for the redemption of
Jerusalem. [39] And when they had accomplished all things that
were according to the law of the Lord, they returned into Galilee,
to their own city Nazareth.

[8] Gr. *bondservant.* [9] Gr. *Master.* [10] Or, *the unveiling of the Gentiles.*
[11] Gr. *advanced in many days.*

[40] And the child grew, and waxed strong, filled[12] with wisdom: and the grace of God was upon him.

[41] And his parents went every year to Jerusalem at the feast of the passover. [42] And when he was twelve years old, they went up after the custom of the feast; [43] and when they had fulfilled the days, as they were returning, the boy Jesus tarried behind in Jerusalem; and his parents knew it not; [44] but supposing him to be in the company, they went a day's journey; and they sought for him among their kinsfolk and acquaintance: [45] and when they found him not, they returned to Jerusalem, seeking for him. [46] And it came to pass, after three days they found him in the temple, sitting in the midst of the teachers,[13] both hearing them, and asking them questions: [47] and all that heard him were amazed at his understanding and his answers. [48] And when they saw him, they were astonished; and his mother said unto him, Son,[14] why hast thou thus dealt with us? behold, thy father and I sought thee sorrowing. [49] And he said unto them, How is it that ye sought me? knew ye not that I must be in[15] my Father's house? [50] And they understood not the saying which he spake unto them. [51] And he went down with them, and came to Nazareth; and he was subject unto them: and his mother kept all *these* sayings[16] in her heart.

[52] And Jesus advanced in wisdom and stature,[17] and in favor[18] with God and men.

III

[1] Now in the fifteenth year of the reign of Tiberius Cæsar, Pontius Pilate being governor of Judæa, and Herod being tetrarch of Galilee, and his brother Philip tetrarch of the region of Ituræa and Trachonitis, and Lysanias tetrarch of Abilene, [2] in the high-priesthood of Annas and Caiaphas, the word of God came unto John the son of Zacharias in the wilderness. [3] And he came into all the region round about the Jordan, preaching the baptism of repentance unto remission of sins; [4] as it is written in the book of the words of Isaiah the prophet,

[12] Gr. *becoming full of wisdom.*
[13] Or, *doctors.* See ch. 5. 17; Acts 5. 34. [14] Gr. *Child.*
[15] Or, *about my Father's business.* Gr. *in the things of my Father.*
[16] Or, *things.* [17] Or, *age.* [18] Or, *grace.*

The voice of one crying in the wilderness,
Make ye ready the way of the Lord,
Make his paths straight.
[5] Every valley shall be filled,
And every mountain and hill shall be brought low;
And the crooked shall become straight,
And the rough ways smooth;
[6] And all flesh shall see the salvation of God.

[7] He said therefore to the multitudes that went out to be baptized of him, Ye offspring of vipers, who warned you to flee from
the wrath to come? [8] Bring forth therefore fruits worthy of
repentance,[1] and begin not to say within yourselves, We have
Abraham to our father: for I say unto you, that God is able of these
stones to raise up children unto Abraham. [9] And even now the
axe also lieth at the root of the trees: every tree therefore that
bringeth not forth good fruit is hewn down, and cast into the fire.
[10] And the multitudes asked him, saying, What then must we do?
[11] And he answered and said unto them, He that hath two coats,
let him impart to him that hath none; and he that hath food, let
him do likewise. [12] And there came also publicans[2] to be baptized,
and they said unto him, Teacher, what must we do? [13] And he
said unto them, Extort no more than that which is appointed you.
[14] And soldiers[3] also asked him, saying, And we, what must we
do? And he said unto them, Extort from no man by violence,
neither accuse *any one* wrongfully; and be content with your wages.

[15] And as the people were in expectation, and all men reasoned
in their hearts concerning John, whether haply he were the Christ;
[16] John answered, saying unto them all, I indeed baptize you with
water; but there cometh he that is mightier than I, the latchet of
whose shoes I am not worthy[4] to unloose: he shall baptize you in[5] the
Holy Spirit and *in* fire: [17] whose fan is in his hand, thoroughly to
cleanse his threshing-floor, and to gather the wheat into his garner;
but the chaff he will burn up with unquenchable fire.

[18] With many other exhortations therefore preached he good[6]
tidings unto the people; [19] but Herod the tetrarch, being reproved

[1] Or, *your repentance.*
[2] That is, *collectors or renters of Roman taxes.*
[3] Gr. *soldiers on service.* [4] Gr. *sufficient.* [5] Or, *with.* [6] Or, *the gospel.*

by him for Herodias his brother's wife, and for all the evil things which Herod had done, [20] added this also to them all, that he shut up John in prison.

[21] Now it came to pass, when all the people were baptized, that, Jesus also having been baptized, and praying, the heaven was opened, [22] and the Holy Spirit descended in a bodily form, as a dove, upon him, and a voice came out of heaven, Thou art my beloved Son; in thee I am well pleased.

[23] And Jesus himself, when he began *to teach,* was about thirty years of age, being the son (as was supposed) of Joseph, the *son* of Heli, [24] the *son* of Matthat, the *son* of Levi, the *son* of Melchi, the *son* of Jannai, the *son* of Joseph, [25] the *son* of Mattathias, the *son* of Amos, the *son* of Nahum, the *son* of Esli, the *son* of Naggai, [26] the *son* of Maath, the *son* of Mattathias, the *son* of Semein, the *son* of Josech, the *son* of Joda, [27] the *son* of Joanan, the *son* of Rhesa, the *son* of Zerubbabel, the *son* of Shealtiel,[7] the *son* of Neri, [28] the *son* of Melchi, the *son* of Addi, the *son* of Cosam, the *son* of Elmadam, the *son* of Er, [29] the *son* of Jesus, the *son* of Eliezer, the *son* of Jorim, the *son* of Matthat, the *son* of Levi, [30] the *son* of Symeon, the *son* of Judas, the *son* of Joseph, the *son* of Jonam, the *son* of Eliakim, [31] the *son* of Melea, the *son* of Menna, the *son* of Mattatha, the *son* of Nathan, the *son* of David, [32] the *son* of Jesse, the *son* of Obed, the *son* of Boaz, the *son* of Salmon,[8] the *son* of Nahshon, [33] the *son* of Amminadab, the[9] *son* of Arni,[10] the *son* of Hezron, the *son* of Perez, the *son* of Judah, [34] the *son* of Jacob, the *son* of Isaac, the *son* of Abraham, the *son* of Terah, the *son* of Nahor, [35] the *son* of Serug, the *son* of Reu, the *son* of Peleg, the *son* of Eber, the *son* of Shelah, [36] the *son* of Cainan, the *son* of Arphaxad, the *son* of Shem, the *son* of Noah, the *son* of Lamech, [37] the *son* of Methuselah, the *son* of Enoch, the *son* of Jared, the *son* of Mahalaleel, the *son* of Cainan, [38] the *son* of Enos, the *son* of Seth, the *son* of Adam, the *son* of God.

IV

[1] AND Jesus, full of the Holy Spirit, returned from the Jordan, and was led in the Spirit in the wilderness [2] during forty days,

[7] Gr. *Salathiel.* [8] Some ancient authorities write *Sala.*

[9] Many ancient authorities insert *the* son *of Admin:* and one writes *Admin* for *Amminadab.* [10] Some ancient authorities write *Aram.*

being tempted of the devil. And he did eat nothing in those days: and when they were completed, he hungered. [3] And the devil said unto him, If thou art the Son of God, command this stone that it become bread.[1] [4] And Jesus answered unto him, It is written, Man shall not live by bread alone. [5] And he led him up, and showed him all the kingdoms of the[2] world in a moment of time. [6] And the devil said unto him, To thee will I give all this authority, and the glory of them: for it hath been delivered unto me; and to whomsoever I will I give it. [7] If thou therefore wilt worship[3] before me, it shall all be thine. [8] And Jesus answered and said unto him, It is written, Thou shalt worship the Lord thy God, and him only shalt thou serve. [9] And he led him to Jerusalem, and set him on the pinnacle[4] of the temple, and said unto him, If thou art the Son of God, cast thyself down from hence: [10] for it is written,

He shall give his angels charge concerning thee, to guard thee:
[11] and,
On their hands they shall bear thee up,
Lest haply thou dash thy foot against a stone.

[12] And Jesus answering said unto him, It is said, Thou shalt not make trial of the Lord thy God.

[13] And when the devil had completed every temptation, he departed from him for[5] a season.

[14] And Jesus returned in the power of the Spirit into Galilee: and a fame went out concerning him through all the region round about. [15] And he taught in their synagogues, being glorified of all.

[16] And he came to Nazareth, where he had been brought up: and he entered, as his custom was, into the synagogue on the sabbath day, and stood up to read. [17] And there was delivered unto him the[6] book of the prophet Isaiah. And he opened the book,[7] and found the place where it was written,

[18] The Spirit of the Lord is upon me,
Because[8] he anointed me to preach good[9] tidings to the poor:
He hath sent me to proclaim release to the captives,

[1] Or, *a loaf*. [2] Gr. *the inhabited earth*. [3] The Greek word denotes an act of reverence, whether paid to a creature, or to the Creator (comp. marginal note on Mt. 2. 2). [4] Gr. *wing*. [5] Or, *until*. [6] Or, *a roll*. [7] Or, *roll*.
[8] Or, *Wherefore*. [9] Or, *the gospel*.

And recovering of sight to the blind,
To set at liberty them that are bruised,
[19] To proclaim the acceptable year of the Lord.
[20] And he closed the book,[10] and gave it back to the attendant,
and sat down: and the eyes of all in the synagogue were fastened
on him. [21] And he began to say unto them, To-day hath this
scripture been fulfilled in your ears. [22] And all bare him witness,
and wondered at the words of grace which proceeded out of his
mouth: and they said, Is not this Joseph's son? [23] And he said
unto them, Doubtless ye will say unto me this parable, Physician,
heal thyself: whatsoever we have heard done at Capernaum, do
also here in thine own country. [24] And he said, Verily I say unto
you, No prophet is acceptable in his own country. [25] But of a
truth I say unto you, There were many widows in Israel in the days
of Elijah, when the heaven was shut up three years and six months,
when there came a great famine over all the land; [26] and unto
none of them was Elijah sent, but only to Zarephath,[11] in the land
of Sidon, unto a woman that was a widow. [27] And there were
many lepers in Israel in the time of Elisha the prophet; and none of
them was cleansed, but only Naaman the Syrian. [28] And they
were all filled with wrath in the synagogue, as they heard these
things; [29] and they rose up, and cast him forth out of the city, and
led him unto the brow of the hill whereon their city was built, that
they might throw him down headlong. [30] But he passing through
the midst of them went his way.

[31] And he came down to Capernaum, a city of Galilee. And
he was teaching them on the sabbath day: [32] and they were
astonished at his teaching; for his word was with authority. [33]
And in the synagogue there was a man, that had a spirit of an
unclean demon; and he cried out with a loud voice, [34] Ah![12]
what have we to do with thee, Jesus thou Nazarene? art thou come
to destroy us? I know thee who thou art, the Holy One of God.
[35] And Jesus rebuked him, saying, Hold thy peace, and come out
of him. And when the demon had thrown him down in the midst,
he came out of him, having done him no hurt. [36] And amazement came upon all, and they spake together, one with another,

[10] Or, *roll.* [11] Gr. *Sarepta.* [12] Or, *Let alone.*

saying, What is this[13] word? for with authority and power he commandeth the unclean spirits, and they come out. [37] And there went forth a rumor concerning him into every place of the region round about.

[38] And he rose up from the synagogue, and entered into the house of Simon. And Simon's wife's mother was holden with a great fever; and they besought him for her. [39] And he stood over her, and rebuked the fever; and it left her: and immediately she rose up and ministered unto them.

[40] And when the sun was setting, all they that had any sick with divers diseases brought them unto him; and he laid his hands on every one of them, and healed them. [41] And demons also came out from many, crying out, and saying, Thou art the Son of God. And rebuking them, he suffered them not to speak, because they knew that he was the Christ.

[42] And when it was day, he came out and went into a desert place: and the multitudes sought after him, and came unto him and would have stayed him, that he should not go from them. [43] But he said unto them, I must preach the[9] good tidings of the kingdom of God to the other cities also: for therefore was I sent.

[44] And he was preaching in the synagogues of Galilee.[14]

V

[1] Now it came to pass, while the multitude pressed upon him and heard the word of God, that he was standing by the lake of Gennesaret; [2] and he saw two boats standing by the lake: but the fishermen had gone out of them, and were washing their nets. [3] And he entered into one of the boats, which was Simon's, and asked him to put out a little from the land. And he sat down and taught the multitudes out of the boat. [4] And when he had left speaking, he said unto Simon, Put out into the deep, and let down your nets for a draught. [5] And Simon answered and said, Master, we toiled all night, and took nothing: but at thy word I will let down the nets. [6] And when they had done this, they inclosed a great multitude of fishes; and their nets were breaking; [7] and they beckoned unto

[13] Or, *this word, that with authority . . . come out?*
[14] Very many ancient authorities read *Judæa.*

their partners in the other boat, that they should come and help them. And they came, and filled both the boats, so that they began to sink. [8] But Simon Peter, when he saw it, fell down at Jesus' knees, saying, Depart from me; for I am a sinful man, O Lord. [9] For he was amazed, and all that were with him, at the draught of the fishes which they had taken; [10] and so were also James[1] and John, sons of Zebedee, who were partners with Simon. And Jesus said unto Simon, Fear not; from henceforth thou shalt catch[2] men. [11] And when they had brought their boats to land, they left all, and followed him.

[12] And it came to pass, while he was in one of the cities, behold, a man full of leprosy: and when he saw Jesus, he fell on his face, and besought him, saying, Lord, if thou wilt, thou canst make me clean. [13] And he stretched forth his hand, and touched him, saying, I will; be thou made clean. And straightway the leprosy departed from him. [14] And he charged him to tell no man: but go thy way, and show thyself to the priest, and offer for thy cleansing, according as Moses commanded, for a testimony unto them. [15] But so much the more went abroad the report concerning him: and great multitudes came together to hear, and to be healed of their infirmities. [16] But he withdrew himself in the deserts, and prayed.

[17] And it came to pass on one of those days, that he was teaching; and there were Pharisees and doctors of the law sitting by, who were come out of every village of Galilee and Judæa and Jerusalem: and the power of the Lord was with him to[3] heal. [18] And behold, men bring on a bed a man that was palsied: and they sought to bring him in, and to lay him before him. [19] And not finding by what *way* they might bring him in because of the multitude, they went up to the housetop, and let him down through the tiles with his couch into the midst before Jesus. [20] And seeing their faith, he said, Man, thy sins are forgiven thee. [21] And the scribes and the Pharisees began to reason, saying, Who is this that speaketh blasphemies? Who can forgive sins, but God alone? [22] But Jesus perceiving their reasonings,[4] answered and said unto them, Why[5] reason ye in your hearts? [23] Which is easier, to say, Thy

[1] Or, *Jacob*. [2] Gr. *take alive*.
[3] Gr. *that he should heal*. Many ancient authorities read *that* he *should heal them*.
[4] Or, *questionings*. [5] Or, *What*.

sins are forgiven thee; or to say, Arise and walk? [24] But that ye may know that the Son of man hath authority on earth to forgive sins (he said unto him that was palsied), I say unto thee, Arise, and take up thy couch, and go unto thy house. [25] And immediately he rose up before them, and took up that whereon he lay, and departed to his house, glorifying God. [26] And amazement took hold on all, and they glorified God; and they were filled with fear, saying, We have seen strange things to-day.

[27] And after these things he went forth, and beheld a publican,[6] named Levi, sitting at the place of toll, and said unto him, Follow me. [28] And he forsook all, and rose up and followed him.

[29] And Levi made him a great feast in his house: and there was a great multitude of publicans[6] and of others that were sitting at meat with them. [30] And the[7] Pharisees and their scribes murmured against his disciples, saying, Why do ye eat and drink with the publicans[6] and sinners? [31] And Jesus answering said unto them, They that are in[8] health have no need of a physician; but they that are sick. [32] I am not come to call the righteous but sinners to repentance.

[33] And they said unto him, The disciples of John fast often, and make supplications; likewise also the *disciples* of the Pharisees; but thine eat and drink. [34] And Jesus said unto them, Can ye make the sons[9] of the bride-chamber fast, while the bridegroom is with them? [35] But the days will come; and when the bridegroom shall be taken away from them, then will they fast in those days. [36] And he spake also a parable unto them: No man rendeth a piece from a new garment and putteth it upon an old garment; else he will rend the new, and also the piece from the new will not agree with the old. [37] And no man putteth new wine into old wine-skins;[10] else the new wine will burst the skins, and itself will be spilled, and the skins will perish. [38] But new wine must be put into fresh wine-skins. [39] And no man having drunk old *wine* desireth new; for he saith, The old is good.[11]

[6] See marginal note on ch. 3. 12. [7] Or, *the Pharisees and the scribes among them.*
[8] Gr. *sound.* [9] That is, *companions of the bridegroom.*
[10] That is, *skins used as bottles.* [11] Many ancient authorities read *better.*

VI

[1] Now it came to pass on a sabbath,[1] that he was going through the grainfields; and his disciples plucked the ears, and did eat, rubbing them in their hands. [2] But certain of the Pharisees said, Why do ye that which it is not lawful to do on the sabbath day? [3] And Jesus answering them said, Have ye not read even this, what David did, when he was hungry, he, and they that were with him; [4] how he entered into the house of God, and took and ate the show-bread, and gave also to them that were with him; which it is not lawful to eat save for the priests alone? [5] And he said unto them, The Son of man is lord of the sabbath.

[6] And it came to pass on another sabbath, that he entered into the synagogue and taught: and there was a man there, and his right hand was withered. [7] And the scribes and the Pharisees watched him, whether he would heal on the sabbath; that they might find how to accuse him. [8] But he knew their thoughts; and he said to the man that had his hand withered, Rise up, and stand forth in the midst. And he arose and stood forth. [9] And Jesus said unto them, I ask you, Is it lawful on the sabbath to do good, or to do harm? to save a life, or to destroy it? [10] And he looked round about on them all, and said unto him, Stretch forth thy hand. And he did *so:* and his hand was restored. [11] But they were filled with madness;[2] and communed one with another what they might do to Jesus.

[12] And it came to pass in these days, that he went out into the mountain to pray; and he continued all night in prayer to God. [13] And when it was day, he called his disciples; and he chose from them twelve, whom also he named apostles: [14] Simon, whom he also named Peter, and Andrew his brother, and James[3] and John, and Philip and Bartholomew, [15] and Matthew and Thomas, and James[3] *the son* of Alphæus, and Simon who was called the Zealot, [16] and Judas *the son*[4] of James,[3] and Judas Iscariot, who became a traitor; [17] and he came down with them, and stood on a level place, and a great multitude of his disciples, and a great number of

[1] Many ancient authorities insert *second-first.*
[2] Or, *foolishness.* [3] Or, *Jacob.* [4] Or, brother. See Jude 1.

the people from all Judæa and Jerusalem, and the sea coast of Tyre
and Sidon, who came to hear him, and to be healed of their diseases;
[18] and they that were troubled with unclean spirits were healed.
[19] And all the multitude sought to touch him; for power came
forth from him, and healed *them* all.

[20] And he lifted up his eyes on his disciples, and said, Blessed
are ye poor: for yours is the kingdom of God. [21] Blessed *are* ye
that hunger now: for ye shall be filled. Blessed *are* ye that weep now:
for ye shall laugh. [22] Blessed are ye, when men shall hate you,
and when they shall separate you *from their company,* and reproach
you, and cast out your name as evil, for the Son of man's sake. [23]
Rejoice in that day, and leap *for joy:* for behold, your reward is
great in heaven; for in the same manner did their fathers unto the
prophets. [24] But woe unto you that are rich! for ye have received
your consolation. [25] Woe unto you, ye that are full now! for ye
shall hunger. Woe *unto you,* ye that laugh now! for ye shall mourn
and weep. [26] Woe *unto you,* when all men shall speak well of
you! for in the same manner did their fathers to the false prophets.

[27] But I say unto you that hear, Love your enemies, do good
to them that hate you, [28] bless them that curse you, pray for them
that despitefully use you. [29] To him that smiteth thee on the *one*
cheek offer also the other; and from him that taketh away thy
cloak withhold not thy coat also. [30] Give to every one that asketh
thee; and of him that taketh away thy goods ask them not again.
[31] And as ye would that men should do to you, do ye also to them
likewise. [32] And if ye love them that love you, what thank have
ye? for even sinners love those that love them. [33] And if ye do
good to them that do good to you, what thank have ye? for even
sinners do the same. [34] And if ye lend to them of whom ye hope
to receive, what thank have ye? even sinners lend to sinners, to
receive again as much. [35] But love your enemies, and do *them*
good, and lend, never[5] despairing; and your reward shall be great,
and ye shall be sons of the Most High: for he is kind toward the
unthankful and evil. [36] Be ye merciful, even as your Father is
merciful. [37] And judge not, and ye shall not be judged: and
condemn not, and ye shall not be condemned: release, and ye shall

[5] Some ancient authorities read *despairing of no man.*

be released: [38] give, and it shall be given unto you; good measure, pressed down, shaken together, running over, shall they give into your bosom. For with what measure ye mete it shall be measured to you again.

[39] And he spake also a parable unto them, Can the blind guide the blind? shall they not both fall into a pit? [40] The disciple is not above his teacher: but every one when he is perfected shall be as his teacher. [41] And why beholdest thou the mote that is in thy brother's eye, but considerest not the beam that is in thine own eye? [42] Or how canst thou say to thy brother, Brother, let me cast out the mote that is in thine eye, when thou thyself beholdest not the beam that is in thine own eye? Thou hypocrite, cast out first the beam out of thine own eye, and then shalt thou see clearly to cast out the mote that is in thy brother's eye. [43] For there is no good tree that bringeth forth corrupt fruit; nor again a corrupt tree that bringeth forth good fruit. [44] For each tree is known by its own fruit. For of thorns men do not gather figs, nor of a bramble bush gather they grapes. [45] The good man out of the good treasure of his heart bringeth forth that which is good; and the evil *man* out of the evil *treasure* bringeth forth that which is evil: for out of the abundance of the heart his mouth speaketh.

[46] And why call ye me, Lord, Lord, and do not the things which I say? [47] Every one that cometh unto me, and heareth my words, and doeth them, I will show you to whom he is like: [48] he is like a man building a house, who digged and went deep, and laid a foundation upon the rock: and when a flood arose, the stream brake against that house, and could not shake it: because[6] it had been well builded. [49] But he that heareth,[7] and doeth[8] not, is like a man that built a house upon the earth without a foundation; against which the stream brake, and straightway it fell in; and the ruin of that house was great.

VII

[1] After he had ended all his sayings in the ears of the people, he entered into Capernaum.

[6] Many ancient authorities read *for it had been founded upon the rock:* as in Mt. 7. 25. [7] Gr. *heard.* [8] Gr. *did not.*

[2] And a certain centurion's servant,[1] who was dear[2] unto him, was sick and at the point of death. [3] And when he heard concerning Jesus, he sent unto him elders of the Jews, asking him that he would come and save his servant.[1] [4] And they, when they came to Jesus, besought him earnestly, saying, He is worthy that thou shouldest do this for him; [5] for he loveth our nation, and himself built us our synagogue. [6] And Jesus went with them. And when he was now not far from the house, the centurion sent friends to him, saying unto him, Lord, trouble not thyself; for I am not worthy[3] that thou shouldest come under my roof: [7] wherefore neither thought I myself worthy to come unto thee: but say the[4] word, and my servant[5] shall be healed. [8] For I also am a man set under authority, having under myself soldiers: and I say to this one, Go, and he goeth; and to another, Come, and he cometh; and to my servant,[6] Do this, and he doeth it. [9] And when Jesus heard these things, he marvelled at him, and turned and said unto the multitude that followed him, I say unto you, I have not found so great faith, no, not in Israel. [10] And they that were sent, returning to the house, found the servant[6] whole.

[11] And it came to pass soon[7] afterwards, that he went to a city called Nain; and his disciples went with him, and a great multitude. [12] Now when he drew near to the gate of the city, behold, there was carried out one that was dead, the only son of his mother, and she was a widow: and much people of the city was with her. [13] And when the Lord saw her, he had compassion on her, and said unto her, Weep not. [14] And he came nigh and touched the bier: and the bearers stood still. And he said, Young man, I say unto thee, Arise. [15] And he that was dead sat up, and began to speak. And he gave him to his mother. [16] And fear took hold on all: and they glorified God, saying, A great prophet is arisen among us: and, God hath visited his people. [17] And this report went forth concerning him in the whole of Judæa, and all the region round about.

[18] And the disciples of John told him of all these things. [19] And John calling unto him two[8] of his disciples sent them to the

[1] Gr. *bondservant.* [2] Or, *precious to him.* Or, *honorable with him.*
[3] Gr. *sufficient.* [4] Gr. *with a word.* [5] Or, *boy.* [6] Gr. *bondservant.*
[7] Many ancient authorities read *on the next day.* [8] Gr. *certain two.*

Lord, saying, Art thou he that cometh, or look we for another? [20] And when the men were come unto him, they said, John the Baptist hath sent us unto thee, saying, Art thou he that cometh, or look we for another? [21] In that hour he cured many of diseases and plagues[9] and evil spirits; and on many that were blind he bestowed sight. [22] And he answered and said unto them, Go and tell John the things which ye have seen and heard; the blind receive their sight, the lame walk, the lepers are cleansed, and the deaf hear, the dead are raised up, the poor have good[10] tidings preached to them. [23] And blessed is he, whosoever shall find no occasion of stumbling in me.

[24] And when the messengers of John were departed, he began to say unto the multitudes concerning John, What went ye out into the wilderness to behold? a reed shaken with the wind? [25] But what went ye out to see? a man clothed in soft raiment? Behold, they that are gorgeously apparelled, and live delicately, are in kings' courts. [26] But what went ye out to see? a prophet? Yea, I say unto you, and much more than a prophet. [27] This is he of whom it is written,

> Behold, I send my messenger before thy face,
> Who shall prepare thy way before thee.

[28] I say unto you, Among them that are born of women there is none greater than John: yet he that is but[11] little in the kingdom of God is greater than he. [29] And all the people when they heard, and the publicans,[12] justified God, being[13] baptized with the baptism of John. [30] But the Pharisees and the lawyers rejected for themselves the counsel of God, being[14] not baptized of him. [31] Whereunto then shall I liken the men of this generation, and to what are they like? [32] They are like unto children that sit in the marketplace, and call one to another; who say, We piped unto you, and ye did not dance; we wailed, and ye did not weep. [33] For John the Baptist is come eating no bread nor drinking wine; and ye say, He hath a demon. [34] The Son of man is come eating and drinking; and ye say, Behold, a gluttonous man, and a winebibber, a friend of

[9] Gr. *scourges.* [10] Or, *the gospel.* [11] Gr. *lesser.*
[12] See marginal note on ch. 3. 12. [13] Or, *having been.* [14] Or, *not having been.*

publicans[15] and sinners! [35] And wisdom is[16] justified of all her children.

[36] And one of the Pharisees desired him that he would eat with him. And he entered into the Pharisee's house, and sat[17] down to meat. [37] And behold, a woman who was in the city, a sinner; and when she knew that he was sitting[18] at meat in the Pharisee's house, she brought an[19] alabaster cruse of ointment, [38] and standing behind at his feet, weeping, she began to wet his feet with her tears, and wiped them with the hair of her head, and kissed[20] his feet, and anointed them with the ointment. [39] Now when the Pharisee that had bidden him saw it, he spake within himself, saying, This man, if he were a[21] prophet, would have perceived who and what manner of woman this is that toucheth him, that she is a sinner. [40] And Jesus answering said unto him, Simon, I have somewhat to say unto thee. And he saith, Teacher, say on. [41] A certain lender had two debtors: the one owed five hundred shillings,[22] and the other fifty. [42] When they had not *wherewith* to pay, he forgave them both. Which of them therefore will love him most? [43] Simon answered and said, He, I suppose, to whom he forgave the most. And he said unto him, Thou hast rightly judged. [44] And turning to the woman, he said unto Simon, Seest thou this woman? I entered into thy house, thou gavest me no water for my feet: but she hath wetted my feet with her tears, and wiped them with her hair. [45] Thou gavest me no kiss: but she, since the time I came in, hath not ceased to kiss[23] my feet. [46] My head with oil thou didst not anoint: but she hath anointed my feet with ointment. [47] Wherefore I say unto thee, Her sins, which are many, are forgiven; for she loved much: but to whom little is forgiven, *the same* loveth little. [48] And he said unto her, Thy sins are forgiven. [49] And they that sat[24] at meat with him began to say within[25] themselves, Who is this that even forgiveth sins? [50] And he said unto the woman, Thy faith hath saved thee; go in peace.

[15] See marginal note on ch. 3. 12. [16] Or, *was.* [17] Or, *reclined at table.*
[18] Or, *reclining at table.* [19] Or, *a flask.*
[20] Gr. *kissed much.* [21] Some ancient authorities read *the prophet.* See Jn. 1. 21, 25. [22] The word in the Greek denotes a coin worth about eight pence halfpenny, or nearly seventeen cents. [23] Gr. *kiss much.*
[24] Gr. *reclined.* [25] Or, *among.*

VIII

[1] And it came to pass soon afterwards, that he went about through cities and villages, preaching and bringing the good[1] tidings of the kingdom of God, and with him the twelve, [2] and certain women who had been healed of evil spirits and infirmities: Mary that was called Magdalene, from whom seven demons had gone out, [3] and Joanna the wife of Chuzas Herod's steward, and Susanna, and many others, who ministered unto them[2] of their substance.

[4] And when a great multitude came together, and they of every city resorted unto him, he spake by a parable: [5] The sower went forth to sow his seed: and as he sowed, some fell by the way side; and it was trodden under foot, and the birds of the heaven devoured it. [6] And other fell on the rock; and as soon as it grew, it withered away, because it had no moisture. [7] And other fell amidst the thorns; and the thorns grew with it, and choked it. [8] And other fell into the good ground, and grew, and brought forth fruit a hundredfold. As he said these things, he cried, He that hath ears to hear, let him hear.

[9] And his disciples asked him what this parable might be. [10] And he said, Unto you it is given to know the mysteries of the kingdom of God: but to the rest in parables; that seeing they may not see, and hearing they may not understand. [11] Now the parable is this: The seed is the word of God. [12] And those by the way side are they that have heard; then cometh the devil, and taketh away the word from their heart, that they may not believe and be saved. [13] And those on the rock *are* they who, when they have heard, receive the word with joy; and these have no root, who for a while believe, and in time of temptation fall away. [14] And that which fell among the thorns, these are they that have heard, and as they go on their way they are choked with cares and riches and pleasures of *this* life, and bring no fruit to perfection. [15] And that in the good ground, these are such as in an honest and good heart, having heard the word, hold it fast, and bring forth fruit with patience.[3]

[16] And no man, when he hath lighted a lamp, covereth it with a vessel, or putteth it under a bed; but putteth it on a stand, that they

[1] Or, *gospel.* [2] Many ancient authorities read *him.* [3] Or, *stedfastness.*

that enter in may see the light. [17] For nothing is hid, that shall not be made manifest; nor *anything* secret, that shall not be known and come to light. [18] Take heed therefore how ye hear: for whosoever hath, to him shall be given; and whosoever hath not, from him shall be taken away even that which he thinketh[4] he hath.

[19] And there came to him his mother and brethren, and they could not come at him for the crowd. [20] And it was told him, Thy mother and thy brethren stand without, desiring to see thee. [21] But he answered and said unto them, My mother and my brethren are these that hear the word of God, and do it.

[22] Now it came to pass on one of those days, that he entered into a boat, himself and his disciples; and he said unto them, Let us go over unto the other side of the lake: and they launched forth. [23] But as they sailed he fell asleep: and there came down a storm of wind on the lake; and they were filling *with water,* and were in jeopardy. [24] And they came to him, and awoke him, saying, Master, master we perish. And he awoke, and rebuked the wind and the raging of the water: and they ceased, and there was a calm. [25] And he said unto them, Where is your faith? And being afraid they marvelled, saying one to another, Who then is this, that he commandeth even the winds and the water, and they obey him?

[26] And they arrived at the country of the Gerasenes,[5] which is over against Galilee. [27] And when he was come forth upon the land, there met him a certain man out of the city, who had demons; and for a long time he had worn no clothes, and abode not in *any* house, but in the tombs. [28] And when he saw Jesus, he cried out, and fell down before him, and with a loud voice said, What have I to do with thee, Jesus, thou Son of the Most High God? I beseech thee, torment me not. [29] For he was commanding the unclean spirit to come out from the man. For often-times[6] it had seized him: and he was kept under guard, and bound with chains and fetters; and breaking the bands asunder, he was driven of the demon into the deserts. [30] And Jesus asked him, What is thy name? And he said, Legion; for many demons were entered into him. [31] And they entreated him that he would not command them to depart into

[4] Or, *seemeth to have.*

[5] Many ancient authorities read *Gergesenes:* others, *Gadarenes:* and so in ver. 37.

[6] Or, *of a long time.*

the abyss. [32] Now there was there a herd of many swine feeding
on the mountain: and they entreated him that he would give them
leave to enter into them. And he gave them leave. [33] And the
demons came out from the man, and entered into the swine: and the
herd rushed down the steep into the lake, and were drowned. [34]
And when they that fed them saw what had come to pass, they fled,
and told it in the city and in the country. [35] And they went out
to see what had come to pass; and they came to Jesus, and found the
man, from whom the demons were gone out, sitting, clothed and in
his right mind, at the feet of Jesus: and they were afraid. [36] And
they that saw it told them how he that was possessed with demons
was made[7] whole. [37] And all the people of the country of the
Gerasenes round about asked him to depart from them; for they were
holden with great fear: and he entered into a boat, and returned.
[38] But the man from whom the demons were gone out prayed him
that he might be with him: but he sent him away, saying, [39] Return to thy house, and declare how great things God hath done for
thee. And he went his way, publishing throughout the whole city
how great things Jesus had done for him.

[40] And as Jesus returned, the multitude welcomed him; for they
were all waiting for him. [41] And behold, there came a man named
Jaïrus, and he was a ruler of the synagogue: and he fell down at
Jesus' feet, and besought him to come into his house; [42] for he had
an only daughter, about twelve years of age, and she was dying.
But as he went the multitudes thronged him.

[43] And a woman having an issue of blood twelve years, who
had[8] spent all her living upon physicians, and could not be healed of
any, [44] came behind him, and touched the border of his garment:
and immediately the issue of her blood stanched. [45] And Jesus
said, Who is it that touched me? And when all denied, Peter said,
and[9] they that were with him, Master, the multitudes press thee and
crush *thee*. [46] But Jesus said, Some one did touch me; for I perceived that power had gone forth from me. [47] And when the
woman saw that she was not hid, she came trembling, and falling
down before him declared in the presence of all the people for what

[7] Or, *saved*.
[8] Some ancient authorities omit *had spent all her living upon physicians, and.*
[9] Some ancient authorities omit *and they that were with him.*

cause she touched him, and how she was healed immediately. [48] And he said unto her, Daughter, thy faith hath made[10] thee whole; go in peace.

[49] While he yet spake, there cometh one from the ruler of the synagogue's *house,* saying, Thy daughter is dead; trouble not the Teacher. [50] But Jesus hearing it, answered him, Fear not: only believe, and she shall be made[11] whole. [51] And when he came to the house, he suffered not any man to enter in with him, save Peter, and John, and James, and the father of the maiden and her mother. [52] And all were weeping, and bewailing her: but he said, Weep not; for she is not dead, but sleepeth. [53] And they laughed him to scorn, knowing that she was dead. [54] But he, taking her by the hand, called, saying, Maiden, arise. [55] And her spirit returned, and she rose up immediately: and he commanded that *something* be given her to eat. [56] And her parents were amazed: but he charged them to tell no man what had been done.

IX

[1] And he called the twelve together, and gave them power and authority over all demons, and to cure diseases. [2] And he sent them forth to preach the kingdom of God, and to heal the[1] sick. [3] And he said unto them, Take nothing for your journey, neither staff, nor wallet, nor bread, nor money; neither have two coats. [4] And into whatsoever house ye enter, there abide, and thence depart. [5] And as many as receive you not, when ye depart from that city, shake off the dust from your feet for a testimony against them. [6] And they departed, and went throughout the villages, preaching the gospel,[2] and healing everywhere.

[7] Now Herod the tetrarch heard of all that was done: and he was much perplexed, because that it was said by some, that John was risen from the dead; [8] and by some, that Elijah had appeared; and by others, that one of the old prophets was risen again. [9] And Herod said, John I beheaded: but who is this, about whom I hear such things? And he sought to see him.

[10] Or, *saved thee.* [11] Or, *saved.*
[1] Some ancient authorities omit *the sick.* [2] Or, *good tidings.*

[10] And the apostles, when they were returned, declared unto him what things they had done. And he took them, and withdrew apart to a city called Bethsaida. [11] But the multitudes perceiving it followed him: and he welcomed them, and spake to them of the kingdom of God, and them that had need of healing he cured. [12] And the day began to wear away; and the twelve came, and said unto him, Send the multitude away, that they may go into the villages and country round about, and lodge, and get provisions: for we are here in a desert place. [13] But he said unto them, Give ye them to eat. And they said, We have no more than five loaves and two fishes; except we should go and buy food for all this people. [14] For they were about five thousand men. And he said unto his disciples, Make them sit[3] down in companies, about fifty each. [15] And they did so, and made them all sit[3] down. [16] And he took the five loaves and the two fishes, and looking up to heaven, he blessed them, and brake; and gave to the disciples to set before the multitude. [17] And they ate, and were all filled: and there was taken up that which remained over to them of broken pieces, twelve baskets.

[18] And it came to pass, as he was praying apart, the disciples were with him: and he asked them, saying, Who do the multitudes say that I am? [19] And they answering said, John the Baptist; but others *say,* Elijah; and others, that one of the old prophets is risen again. [20] And he said unto them, But who say ye that I am? And Peter answering said, The Christ of God. [21] But he charged them, and commanded *them* to tell this to no man; [22] saying, The Son of man must suffer many things, and be rejected of the elders and chief priests and scribes, and be killed, and the third day be raised up. [23] And he said unto all, If any man would come after me, let him deny himself, and take up his cross daily, and follow me. [24] For whosoever would save his life shall lose it; but whosoever shall lose his life for my sake, the same shall save it. [25] For what is a man profited, if he gain the whole world, and lose or forfeit his own self? [26] For whosoever shall be ashamed of me and of my words, of him shall the Son of man be ashamed, when he cometh in his own glory, and *the glory* of the Father, and of the holy angels. [27] But I tell you of a truth, There are some of them that stand

[3] Gr. *recline.*

here, who shall in no wise taste of death, till they see the kingdom of God.

[28] And it came to pass about eight days after these sayings, that he took with him Peter and John and James, and went up into the mountain to pray. [29] And as he was praying, the fashion of his countenance was altered, and his raiment *became* white *and* dazzling. [30] And behold, there talked with him two men, who were Moses and Elijah; [31] who appeared in glory, and spake of his decease[4] which he was about to accomplish at Jerusalem. [32] Now Peter and they that were with him were heavy with sleep: but when[5] they were fully awake, they saw his glory, and the two men that stood with him. [33] And it came to pass, as they were parting from him, Peter said unto Jesus, Master, it is good for us to be here: and let us make three tabernacles;[6] one for thee, and one for Moses, and one for Elijah: not knowing what he said. [34] And while he said these things, there came a cloud, and overshadowed them: and they feared as they entered into the cloud. [35] And a voice came out of the cloud, saying, This is my[7] Son, my chosen: hear ye him. [36] And when the voice came,[8] Jesus was found alone. And they held their peace, and told no man in those days any of the things which they had seen.

[37] And it came to pass, on the next day, when they were come down from the mountain, a great multitude met him. [38] And behold, a man from the multitude cried, saying, Teacher, I beseech thee to look upon my son; for he is mine only child: [39] and behold, a spirit taketh him, and he suddenly crieth out; and it teareth[9] him that he foameth, and it hardly departeth from him, bruising him sorely. [40] And I besought thy disciples to cast it out; and they could not. [41] And Jesus answered and said, O faithless and perverse generation, how long shall I be with you, and bear with you? bring hither thy son. [42] And as he was yet a coming, the demon dashed[10] him down, and tare[11] *him* grievously. But Jesus rebuked the unclean spirit, and healed the boy, and gave him back to his father. [43] And they were all astonished at the majesty of God.

[4] Or, *departure*. [5] Or, *having remained awake*.
[6] Or, *booths*. [7] Many ancient authorities read *my beloved Son*. See Mt. 17. 5; Mk. 9. 7.
[8] Or, *was past*. [9] Or, *convulseth*. [10] Or, *rent him*. [11] Or, *convulsed*.

But while all were marvelling at all the things which he did, he said unto his disciples, [44] Let these words sink into your ears: for the Son of man shall be delivered[12] up into the hands of men. [45] But they understood not this saying, and it was concealed from them, that they should not perceive it; and they were afraid to ask him about this saying.

[46] And there arose a reasoning[13] among them, which of them was the greatest.[14] [47] But when Jesus saw the reasoning[13] of their heart, he took a little child, and set him by his side, [48] and said unto them, Whosoever shall receive this little child in my name receiveth me: and whosoever shall receive me receiveth him that sent me: for he that is least[15] among you all, the same is great.

[49] And John answered and said, Master, we saw one casting out demons in thy name; and we forbade him, because he followeth not with us. [50] But Jesus said unto him, Forbid *him* not: for he that is not against you is for you.

[51] And it came to pass, when the days were[16] well-nigh come that he should be received up, he stedfastly set his face to go to Jerusalem, and sent messengers before his face: [52] and they went, and entered into a village of the Samaritans, to make ready for him. [53] And they did not receive him, because his face was *as though he were* going to Jerusalem. [54] And when his disciples James and John saw *this,* they said, Lord, wilt thou that we bid fire to come down from heaven, and consume them?[17] [55] But he turned, and rebuked them.[18] [56] And they went to another village.

[57] And as they went on the way, a certain man said unto him, I will follow thee whithersoever thou goest. [58] And Jesus said unto him, The foxes have holes, and the birds of the heaven *have* nests;[19] but the Son of man hath not where to lay his head. [59] And he said unto another, Follow me. But he said, Lord, suffer me first to go and bury my father. [60] But he said unto him, Leave the dead to bury their own dead; but go thou and publish abroad the

[12] Or, *betrayed.* [13] Or, *questioning.* [14] Gr. *greater.* [15] Gr. *lesser.*
[16] Gr. *were being fulfilled.*
[17] Many ancient authorities add *even as Elijah did.* Comp. 2 K. 1. 10–12.
[18] Some ancient authorities add *and said, Ye know not what manner of spirit ye are of.* Some, but fewer, add also *For the Son of man came not to destroy men's lives, but to save* them. Comp. ch. 19. 10; Jn. 3. 17; 12. 47.
[19] Gr. *lodging-places.*

kingdom of God. [61] And another also said, I will follow thee, Lord; but first suffer me to bid farewell to them that are at my house. [62] But Jesus said unto him, No man, having put his hand to the plow, and looking back, is fit for the kingdom of God.

X

[1] Now after these things the Lord appointed seventy others,[1] and sent them two and two before his face into every city and place, whither he himself was about to come. [2] And he said unto them, The harvest indeed is plenteous, but the laborers are few: pray ye therefore the Lord of the harvest, that he send forth laborers into his harvest. [3] Go your ways; behold, I send you forth as lambs in the midst of wolves. [4] Carry no purse, no wallet, no shoes; and salute no man on the way. [5] And into whatsoever house ye shall enter,[2] first say, Peace *be* to this house. [6] And if a son of peace be there, your peace shall rest upon him:[3] but if not, it shall turn to you again. [7] And in that same house remain, eating and drinking such things as they give: for the laborer is worthy of his hire. Go not from house to house. [8] And into whatsoever city ye enter, and they receive you, eat such things as are set before you: [9] and heal the sick that are therein, and say unto them, The kingdom of God is come nigh unto you. [10] But into whatsoever city ye shall enter, and they receive you not, go out into the streets thereof and say, [11] Even the dust from your city, that cleaveth to our feet, we wipe off against you: nevertheless know this, that the kingdom of God is come nigh. [12] I say unto you, It shall be more tolerable in that day for Sodom, than for that city. [13] Woe unto thee, Chorazin! woe unto thee, Bethsaida! for if the mighty[4] works had been done in Tyre and Sidon, which were done in you, they would have repented long ago, sitting in sackcloth and ashes. [14] But it shall be more tolerable for Tyre and Sidon in the judgment, than for you. [15] And thou, Capernaum, shalt thou be exalted unto heaven? thou shalt be brought down unto Hades. [16] He that heareth you heareth me; and he that rejecteth you rejecteth me; and he that rejecteth me rejecteth him that sent me.

[1] Many ancient authorities add *and two:* and so in ver. 17.
[2] Or, *enter first, say.* [3] Or, *it.* [4] Gr. *powers.*

[17] And the seventy returned with joy, saying, Lord, even the demons are subject unto us in thy name. [18] And he said unto them, I beheld Satan fallen as lightning from heaven. [19] Behold, I have given you authority to tread upon serpents and scorpions, and over all the power of the enemy: and nothing shall in any wise hurt you. [20] Nevertheless in this rejoice not, that the spirits are subject unto you; but rejoice that your names are written in heaven.

[21] In that same hour he rejoiced in[5] the Holy Spirit, and said, I thank[6] thee, O Father, Lord of heaven and earth, that thou didst hide these things from the wise and understanding, and didst reveal them unto babes: yea, Father; for[7] so it was well-pleasing in thy sight. [22] All things have been delivered unto me of my Father: and no one knoweth who the Son is, save the Father; and who the Father is, save the Son, and he to whomsoever the Son willeth to reveal *him*. [23] And turning to the disciples, he said privately, Blessed *are* the eyes which see the things that ye see: [24] for I say unto you, that many prophets and kings desired to see the things which ye see, and saw them not; and to hear the things which ye hear, and heard them not.

[25] And behold, a certain lawyer stood up and made trial of him, saying, Teacher, what shall I do to inherit eternal life? [26] And he said unto him, What is written in the law? how readest thou? [27] And he answering said, Thou shalt love the Lord thy God with[8] all thy heart, and with all thy soul, and with all thy strength, and with all thy mind; and thy neighbor as thyself. [28] And he said unto him, Thou hast answered right: this do, and thou shalt live. [29] But he, desiring to justify himself, said unto Jesus, And who is my neighbor? [30] Jesus made answer and said, A certain man was going down from Jerusalem to Jericho; and he fell among robbers, who both stripped him and beat him, and departed, leaving him half dead. [31] And by chance a certain priest was going down that way: and when he saw him, he passed by on the other side. [32] And in like manner a Levite also, when he came to the place, and saw him, passed by on the other side. [33] But a certain Samaritan, as he journeyed, came where he was: and when he saw him, he was moved with compassion, [34] and came to him, and bound up his

[5] Or, *by*. [6] Or, *praise*. [7] Or, *that*. [8] Gr. *from*.

wounds, pouring on *them* oil and wine; and he set him on his own beast, and brought him to an inn, and took care of him. [35] And on the morrow he took out two shillings,[9] and gave them to the host, and said, Take care of him; and whatsoever thou spendest more, I, when I come back again, will repay thee. [36] Which of these three, thinkest thou, proved neighbor unto him that fell among the robbers? [37] And he said, He that showed mercy on him. And Jesus said unto him, Go, and do thou likewise.

[38] Now as they went on their way, he entered into a certain village: and a certain woman named Martha received him into her house. [39] And she had a sister called Mary, who also sat at the Lord's feet, and heard his word. [40] But Martha was cumbered[10] about much serving; and she came up to him, and said, Lord, dost thou not care that my sister did leave me to serve alone? bid her therefore that she help me. [41] But the Lord answered and said unto her, Martha,[11] Martha, thou art anxious and troubled about many things: [42] but[12] one thing is needful: for Mary hath chosen the good part, which shall not be taken away from her.

XI

[1] AND it came to pass, as he was praying in a certain place, that when he ceased, one of his disciples said unto him, Lord, teach us to pray, even as John also taught his disciples. [2] And he said unto them, When ye pray, say, Father,[1] Hallowed be thy name. Thy kingdom come.[2] [3] Give us day by day our[3] daily bread. [4] And forgive us our sins; for we ourselves also forgive every one that is indebted to us. And bring us not into temptation.[4]

[5] And he said unto them, Which of you shall have a friend, and shall go unto him at midnight, and say to him, Friend, lend me three loaves; [6] for a friend of mine is come to me from a journey, and I have nothing to set before him; [7] and he from within shall answer

[9] See marginal note on ch. 7. 41.

[10] Gr. *distracted.* [11] A few ancient authorities read *Martha, Martha, thou art troubled; Mary hath chosen &c.* [12] Many ancient authorities read *but few things are needful, or one.*

[1] Many ancient authorities read *Our Father, who art in heaven.* See Mt. 6. 9.

[2] Many ancient authorities add *Thy will be done, as in heaven, so on earth.* See Mt. 6. 10. [3] Gr. *our bread for the coming day.* Or, *our needful bread:* as in Mt 6. 11. [4] Many ancient authorities add *but deliver us from the evil* one (or, *from evil*). See Mt. 6. 13.

and say, Trouble me not: the door is now shut, and my children are with me in bed; I cannot rise and give thee? [8] I say unto you, Though he will not rise and give him because he is his friend, yet because of his importunity he will arise and give him as[5] many as he needeth. [9] And I say unto you, Ask, and it shall be given you; seek, and ye shall find; knock, and it shall be opened unto you. [10] For every one that asketh receiveth; and he that seeketh findeth; and to him that knocketh it shall be opened. [11] And of which of you that is a father shall his son ask a[6] loaf, and he give him a stone? or a fish, and he for a fish give him a serpent? [12] Or *if* he shall ask an egg, will he give him a scorpion? [13] If ye then, being evil, know how to give good gifts unto your children, how much more shall *your* heavenly Father give the Holy Spirit to them that ask him?

[14] And he was casting out a demon *that was* dumb. And it came to pass, when the demon was gone out, the dumb man spake; and the multitudes marvelled. [15] But some of them said, By[7] Beelzebub[8] the prince of the demons casteth he out demons. [16] And others, trying *him,* sought of him a sign from heaven. [17] But he, knowing their thoughts, said unto them, Every kingdom divided against itself is brought to desolation; and[9] a house *divided* against a house falleth. [18] And if Satan also is divided against himself, how shall his kingdom stand? because ye say that I cast out demons by[7] Beelzebub.[8] [19] And if I by[7] Beelzebub[8] cast out demons, by whom do your sons cast them out? therefore shall they be your judges. [20] But if I by the finger of God cast out demons, then is the kingdom of God come upon you. [21] When the strong *man* fully armed guardeth his own court, his goods are in peace: [22] but when a stronger than he shall come upon him, and overcome him, he taketh from him his whole armor wherein he trusted, and divideth his spoils. [23] He that is not with me is against me; and he that gathereth not with me scattereth. [24] The unclean spirit when he[10] is gone out of the man, passeth through waterless places, seeking rest; and finding none, he[10] saith, I will turn back unto my house whence I came out. [24] And when he[10] is come he[10] findeth it swept and garnished. [26] Then goeth he,[10] and taketh *to him* seven other

[5] Or, *whatsoever things.*
[6] Some ancient authorities omit *a loaf, and he give him a stone? or.*
[7] Or, *In.* [8] Gr. *Beelzebul.* [9] Or, *and house falleth upon house.* [10] Or, *it.*

spirits more evil than himself;[11] and they enter in and dwell there: and the last state of that man becometh worse than the first.

[27] And it came to pass, as he said these things, a certain woman out of the multitude lifted up her voice, and said unto him, Blessed is the womb that bare thee, and the breasts which thou didst suck. [28] But he said, Yea rather, blessed are they that hear the word of God, and keep it.

[29] And when the multitudes were gathering together unto him, he began to say, This generation is an evil generation: it seeketh after a sign; and there shall no sign be given to it but the sign of Jonah. [30] For even as Jonah became a sign unto the Ninevites, so shall also the Son of man be to this generation. [31] The queen of the south shall rise up in the judgment with the men of this generation, and shall condemn them: for she came from the ends of the earth to hear the wisdom of Solomon; and behold, a[12] greater than Solomon is here. [32] The men of Nineveh shall stand up in the judgment with this generation, and shall condemn it: for they repented at the preaching of Jonah; and behold, a[12] greater than Jonah is here.

[33] No man, when he hath lighted a lamp, putteth it in a cellar, neither under the bushel, but on the stand, that they which enter in may see the light. [34] The lamp of thy body is thine eye: when thine eye is single, thy whole body also is full of light; but when it is evil, thy body also is full of darkness. [35] Look therefore whether the light that is in thee be not darkness. [36] If therefore thy whole body be full of light, having no part dark, it shall be wholly full of light, as when the lamp with its bright shining doth give thee light.

[37] Now as he spake, a Pharisee asketh him to dine[13] with him: and he went in, and sat down to meat. [38] And when the Pharisee saw it, he marvelled that he had not first bathed himself before dinner.[13] [39] And the Lord said unto him, Now ye the Pharisees cleanse the outside of the cup and of the platter; but your inward part is full of extortion and wickedness. [40] Ye foolish ones, did not he that made the outside make the inside also? [41] But give for alms those things which are[14] within; and behold, all things are clean unto you.

[11] Or, *itself.* [12] Gr. *more than.* [13] Gr. *breakfast.* [14] Or, *ye can.*

[42] But woe unto you Pharisees! for ye tithe mint and rue and every herb, and pass over justice and the love of God: but these ought ye to have done, and not to leave the other undone. [43] Woe unto you Pharisees! for ye love the chief seats in the synagogues, and the salutations in the marketplaces. [44] Woe unto you! for ye are as the tombs which appear not, and the men that walk over *them* know it not.

[45] And one of the lawyers answering saith unto him, Teacher, in saying this thou reproachest us also. [46] And he said, Woe unto you lawyers also! for ye load men with burdens grievous to be borne, and ye yourselves touch not the burdens with one of your fingers. [47] Woe unto you! for ye build the tombs of the prophets, and your fathers killed them. [48] So ye are witnesses and consent unto the works of your fathers: for they killed them, and ye build *their tombs*. [49] Therefore also said the wisdom of God, I will send unto them prophets and apostles; and *some* of them they shall kill and persecute; [50] that the blood of all the prophets, which was shed from the foundation of the world, may be required of this generation; [51] from the blood of Abel unto the blood of Zachariah, who perished between the altar and the sanctuary:[15] yea, I say unto you, it shall be required of this generation. [52] Woe unto you lawyers! for ye took away the key of knowledge: ye entered not in yourselves, and them that were entering in ye hindered.

[53] And when he was come out from thence, the scribes and the Pharisees began to press[16] upon *him* vehemently, and to provoke him to speak of many[17] things; [54] laying wait for him, to catch something out of his mouth.

XII

[1] In the mean time, when the[1] many thousands of the multitude were gathered together, insomuch that they trod one upon another, he began to say[2] unto his disciples first of all, Beware ye of the leaven of the Pharisees, which is hypocrisy. [2] But there is nothing covered up, that shall not be revealed; and hid, that shall not be known. [3] Wherefore whatsoever ye have said in the darkness shall be heard in

[15] Gr. *house*. [16] Or, *set themselves vehemently against* him. [17] Or, *more*.
[1] Gr. *the myriads of*. [2] Or, *say unto his disciples, First of all beware ye*.

the light; and what ye have spoken in the ear in the inner chambers shall be proclaimed upon the housetops. [4] And I say unto you my friends, Be not afraid of them that kill the body, and after that have no more that they can do. [5] But I will warn you whom ye shall fear: Fear him, who after he hath killed hath power[3] to cast into hell;[4] yea, I say unto you, Fear him. [6] Are not five sparrows sold for two pence? and not one of them is forgotten in the sight of God. [7] But the very hairs of your head are all numbered. Fear not: ye are of more value than many sparrows. [8] And I say unto you, Every one who shall confess me[5] before men, him[6] shall the Son of man also confess before the angels of God: [9] but he that denieth me in the presence of men shall be denied in the presence of the angels of God. [10] And every one who shall speak a word against the Son of man, it shall be forgiven him: but unto him that blasphemeth against the Holy Spirit it shall not be forgiven. [11] And when they bring you before the synagogues, and the rulers, and the authorities, be not anxious how or what ye shall answer, or what ye shall say: [12] for the Holy Spirit shall teach you in that very hour what ye ought to say.

[13] And one out of the multitude said unto him, Teacher, bid my brother divide the inheritance with me. [14] But he said unto him, Man, who made me a judge or a divider over you? [15] And he said unto them, Take heed, and keep yourselves from all covetousness: for[7] a man's life consisteth not in the abundance of the things which he possesseth. [16] And he spake a parable unto them, saying, The ground of a certain rich man brought forth plentifully: [17] and he reasoned within himself, saying, What shall I do, because I have not where to bestow my fruits? [18] And he said, This will I do: I will pull down my barns, and build greater; and there will I bestow all my grain and my goods. [19] And I will say to my soul,[8] Soul,[8] thou hast much goods laid up for many years; take thine ease, eat, drink, be merry. [20] But God said unto him, Thou foolish one, this night is[9] thy soul[8] required of thee; and the things which thou hast prepared, whose shall they be? [21] So is he that layeth up treasure for himself, and is not rich toward God.

[3] Or, *authority*. [4] Gr. *Gehenna*. [5] Gr. *in me*. [6] Gr. *in him*.

[7] Or, *for* even *in a man's abundance his life is not from the things which he possesseth*. [8] Or, *life*. [9] Gr. *they require thy soul*.

[22] And he said unto his disciples, Therefore I say unto you, Be not anxious for *your* life,[10] what ye shall eat; nor yet for your body, what ye shall put on. [23] For the life[10] is more than the food, and the body than the raiment. [24] Consider the ravens, that they sow not, neither reap; which have no store-chamber nor barn; and God feedeth them: of how much more value are ye than the birds! [25] And which of you by being anxious can add a cubit unto the[11] measure of his life? [26] If then ye are not able to do even that which is least, why are ye anxious concerning the rest? [27] Consider the lilies, how they grow: they toil not, neither do they spin; yet I say unto you, Even Solomon in all his glory was not arrayed like one of these. [28] But if God doth so clothe the grass in the field, which to-day is, and to-morrow is cast into the oven; how much more *shall he clothe* you, O ye of little faith? [29] And seek not ye what ye shall eat, and what ye shall drink, neither be ye of doubtful mind. [30] For all these things do the nations of the world seek after: but your Father knoweth that ye have need of these things. [31] Yet seek ye his[12] kingdom, and these things shall be added unto you. [32] Fear not, little flock; for it is your Father's good pleasure to give you the kingdom. [33] Sell that which ye have, and give alms; make for yourselves purses which wax not old, a treasure in the heavens that faileth not, where no thief draweth near, neither moth destroyeth. [34] For where your treasure is, there will your heart be also.

[35] Let your loins be girded about, and your lamps burning; [36] and be ye yourselves like unto men looking for their lord, when he shall return from the marriage feast; that, when he cometh and knocketh, they may straightway open unto him. [37] Blessed are those servants,[13] whom the lord when he cometh shall find watching: verily I say unto you, that he shall gird himself, and make them sit down to meat, and shall come and serve them. [38] And if he shall come in the second watch, and if in the third, and find *them* so, blessed are those *servants*. [39] But[14] know this, that if the master of the house had known in what hour the thief

[10] Or, *soul*. [11] Or, *his stature*. [12] Many ancient authorities read *the kingdom of God*. [13] Gr. *bondservants*. [14] Or, *But this ye know*.

was coming, he would have watched, and not have left his house to be broken[15] through. [40] Be ye also ready: for in an hour that ye think not the Son of man cometh.

[41] And Peter said, Lord, speakest thou this parable unto us, or even unto all? [42] And the Lord said, Who then is the[16] faithful and wise steward, whom his lord shall set over his household, to give them their portion of food in due season? [43] Blessed is that servant,[17] whom his lord when he cometh shall find so doing. [44] Of a truth I say unto you, that he will set him over all that he hath. [45] But if that servant[17] shall say in his heart, My lord delayeth his coming; and shall begin to beat the menservants and the maidservants, and to eat and drink, and to be drunken; [46] the lord of that servant[17] shall come in a day when he expecteth not, and in an hour when he knoweth not, and shall cut[18] him asunder, and appoint his portion with the unfaithful. [47] And that servant,[17] who knew his lord's will, and made not ready, nor did according to his will, shall be beaten with many *stripes;* [48] but he that knew not, and did things worthy of stripes, shall be beaten with few *stripes*. And to whomsoever much is given, of him shall much be required: and to whom they commit much, of him will they ask the more.

[49 I came to cast fire upon the earth; and what[19] do I desire, if it is already kindled? [50] But I have a baptism to be baptized with; and how am I straitened till it be accomplished! [51] Think ye that I am come to give peace in the earth? I tell you, Nay; but rather division: [52] for there shall be from henceforth five in one house divided, three against two, and two against three. [53] They shall be divided, father against son, and son against father; mother against daughter, and daughter against her mother; mother in law against her daughter in law, and daughter in law against her mother in law.

[54] And he said to the multitudes also, When ye see a cloud rising in the west, straightway ye say, There cometh a shower; and so it cometh to pass. [55] And when *ye see* a south wind blowing, ye say, There will be a scorching[20] heat; and it cometh to pass.

15 Gr. *digged through.* 16 Or, *the faithful steward, the wise* man *whom &c.*
17 Gr. *bondservant.* 18 Or, *severely scourge him.*
19 Or, *how would I that it were already kindled!* 20 Or, *hot wind.*

[56] Ye hypocrites, ye know how to interpret[21] the face of the earth and the heaven; but how is it that ye know not how to interpret[21] this time? [57] And why even of yourselves judge ye not what is right? [58] For as thou art going with thine adversary before the magistrate, on the way give diligence to be quit of him; lest haply he drag thee unto the judge, and the judge shall deliver thee to the officer,[22] and the officer[22] shall cast thee into prison. [59] I say unto thee, Thou shalt by no means come out thence, till thou have paid the very last mite.

XIII

[1] Now there were some present at that very season who told him of the Galilæans, whose blood Pilate had mingled with their sacrifices. [2] And he answered and said unto them, Think ye that these Galilæans were sinners above all the Galilæans, because they have suffered these things? [3] I tell you, Nay: but, except ye repent, ye shall all in like manner perish. [4] Or those eighteen, upon whom the tower in Siloam fell, and killed them, think ye that they were offenders[1] above all the men that dwell in Jerusalem? [5] I tell you, Nay: but, except ye repent, ye shall all likewise perish.

[6] And he spake this parable; A certain man had a fig tree planted in his vineyard: and he came seeking fruit thereon, and found none. [7] And he said unto the vine-dresser, Behold, these three years I come seeking fruit on this fig tree, and find none: cut it down; why doth it also cumber the ground? [8] And he answering saith unto him, Lord, let it alone this year also, till I shall dig about it, and dung it: [9] and if it bear fruit thenceforth, *well;* but if not, thou shalt cut it down.

[10] And he was teaching in one of the synagogues on the sabbath day. [11] And behold, a woman that had a spirit of infirmity eighteen years; and she was bowed together, and could in no wise lift herself up. [12] And when Jesus saw her, he called her, and said to her, Woman, thou art loosed from thine infirmity. [13] And he laid his hands upon her: and immediately she was made straight, and glorified God. [14] And the ruler of the synagogue, being moved

[21] Gr. *prove.* [22] Gr. *exactor.*

[1] Gr. *debtors.*

with indignation because Jesus had healed on the sabbath, answered and said to the multitude, There are six days in which men ought to work: in them therefore come and be healed, and not on the day of the sabbath. [15] But the Lord answered him, and said, Ye hypocrites, doth not each one of you on the sabbath loose his ox or his ass from the stall,[2] and lead him away to watering? [16] And ought not this woman, being a daughter of Abraham, whom Satan had bound, lo, *these* eighteen years, to have been loosed from this bond on the day of the sabbath? [17] And as he said these things, all his adversaries were put to shame: and all the multitude rejoiced for all the glorious things that were done by him.

[18] He said therefore, Unto what is the kingdom of God like? and whereunto shall I liken it? [19] It is like unto a grain of mustard seed, which a man took, and cast into his own garden; and it grew, and became a tree; and the birds of the heaven lodged in the branches thereof.

[20] And again he said, Whereunto shall I liken the kingdom of God? [21] It is like unto leaven which a woman took and hid in three measures[3] of meal, till it was all leavened.

[22] And he went on his way through cities and villages, teaching, and journeying on unto Jerusalem. [23] And one said unto him, Lord, are they few that are saved? And he said unto them, [24] Strive to enter in by the narrow door: for many, I say unto you, shall seek to enter in, and shall not be able.[4] [25] When once the master of the house is risen up, and hath shut to the door, and ye begin to stand without, and to knock at the door, saying, Lord, open to us; and he shall answer and say to you, I know you not whence ye are; [26] then shall ye begin to say, We did eat and drink in thy presence, and thou didst teach in our streets; [27] and he shall say, I tell you, I know not whence ye are; depart from me, all ye workers of iniquity. [28] There shall be the weeping and the gnashing of teeth, when ye shall see Abraham, and Isaac, and Jacob, and all the prophets, in the kingdom of God, and yourselves cast forth without. [29] And they shall come from the east and west, and from the north and south, and shall sit[5] down

[2] Gr. *manger.* [3] See marginal note on Mt. 13. 33. [4] Or, *able, when once.*
[5] Gr. *recline.*

in the kingdom of God. [30] And behold, there are last who shall be first, and there are first who shall be last.

[31] In that very hour there came certain Pharisees, saying to him, Get thee out, and go hence: for Herod would fain kill thee. [32] And he said unto them, Go and say to that fox, Behold, I cast out demons and perform cures to-day and to-morrow, and the third *day* I am[6] perfected. [33] Nevertheless I must go on my way to-day and to-morrow and the *day* following: for it cannot be that a prophet perish out of Jerusalem. [34] O Jerusalem, Jerusalem, that killeth the prophets, and stoneth them that are sent unto her! how often would I have gathered thy children together, even as a hen *gathereth* her own brood under her wings, and ye would not! [35] Behold, your house is left unto you *desolate:* and I say unto you, Ye shall not see me, until ye shall say, Blessed *is* he that cometh in the name of the Lord.

XIV

[1] And it came to pass, when he went into the house of one of the rulers of the Pharisees on a sabbath to eat bread, that they were watching him. [2] And behold, there was before him a certain man that had the dropsy. [3] And Jesus answering spake unto the lawyers and Pharisees, saying, Is it lawful to heal on the sabbath, or not? [4] But they held their peace. And he took him, and healed him, and let him go. [5] And he said unto them, Which of you shall have an[1] ass or an ox fallen into a well, and will not straightway draw him up on a sabbath day? [6] And they could not answer again unto these things.

[7] And he spake a parable unto those that were bidden, when he marked how they chose out the chief seats; saying unto them, [8] When thou art bidden of any man to a marriage feast, sit[2] not down in the chief seat; lest haply a more honorable man than thou be bidden of him, [9] and he that bade thee and him shall come and say to thee, Give this man place; and then thou shalt begin with shame to take the lowest place. [10] But when thou art bidden, go and sit down in the lowest place; that when he that

[6] Or, *end my course.*

[1] Many ancient authorities read *a son.* See ch. 13. 15. [2] Gr. *recline not.*

hath bidden thee cometh, he may say to thee, Friend, go up higher: then shalt thou have glory in the presence of all that sit[3] at meat with thee. [11] For every one that exalteth himself shall be humbled; and he that humbleth himself shall be exalted.

[12] And he said to him also that had bidden him, When thou makest a dinner or a supper, call not thy friends, nor thy brethren, nor thy kinsmen, nor rich neighbors; lest haply they also bid thee again, and a recompense be made thee. [13] But when thou makest a feast, bid the poor, the maimed, the lame, the blind: [14] and thou shalt be blessed; because they have not *wherewith* to recompense thee: for thou shalt be recompensed in the resurrection of the just.

[15] And when one of them that sat[4] at meat with him heard these things, he said unto him, Blessed is he that shall eat bread in the kingdom of God. [16] But he said unto him, A certain man made a great supper; and he bade many: [17] and he sent forth his servant[5] at supper time to say to them that were bidden, Come; for *all* things are now ready. [18] And they all with one *consent* began to make excuse. The first said unto him, I have bought a field, and I must needs go out and see it; I pray thee have me excused. [19] And another said, I have bought five yoke of oxen, and I go to prove them; I pray thee have me excused. [20] And another said, I have married a wife, and therefore I cannot come. [21] And the servant[5] came, and told his lord these things. Then the master of the house being angry said to his servant,[5] Go out quickly into the streets and lanes of the city, and bring in hither the poor and maimed and blind and lame. [22] And the servant[5] said, Lord, what thou didst command is done, and yet there is room. [23] And the lord said unto the servant,[5] Go out into the highways and hedges, and constrain *them* to come in, that my house may be filled. [24] For I say unto you, that none of those men that were bidden shall taste of my supper.

[25] Now there went with him great multitudes: and he turned, and said unto them, [26] If any man cometh unto me, and hateth not his own father, and mother, and wife, and children, and brethren,

[3] Gr. *recline.* Comp. ch. 7. 36, 37, marg.
[4] Gr. *reclined.* Comp. ch. 7. 36, 37, marg. [5] Gr. *bondservant.*

and sisters, yea, and his own life also, he cannot be my disciple. [27] Whosoever doth not bear his own cross, and come after me, cannot be my disciple. [28] For which of you, desiring to build a tower, doth not first sit down and count the cost, whether he have *wherewith* to complete it? [29] Lest haply, when he hath laid a foundation, and is not able to finish, all that behold begin to mock him, [30] saying, This man began to build, and was not able to finish. [31] Or what king, as he goeth to encounter another king in war, will not sit down first and take counsel whether he is able with ten thousand to meet him that cometh against him with twenty thousand? [32] Or else, while the other is yet a great way off, he sendeth an ambassage, and asketh conditions of peace. [33] So therefore whosoever he be of you that renounceth not all that he hath, he cannot be my disciple. [34] Salt therefore is good: but if even the salt have lost its savor, wherewith shall it be seasoned? [35] It is fit neither for the land nor for the dunghill: *men* cast it out. He that hath ears to hear, let him hear.

XV

[1] Now all the publicans[1] and sinners were drawing near unto him to hear him. [2] And both the Pharisees and the scribes murmured, saying, This man receiveth sinners, and eateth with them.

[3] And he spake unto them this parable, saying, [4] What man of you, having a hundred sheep, and having lost one of them, doth not leave the ninety and nine in the wilderness, and go after that which is lost, until he find it? [5] And when he hath found it, he layeth it on his shoulders, rejoicing. [6] And when he cometh home, he calleth together his friends and his neighbors, saying unto them, Rejoice with me, for I have found my sheep which was lost. [7] I say unto you, that even so there shall be joy in heaven over one sinner that repenteth, *more* than over ninety and nine righteous persons, who need no repentance.

[8] Or what woman having ten pieces[2] of silver, if she lose one piece, doth not light a lamp, and sweep the house, and seek diligently until she find it? [9] And when she hath found it, she calleth

[1] See marginal note on ch. 3. 12.

[2] Gr. *drachma*, a coin worth about eight pence, or sixteen cents.

together her friends and neighbors, saying, Rejoice with me, for I have found the piece which I had lost. [10] Even so, I say unto you, there is joy in the presence of the angels of God over one sinner that repenteth.

[11] And he said, A certain man had two sons: [12] and the younger of them said to his father, Father, give me the portion of *thy*[3] substance that falleth to me. And he divided unto them his living. [13] And not many days after, the younger son gathered all together and took his journey into a far country; and there he wasted his substance with riotous living. [14] And when he had spent all, there arose a mighty famine in that country; and he began to be in want. [15] And he went and joined himself to one of the citizens of that country; and he sent him into his fields to feed swine. [16] And he would fain have[4] filled his belly with the[5] husks that the swine did eat: and no man gave unto him. [17] But when he came to himself he said, How many hired servants of my father's have bread enough and to spare, and I perish here with hunger! [18] I will arise and go to my father, and will say unto him, Father, I have sinned against heaven, and in thy sight: [19] I am no more worthy to be called thy son: make me as one of thy hired servants. [20] And he arose, and came to his father. But while he was yet afar off, his father saw him, and was moved with compassion, and ran, and fell on his neck, and kissed[6] him. [21] And the son said unto him, Father, I have sinned against heaven, and in thy sight: I am no more worthy to be called thy son.[7] [22] But the father said to his servants,[8] Bring forth quickly the best robe, and put it on him; and put a ring on his hand, and shoes on his feet: [23] and bring the fatted calf, *and* kill it, and let us eat, and make merry: [24] for this my son was dead, and is alive again; he was lost, and is found. And they began to be merry. [25] Now his elder son was in the field: and as he came and drew nigh to the house, he heard music and dancing. [26] And he called to him one of the servants, and inquired what these things might be.

[3] Gr. *the.* [4] Many ancient authorities read *have been filled.*
[5] Gr. *the pods of the carob tree.*
[6] Gr. *kissed him much.* See ch. 7. 38, 45.
[7] Some ancient authorities add *make me as one of thy hired servants.* See ver. 19.
[8] Gr. *bondservants.*

[27] And he said unto him, Thy brother is come; and thy father hath killed the fatted calf, because he hath received him safe and sound. [28] But he was angry, and would not go in: and his father came out, and entreated him. [29] But he answered and said to his father, Lo, these many years do I serve thee, and I never transgressed a commandment of thine; and *yet* thou never gavest me a kid, that I might make merry with my friends: [30] but when this thy son came, who hath devoured thy living with harlots, thou killedst for him the fatted calf. [31] And he said unto him, Son,[9] thou art ever with me, and all that is mine is thine. [32] But it was meet to make merry and be glad: for this thy brother was dead, and is alive *again;* and *was* lost, and is found.

XVI

[1] AND he said also unto the disciples, There was a certain rich man, who had a steward; and the same was accused unto him that he was wasting his goods. [2] And he called him, and said unto him, What is this that I hear of thee? render the account of thy stewardship; for thou canst be no longer steward. [3] And the steward said within himself, What shall I do, seeing that my lord taketh away the stewardship from me? I have not strength to dig; to beg I am ashamed. [4] I am resolved what to do, that, when I am put out of the stewardship, they may receive me into their houses. [5] And calling to him each one of his lord's debtors, he said to the first, How much owest thou unto my lord? [6] And he said, A hundred measures[1] of oil. And he said unto him, Take thy bond,[2] and sit down quickly and write fifty. [7] Then said he to another, And how much owest thou? And he said, A hundred measures[3] of wheat. He saith unto him, Take thy bond,[2] and write fourscore. [8] And his lord commended the[4] unrighteous steward because he had done wisely: for the sons of this world[5] are for their own generations wiser than the sons of the light. [9] And I say unto you, Make to yourselves friends by[6] means of the mammon of unrighteousness; that, when it shall fail, they may receive you into

[9] Gr. *Child.*
[1] Gr. *baths,* the bath being a Hebrew measure. See Ezek. 45. 10, 11, 14.
[2] Gr. *writings.* [3] Gr. *cors,* the cor being a Hebrew measure. See Ezek. 45. 14.
[4] Gr. *the steward of unrighteousness.* [5] Or, *age.* [6] Gr. *out of.*

the eternal tabernacles. [10] He that is faithful in a very little is faithful also in much: and he that is unrighteous in a very little is unrighteous also in much. [11] If therefore ye have not been faithful in the unrighteous mammon, who will commit to your trust the true *riches?* [12] And if ye have not been faithful in that which is another's, who will give you that which is your[7] own? [13] No servant[8] can serve two masters: for either he will hate the one, and love the other; or else he will hold to one, and despise the other. Ye cannot serve God and mammon.

[14] And the Pharisees, who were lovers of money, heard all these things; and they scoffed at him. [15] And he said unto them, Ye are they that justify yourselves in the sight of men; but God knoweth your hearts: for that which is exalted among men is an abomination in the sight of God. [16] The law and the prophets *were* until John: from that time the gospel[9] of the kingdom of God is preached, and every man entereth violently into it. [17] But it is easier for heaven and earth to pass away, than for one tittle of the law to fall.

[18] Every one that putteth away his wife, and marrieth another, committeth adultery: and he that marrieth one that is put away from a husband committeth adultery.

[19] Now there was a certain rich man, and he was clothed in purple and fine linen, faring[10] sumptuously every day: [20] and a certain beggar named Lazarus was laid at his gate, full of sores, [21] and desiring to be fed with the *crumbs* that fell from the rich man's table; yea, even the dogs came and licked his sores. [22] And it came to pass, that the beggar died, and that he was carried away by the angels into Abraham's bosom: and the rich man also died, and was buried. [23] And in Hades he lifted up his eyes, being in torments, and seeth Abraham afar off, and Lazarus in his bosom. [24] And he cried and said, Father Abraham, have mercy on me, and send Lazarus, that he may dip the tip of his finger in water, and cool my tongue; for I am in anguish in this flame. [25] But Abraham said, Son,[11] remember that thou in thy lifetime receivedst thy good things, and Lazarus in like manner evil things: but now

[7] Some ancient authorities read *our own.* [8] Gr. *household-servant.*
[9] Or, *good tidings:* comp. ch. 3. 18. [10] Or, *living in mirth and splendor every day.*
[11] Gr. *Child.*

here he is comforted, and thou art in anguish. [26] And besides[12] all this, between us and you there is a great gulf fixed, that they that would pass from hence to you may not be able, and that none may cross over from thence to us. [27] And he said, I pray thee therefore, father, that thou wouldest send him to my father's house; [28] for I have five brethren; that he may testify unto them, lest they also come into this place of torment. [29] But Abraham saith, They have Moses and the prophets; let them hear them. [30] And he said, Nay, father Abraham: but if one go to them from the dead, they will repent. [31] And he said unto him, If they hear not Moses and the prophets, neither will they be persuaded, if one rise from the dead.

XVII

[1] And he said unto his disciples, It is impossible but that occasions of stumbling should come; but woe unto him, through whom they come! [2] It were well for him if a millstone were hanged about his neck, and he were thrown into the sea, rather than that he should cause one of these little ones to stumble. [3] Take heed to yourselves: if thy brother sin, rebuke him; and if he repent, forgive him. [4] And if he sin against thee seven times in the day, and seven times turn again to thee, saying, I repent; thou shalt forgive him.

[5] And the apostles said unto the Lord, Increase our faith. [6] And the Lord said, If ye had faith as a grain of mustard seed, ye would say unto this sycamine tree, Be thou rooted up, and be thou planted in the sea; and it would obey you. [7] But who is there of you, having a servant[1] plowing or keeping sheep, that will say unto him, when he is come in from the field, Come straightway and sit down to meat; [8] and will not rather say unto him, Make ready wherewith I may sup, and gird thyself, and serve me, till I have eaten and drunken; and afterward thou shalt eat and drink? [9] Doth he thank the servant[1] because he did the things that were commanded? [10] Even so ye also, when ye shall have done all the things that are commanded you, say, We are

[12] Or, *in all these things.*
[1] Gr. *bondservant.*

unprofitable servants;[2] we have done that which it was our duty to do.

[11] And it came to pass, as[3] they were on the way to Jerusalem, that he was passing along[4] the borders of Samaria and Galilee. [12] And as he entered into a certain village, there met him ten men that were lepers, who stood afar off: [13] and they lifted up their voices, saying, Jesus, Master, have mercy on us. [14] And when he saw them, he said unto them, Go and show yourselves unto the priests. And it came to pass, as they went, they were cleansed. [15] And one of them, when he saw that he was healed, turned back, with a loud voice glorifying God; [16] and he fell upon his face at his feet, giving him thanks: and he was a Samaritan. [17] And Jesus answering said, Were not the ten cleansed? but where are the nine? [18] Were[5] there none found that returned to give glory to God, save this stranger?[6] [19] And he said unto him, Arise, and go thy way: thy faith hath made[7] thee whole.

[20] And being asked by the Pharisees, when the kingdom of God cometh, he answered them and said, The kingdom of God cometh not with observation: [21] neither shall they say, Lo, here! or, There! for lo, the kingdom of God is within[8] you.

[22] And he said unto the disciples, The days will come, when ye shall desire to see one of the days of the Son of man, and ye shall not see it. [23] And they shall say to you, Lo, there! Lo, here! go not away, nor follow after *them:* [24] for as the lightning, when it lighteneth out of the one part under the heaven, shineth unto the other part under heaven; so shall the Son of man be in[9] his day. [25] But first must he suffer many things and be rejected of this generation. [26] And as it came to pass in the days of Noah, even so shall it be also in the days of the Son of man. [27] They ate, they drank, they married, they were given in marriage, until the day that Noah entered into the ark, and the flood came, and destroyed them all. [28] Likewise even as it came to pass in the days of Lot; they ate, they drank, they bought, they sold, they planted, they builded; [29] but in the day that Lot went out from

[2] Gr. *bondservants.* [3] Or, *as he was.*
[4] Or, *through the midst of &c.* [5] Or, *There were none found . . . save this stranger.* [6] Or, *alien.* [7] Or, *saved thee.*
[8] Or, *in the midst of you.* [9] Some ancient authorities omit *in his day.*

Sodom it rained fire and brimstone from heaven, and destroyed them all: [30] after the same manner shall it be in the day that the Son of man is revealed. [31] In that day, he that shall be on the housetop, and his goods in the house, let him not go down to take them away: and let him that is in the field likewise not return back. [32] Remember Lot's wife. [33] Whosoever shall seek to gain his life shall lose it: but whosoever shall lose *his life* shall preserve[10] it. [34] I say unto you, In that night there shall be two men on one bed; the one shall be taken, and the other shall be left. [35] There shall be two women grinding together; the one shall be taken, and the other shall be left.[11] [37] And they answering say unto him, Where, Lord? And he said unto them, Where the body *is,* thither will the eagles[12] also be gathered together.

XVIII

[1] AND he spake a parable unto them to the end that they ought always to pray, and not to faint; [2] saying, There was in a city a judge, who feared not God, and regarded not man: [3] and there was a widow in that city; and she came oft unto him, saying, Avenge[1] me of mine adversary. [4] And he would not for a while: but afterward he said within himself, Though I fear not God, nor regard man; [5] yet because this widow troubleth me, I will avenge her, lest[2] she wear[3] me out by her continual coming. [6] And the Lord said, Hear what the[4] unrighteous judge saith. [7] And shall not God avenge his elect, that cry to him day and night, and[5] *yet* he is longsuffering over them? [8] I say unto you, that he will avenge them speedily. Nevertheless, when the Son of man cometh, shall he find faith[6] on the earth?

[9] And he spake also this parable unto certain who trusted in themselves that they were righteous, and set all[7] others at nought: [10] Two men went up into the temple to pray; the one a Pharisee,

[10] Gr. *save it alive.*
[11] Some ancient authorities add ver. 36. *There shall be two men in the field; the one shall be taken, and the other shall be left.* Mt. 24. 40.
[12] Or, *vultures.*
[1] Or, *Do me justice of:* and so in ver. 5, 7, 8.
[2] Or, *lest at last by her coming she wear me out.* [3] Gr. *bruise.*
[4] Gr. *the judge of unrighteousness.* [5] Or, *and is he slow to punish on their behalf?*
[6] Or, *the faith.* [7] Gr. *the rest.*

and the other a publican.[8] [11] The Pharisee stood and prayed thus with himself, God, I thank thee, that I am not as the rest of men, extortioners, unjust, adulterers, or even as this publican.[8] [12] I fast twice in the week; I give tithes of all that I get. [13] But the publican,[8] standing afar off, would not lift up so much as his eyes unto heaven, but smote his breast, saying God, be[9] thou merciful to me a[10] sinner. [14] I say unto you, This man went down to his house justified rather than the other: for every one that exalteth himself shall be humbled; but he that humbleth himself shall be exalted.

[15] And they were bringing unto him also their babes, that he should touch them: but when the disciples saw it, they rebuked them. [16] But Jesus called them unto him, saying, Suffer the little children to come unto me, and forbid them not: for to[11] such belongeth the kingdom of God. [17] Verily I say unto you, Whosoever shall not receive the kingdom of God as a little child, he shall in no wise enter therein.

[18] And a certain ruler asked him, saying, Good Teacher, what shall I do to inherit eternal life? [19] And Jesus said unto him, Why callest thou me good? none is good, save one, *even* God. [20] Thou knowest the commandments, Do not commit adultery, Do not kill, Do not steal, Do not bear false witness, Honor thy father and mother. [21] And he said, All these things have I observed from my youth up. [22] And when Jesus heard it, he said unto him, One thing thou lackest yet: sell all that thou hast, and distribute unto the poor, and thou shalt have treasure in heaven: and come, follow me. [23] But when he heard these things, he became exceeding sorrowful; for he was very rich. [24] And Jesus seeing him said, How hardly shall they that have riches enter into the kingdom of God! [25] For it is easier for a camel to enter in through a needle's eye, than for a rich man to enter into the kingdom of God. [26] And they that heard it said, Then who can be saved? [27] But he said, The things which are impossible with men are possible with God. [28] And Peter said, Lo, we have left our[12] own, and followed thee. [29] And he said unto them, Verily I say unto

[8] See marginal note on ch. 3. 12. [9] Or, *be thou propitiated.* [10] Or, *the sinner.*
[11] Or, *of such is.* [12] Or, *our own* homes. See Jn. 19. 27.

you, There is no man that hath left house, or wife, or brethren,
or parents, or children, for the kingdom of God's sake, [30] who
shall not receive manifold more in this time, and in the world[13] to
come eternal life.

[31] And he took unto him the twelve, and said unto them,
Behold, we go up to Jerusalem, and all the things that are written
through the prophets shall be accomplished unto the Son of man.
[32] For he shall be delivered[14] up unto the Gentiles, and shall be
mocked, and shamefully treated, and spit upon: [33] and they
shall scourge and kill him: and the third day he shall rise again.
[34] And they understood none of these things; and this saying was
hid from them, and they perceived not the things that were said.

[35] And it came to pass, as he drew nigh unto Jericho, a certain
blind man sat by the way side begging: [36] and hearing a multitude going by, he inquired what this meant. [37] And they told
him, that Jesus of Nazareth passeth by. [38] And he cried, saying,
Jesus, thou son of David, have mercy on me. [39] And they that
went before rebuked him, that he should hold his peace: but he
cried out the more a great deal, Thou son of David, have mercy
on me. [40] And Jesus stood, and commanded him to be brought
unto him: and when he was come near, he asked him, [41] What
wilt thou that I should do unto thee? And he said, Lord, that
I may receive my sight. [42] And Jesus said unto him, Receive
thy sight: thy faith hath made[15] thee whole. [43] And immediately
he received his sight, and followed him, glorifying God: and all the
people, when they saw it, gave praise unto God.

XIX

[1] And he entered and was passing through Jericho. [2] And
behold, a man called by name Zacchæus; and he was a chief publican,
and he was rich. [3] And he sought to see Jesus who he was; and
could not for the crowd, because he was little of stature. [4] And
he ran on before, and climbed up into a sycamore tree to see him:
for he was to pass that way. [5] And when Jesus came to the place,
he looked up, and said unto him, Zacchæus, make haste, and come
down; for to-day I must abide at thy house. [6] And he made

[13] Or, *age.* [14] Or, *betrayed.* [15] Or, *saved thee.*

haste, and came down, and received him joyfully. [7] And when they saw it, they all murmured, saying, He is gone in to lodge with a man that is a sinner. [8] And Zacchæus stood, and said unto the Lord, Behold, Lord, the half of my goods I give to the poor; and if I have wrongfully exacted aught of any man, I restore fourfold. [9] And Jesus said unto him, To-day is salvation come to this house, forasmuch as he also is a son of Abraham. [10] For the Son of man came to seek and to save that which was lost.

[11] And as they heard these things, he added and spake a parable, because he was nigh to Jerusalem, and *because* they supposed that the kingdom of God was immediately to appear. [12] He said therefore, A certain nobleman went into a far country, to receive for himself a kingdom, and to return. [13] And he called ten servants[1] of his, and gave them ten pounds,[2] and said unto them, Trade ye *herewith* till I come. [14] But his citizens hated him, and sent an ambassage after him, saying, We will not that this man reign over us. [15] And it came to pass, when he was come back again, having received the kingdom, that he commanded these servants,[1] unto whom he had given the money, to be called to him, that he might know what they had gained by trading. [16] And the first came before him, saying, Lord, thy pound hath made ten pounds more. [17] And he said unto him, Well done, thou good servant:[3] because thou wast found faithful in a very little, have thou authority over ten cities. [18] And the second came, saying, Thy pound, Lord, hath made five pounds. [19] And he said unto him also, Be thou also over five cities. [20] And another[4] came, saying, Lord, behold, *here is* thy pound, which I kept laid up in a napkin: [21] for I feared thee, because thou art an austere man: thou takest up that which thou layedst not down, and reapest that which thou didst not sow. [22] He saith unto him, Out of thine own mouth will I judge thee, thou wicked servant.[3] Thou knewest that I am an austere man, taking up that which I laid not down, and reaping that which I did not sow; [23] then wherefore gavest thou not my money into the bank, and I[5] at my coming should have required it with interest? [24] And he said

[1] Gr. *bondservants.* [2] *Mina,* here translated a pound, is equal to one hundred drachmas. See ch. 15. 8. [3] Gr. *bondservant.*
[4] Gr. *the other.* [5] Or, *I should have gone and required.*

unto them that stood by, Take away from him the pound, and give it unto him that hath the ten pounds. [25] And they said unto him, Lord, he hath ten pounds. [26] I say unto you, that unto every one that hath shall be given; but from him that hath not, even that which he hath shall be taken away from him. [27] But these mine enemies, that would not that I should reign over them, bring hither, and slay them before me.

[28] And when he had thus spoken, he went on before, going up to Jerusalem.

[29] And it came to pass, when he drew nigh unto Bethphage and Bethany, at the mount that is called Olivet, he sent two of the disciples, [30] saying, Go your way into the village over against *you;* in which as ye enter ye shall find a colt tied, whereon no man ever yet sat: loose him, and bring him. [31] And if any one ask you, Why do ye loose him? thus shall ye say, The Lord hath need of him. [32] And they that were sent went away, and found even as he had said unto them. [33] And as they were loosing the colt, the owners thereof said unto them, Why loose ye the colt? [34] And they said, The Lord hath need of him. [35] And they brought him to Jesus: and they threw their garments upon the colt, and set Jesus thereon. [36] And as he went, they spread their garments in the way. [37] And as he was now drawing nigh, *even* at the descent of the mount of Olives, the whole multitude of the disciples began to rejoice and praise God with a loud voice for all the mighty[6] works which they had seen; [38] saying, Blessed *is* the King that cometh in the name of the Lord: peace in heaven, and glory in the highest. [39] And some of the Pharisees from the multitude said unto him, Teacher, rebuke thy disciples. [40] And he answered and said, I tell you that, if these shall hold their peace, the stones will cry out.

[41] And when he drew nigh, he saw the city and wept over it, [42] saying, If[7] thou hadst known in this[8] day, even thou, the things which belong unto peace![9] but now they are hid from thine eyes. [43] For the days shall come upon thee, when thine enemies shall cast up a bank[10] about thee, and compass thee round, and keep

[6] Gr. *powers.* [7] Or, *O that thou hadst known.*
[8] Some ancient authorities read *this thy day.*
[9] Some ancient authorities read *thy peace.* [10] Gr. *palisade.*

thee in on every side, [44] and shall dash thee to the ground, and
thy children within thee; and they shall not leave in thee one stone
upon another; because thou knewest not the time of thy visitation.

[45] And he entered into the temple, and began to cast out them
that sold, [46] saying unto them, It is written, And my house shall
be a house of prayer: but ye have made it a den of robbers.

[47] And he was teaching daily in the temple. But the chief
priests and the scribes and the principal men of the people sought
to destroy him: [48] and they could not find what they might do;
for the people all hung upon him, listening.

XX

[1] And it came to pass, on one of the days, as he was teaching
the people in the temple, and preaching the gospel,[1] there came upon
him the chief priests and the scribes with the elders; [2] and they
spake, saying unto him, Tell us: By what authority doest thou
these things? or who is he that gave thee this authority? [3] And
he answered and said unto them, I also will ask you a question;[2]
and tell me: [4] The baptism of John, was it from heaven, or from
men? [5] And they reasoned with themselves, saying, If we shall
say, From heaven; he will say, Why did ye not believe him?
[6] But if we shall say, From men; all the people will stone us:
for they are persuaded that John was a prophet. [7] And they
answered, that they knew not whence *it was*. [8] And Jesus said
unto them, Neither tell I you by what authority I do these things.

[9] And he began to speak unto the people this parable: A man
planted a vineyard, and let it out to husbandmen, and went into
another country for a long time. [10] And at the season he sent
unto the husbandmen a servant,[3] that they should give him of the
fruit of the vineyard: but the husbandmen beat him, and sent him
away empty. [11] And he sent yet another servant:[3] and him also
they beat, and handled him shamefully, and sent him away empty.
[12] And he sent yet a third: and him also they wounded, and cast
him forth. [13] And the lord of the vineyard said, What shall I
do? I will send my beloved son; it may be they will reverence
him. [14] But when the husbandmen saw him, they reasoned one

[1] Or, *good tidings:* comp. ch. 3. 18. [2] Gr. *word.* [3] Gr. *bondservant.*

with another, saying, This is the heir; let us kill him, that the inheritance may be ours. [15] And they cast him forth out of the vineyard, and killed him. What therefore will the lord of the vineyard do unto them? [16] He will come and destroy these husbandmen, and will give the vineyard unto others. And when they heard it, they said, God[4] forbid. [17] But he looked upon them, and said, What then is this that is written,

> The stone which the builders rejected,
> The same was made the head of the corner?

[18] Every one that falleth on that stone shall be broken to pieces; but on whomsoever it shall fall, it will scatter him as dust.

[19] And the scribes and the chief priests sought to lay hands on him in that very hour; and they feared the people: for they perceived that he spake this parable against them. [20] And they watched him, and sent forth spies, who feigned themselves to be righteous, that they might take hold of his speech, so as to deliver him up to the rule[5] and to the authority of the governor. [21] And they asked him, saying, Teacher, we know that thou sayest and teachest rightly, and acceptest not the person *of any,* but of a truth teachest the way of God: [22] Is it lawful for us to give tribute unto Cæsar, or not? [23] But he perceived their craftiness, and said unto them, [24] Show me a denarius.[6] Whose image and superscription hath it? And they said, Cæsar's. [25] And he said unto them, Then render unto Cæsar the things that are Cæsar's, and unto God the things that are God's. [26] And they were not able to take hold of the saying before the people: and they marvelled at his answer, and held their peace.

[27] And there came to him certain of the Sadducees, they that say that there is no resurrection; [28] and they asked him, saying, Teacher, Moses wrote unto us, that if a man's brother die, having a wife, and he be childless, his brother should take the wife, and raise up seed unto his brother. [29] There were therefore seven brethren: and the first took a wife, and died childless; [30] and the second; [31] and the third took her; and likewise the seven also left no children, and died. [32] Afterward the woman also

[4] Gr. *Be it not so.* [5] Or, *ruling power.* [6] See marginal note on ch. 7. 41.

died. [33] In the resurrection therefore whose wife of them shall she be? for the seven had her to wife. [34] And Jesus said unto them, The sons of this world[7] marry, and are given in marriage: [35] but they that are accounted worthy to attain to that world,[7] and the resurrection from the dead, neither marry, nor are given in marriage: [36] for neither can they die any more: for they are equal unto the angels; and are sons of God, being sons of the resurrection. [37] But that the dead are raised, even Moses showed, in *the place concerning* the Bush, when he calleth the Lord the God of Abraham, and the God of Isaac, and the God of Jacob. [38] Now he is not the God of the dead, but of the living: for all live unto him. [39] And certain of the scribes answering said, Teacher, thou hast well said. [40] For they durst not any more ask him any question.

[41] And he said unto them, How say they that the Christ is David's son? [42] For David himself saith in the book of Psalms,

The Lord said unto my Lord,
Sit thou on my right hand,

[43] Till I make thine enemies the footstool of thy feet.
[44] David therefore calleth him Lord, and how is he his son?

[45] And in the hearing of all the people he said unto his disciples, [46] Beware of the scribes, who desire to walk in long robes, and love salutations in the market-places, and chief seats in the synagogues, and chief places at feasts; [47] who devour widows' houses, and for a pretence make long prayers: these shall receive greater condemnation.

XXI

[1] And he looked up, and[1] saw the rich men that were casting their gifts into the treasury. [2] And he saw a certain poor widow casting in thither two mites. [3] And he said, Of a truth I say unto you, This poor widow cast in more than they all: [4] for all these did of their superfluity cast in unto the gifts; but she of her want did cast in all the living that she had.

[5] And as some spake of the temple, how it was adorned with goodly stones and offerings, he said, [6] As for these things which ye

[7] Or, *age*. [1] Or, *and saw them that . . . treasury, and they were rich.*

behold, the days will come, in which there shall not be left here one stone upon another, that shall not be thrown down. [7] And they asked him, saying, Teacher, when therefore shall these things be? and what *shall be* the sign when these things are about to come to pass? [8] And he said, Take heed that ye be not led astray: for many shall come in my name, saying, I am *he;* and, The time is at hand: go ye not after them. [9] And when ye shall hear of wars and tumults, be not terrified: for these things must needs come to pass first; but the end is not immediately.

[10] Then said he unto them, Nation shall rise against nation, and kingdom against kingdom; [11] and there shall be great earthquakes, and in divers places famines and pestilences; and there shall be terrors and great signs from heaven. [12] But before all these things, they shall lay their hands on you, and shall persecute you, delivering you up to the synagogues and prisons, bringing[2] you before kings and governors for my name's sake. [13] It shall turn out unto you for a testimony. [14] Settle it therefore in your hearts, not to meditate beforehand how to answer: [15] for I will give you a mouth and wisdom, which all your adversaries shall not be able to withstand or to gainsay. [16] But ye shall be delivered[3] up even by parents, and brethren, and kinsfolk, and friends; and *some* of you shall[4] they cause to be put to death. [17] And ye shall be hated of all men for my name's sake. [18] And not a hair of your head shall perish. [19] In your patience[5] ye shall win your souls.[6]

[20] But when ye see Jerusalem compassed with armies, then know that her desolation is at hand. [21] Then let them that are in Judæa flee unto the mountains; and let them that are in the midst of her depart out; and let not them that are in the country enter therein. [22] For these are days of vengeance, that all things which are written may be fulfilled. [23] Woe unto them that are with child and to them that give suck in those days! for there shall be great distress upon the land,[7] and wrath unto this people. [24] And they shall fall by the edge of the sword, and shall be led captive into all the nations: and Jerusalem shall be trodden down of the Gentiles, until the times of the Gentiles be fulfilled.

[2] Gr. you *being brought.* [3] Or, *betrayed.* [4] Or, *shall they put to death.*
[5] Or, *stedfastness.* [6] Or, *lives.* [7] Or, *earth.*

[25] And there shall be signs in sun and moon and stars; and upon the earth distress of nations, in perplexity for the roaring of the sea and the billows; [26] men fainting[8] for fear, and for expectation of the things which are coming on the world[9]: for the powers of the heavens shall be shaken. [27] And then shall they see the Son of man coming in a cloud with power and great glory. [28] But when these things begin to come to pass, look up, and lift up your heads; because your redemption draweth nigh.

[29] And he spake to them a parable: Behold the fig tree, and all the trees: [30] when they now shoot forth, ye see it and know of your own selves that the summer is now nigh. [31] Even so ye also, when ye see these things coming to pass, know ye that the kingdom of God is nigh. [32] Verily I say unto you, This generation shall not pass away, till all things be accomplished. [33] Heaven and earth shall pass away: but my words shall not pass away.

[34] But take heed to yourselves, lest haply your hearts be overcharged with surfeiting, and drunkenness, and cares of this life, and that day come on you suddenly as a snare: [35] for *so* shall it come upon all them that dwell on the face of all the earth. [36] But watch ye at every season, making supplication, that ye may prevail to escape all these things that shall come to pass, and to stand before the Son of man.

[37] And every day he was teaching in the temple; and every night he went out, and lodged in the mount that is called Olivet. [38] And all the people came early in the morning to him in the temple, to hear him.

XXII

[1] Now the feast of unleavened bread drew nigh, which is called the Passover. [2] And the chief priests and the scribes sought how they might put him to death; for they feared the people.

[3] And Satan entered into Judas who was called Iscariot, being of the number of the twelve. [4] And he went away, and communed with the chief priests and captains, how he might deliver[1] him unto them. [5] And they were glad, and covenanted to give

[8] Or, *expiring.* [9] Gr. *the inhabited earth.*
[1] Or, *betray.*

him money. [6] And he consented, and sought opportunity to deliver[1] him unto them in[2] the absence of the multitude.

[7] And the day of unleavened bread came, on which the passover must be sacrificed. [8] And he sent Peter and John, saying, Go and make ready for us the passover, that we may eat. [9] And they said unto him, Where wilt thou that we make ready? [10] And he said unto them, Behold, when ye are entered into the city, there shall meet you a man bearing a pitcher of water; follow him into the house whereinto he goeth. [11] And ye shall say unto the master of the house, The Teacher saith unto thee, Where is the guest-chamber, where I shall eat the passover with my disciples? [12] And he will show you a large upper room furnished: there make ready. [13] And they went, and found as he had said unto them: and they made ready the passover.

[14] And when the hour was come, he sat down, and the apostles with him. [15] And he said unto them, With desire I have desired to eat this passover with you before I suffer: [16] for I say unto you, I shall not eat it, until it be fulfilled in the kingdom of God. [17] And he received a cup, and when he had given thanks, he said, Take this, and divide it among yourselves: [18] for I say unto you, I shall not drink from henceforth of the fruit of the vine, until the kingdom of God shall come. [19] And he took bread,[3] and when he had given thanks, he brake it, and gave to them, saying, This is my body which[4] is given for you: this do in remembrance of me. [20] And the cup in like manner after supper, saying, This cup is the new covenant in my blood, *even* that which is poured out for you. [21] But behold, the hand of him that betrayeth[5] me is with me on the table. [22] For the Son of man indeed goeth, as it hath been determined: but woe unto that man through whom he is betrayed![5] [23] And they began to question among themselves, which of them it was that should do this thing.

[24] And there arose also a contention among them, which of them was accounted to be greatest.[6] [25] And he said unto them, The kings of the Gentiles have lordship over them; and they that have authority over them are called Benefactors. [26] But ye *shall*

[2] Or, *without tumult.* [3] Or, *a loaf.* [4] Some ancient authorities omit *which is given for you . . . which is poured out for you.* [5] See ver. 4. [6] Gr. *greater.*

not *be* so: but he that is the greater among you, let him become as the younger; and he that is chief, as he that doth serve. [27] For which is greater, he that sitteth[7] at meat, or he that serveth? is not he that sitteth[7] at meat? but I am in the midst of you as he that serveth. [28] But ye are they that have continued with me in my temptations; [29] and I[8] appoint unto you a kingdom, even as my Father appointed unto me, [30] that ye may eat and drink at my table in my kingdom; and ye shall sit on thrones judging the twelve tribes of Israel.

[31] Simon, Simon, behold, Satan asked[9] to have you, that he might sift you as wheat: [32] but I made supplication for thee, that thy faith fail not; and do thou, when once thou hast turned again, establish thy brethren. [33] And he said unto him, Lord, with thee I am ready to go both to prison and to death. [34] And he said, I tell thee, Peter, the cock shall not crow this day, until thou shalt thrice deny that thou knowest me.

[35] And he said unto them, When I sent you forth without purse, and wallet, and shoes, lacked ye anything? And they said, Nothing. [36] And he said unto them, But now, he that hath a purse, let him take it, and likewise a wallet; and[10] he that hath none, let him sell his cloak, and buy a sword. [37] For I say unto you, that this which is written must be fulfilled in me, And he was reckoned with transgressors: for that which concerneth me hath fulfilment.[11] [38] And they said, Lord, behold, here are two swords. And he said unto them, It is enough.

[39] And he came out, and went, as his custom was, unto the mount of Olives; and the disciples also followed him. [40] And when he was at the place, he said unto them, Pray that ye enter not into temptation. [41] And he was parted from them about a stone's cast; and he kneeled down and prayed, [42] saying, Father, if thou be willing, remove this cup from me: nevertheless not my will, but thine, be done. [43] And[12] there appeared unto him an angel from heaven, strengthening him. [44] And being in an agony he prayed

[7] Gr. *reclineth.*

[8] Or, *I appoint unto you, even as my Father appointed unto me a kingdom, that ye may eat and drink &c.* [9] Or, *obtained you by asking.*

[10] Or, *and he that hath no sword, let him sell his cloak, and buy one.*

[11] Gr. *end.* [12] Many ancient authorities omit ver. 43, 44.

more earnestly; and his sweat became as it were great drops of blood falling down upon the ground. [45] And when he rose up from his prayer, he came unto the disciples, and found them sleeping for sorrow, [46] and said unto them, Why sleep ye? rise and pray, that ye enter not into temptation.

[47] While he yet spake, behold, a multitude, and he that was called Judas, one of the twelve, went before them; and he drew near unto Jesus to kiss him. [48] But Jesus said unto him, Judas, betrayest[5] thou the Son of man with a kiss? [49] And when they that were about him saw what would follow, they said, Lord, shall we smite with the sword? [50] And a certain one of them smote the servant[13] of the high priest, and struck off his right ear. [51] But Jesus answered and said, Suffer ye *them* thus far. And he touched his ear, and healed him. [52] And Jesus said unto the chief priests, and captains of the temple, and elders, that were come against him, Are ye come out, as against a robber, with swords and staves? [53] When I was daily with you in the temple, ye stretched not forth your hands against me: but this is your hour, and the power of darkness.

[54] And they seized him, and led him *away,* and brought him into the high priest's house. But Peter followed afar off. [55] And when they had kindled a fire in the midst of the court, and had sat down together, Peter sat in the midst of them. [56] And a certain maid seeing him as he sat in the light *of the fire,* and looking stedfastly upon him, said, This man also was with him. [57] But he denied, saying, Woman, I know him not. [58] And after a little while another saw him, and said, Thou also art *one* of them. But Peter said, Man, I am not. [59] And after the space of about one hour another confidently affirmed, saying, Of a truth this man also was with him; for he is a Galilæan. [60] But Peter said, Man, I know not what thou sayest. And immediately, while he yet spake, the cock crew. [61] And the Lord turned, and looked upon Peter. And Peter remembered the word of the Lord, how that he said unto him, Before the cock crow this day, thou shalt deny me thrice. [62] And he went out, and wept bitterly.

[63] And the men that held *Jesus*[14] mocked him, and beat him. [64] And they blindfolded him, and asked him, saying, Prophesy:

[13] Gr. *bondservant.* [14] Gr. *him.*

who is he that struck thee? [65] And many other things spake they against him, reviling him.

[66] And as soon as it was day, the assembly of the elders of the people was gathered together, both chief priests and scribes; and they led him away into their council, saying, [67] If thou art the Christ, tell us. But he said unto them, If I tell you, ye will not believe: [68] and if I ask *you,* ye will not answer. [69] But from henceforth shall the Son of man be seated at the right hand of the power of God. [70] And they all said, Art thou then the Son of God? And he said unto them, Ye[15] say that I am. [71] And they said, What further need have we of witness? for we ourselves have heard from his own mouth.

XXIII

[1] AND the whole company of them rose up, and brought him before Pilate. [2] And they began to accuse him, saying, We found this man perverting our nation, and forbidding to give tribute to Cæsar, and saying that he himself is Christ a king. [3] And Pilate asked him, saying, Art thou the King of the Jews? And he answered him and said, Thou sayest. [4] And Pilate said unto the chief priests and the multitudes, I find no fault in this man. [5] But they were the more urgent, saying, He stirreth up the people, teaching throughout all Judæa, and beginning from Galilee even unto this place. [6] But when Pilate heard it, he asked whether the man were a Galilæan. [7] And when he knew that he was of Herod's jurisdiction, he sent him unto Herod, who himself also was at Jerusalem in these days.

[8] Now when Herod saw Jesus, he was exceeding glad: for he was of a long time desirous to see him, because he had heard concerning him; and he hoped to see some miracle[1] done by him. [9] And he questioned him in many words; but he answered him nothing. [10] And the chief priests and the scribes stood, vehemently accusing him. [11] And Herod with his soldiers set him at nought, and mocked him, and arraying him in gorgeous apparel sent him back to Pilate. [12] And Herod and Pilate became friends with each

[15] Or, *Ye say* it, *because I am.*
[1] Gr. *sign.*

other that very day: for before they were at enmity between themselves.

[13] And Pilate called together the chief priests and the rulers and the people, [14] and said unto them, Ye brought unto me this man, as one that perverteth the people: and behold, I, having examined him before you, found no fault in this man touching those things whereof ye accuse him: [15] no, nor yet Herod: for he[2] sent him back unto us; and behold, nothing worthy of death hath been done by him. [16] I will therefore chastise him, and release him.[3] [18] But they cried out all together, saying, Away with this man, and release unto us Barabbas:—[19] one who for a certain insurrection made in the city, and for murder, was cast into prison. [20] And Pilate spake unto them again, desiring to release Jesus; [21] but they shouted, saying, Crucify, crucify him. [22] And he said unto them the third time, Why, what evil hath this man done? I have found no cause of death in him: I will therefore chastise him and release him. [23] But they were urgent with loud voices, asking that he might be crucified. And their voices prevailed. [24] And Pilate gave sentence that what they asked for should be done. [25] And he released him that for insurrection and murder had been cast into prison, whom they asked for; but Jesus he delivered up to their will.

[26] And when they led him away, they laid hold upon one Simon of Cyrene, coming from the country, and laid on him the cross, to bear it after Jesus.

[27] And there followed him a great multitude of the people, and of women who bewailed and lamented him. [28] But Jesus turning unto them said, Daughters of Jerusalem, weep not for me, but weep for yourselves, and for your children. [29] For behold, the days are coming, in which they shall say, Blessed are the barren, and the wombs that never bare, and the breasts that never gave suck. [30] Then shall they begin to say to the mountains, Fall on us; and to the hills, Cover us. [31] For if they do these things in the green tree, what shall be done in the dry?

[2] Many ancient authorities read *I sent you to him.*

[3] Many ancient authorities insert ver. 17. *Now he must needs release unto them at the feast one* prisoner. Comp. Mt. 27. 15; Mk. 15. 6; Jn. 18. 39. Others add the same words after ver. 19.

[32] And there were also two others, malefactors, led with him to be put to death.

[33] And when they came unto the place which is called The skull,[4] there they crucified him, and the malefactors, one on the right hand and the other on the left. [34] And[5] Jesus said, Father, forgive them; for they know not what they do. And parting his garments among them, they cast lots. [35] And the people stood beholding. And the rulers also scoffed at him, saying, He saved others; let him save himself, if this is the Christ of God, his chosen. [36] And the soldiers also mocked him, coming to him, offering him vinegar, [37] and saying, If thou art the King of the Jews, save thyself. [38] And there was also a superscription over him, THIS IS THE KING OF THE JEWS.

[39] And one of the malefactors that were hanged railed on him, saying, Art not thou the Christ? save thyself and us. [40] But the other answered, and rebuking him said, Dost thou not even fear God, seeing thou art in the same condemnation? [41] And we indeed justly; for we receive the due reward of our deeds: but this man hath done nothing amiss. [42] And he said, Jesus, remember me when thou comest in[6] thy kingdom. [43] And he said unto him, Verily I say unto thee, To-day shalt thou be with me in Paradise.

[44] And it was now about the sixth hour, and a darkness came over the whole land[7] until the ninth hour, [45] the sun's[8] light failing: and the veil of the temple[9] was rent in the midst. [46] And[10] Jesus, crying with a loud voice, said, Father, into thy hands I commend my spirit: and having said this, he gave up the ghost. [47] And when the centurion saw what was done, he glorified God, saying, Certainly this was a righteous man. [48] And all the multitudes that came together to this sight, when they beheld the things that were done, returned smiting their breasts. [49] And all his acquaintance, and the women that followed with him from Galilee, stood afar off, seeing these things.

[4] According to the Latin, *Calvary,* which has the same meaning.

[5] Some ancient authorities omit *And Jesus said, Father, forgive them; for they know not what they do.* [6] Some ancient authorities read *into thy kingdom.*

[7] Or, *earth.* [8] Gr. *the sun failing.* [9] Or, *sanctuary.*

[10] Or, *And when Jesus had cried with a loud voice, he said*

[50] And behold, a man named Joseph, who was a councillor, a good and righteous man [51] (he had not consented to their counsel and deed), *a man* of Arimathæa, a city of the Jews, who was looking for the kingdom of God: [52] this man went to Pilate, and asked for the body of Jesus. [53] And he took it down, and wrapped it in a linen cloth, and laid him in a tomb that was hewn in stone, where never man had yet lain. [54] And it was the day of the Preparation, and the sabbath drew[11] on. [55] And the women, who had come with him out of Galilee, followed after, and beheld the tomb, and how his body was laid. [56] And they returned, and prepared spices and ointments.

And on the sabbath they rested according to the commandment.

XXIV

[1] But on the first day of the week, at early dawn, they came unto the tomb, bringing the spices which they had prepared. [2] And they found the stone rolled away from the tomb. [3] And they entered in, and found not the body of[1] the Lord Jesus. [4] And it came to pass, while they were perplexed thereabout, behold, two men stood by them in dazzling apparel: [5] and as they were affrighted and bowed down their faces to the earth, they said unto them, Why seek ye the[2] living among the dead? [6] He[3] is not here, but is risen: remember how he spake unto you when he was yet in Galilee, [7] saying that the Son of man must be delivered up into the hands of sinful men, and be crucified, and the third day rise again. [8] And they remembered his words, [9] and returned from[4] the tomb, and told all these things to the eleven, and to all the rest. [10] Now they were Mary Magdalene, and Joanna, and Mary the *mother* of James: and the other women with them told these things unto the apostles. [11] And these words appeared in their sight as idle talk; and they disbelieved them. [12] But[5] Peter arose, and ran unto the tomb; and stooping and looking in, he seeth the linen cloths by themselves;

[11] Gr. *began to dawn.*
[1] Some ancient authorities omit *of the Lord Jesus.*
[2] Gr. *him that liveth.*
[3] Some ancient authorities omit *He is not here, but is risen.*
[4] Some ancient authorities omit *from the tomb.*
[5] Some ancient authorities omit ver. 12.

and he departed[6] to his home, wondering at that which was come to pass.

[13] And behold, two of them were going that very day to a village named Emmaus, which was threescore furlongs from Jerusalem. [14] And they communed with each other of all these things which had happened. [15] And it came to pass, while they communed and questioned together, that Jesus himself drew near, and went with them. [16] But their eyes were holden that they should not know him. [17] And he said unto them, What[7] communications are these that ye have one with another, as ye walk? And they stood still, looking sad. [18] And one of them, named Cleopas, answering said unto him, Dost[8] thou alone sojourn in Jerusalem and not know the things which are come to pass there in these days? [19] And he said unto them, What things? And they said unto him, The things concerning Jesus the Nazarene, who was a prophet mighty in deed and word before God and all the people: [20] and how the chief priests and our rulers delivered him up to be condemned to death, and crucified him. [21] But we hoped that it was he who should redeem Israel. Yea and besides all this, it is now the third day since these things came to pass. [22] Moreover certain women of our company amazed us, having been early at the tomb; [23] and when they found not his body, they came, saying, that they had also seen a vision of angels, who said that he was alive. [24] And certain of them that were with us went to the tomb, and found it even so as the women had said: but him they saw not. [25] And he said unto them, O foolish men, and slow of heart to believe in[9] all that the prophets have spoken! [26] Behooved it not the Christ to suffer these things, and to enter into his glory? [27] And beginning from Moses and from all the prophets, he interpreted to them in all the scriptures the things concerning himself. [28] And they drew nigh unto the village, whither they were going: and he made as though he would go further. [29] And they constrained him, saying, Abide with us; for it is toward evening, and the day is now far spent. And he went in to abide with them. [30] And it came to pass, when he had sat down with them

[6] Or, *departed, wondering with himself.*
[7] Gr. *What words are these that ye exchange one with another.*
[8] Or, *Dost thou sojourn alone in Jerusalem, and knowest thou not the things.*
[9] Or, *after.*

to meat, he took the bread[10] and blessed; and breaking *it* he gave to them. [31] And their eyes were opened, and they knew him; and he vanished out of their sight. [32] And they said one to another, Was not our heart burning within us, while he spake to us in the way, while he opened to us the scriptures? [33] And they rose up that very hour, and returned to Jerusalem, and found the eleven gathered together, and them that were with them, [34] saying, The Lord is risen indeed, and hath appeared to Simon. [35] And they rehearsed the things *that happened* in the way, and how he was known of them in the breaking of the bread.

[36] And as they spake these things, he himself stood in the midst of them, and[11] saith unto them, Peace *be* unto you. [37] But they were terrified and affrighted, and supposed that they beheld a spirit. [38] And he said unto them, Why are ye troubled? and wherefore do questionings arise in your heart? [39] See my hands and my feet, that it is I myself: handle me, and see; for a spirit hath not flesh and bones, as ye behold me having. [40] And[12] when he had said this, he showed them his hands and his feet. [41] And while they still disbelieved for joy, and wondered, he said unto them, Have ye here anything to eat? [42] And they gave him a piece of a broiled fish.[13] [43] And he took it, and ate before them.

[44] And he said unto them, These are my words which I spake unto you, while I was yet with you, that all things must needs be fulfilled, which are written in the law of Moses, and the prophets, and the psalms, concerning me. [45] Then opened he their mind, that they might understand the scriptures; [46] and he said unto them, Thus it is written, that the Christ should suffer, and rise again from the dead the third day; [47] and that repentance and[14] remission of sins should be preached in his name unto all the nations,[15] beginning from Jerusalem. [48] Ye are witnesses of these things. [49] And behold, I send forth the promise of my Father upon you: but tarry ye in the city, until ye be clothed with power from on high.

[10] Or, *loaf.*

[11] Some ancient authorities omit *and saith unto them, Peace* be *unto you.*

[12] Some ancient authorities omit ver. 40.

[13] Many ancient authorities add *and a honeycomb.*

[14] Some ancient authorities read *unto.* [15] Or, *nations. Beginning from Jerusalem, ye are witnesses.*

[50] And he led them out until *they were* over against Bethany:
and he lifted up his hands, and blessed them. [51] And it came to
pass, while he blessed them, he parted from them, and[16] was carried
up into heaven. [52] And they worshipped[17] him, and returned to
Jerusalem with great joy: [53] and were continually in the temple,
blessing God.

[16] Some ancient authorities omit *and was carried up into heaven.*

[17] Some ancient authorities omit *worshipped him, and.* See marginal note on ch. 4. 7.

(CHRISTIAN)

THE ACTS OF THE APOSTLES

INTRODUCTORY NOTE

The author of "Luke" related in that gospel the story of the life and teachings of Christ, culminating in his rejection and crucifixion by the Jews. In his continuation, "The Acts of the Apostles," the same writer narrates the establishment of the religion of Christ among both Jews and Gentiles, and the beginning of its conquest of the western world. The question of authorship has been touched on in the introductory note to "Luke." The date of composition of the "Acts" is later than that of the gospel, perhaps between 80 and 90 A. D.

Though called "The Acts of the Apostles," this book describes in detail the careers of only two of the apostles, Peter and Paul. The first twelve chapters deal with the founding of the Church in Judæa, Samaria, and Syria, and the beginning of the evangelization of the Gentiles. The main figure in this part is Peter, but his career is not followed to its close. The second part is chiefly occupied with accounts of the missionary journeys of Paul, and the spread of Christianity in the Græco-Roman world. It closes with the establishment of his ministry in Rome.

In chapters xvi, xx, xxi, and xxvii will be found passages in which the use of "we" seems to imply that the author was himself a member of Paul's party, and it is in this so-called "Diary" that the hand of Luke is most generally acknowledged, even by those critics who do not hold that Luke was the compiler of the gospel and the "Acts" as a whole.

The interest of this book is not confined to the narrative of the travels and work of organization performed by the two apostles; it is enormously increased by the accounts of their preaching. In the reports of the addresses to believers and unbelievers of Peter, Stephen, and Paul, we have an invaluable picture of what the earliest Christian missionaries regarded as the essentials of the new religion, and of the form in which Christianity began its victorious contest with Judaism on the one hand, and paganism on the other.

THE ACTS OF THE APOSTLES

[1] I

THE former[1] treatise I made, O Theophilus, concerning all
that Jesus began both to do and to teach, [2] until the day
in which he was received up, after that he had given commandment through the Holy Spirit unto the apostles whom he had
chosen: [3] to whom he also showed[2] himself alive after his passion
by many proofs, appearing unto them by the space of forty days,
and speaking the things concerning the kingdom of God: [4] and,
being[3] assembled together with them, he charged them not to depart
from Jerusalem, but to wait for the promise of the Father, which,
said he, ye heard from me: [5] for John indeed baptized with water;
but ye shall be baptized in[4] the Holy Spirit not many days hence.
[6] They therefore, when they were come together, asked him,
saying, Lord, dost thou at this time restore the kingdom to Israel?
[7] And he said unto them, It is not for you to know times or
seasons, which the Father hath set[5] within his own authority. [8]
But ye shall receive power, when the Holy Spirit is come upon you:
and ye shall be my witnesses both in Jerusalem, and in all Judæa
and Samaria, and unto the uttermost part of the earth. [9] And
when he had said these things, as they were looking, he was taken
up; and a cloud received him out of their sight. [10] And while
they were looking stedfastly into heaven as he went, behold, two
men stood by them in white apparel; [11] who also said, Ye men of
Galilee, why stand ye looking into heaven? this Jesus, who was
received up from you into heaven, shall so come in like manner as
ye beheld him going into heaven.

[12] Then returned they unto Jerusalem from the mount called
Olivet, which is nigh unto Jerusalem, a sabbath day's journey off.

[1] Gr. *first.* [2] Gr. *presented.* [3] Or, *eating with them.*
[4] Or, *with.* [5] Or, *appointed by.*

[13] And when they were come in, they went up into the upper chamber, where they were abiding; both Peter and John and James[6] and Andrew, Philip and Thomas, Bartholomew and Matthew, James[6] *the son* of Alphæus, and Simon the Zealot, and Judas *the son*[7] of James.[6] [14] These all with one accord continued stedfastly in prayer, with[8] the women, and Mary the mother of Jesus, and with his brethren.

[15] And in these days Peter stood up in the midst of the brethren, and said (and there was a multitude of persons[9] *gathered* together, about a hundred and twenty), [16] Brethren, it was needful that the scripture should be fulfilled, which the Holy Spirit spake before by the mouth of David concerning Judas, who was guide to them that took Jesus. [17] For he was numbered among us, and received his portion[10] in this ministry. [18] (Now this man obtained a field with the reward of his iniquity; and falling headlong, he burst asunder in the midst, and all his bowels gushed out. [19] And it became known to all the dwellers at Jerusalem; insomuch that in their language that field was called Akeldama, that is, The field of blood.) [20] For it is written in the book of Psalms,

> Let his habitation be made desolate,
> And let no man dwell therein:

and,

> His office[11] let another take.

[21] Of the men therefore that have companied with us all the time that the Lord Jesus went in and went out among[12] us, [22] beginning from the baptism of John, unto the day that he was received up from us, of these must one become a witness with us of his resurrection. [23] And they put forward two, Joseph called Barsabbas, who was surnamed Justus, and Matthias. [24] And they prayed, and said, Thou, Lord, who knowest the hearts of all men, show of these two the one whom thou hast chosen, [25] to take the place in this ministry and apostleship from which Judas fell away, that he might go to his own place. [26] And they gave lots for[13] them; and the lot fell upon Matthias; and he was numbered with the eleven apostles.

[6] Or, *Jacob.* [7] Or, brother. See Jude 1. [8] Or, *with* certain *women.*
[9] Gr. *names.* See Rev. 3. 4. [10] Or, *lot.*
[11] Gr. *overseership.* [12] Or, *over.* [13] Or, *unto.*

II

[1] And when the day of Pentecost was[1] now come, they were all together in one place. [2] And suddenly there came from heaven a sound as of the rushing of a mighty wind, and it filled all the house where they were sitting. [3] And there appeared unto them tongues parting[2] asunder, like as of fire; and it sat upon each one of them. [4] And they were all filled with the Holy Spirit, and began to speak with other tongues, as the Spirit gave them utterance.

[5] Now there were dwelling at Jerusalem Jews, devout men, from every nation under heaven. [6] And when this sound was heard, the multitude came together, and were confounded, because that every man heard them speaking in his own language. [7] And they were all amazed and marvelled, saying, Behold, are not all these that speak Galilæans? [8] And how hear we, every man in our own language wherein we were born? [9] Parthians and Medes and Elamites, and the dwellers in Mesopotamia, in Judæa and Cappadocia, in Pontus and Asia, [10] in Phrygia and Pamphylia, in Egypt and the parts of Libya about Cyrene, and sojourners from Rome, both Jews and proselytes, [11] Cretans and Arabians, we hear them speaking in our tongues the mighty works of God. [12] And they were all amazed, and were perplexed, saying one to another, What meaneth this? [13] But others mocking said, They are filled with new wine.

[14] But Peter, standing up with the eleven, lifted up his voice, and spake forth unto them, *saying,* Ye men of Judæa, and all ye that dwell at Jerusalem, be this known unto you, and give ear unto my words. [15] For these are not drunken, as ye suppose; seeing it is *but* the third hour of the day; [16] but this is that which hath been spoken through the prophet Joel:

[17] And it shall be in the last days, saith God,
I will pour forth of my Spirit upon all flesh:
And your sons and your daughters shall prophesy,
And your young men shall see visions,
And your old men shall dream dreams:

[1] Gr. *was being fulfilled.* [2] Or, *parting among them.* Or, *distributing themselves.*

[18] Yea and on my servants[3] and on my handmaidens[4] in those days
Will I pour forth of my Spirit; and they shall prophesy.
[19] And I will show wonders in the heaven above,
And signs on the earth beneath;
Blood, and fire, and vapor of smoke:
[20] The sun shall be turned into darkness,
And the moon into blood,
Before the day of the Lord come,
That great and notable *day:*
[21] And it shall be, that whosoever shall call on the name of the Lord shall be saved.

[22] Ye men of Israel, hear these words: Jesus of Nazareth, a man
approved of God unto you by mighty[5] works and wonders and
signs which God did by him in the midst of you, even as ye yourselves know; [23] him, being delivered up by the determinate counsel and foreknowledge of God, ye by the hand of lawless[6] men did
crucify and slay: [24] whom God raised up, having loosed the
pangs of death: because it was not possible that he should be holden
of it.

[25] For David saith concerning him,
I beheld the Lord always before my face;
For he is on my right hand, that I should not be moved:
[26] Therefore my heart was glad, and my tongue rejoiced;
Moreover my flesh also shall dwell[7] in hope:
[27] Because thou wilt not leave my soul unto Hades,
Neither wilt thou give thy Holy One to see corruption.
[28] Thou madest known unto me the ways of life;
Thou shalt make me full of gladness with[8] thy countenance.

[29] Brethren, I may say unto you freely of the patriarch David,
that he both died and was buried, and his tomb is with us unto this
day. [30] Being therefore a prophet, and knowing that God had
sworn with an oath to him, that of the fruit of his loins he[9] would
set *one* upon his throne; [31] he foreseeing *this* spake of the resurrection of the Christ, that neither was he left unto Hades, nor did

[3] Gr. *bondmen.* [4] Gr. *bondmaidens.* [5] Gr. *powers.*
[6] Or, *men without the law.* See Rom. 2. 21. [7] Or, *tabernacle.*
[8] Or, *in thy presence.* [9] Or, one *should sit.*

his flesh see corruption. [32] This Jesus did God raise up, whereof[10] we all are witnesses. [33] Being therefore by[11] the right hand of God exalted, and having received of the Father the promise of the Holy Spirit, he hath poured forth this, which ye see and hear. [34] For David ascended not into the heavens: but he saith himself,

The Lord said unto my Lord, Sit thou on my right hand,
[35] Till I make thine enemies the footstool of thy feet.

[36] Let all[12] the house of Israel therefore know assuredly, that God hath made him both Lord and Christ, this Jesus whom ye crucified.

[37] Now when they heard *this,* they were pricked in their heart, and said unto Peter and the rest of the apostles, Brethren, what shall we do? [38] And Peter *said* unto them, Repent ye, and be baptized every one of you in the name of Jesus Christ unto the remission of your sins; and ye shall receive the gift of the Holy Spirit. [39] For to you is the promise, and to your children, and to all that are afar off, *even* as many as the Lord our God shall call unto him. [40] And with many other words he testified, and exhorted them, saying, Save yourselves from this crooked generation. [41] They then that[13] received his word were baptized: and there were added *unto them* in that day about three thousand souls. [42] And they continued stedfastly in the apostles' teaching and fellowship,[14] in the breaking of bread and the prayers.

[43] And fear came upon every soul: and many wonders and signs were done through the apostles.[15] [44] And all that believed were together, and had all things common; [45] and they sold their possessions and goods, and parted them to all, according as any man had need. [46] And day by day, continuing stedfastly with one accord in the temple, and breaking bread at home, they took their food with gladness and singleness of heart, [47] praising God, and having favor with all the people. And the Lord added to[16] them day by day those that were[17] saved.

[10] Or, *of whom.* [11] Or, *at.*
[12] Or, *every house.* [13] Or, *having received.* [14] Or, *in fellowship.*
[15] Many ancient authorities add *in Jerusalem; and great fear was upon all.*
[16] Gr. *together.* [17] Or, *were being saved.*

III

[1] Now Peter and John were going up into the temple at the
hour of prayer, *being* the ninth *hour*. [2] And a certain man that
was lame from his mother's womb was carried, whom they laid
daily at the door of the temple which is called Beautiful, to ask alms
of them that entered into the temple; [3] who seeing Peter and
John about to go into the temple, asked to receive an alms. [4] And
Peter, fastening his eyes upon him, with John, said, Look on us.
[5] And he gave heed unto them, expecting to receive something
from them. [6] But Peter said, Silver and gold have I none; but
what I have, that give I thee. In the name of Jesus Christ of Nazareth, walk. [7] And he took him by the right hand and raised him
up: and immediately his feet and his ankle-bones received strength.
[8] And leaping up, he stood, and began to walk; and he entered
with them into the temple, walking, and leaping, and praising God.
[9] And all the people saw him walking and praising God: [10]
and they took knowledge of him, that it was he that sat for alms
at the Beautiful Gate of the temple; and they were filled with
wonder and amazement at that which had happened unto him.

[11] And as he held Peter and John, all the people ran together
unto them in the porch[1] that is called Solomon's, greatly wondering.
[12] And when Peter saw it, he answered unto the people, Ye men
of Israel, why marvel ye at this man?[2] or why fasten ye your eyes
on us, as though by our own power or godliness we had made him
to walk? [13] The God of Abraham, and of Isaac, and of Jacob,
the God of our fathers, hath glorified his Servant[3] Jesus; whom ye
delivered up, and denied before the face of Pilate, when he had
determined to release him. [14] But ye denied the Holy and Righteous One, and asked for a murderer to be granted unto you, [15]
and killed the Prince[4] of life; whom God raised from the dead;
whereof[5] we are witnesses. [16] And by[6] faith in his name hath his
name made this man strong, whom ye behold and know: yea, the
faith which is through him hath given him this perfect soundness
in the presence of you all. [17] And now, brethren, I know that in

[1] Or, *portico*. [2] Or, *thing*. [3] Or, *Child*. See Mt. 12. 18; Is. 42. 1; 52. 13; 53. 11.
[4] Or, *Author*. [5] Or, *of whom*. [6] Or, *on the ground of*.

ignorance ye did it, as did also your rulers. [18] But the things which God foreshowed by the mouth of all the prophets, that his Christ should suffer, he thus fulfilled. [19] Repent ye therefore, and turn again, that your sins may be blotted out, that so there may come seasons of refreshing from the presence of the Lord; [20] and that he may send the Christ who hath been appointed for you, *even* Jesus: [21] whom the heaven must receive until the times of restoration of all things, whereof God spake by the mouth of his holy prophets that have been from of old. [22] Moses indeed said, A prophet shall the Lord God raise up unto you from among your brethren, like[7] unto me; to him shall ye hearken in all things whatsoever he shall speak unto you. [23] And it shall be, that every soul that shall not hearken to that prophet, shall be utterly destroyed from among the people. [24] Yea and all the prophets from Samuel and them that followed after, as many as have spoken, they also told of these days. [25] Ye are the sons of the prophets, and of the covenant which God made[8] with your fathers, saying unto Abraham, And in thy seed shall all the families of the earth be blessed. [26] Unto you first God, having raised up his Servant,[3] sent him to bless you, in turning away every one of you from your iniquities.

IV

[1] AND as they spake unto the people, the[1] priests and the captain of the temple and the Sadducees came upon them, [2] being sore troubled because they taught the people, and proclaimed in Jesus the resurrection from the dead. [3] And they laid hands on them, and put them in ward unto the morrow: for it was now eventide. [4] But many of them that heard the word believed; and the number of the men came to be about five thousand.

[5] And it came to pass on the morrow, that their rulers and elders and scribes were gathered together in Jerusalem; [6] and Annas the high priest *was there,* and Caiaphas, and John, and Alexander, and as many as were of the kindred of the high priest. [7] And when they had set them in the midst, they inquired, By what power, or in what name, have ye done this? [8] Then Peter, filled with the Holy

[7] Or, *as* he raised up *me*. [8] Gr. *covenanted.*
[1] Some ancient authorities read *the chief priests.*

Spirit, said unto tnem, Ye rulers of the people, and elders, [9] if we this day are examined concerning a good deed done to an impotent man, by[2] what means this man is made whole; [10] be it known unto you all, and to all the people of Israel, that in the name of Jesus Christ of Nazareth, whom ye crucified, whom God raised from the dead, *even* in him[3] doth this man stand here before you whole. [11] He is the stone which was set at nought of you the builders, which was made the head of the corner. [12] And in none other is there salvation: for neither is there any other name under heaven, that is given among men, wherein we must be saved.

[13] Now when they beheld the boldness of Peter and John, and had perceived that they were unlearned and ignorant men, they marvelled; and they took knowledge of them, that they had been with Jesus. [14] And seeing the man that was healed standing with them, they could say nothing against it. [15] But when they had commanded them to go aside out of the council, they conferred among themselves, [16] saying, What shall we do to these men? for that indeed a notable miracle[4] hath been wrought through them, is manifest to all that dwell in Jerusalem; and we cannot deny it. [17] But that it spread no further among the people, let us threaten them, that they speak henceforth to no man in this name. [18] And they called them, and charged them not to speak at all nor teach in the name of Jesus. [19] But Peter and John answered and said unto them, Whether it is right in the sight of God to hearken unto you rather than unto God, judge ye: [20] for we cannot but speak the things which we saw and heard. [21] And they, when they had further threatened them, let them go, finding nothing how they might punish them, because of the people; for all men glorified God for that which was done. [22] For the man was more than forty years old, on whom this miracle[4] of healing was wrought.

[23] And being let go, they came to their own company, and reported all that the chief priests and the elders had said unto them. [24] And they, when they heard it, lifted up their voice to God with one accord, and said, O Lord,[5] thou[6] that didst make the heaven and the earth and the sea, and all that in them is: [25] who[7] by the Holy

[2] Or, *in whom*. [3] Or, *this name*. [4] Gr. *sign*.
[5] Gr. *Master*. [6] Or, *thou* art *he that did make*.
[7] The Greek text in this clause is somewhat uncertain.

Spirit, *by* the mouth of our father David thy servant, didst say,
Why did the Gentiles[8] rage,
And the peoples imagine[9] vain things?
[26] The kings of the earth set themselves in array,
And the rulers were gathered together,
Against the Lord, and against his Anointed:[10]
[27] for of a truth in this city against thy holy Servant[11] Jesus, whom
thou didst anoint, both Herod and Pontius Pilate, with the Gentiles[8]
and the peoples of Israel, were gathered together, [28] to do whatsoever thy hand and thy counsel foreordained to come to pass.
[29] And now, Lord, look upon their threatenings: and grant unto
thy servants[12] to speak thy word with all boldness, [30] while thou
stretchest forth thy hand to heal; and that signs and wonders may
be done through the name of thy holy Servant[11] Jesus. [31] And
when they had prayed, the place was shaken wherein they were
gathered together; and they were all filled with the Holy Spirit, and
they spake the word of God with boldness.

[32] And the multitude of them that believed were of one heart
and soul: and not one *of them* said that aught of the things which
he possessed was his own; but they had all things common. [33]
And with great power gave the apostles their witness of the resurrection of the Lord Jesus:[13] and great grace was upon them all.
[34] For neither was there among them any that lacked: for as many
as were possessors of lands or houses sold them, and brought the
prices of the things that were sold, [35] and laid them at the apostles'
feet: and distribution was made unto each, according as any one
had need.

[36] And Joseph, who by the apostles was surnamed Barnabas
(which is, being interpreted, Son of exhortation),[14] a Levite, a man
of Cyprus by race, [37] having a field, sold it, and brought the
money and laid it at the apostles' feet.

[8] Gr. *nations*. [9] Or, *meditate*. [10] Gr. *Christ*.
[11] Or, *Child*. See marginal note on ch. 3. 13. [12] Gr. *bondservants*.
[13] Some ancient authorities add *Christ*.
[14] Or, *consolation*. See Lk. 2. 25; ch. 9. 31; 15. 31; 2 Cor. 1. 3-7, in the Gr.

V

[1] But a certain man named Ananias, with Sapphira his wife, sold a possession, [2] and kept back *part* of the price, his wife also being privy to it, and brought a certain part, and laid it at the apostles' feet. [3] But Peter said, Ananias, why hath Satan filled thy heart to lie[1] to the Holy Spirit, and to keep back *part* of the price of the land? [4] While it remained, did it not remain thine own? and after it was sold, was it not in thy power? How is it that thou hast conceived this thing in thy heart? thou hast not lied unto men, but unto God. [5] And Ananias hearing these words fell down and gave up the ghost: and great fear came upon all that heard it. [6] And the young[2] men arose and wrapped him round, and they carried him out and buried him.

[7] And it was about the space of three hours after, when his wife, not knowing what was done, came in. [8] And Peter answered unto her, Tell me whether ye sold the land for so much. And she said, Yea, for so much. [9] But Peter *said* unto her, How is it that ye have agreed together to try the Spirit of the Lord? behold, the feet of them that have buried thy husband are at the door, and they shall carry thee out. [10] And she fell down immediately at his feet, and gave up the ghost: and the young men came in and found her dead, and they carried her out and buried her by her husband. [11] And great fear came upon the whole church, and upon all that heard these things.

[12] And by the hands of the apostles were many signs and wonders wrought among the people; and they were all with one accord in Solomon's porch.[3] [13] But of the rest durst no man join himself to them: howbeit the people magnified them; [14] and[4] believers were the more added to the Lord, multitudes both of men and women; [15] insomuch that they even carried out the sick into the streets, and laid them on beds and couches,[5] that, as Peter came by, at the least his shadow might overshadow some one of them. [16] And there also came together the multitude from the cities round about Jerusalem, bringing sick folk, and them that were vexed with unclean spirits: and they were healed every one.

[1] Or, *deceive*. [2] Gr. *younger*. [3] Or, *portico*.
[4] Or, *and there were the more added* to them, *believing on the Lord*. [5] Or, *pallets*.

[17] But the high priest rose up, and all they that were with him (which is the sect of the Sadducees), and they were filled with jealousy, [18] and laid hands on the apostles, and put them in public ward. [19] But an angel of the Lord by night opened the prison doors, and brought them out, and said, [20] Go ye, and stand and speak in the temple to the people all the words of this Life. [21] And when they heard *this,* they entered into the temple about daybreak, and taught. But the high priest came, and they that were with him, and called the council together, and all the senate of the children of Israel, and sent to the prison-house to have them brought. [22] But the officers that came found them not in the prison; and they returned, and told, [23] saying, The prison-house we found shut in all safety, and the keepers standing at the doors: but when we had opened, we found no man within. [24] Now when the captain of the temple and the chief priests heard these words, they were much perplexed concerning them whereunto this would grow. [25] And there came one and told them, Behold, the men whom ye put in the prison are in the temple standing and teaching the people. [26] Then went the captain with the officers, and brought them, *but* without violence; for they feared the people, lest they should be stoned. [27] And when they had brought them, they set them before the council. And the high priest asked them, [28] saying, We strictly charged you not to teach in this name: and behold, ye have filled Jerusalem with your teaching, and intend to bring this man's blood upon us. [29] But Peter and the apostles answered and said, We must obey God rather than men. [30] The God of our fathers raised up Jesus, whom ye slew, hanging him on a tree. [31] Him did God exalt with[6] his right hand *to be* a Prince and a Saviour, to give repentance to Israel, and remission of sins. [32] And we are witnesses of[7] these things;[8] and[9] *so is* the Holy Spirit, whom God hath given to them that obey him.

[33] But they, when they heard this, were cut to the heart, and were minded to slay them. [34] But there stood up one in the council, a Pharisee, named Gamaliel, a doctor of the law, had in honor of all the people, and commanded to put the men forth a

[6] Or, *at.* [7] Some ancient authorities add *in him.* [8] Gr. *sayings.*

[9] Some ancient authorities read *and God hath given the Holy Spirit to them that obey him.*

little while. [35] And he said unto them, Ye men of Israel, take heed to yourselves as touching these men, what ye are about to do. [36] For before these days rose up Theudas, giving himself out to be somebody; to whom a number of men, about four hundred, joined themselves: who was slain; and all, as many as obeyed him, were dispersed, and came to nought. [37] After this man rose up Judas of Galilee in the days of the enrolment, and drew away *some of the* people after him: he also perished; and all, as many as obeyed him, were scattered abroad. [38] And now I say unto you, Refrain from these men, and let them alone: for if this counsel or this work be of men, it will be overthrown: [39] but if it is of God, ye will not be able to overthrow them; lest haply ye be found even to be fighting against God. [40] And to him they agreed: and when they had called the apostles unto them, they beat them and charged them not to speak in the name of Jesus, and let them go. [41] They therefore departed from the presence of the council, rejoicing that they were counted worthy to suffer dishonor for the Name. [42] And every day, in the temple and at home, they ceased not to teach and to preach[10] Jesus *as* the Christ.

VI

[1] Now in these days, when the number of the disciples was multiplying, there arose a murmuring of the Grecian[1] Jews against the Hebrews, because their widows were neglected in the daily ministration. [2] And the twelve called the multitude of the disciples unto them, and said, It is not fit[2] that we should forsake the word of God, and serve[3] tables. [3] Look[4] ye out therefore, brethren, from among you seven men of good report, full of the Spirit and of wisdom, whom we may appoint over this business. [4] But we will continue stedfastly in prayer, and in the ministry of the word. [5] And the saying pleased the whole multitude: and they chose Stephen, a man full of faith and of the Holy Spirit, and Philip, and Prochorus, and Nicanor, and Timon, and Parmenas, and Nicolaüs a proselyte of Antioch; [6] whom they set before the apostles: and when they had prayed, they laid their hands upon them.

[10] Gr. *bring good tidings of.* See ch. 13. 32; 14. 15.
[1] Gr. *Hellenists.* [2] Gr. *pleasing.* [3] Or, *minister to tables.*
[4] Some ancient authorities read *But, brethren, look ye out from among you.*

[7] And the word of God increased; and the number of the disciples multiplied in Jerusalem exceedingly; and a great company of the priests were obedient to the faith.

[8] And Stephen, full of grace and power, wrought great wonders and signs among the people. [9] But there arose certain of them that were of the synagogue called *the synagogue* of the Libertines,[5] and of the Cyrenians, and of the Alexandrians, and of them of Cilicia and Asia, disputing with Stephen. [10] And they were not able to withstand the wisdom and the Spirit by which he spake. [11] Then they suborned men, who said, We have heard him speak blasphemous words against Moses, and *against* God. [12] And they stirred up the people, and the elders, and the scribes, and came upon him, and seized him, and brought him into the council, [13] and set up false witnesses, who said, This man ceaseth not to speak words against this holy place, and the law: [14] for we have heard him say, that this Jesus of Nazareth shall destroy this place, and shall change the customs which Moses delivered unto us. [15] And all that sat in the council, fastening their eyes on him, saw his face as it had been the face of an angel.

VII

[1] AND the high priest said, Are these things so? [2] And he said,

Brethren and fathers, hearken: The God of glory appeared unto our father Abraham, when he was in Mesopotamia, before he dwelt in Haran, [3] and said unto him, Get thee out of thy land, and from thy kindred, and come into the land which I shall show thee. [4] Then came he out of the land of the Chaldæans, and dwelt in Haran: and from thence, when his father was dead, *God* removed him into this land, wherein ye now dwell: [5] and he gave him none inheritance in it, no, not so much as to set his foot on: and he promised that he would give it to him in possession, and to his seed after him, when *as yet* he had no child. [6] And God spake on this wise, that his seed should sojourn in a strange land, and that they should bring them into bondage, and treat them ill, four hundred years. [7] And the nation to which they shall be in bondage will I judge, said God:

[5] Or, *Freedmen.*

and after that shall they come forth, and serve me in this place.
[8] And he gave him the covenant of circumcision: and so *Abraham*
begat Isaac, and circumcised him the eighth day; and Isaac *begat*
Jacob, and Jacob the twelve patriarchs. [9] And the patriarchs,
moved with jealousy against Joseph, sold him into Egypt: and God
was with him, [10] and delivered him out of all his afflictions, and
gave him favor and wisdom before Pharaoh king of Egypt; and he
made him governor over Egypt and all his house. [11] Now there
came a famine over all Egypt and Canaan, and great affliction: and
our fathers found no sustenance. [12] But when Jacob heard that
there was grain in Egypt, he sent forth our fathers the first time.
[13] And at the second time Joseph was made known to his brethren;
and Joseph's race became manifest unto Pharaoh. [14] And Joseph
sent, and called to him Jacob his father, and all his kindred, threescore and fifteen souls. [15] And Jacob went down into Egypt; and
he died, himself and our fathers; [16] and they were carried over
unto Shechem, and laid in the tomb that Abraham bought for a
price in silver of the sons of Hamor[1] in Shechem. [17] But as the
time of the promise drew nigh which God vouchsafed unto Abraham, the people grew and multiplied in Egypt, [18] till there arose
another king over Egypt, who knew not Joseph. [19] The same
dealt craftily with our race, and ill-treated our fathers, that they[2]
should cast out their babes to the end they might not live.[3] [20] At
which season Moses was born, and was exceeding[4] fair; and he was
nourished three months in his father's house: [21] and when he was
cast out, Pharaoh's daughter took him up, and nourished him for
her own son. [22] And Moses was instructed in all the wisdom of
the Egyptians; and he was mighty in his words and works. [23]
But when he was well-nigh forty years old, it came into his heart to
visit his brethren the children of Israel. [24] And seeing one
of them suffer wrong, he defended him, and avenged him that was
oppressed, smiting the Egyptian: [25] and he supposed that his
brethren understood that God by his hand was giving them deliverance;[5] but they understood not. [26] And the day following he
appeared unto them as they strove, and would have set them at one

[1] Gr. *Emmor.* [2] Or, *he.* [3] Gr. *be preserved alive.*
[4] Or, *fair unto God.* Comp. 2 Cor. 10. 4. [5] Or, *salvation.*

again, saying, Sirs, ye are brethren; why do ye wrong one to
another? [27] But he that did his neighbor wrong thrust him away,
saying, Who made thee a ruler and a judge over us? [28] Wouldest
thou kill me, as thou killedst the Egyptian yesterday? [29] And
Moses fled at this saying, and became a sojourner in the land of
Midian, where he begat two sons. [30] And when forty years were
fulfilled, an angel appeared to him in the wilderness of mount Sinai,
in a flame of fire in a bush. [31] And when Moses saw it, he wondered at the sight: and as he drew near to behold, there came a voice
of the Lord, [32] I am the God of thy fathers, the God of Abraham,
and of Isaac, and of Jacob. And Moses trembled, and durst not
behold. [33] And the Lord said unto him, Loose the shoes from thy
feet: for the place whereon thou standest is holy ground. [34] I have
surely seen the affliction of my people that is in Egypt, and have
heard their groaning, and I am come down to deliver them: and
now come, I will send thee into Egypt. [35] This Moses whom they
refused, saying, Who made thee a ruler and a judge? him hath God
sent *to be* both a ruler and a deliverer[6] with the hand of the angel
that appeared to him in the bush. [36] This man led them forth,
having wrought wonders and signs in Egypt, and in the Red sea,
and in the wilderness forty years. [37] This is that Moses, who said
unto the children of Israel, A prophet shall God raise up unto you
from among your brethren, like[7] unto me. [38] This is he that was
in the church[8] in the wilderness with the angel that spake to him
in the mount Sinai, and with our fathers: who received living oracles
to give unto us: [39] to whom our fathers would not be obedient,
but thrust him from them, and turned back in their hearts unto
Egypt, [40] saying unto Aaron, Make us gods that shall go before
us: for as for this Moses, who led us forth out of the land of Egypt,
we know not what is become of him. [41] And they made a calf in
those days, and brought a sacrifice unto the idol, and rejoiced in the
works of their hands. [42] But God turned, and gave them up to
serve the host of heaven; as it is written in the book of the prophets,

Did ye offer unto me slain beasts and sacrifices
Forty years in the wilderness, O house of Israel?

[6] Gr. *redeemer*. [7] Or, *as* he raised up *me*.
[8] Or, *congregation*.

[43] And ye took up the tabernacle of Moloch,
And the star of the god Rephan,
The figures which ye made to worship them:
And I will carry you away beyond Babylon.

[44] Our fathers had the tabernacle of the testimony in the wilderness, even as he appointed who spake unto Moses, that he should
make it according to the figure that he had seen. [45] Which also
our fathers, in their turn, brought in with Joshua[9] when they entered
on the possession of the nations,[10] that God thrust out before the face
of our fathers, unto the days of David; [46] who found favor in the
sight of God, and asked to find a habitation for the God of Jacob.
[47] But Solomon built him a house. [48] Howbeit the Most High
dwelleth not in *houses* made with hands; as saith the prophet,

[49] The heaven is my throne,
And the earth the footstool of my feet:
What manner of house will ye build me? saith the Lord:
Or what is the place of my rest?
[50] Did not my hand make all these things?

[51] Ye stiffnecked and uncircumcised in heart and ears, ye do
always resist the Holy Spirit: as your fathers did, so do ye. [52]
Which of the prophets did not your fathers persecute? and they
killed them that showed before of the coming of the Righteous One;
of whom ye have now become betrayers and murderers; [53] ye who
received the law as[11] it was ordained by angels, and kept it not.

[54] Now when they heard these things, they were cut to the
heart, and they gnashed on him with their teeth. [55] But he, being
full of the Holy Spirit, looked up stedfastly into heaven, and saw
the glory of God, and Jesus standing on the right hand of God, [56]
and said, Behold, I see the heavens opened, and the Son of man
standing on the right hand of God. [57] But they cried out with a
loud voice, and stopped their ears, and rushed upon him with one
accord; [58] and they cast him out of the city, and stoned him: and
the witnesses laid down their garments at the feet of a young man
named Saul. [59] And they stoned Stephen, calling upon *the Lord,*
and saying, Lord Jesus, receive my spirit. [60] And he kneeled

[9] Gr. *Jesus.* Comp. Heb. 4. 8. [10] Or, *Gentiles.* Comp. ch. 4. 25.
[11] Or, *as the ordinance of angels.* Gr. *unto ordinances of angels.*

down, and cried with a loud voice, Lord, lay not this sin to their charge. And when he had said this, he fell asleep.

VIII

[1] AND Saul was consenting unto his death.

And there arose on that day a great persecution against the church which was in Jerusalem; and they were all scattered abroad throughout the regions of Judæa and Samaria, except the apostles. [2] And devout men buried Stephen, and made great lamentation over him. [3] But Saul laid waste the church, entering into every house, and dragging men and women committed them to prison.

[4] They therefore that were scattered abroad went about preaching[1] the word. [5] And Philip went down to the city of Samaria, and proclaimed unto them the Christ. [6] And the multitudes gave heed with one accord unto the things that were spoken by Philip, when they heard, and saw the signs which he did. [7] For[2] *from* many of those that had unclean spirits, they came out, crying with a loud voice: and many that were palsied, and that were lame, were healed. [8] And there was much joy in that city.

[9] But there was a certain man, Simon by name, who beforetime in the city used sorcery, and amazed the people[3] of Samaria, giving out that himself was some great one: [10] to whom they all gave heed, from the least to the greatest, saying, This man is that power of God which is called Great. [11] And they gave heed to him, because that of long time he had amazed them with his sorceries. [12] But when they believed Philip preaching[1] good tidings concerning the kingdom of God and the name of Jesus Christ, they were baptized, both men and women. [13] And Simon also himself believed: and being baptized, he continued with Philip; and beholding signs and great miracles[4] wrought, he was amazed.

[14] Now when the apostles that were at Jerusalem heard that Samaria had received the word of God, they sent unto them Peter and John: [15] who, when they were come down, prayed for them, that they might receive the Holy Spirit: [16] for as yet it was fallen upon none of them: only they had been baptized into the name of

[1] Comp. marg. note on ch. 5. 42.

[2] Or, *For many of those that had unclean spirits that cried with a loud voice came forth.* [3] Gr. *nation.* [4] Gr. *powers.*

the Lord Jesus. [17] Then laid they their hands on them, and they
received the Holy Spirit. [18] Now when Simon saw that through
the laying on of the apostles' hands the Holy[5] Spirit was given, he
offered them money, [19] saying, Give me also this power, that on
whomsoever I lay my hands, he may receive the Holy Spirit. [20]
But Peter said unto him, Thy silver perish with thee, because thou
hast thought to obtain the gift of God with money. [21] Thou hast
neither part nor lot in this matter:[6] for thy heart is not right before
God. [22] Repent therefore of this thy wickedness, and pray the
Lord, if perhaps the thought of thy heart shall be forgiven thee.
[23] For I see that thou art[7] in the gall of bitterness and in the bond
of iniquity. [24] And Simon answered and said, Pray ye for me to
the Lord, that none of the things which ye have spoken come upon
me.

[25] They therefore, when they had testified and spoken the word
of the Lord, returned to Jerusalem, and preached[8] the gospel to many
villages of the Samaritans.

[26] But an angel of the Lord spake unto Philip, saying, Arise,
and go toward[9] the south unto the way that goeth down from
Jerusalem unto Gaza: the same is desert. [27] And he arose and
went: and behold, a man of Ethiopia, a eunuch of great authority
under Candace, queen of the Ethiopians, who was over all her
treasure, who had come to Jerusalem to worship; [28] and he was
returning and sitting in his chariot, and was reading the prophet
Isaiah. [29] And the Spirit said unto Philip, Go near, and join
thyself to this chariot. [30] And Philip ran to him, and heard him
reading Isaiah the prophet, and said, Understandest thou what thou
readest? [31] And he said, How can I, except some one shall
guide me? And he besought Philip to come up and sit with him.
[32] Now the passage of the scripture which he was reading was
this,

He was led as a sheep to the slaughter;
And as a lamb before his shearer is dumb,
So he openeth not his mouth:

[5] Some ancient authorities omit *Holy*. [6] Gr. *word*.

[7] Or, *wilt become gall* (or, *a gall root*) *of bitterness and a bond of iniquity*. Comp. Deut 29. 18; Heb. 12. 15. [8] Gr. *brought good tidings*. Comp. ch. 5 42. [9] Or, *at noon*. Comp. ch. 22. 6.

[33] In his humiliation his judgment was taken away:
His generation who shall declare?
For his life is taken from the earth.
[34] And the eunuch answered Philip, and said, I pray thee, of whom
speaketh the prophet this? of himself, or of some other? [35] And
Philip opened his mouth, and beginning from this scripture,
preached[10] unto him Jesus. [36] And as they went on the way, they
came unto a certain water; and the eunuch saith, Behold, *here is*
water; what doth hinder me to be baptized?[11] [38] And he commanded the chariot to stand still: and they both went down into the
water, both Philip and the eunuch; and he baptized him. [39] And
when they came up out of the water, the Spirit of the Lord caught
away Philip; and the eunuch saw him no more, for he went on his
way rejoicing. [40] But Philip was found at Azotus: and passing
through he preached[10] the gospel to all the cities, till he came to
Cæsarea.

IX

[1] BUT Saul, yet breathing threatening and slaughter against the
disciples of the Lord, went unto the high priest, [2] and asked of him
letters to Damascus unto the synagogues, that if he found any that
were of the Way, whether men or women, he might bring them
bound to Jerusalem. [3] And as he journeyed, it came to pass that
he drew nigh unto Damascus: and suddenly there shone round about
him a light out of heaven: [4] and he fell upon the earth, and heard
a voice saying unto him, Saul, Saul, why persecutest thou me? [5]
And he said, Who art thou, Lord? and he *said,* I am Jesus whom
thou persecutest: [6] but rise, and enter into the city, and it shall
be told thee what thou must do. [7] And the men that journeyed
with him stood speechless, hearing the voice,[1] but beholding no man.
[8] And Saul arose from the earth; and when his eyes were opened,
he saw nothing; and they led him by the hand, and brought him
into Damascus. [9] And he was three days without sight, and did
neither eat nor drink.

[10] See marg. note on ch. 5. 42.

[11] Some ancient authorities insert, wholly or in part, ver. 37. *And Philip said, If thou believest with all thy heart, thou mayest. And he answered and said, I believe that Jesus Christ is the Son of God.* [1] Or, *sound.*

[10] Now there was a certain disciple at Damascus, named Ananias; and the Lord said unto him in a vision, Ananias. And he said, Behold, I *am here,* Lord. [11] And the Lord *said* unto him, Arise, and go to the street which is called Straight, and inquire in the house of Judas for one named Saul, a man of Tarsus: for behold, he prayeth; [12] and he hath seen a man named Ananias coming in, and laying his hands on him, that he might receive his sight. [13] But Ananias answered, Lord, I have heard from many of this man, how much evil he did to thy saints at Jerusalem: [14] and here he hath authority from the chief priests to bind all that call upon thy name. [15] But the Lord said unto him, Go thy way: for he is a chosen[2] vessel unto me, to bear my name before the Gentiles and kings, and the children of Israel: [16] for I will show him how many things he must suffer for my name's sake. [17] And Ananias departed, and entered into the house; and laying his hands on him said, Brother Saul, the Lord, *even* Jesus, who appeared unto thee in the way which thou camest, hath sent me, that thou mayest receive thy sight, and be filled with the Holy Spirit. [18] And straightway there fell from his eyes as it were scales, and he received his sight; and he arose and was baptized; [19] and he took food and was strengthened.

And he was certain days with the disciples that were at Damascus. [20] And straightway in the synagogues he proclaimed Jesus, that he is the Son of God. [21] And all that heard him were amazed, and said, Is not this he that in Jerusalem made havoc of them that called on this name? and he had come hither for this intent, that he might bring them bound before the chief priests. [22] But Saul increased the more in strength, and confounded the Jews that dwelt at Damascus, proving that this is the Christ.

[23] And when many days were fulfilled, the Jews took counsel together to kill him: [24] but their plot became known to Saul. And they watched the gates also day and night that they might kill him: [25] but his disciples took him by night, and let him down through the wall, lowering him in a basket.

[26] And when he was come to Jerusalem, he assayed to join himself to the disciples: and they were all afraid of him, not believing that he was a disciple. [27] But Barnabas took him, and brought him to

[2] Gr. *vessel of election.*

the apostles, and declared unto them how he had seen the Lord in the way, and that he had spoken to him, and how at Damascus he had preached boldly in the name of Jesus. [28] And he was with them going in and going out at Jerusalem, [29] preaching boldly in the name of the Lord: and he spake and disputed against the Grecian[3] Jews; but they were seeking to kill him. [30] And when the brethren knew it, they brought him down to Cæsarea, and sent him forth to Tarsus.

[31] So the church throughout all Judæa and Galilee and Samaria had peace, being edified;[4] and, walking in[5] the fear of the Lord and in[5] the comfort of the Holy Spirit, was multiplied.

[32] And it came to pass, as Peter went throughout all parts, he came down also to the saints that dwelt at Lydda. [33] And there he found a certain man named Æneas, who had kept his bed eight years; for he was palsied. [34] And Peter said unto him, Æneas, Jesus Christ healeth thee: arise, and make thy bed. And straightway he arose. [35] And all that dwelt at Lydda and in Sharon saw him, and they turned to the Lord.

[36] Now there was at Joppa a certain disciple named Tabitha, which by interpretation is called Dorcas:[6] this woman was full of good works and almsdeeds which she did. [37] And it came to pass in those days, that she fell sick, and died: and when they had washed her, they laid her in an upper chamber. [38] And as Lydda was nigh unto Joppa, the disciples, hearing that Peter was there, sent two men unto him, entreating him, Delay not to come on unto us. [39] And Peter arose and went with them. And when he was come, they brought him into the upper chamber: and all the widows stood by him weeping, and showing the coats and garments which Dorcas made, while she was with them. [40] But Peter put them all forth, and kneeled down, and prayed; and turning to the body, he said, Tabitha, arise. And she opened her eyes; and when she saw Peter, she sat up. [41] And he gave her his hand, and raised her up; and calling the saints and widows, he presented her alive. [42] And it became known throughout all Joppa: and many believed on the Lord. [43] And it came to pass, that he abode many days in Joppa with one Simon a tanner.

[3] Gr. *Hellenists.* [4] Gr. *builded up.*
[5] Or, *by.* [6] That is, *Gazelle.*

X

[1] Now *there was* a certain man in Cæsarea, Cornelius by name, a centurion of the band[1] called the Italian *band,* [2] a devout man, and one that feared God with all his house, who gave much alms to the people, and prayed to God always. [3] He saw in a vision openly, as it were about the ninth hour of the day, an angel of God coming in unto him, and saying to him, Cornelius. [4] And he, fastening his eyes upon him, and being affrighted, said, What is it, Lord? And he said unto him, Thy prayers and thine alms are gone up for a memorial before God. [5] And now send men to Joppa, and fetch one Simon, who is surnamed Peter: [6] he lodgeth with one Simon a tanner, whose house is by the sea side. [7] And when the angel that spake unto him was departed, he called two of his household-servants, and a devout soldier of them that waited on him continually; [8] and having rehearsed all things unto them, he sent them to Joppa.

[9] Now on the morrow, as they were on their journey, and drew nigh unto the city, Peter went up upon the housetop to pray, about the sixth hour: [10] and he became hungry, and desired to eat: but while they made ready, he fell into a trance; [11] and he beholdeth the heaven opened, and a certain vessel descending, as it were a great sheet, let down by four corners upon the earth: [12] wherein were all manner of four-footed beasts and creeping things of the earth and birds of the heaven. [13] And there came a voice to him, Rise, Peter; kill and eat. [14] But Peter said, Not so, Lord; for I have never eaten anything that is common and unclean. [15] And a voice *came* unto him again the second time, What God hath cleansed, make not thou common. [16] And this was done thrice: and straightway the vessel was received up into heaven.

[17] Now while Peter was much perplexed in himself what the vision which he had seen might mean, behold, the men that were sent by Cornelius, having made inquiry for Simon's house, stood before the gate, [18] and called and asked whether Simon, who was surnamed Peter, were lodging there. [19] And while Peter thought

[1] Or, *cohort.*

on the vision, the Spirit said unto him, Behold, three men seek thee. [20] But arise, and get thee down, and go with them, nothing doubting: for I have sent them. [21] And Peter went down to the men, and said, Behold, I am he whom ye seek: what is the cause wherefore ye are come? [22] And they said, Cornelius a centurion, a righteous man and one that feareth God, and well reported of by all the nation of the Jews, was warned *of God* by a holy angel to send for thee into his house, and to hear words from thee. [23] So he called them in and lodged them.

And on the morrow he arose and went forth with them, and certain of the brethren from Joppa accompanied him. [24] And on the morrow they[2] entered into Cæsarea. And Cornelius was waiting for them, having called together his kinsmen and his near friends. [25] And when it came to pass that Peter entered, Cornelius met him, and fell down at his feet, and worshipped[3] him. [26] But Peter raised him up, saying, Stand up; I myself also am a man. [27] And as he talked with him, he went in, and findeth many come together: [28] and he said unto them, Ye yourselves know how[4] it is an unlawful thing for a man that is a Jew to join himself or come unto one of another nation; and *yet* unto me hath God showed that I should not call any man common or unclean: [29] wherefore also I came without gainsaying, when I was sent for. I ask therefore with what intent ye sent for me. [30] And Cornelius said, Four days ago, until this hour, I was keeping the ninth hour of prayer in my house; and behold, a man stood before me in bright apparel, [31] and saith, Cornelius, thy prayer is heard, and thine alms are had in remembrance in the sight of God. [32] Send therefore to Joppa, and call unto thee Simon, who is surnamed Peter; he lodgeth in the house of Simon a tanner, by the sea side. [33] Forthwith therefore I sent to thee; and thou hast well done that thou art come. Now therefore we are all here present in the sight of God, to hear all things that have been commanded thee of the Lord. [34] And Peter opened his mouth, and said,

Of a truth I perceive that God is no respecter of persons: [35] but

[2] Some ancient authorities read *he*.

[3] The Greek word denotes an act of reverence, whether paid to a creature or to the Creator. [4] Or, *how unlawful it is for a man &c.*

in every nation he that feareth him, and worketh righteousness, is acceptable to him. [36] The[5] word which he sent unto the children of Israel, preaching good[6] tidings of peace by Jesus Christ (he is Lord of all)—[37] that saying ye yourselves know, which was published throughout all Judæa, beginning from Galilee, after the baptism which John preached; [38] *even* Jesus of Nazareth, how God anointed him with the Holy Spirit and with power: who went about doing good, and healing all that were oppressed of the devil; for God was with him. [39] And we are witnesses of all things which he did both in the country of the Jews, and in Jerusalem; whom also they slew, hanging him on a tree. [40] Him God raised up the third day, and gave him to be made manifest, [41] not to all the people, but unto witnesses that were chosen before of God, *even* to us, who ate and drank with him after he rose from the dead. [42] And he charged us to preach unto the people, and to testify that this is he who is ordained of God *to be* the Judge of the living and the dead. [43] To him bear all the prophets witness, that through his name every one that believeth on him shall receive remission of sins.

[44] While Peter yet spake these words, the Holy Spirit fell on all them that heard the word. [45] And they of the circumcision that believed were amazed, as many as came with Peter, because that on the Gentiles also was poured out the gift of the Holy Spirit. [46] For they heard them speak with tongues, and magnify God. Then answered Peter, [47] Can any man forbid the water, that these should not be baptized, who have received the Holy Spirit as well as we? [48] And he commanded them to be baptized in the name of Jesus Christ. Then prayed they him to tarry certain days.

XI

[1] Now the apostles and the brethren that were in Judæa heard that the Gentiles also had received the word of God. [2] And when Peter was come up to Jerusalem, they that were of the circumcision contended with him, [3] saying, Thou wentest in to men uncircumcised, and didst eat with them. [4] But Peter began, and expounded *the matter* unto them in order, saying, [5] I was in the city of Joppa praying: and in a trance I saw a vision, a certain vessel

[5] Many ancient authorities read *He sent the word unto.* [6] Or, *the gospel.*

descending, as it were a great sheet let down from heaven by four
corners; and it came even unto me: [6] upon which when I had
fastened mine eyes, I considered, and saw the four-footed beasts of
the earth and wild beasts and creeping things and birds of the
heaven. [7] And I heard also a voice saying unto me, Rise, Peter;
kill and eat. [8] But I said, Not so, Lord; for nothing common or
unclean hath ever entered into my mouth. [9] But a voice answered
the second time out of heaven, What God hath cleansed, make not
thou common. [10] And this was done thrice: and all were drawn
up again into heaven. [11] And behold, forthwith three men stood
before the house in which we were, having been sent from Cæsarea
unto me. [12] And the Spirit bade me go with them, making no
distinction. And these six brethren also accompanied me; and we
entered into the man's house: [13] and he told us how he had seen
the angel standing in his house, and saying, Send to Joppa, and
fetch Simon, whose surname is Peter; [14] who shall speak unto
thee words, whereby thou shalt be saved, thou and all thy house.
[15] And as I began to speak, the Holy Spirit fell on them, even as
on us at the beginning. [16] And I remembered the word of the
Lord, how he said, John indeed baptized with water; but ye shall
be baptized in[1] the Holy Spirit. [17] If then God gave unto them
the like gift as *he did* also unto us, when we believed on the Lord
Jesus Christ, who was I, that I could withstand God? [18] And
when they heard these things, they held their peace, and glorified
God, saying, Then to the Gentiles also hath God granted repentance
unto life.

[19] They therefore that were scattered abroad upon the tribula-
tion that arose about Stephen travelled as far as Phœnicia, and
Cyprus, and Antioch, speaking the word to none save only to Jews.
[20] But there were some of them, men of Cyprus and Cyrene, who,
when they were come to Antioch, spake unto the Greeks[2] also,
preaching[3] the Lord Jesus. [21] And the hand of the Lord was with
them: and a great number that believed turned unto the Lord. [22]
And the report concerning them came to the ears of the church
which was in Jerusalem: and they sent forth Barnabas as far as

[1] Or, *with*.
[2] Many ancient authorities read *Grecian Jews*. See ch. 6. 1.
[3] See marginal note on ch. 5. 42.

Antioch: [23] who, when he was come, and had seen the grace of God, was glad; and he exhorted them all, that[4] with purpose of heart they would cleave unto the Lord: [24] for he was a good man, and full of the Holy Spirit and of faith: and much people was added unto the Lord. [25] And he went forth to Tarsus to seek for Saul; [26] and when he had found him, he brought him unto Antioch. And it came to pass, that even for a whole year they were gathered together with[5] the church, and taught much people; and that the disciples were called Christians first in Antioch.

[27] Now in these days there came down prophets from Jerusalem unto Antioch. [28] And there stood up one of them named Agabus, and signified by the Spirit that there should be a great famine over all the[6] world: which came to pass in the days of Claudius. [29] And the disciples, every man according to his ability, determined to send relief[7] unto the brethren that dwelt in Judæa: [30] which also they did, sending it to the elders by the hand of Barnabas and Saul.

XII

[1] Now about that time Herod the king put forth his hands to afflict certain of the church. [2] And he killed James the brother of John with the sword. [3] And when he saw that it pleased the Jews, he proceeded to seize Peter also. And *those* were the days of unleavened bread. [4] And when he had taken him, he put him in prison, and delivered him to four quaternions of soldiers to guard him; intending after the Passover to bring him forth to the people. [5] Peter therefore was kept in the prison: but prayer was made earnestly of the church unto God for him. [6] And when Herod was about to bring him forth, the same night Peter was sleeping between two soldiers, bound with two chains: and guards before the door kept the prison. [7] And behold, an angel of the Lord stood by him, and a light shined in the cell: and he smote Peter on the side, and awoke him, saying, Rise up quickly. And his chains fell off from his hands. [8] And the angel said unto him, Gird thyself, and bind on thy sandals. And he did so. And he saith unto him, Cast thy garment about thee, and follow me. [9] And he went

[4] Some ancient authorities read *that they would cleave unto the purpose of their heart in the Lord.* [5] Gr. *in.* [6] Gr. *the inhabited earth.*
[7] Gr. *for ministry.* Comp. ch. 6. 1.

out, and followed; and he knew not that it was true which was done by[1] the angel, but thought he saw a vision. [10] And when they were past the first and the second guard, they came unto the iron gate that leadeth into the city; which opened to them of its own accord: and they went out, and passed on through one street and straightway the angel departed from him. [11] And when Peter was come to himself, he said, Now I know of a truth, that the Lord hath sent forth his angel and delivered me out of the hand of Herod, and from all the expectation of the people of the Jews. [12] And when he had considered *the thing,* he came to the house of Mary the mother of John whose surname was Mark; where many were gathered together and were praying. [13] And when he knocked at the door of the gate, a maid came to answer, named Rhoda. [14] And when she knew Peter's voice, she opened not the gate for joy, but ran in, and told that Peter stood before the gate. [15] And they said unto her, Thou art mad. But she confidently affirmed that it was even so. And they said, It is his angel. [16] But Peter continued knocking: and when they had opened, they saw him, and were amazed. [17] But he, beckoning unto them with the hand to hold their peace, declared unto them how the Lord had brought him forth out of the prison. And he said, Tell these things unto James, and to the brethren. And he departed, and went to another place. [18] Now as soon as it was day, there was no small stir among the soldiers, what was become of Peter. [19] And when Herod had sought for him, and found him not, he examined the guards, and commanded that they should be put[2] to death. And he went down from Judæa to Cæsarea, and tarried there.

[20] Now he was highly displeased with them of Tyre and Sidon: and they came with one accord to him, and, having made Blastus the king's chamberlain their friend, they asked for peace, because their country was fed from the king's country. [21] And upon a set day Herod arrayed himself in royal apparel, and sat on the throne,[3] and made an oration unto them. [22] And the people shouted, *saying,* The voice of a god, and not of a man. [23] And immediately an angel of the Lord smote him, because he gave not

[1] Gr. *through.*
[2] Gr. *led away to death.* [3] Or, *judgment-seat.* See Mt. 27. 19.

God the glory: and he was eaten of worms, and gave up the ghost.
[24] But the word of God grew and multiplied.
[25] And Barnabas and Saul returned from[4] Jerusalem, when
they had fulfilled their ministration, taking with them John whose
surname was Mark.

XIII

[1] Now there were at Antioch, in the church that was *there,*
prophets and teachers, Barnabas, and Symeon that was called Niger,
and Lucius of Cyrene, and Manaen the foster-brother of Herod the
tetrarch, and Saul. [2] And as they ministered to the Lord, and
fasted, the Holy Spirit said, Separate me Barnabas and Saul for the
work whereunto I have called them. [3] Then, when they had
fasted and prayed and laid their hands on them, they sent them
away.
[4] So they, being sent forth by the Holy Spirit, went down to
Seleucia; and from thence they sailed to Cyprus. [5] And when
they were at Salamis, they proclaimed the word of God in the
synagogues of the Jews: and they had also John as their attendant.
[6] And when they had gone through the whole island unto Paphos,
they found a certain sorcerer,[1] a false prophet, a Jew, whose name
was Bar-Jesus; [7] who was with the proconsul, Sergius Paulus, a
man of understanding. The same called unto him Barnabas and
Saul, and sought to hear the word of God. [8] But Elymas the
sorcerer[1] (for so is his name by interpretation) withstood them,
seeking to turn aside the proconsul from the faith. [9] But Saul,
who is also *called* Paul, filled with the Holy Spirit, fastened his eyes
on him, [10] and said, O full of all guile and all villany, thou son
of the devil, thou enemy of all righteousness, wilt thou not cease
to pervert the right ways of the Lord? [11] And now, behold, the
hand of the Lord is upon thee, and thou shalt be blind, not seeing
the sun for[2] a season. And immediately there fell on him a mist and
a darkness; and he went about seeking some to lead him by the
hand. [12] Then the proconsul, when he saw what was done,
believed, being astonished at the teaching of the Lord.

[4] Many ancient authorities read *to Jerusalem.*
[1] Gr. *Magus:* as in Mt. 2. 1, 7, 16. [2] Or, *until.*

[13] Now Paul and his company set sail from Paphos, and came to Perga in Pamphylia: and John departed from them and returned to Jerusalem. [14] But they, passing through from Perga, came to Antioch of Pisidia; and they went into the synagogue on the sabbath day, and sat down. [15] And after the reading of the law and the prophets the rulers of the synagogue sent unto them, saying, Brethren, if ye have any word of exhortation for the people, say on. [16] And Paul stood up, and beckoning with the hand said,

Men of Israel, and ye that fear God, hearken: [17] The God of this people Israel chose our fathers, and exalted the people when they sojourned in the land of Egypt, and with a high arm led he them forth out of it. [18] And for about the time of forty years as[3] a nursing-father bare he them in the wilderness. [19] And when he had destroyed seven nations in the land of Canaan, he gave *them* their land for an inheritance, for about four hundred and fifty years: [20] and after these things he gave *them* judges until Samuel the prophet. [21] And afterward they asked for a king: and God gave unto them Saul the son of Kish, a man of the tribe of Benjamin, for the space of forty years. [22] And when he had removed him, he raised up David to be their king; to whom also he bare witness and said, I have found David the son of Jesse, a man after my heart, who shall do all my will.[4] [23] Of this man's seed hath God according to promise brought unto Israel a Saviour, Jesus; [24] when John had first preached before[5] his coming the baptism of repentance to all the people of Israel. [25] And as John was fulfilling his course, he said, What suppose ye that I am? I am not *he*. But behold, there cometh one after me the shoes of whose feet I am not worthy to unloose. [26] Brethren, children of the stock of Abraham, and those among you that fear God, to us is the word of this salvation sent forth. [27] For they that dwell in Jerusalem, and their rulers, because they knew him not, nor the voices of the prophets which are read every sabbath, fulfilled *them* by condemning *him*. [28] And though they found no cause of death *in him,* yet asked they of Pilate that he should be slain. [29] And when they had fulfilled all things that were written of him, they took him down from the tree,

[3] Many ancient authorities read *suffered he their manners in the wilderness.* See Deut. 9. 7. [4] Gr. *wills.* [5] Gr. *before the face of his entering in.*

and laid him in a tomb. [30] But God raised him from the dead: [31] and he was seen for many days of them that came up with him from Galilee to Jerusalem, who are now his witnesses unto the people. [32] And we bring you good tidings of the promise made unto the fathers, [33] that God hath fulfilled the same unto our children, in that he raised up Jesus; as also it is written in the second psalm, Thou art my Son, this day have I begotten thee. [34] And as concerning that he raised him up from the dead, now no more to return to corruption, he hath spoken on this wise, I will give you the holy and sure *blessings* of David. [35] Because he saith also in another *psalm,* Thou wilt not give thy Holy One to see corruption. [36] For David, after he had in[6] his own generation served the counsel of God, fell asleep, and was laid unto his fathers, and saw corruption: [37] but he whom God raised up saw no corruption. [38] Be it known unto you therefore, brethren, that through this man is proclaimed unto you remission of sins: [39] and by him every one that believeth is justified from all things, from which ye could not be justified by the law of Moses. [40] Beware therefore, lest that come upon *you* which is spoken in the prophets:

[41] Behold, ye despisers, and wonder, and perish;[7]
For I work a work in your days,
A work which ye shall in no wise believe, if one declare it unto you.

[42] And as they went out, they besought that these words might be spoken to them the next sabbath. [43] Now when the synagogue broke up, many of the Jews and of the devout proselytes followed Paul and Barnabas; who, speaking to them, urged them to continue in the grace of God.

[44] And the next sabbath almost the whole city was gathered together to hear the word of God.[8] [45] But when the Jews saw the multitudes, they were filled with jealousy, and contradicted the things which were spoken by Paul, and blasphemed.[9] [46] And Paul and Barnabas spake out boldly, and said, It was necessary that the word of God should first be spoken to you. Seeing ye thrust it from

[6] Or, *served his own generation by the counsel of God, fell asleep.* Or, *served his own generation, fell asleep by the counsel of God.*

[7] Or, *vanish away.* Jas. 4. 14. [8] Many ancient authorities read *the Lord.*

[9] Or, *railed.*

you, and judge yourselves unworthy of eternal life, lo, we turn to
the Gentiles. [47] For so hath the Lord commanded us, *saying,*

I have set thee for a light of the Gentiles,
That thou shouldest be for salvation unto the uttermost part
of the earth.

[48] And as the Gentiles heard this, they were glad, and glorified
the word of God:[8] and as many as were ordained to eternal life
believed. [49] And the word of the Lord was spread abroad throughout all the region. [50] But the Jews urged on the devout women
of honorable estate, and the chief men of the city, and stirred up
a persecution against Paul and Barnabas, and cast them out of their
borders. [51] But they shook off the dust of their feet against them,
and came unto Iconium. [52] And the disciples were filled with
joy and with the Holy Spirit.

XIV

[1] And it came to pass in Iconium that they entered together
into the synagogue of the Jews, and so spake that a great multitude
both of Jews and of Greeks believed. [2] But the Jews that were
disobedient stirred up the souls of the Gentiles, and made them evil
affected against the brethren. [3] Long time therefore they tarried
there speaking boldly in the Lord, who bare witness unto the word
of his grace, granting signs and wonders to be done by their hands.
[4] But the multitude of the city was divided; and part held with
the Jews, and part with the apostles. [5] And when there was made
an onset both of the Gentiles and of the Jews with their rulers, to
treat them shamefully and to stone them, [6] they became aware of
it, and fled unto the cities of Lycaonia, Lystra and Derbe, and the
region round about: [7] and there they preached[1] the gospel.

[8] And at Lystra there sat a certain man, impotent in his feet,
a cripple from his mother's womb, who never had walked. [9] The
same heard Paul speaking: who, fastening his eyes upon him, and
seeing that he had faith to be made whole, [10] said with a loud
voice, Stand upright on thy feet. And he leaped up and walked.
[11] And when the multitudes saw what Paul had done, they lifted

[1] See marginal note on ch. 5. 42.

up their voice, saying in the speech of Lycaonia, The gods are come
down to us in the likeness of men. [12] And they called Barnabas,
Jupiter;[2] and Paul, Mercury,[3] because he was the chief speaker. [13]
And the priest of Jupiter[2] whose *temple* was before the city, brought
oxen and garlands unto the gates, and would have done sacrifice
with the multitudes. [14] But when the apostles, Barnabas and Paul,
heard of it, they rent their garments, and sprang forth among the
multitude, crying out [15] and saying, Sirs, why do ye these things?
We also are men of like passions[4] with you, and bring you good
tidings, that ye should turn from these vain things unto a living God,
who made the heaven and the earth and the sea, and all that in
them is: [16] who in the generations gone by suffered all the nations[5]
to walk in their own ways. [17] And yet he left not himself without
witness, in that he did good and gave you from heaven rains and
fruitful seasons, filling your hearts with food and gladness. [18] And
with these sayings scarce restrained they the multitudes from doing
sacrifice unto them.

[19] But there came Jews thither from Antioch and Iconium: and
having persuaded the multitudes, they stoned Paul, and dragged him
out of the city, supposing that he was dead. [20] But as the disciples
stood round about him, he rose up, and entered into the city: and
on the morrow he went forth with Barnabas to Derbe. [21] And
when they had preached[6] the gospel to that city, and had made many
disciples, they returned to Lystra, and to Iconium, and to Antioch,
[22] confirming the souls of the disciples, exhorting them to continue in the faith, and that through many tribulations we must enter
into the kingdom of God. [23] And when they had appointed for
them elders in every church, and had prayed with fasting, they
commended them to the Lord, on whom they had believed. [24]
And they passed through Pisidia, and came to Pamphylia. [25] And
when they had spoken the word in Perga, they went down to
Attalia; [26] and thence they sailed to Antioch, from whence they
had been committed to the grace of God for the work which they
had fulfilled. [27] And when they were come, and had gathered the
church together, they rehearsed all things that God had done with

[2] Gr. *Zeus.* [3] Gr. *Hermes.* [4] Or, *nature.* [5] Or, *Gentiles.* See ch. 4. **25.**
[6] Gr. *brought the good tidings.* Comp. ch. 5. 42.

them, and that he had opened a door of faith unto the Gentiles. [28] And they tarried no little time with the disciples.

XV

[1] And certain men came down from Judæa and taught the brethren, *saying,* Except ye be circumcised after the custom of Moses, ye cannot be saved. [2] And when Paul and Barnabas had no small dissension and questioning with them, *the brethren* appointed that Paul and Barnabas, and certain other of them, should go up to Jerusalem unto the apostles and elders about this question. [3] They therefore, being brought on their way by the church, passed through both Phœnicia and Samaria, declaring the conversion of the Gentiles: and they caused great joy unto all the brethren. [4] And when they were come to Jerusalem, they were received of the church and the apostles and the elders, and they rehearsed all things that God had done with them. [5] But there rose up certain of the sect of the Pharisees who believed, saying, It is needful to circumcise them, and to charge them to keep the law of Moses.

[6] And the apostles and the elders were gathered together to consider of this matter. [7] And when there had been much questioning, Peter rose up, and said unto them,

Brethren, ye know that a[1] good while ago God made choice among you, that by my mouth the Gentiles should hear the word of the gospel,[2] and believe. [8] And God, who knoweth the heart, bare them witness, giving them the Holy Spirit, even as he did unto us; [9] and he made no distinction between us and them, cleansing their hearts by faith. [10] Now therefore why make ye trial of God, that ye should put a yoke upon the neck of the disciples which neither our fathers nor we were able to bear? [11] But we believe that we shall be saved through the grace of the Lord Jesus, in like manner as they.

[12] And all the multitude kept silence; and they hearkened unto Barnabas and Paul rehearsing what signs and wonders God had wrought among the Gentiles through them. [13] And after they had held their peace, James answered, saying,

[1] Gr. *from early days.* [2] Or, *good tidings.*

Brethren, hearken unto me: [14] Symeon hath rehearsed how first God visited the Gentiles,[3] to take out of them a people for his name. [15] And to this agree the words of the prophets; as it is written,

[16] After these things I will return,
And I will build again the tabernacle of David, which is fallen;
And I will build again the ruins thereof,
And I will set it up:
[17] That the residue of men may seek after the Lord,
And all the Gentiles,[4] upon whom my name is called,
[18] Saith the Lord, who[5] maketh these things known from of old.

[19] Wherefore my judgment is, that we trouble not them that from among the Gentiles turn to God; [20] but that we write[6] unto them, that they abstain from the pollutions of idols, and from fornication, and from what is strangled, and from blood. [21] For Moses from generations of old hath in every city them that preach him, being read in the synagogues every sabbath.

[22] Then it seemed good to the apostles and the elders, with the whole church, to choose men out of their company, and send them to Antioch with Paul and Barnabas; *namely,* Judas called Barsabbas, and Silas, chief men among the brethren: [23] and they wrote *thus* by them, The[7] apostles and the elders, brethren, unto the brethren who are of the Gentiles in Antioch and Syria and Cilicia, greeting: [24] Forasmuch as we have heard that certain who[8] went out from us have troubled you with words, subverting your souls; to whom we gave no commandment; [25] it seemed good unto us, having come to one accord, to choose out men and send them unto you with our beloved Barnabas and Paul, [26] men that have hazarded their lives for the name of our Lord Jesus Christ. [27] We have sent therefore Judas and Silas, who themselves also shall tell you the same things by word of mouth. [28] For it seemed good to the Holy Spirit, and to us, to lay upon you no greater burden than these necessary things: [29] that ye abstain from things sacrificed to idols, and from blood, and from things strangled, and from fornication;

[3] See marginal note on ch. 4. 25. [4] See marginal note on ch. 4. 25.
[5] Or, *who doeth these things* which were *known &c.*
[6] Or, *enjoin them.* [7] Or, *The apostles and the elder brethren.*
[8] Some ancient authorities omit *who went out.*

from which if ye keep yourselves, it shall be well with you. Fare ye well.

[30] So they, when they were dismissed, came down to Antioch; and having gathered the multitude together, they delivered the epistle. [31] And when they had read it, they rejoiced for the consolation.[9] [32] And Judas and Silas, being themselves also prophets, exhorted[10] the brethren with many words, and confirmed them. [33] And after they had spent some time *there,* they were dismissed in peace from the brethren unto those that had sent them forth.[11] [35] But Paul and Barnabas tarried in Antioch, teaching and preaching[12] the word of the Lord, with many others also.

[36] And after some days Paul said unto Barnabas, Let us return now and visit the brethren in every city wherein we proclaimed the word of the Lord, *and see* how they fare. [37] And Barnabas was minded to take with them John also, who was called Mark. [38] But Paul thought not good to take with them him who withdrew from them from Pamphylia, and went not with them to the work. [39] And there arose a sharp contention, so that they parted asunder one from the other, and Barnabas took Mark with him, and sailed away unto Cyprus; [40] but Paul chose Silas, and went forth, being commended by the brethren to the grace of the Lord. [41] And he went through Syria and Cilicia, confirming the churches.

XVI

[1] AND he came also to Derbe and to Lystra: and behold, a certain disciple was there, named Timothy, the son of a Jewess that believed; but his father was a Greek. [2] The same was well reported of by the brethren that were at Lystra and Iconium. [3] Him would Paul have to go forth with him; and he took and circumcised him because of the Jews that were in those parts: for they all knew that his father was a Greek. [4] And as they went on their way through the cities, they delivered them the decrees to keep which had been ordained of the apostles and elders that were at Jerusalem. [5] So the churches were strengthened in[1] the faith, and increased in number daily.

[9] Or, *exhortation.* [10] Or, *comforted.*

[11] Some ancient authorities insert, with variations, ver. 34 *But it seemed good unto Silas to abide there.* [12] Comp. marg. note on ch. 5. 42. [1] Or, *in faith.*

[6] And they went through the[2] region of Phrygia and Galatia,
having been forbidden of the Holy Spirit to speak the word in Asia;
[7] and when they were come over against Mysia, they assayed to
go into Bithynia; and the Spirit of Jesus suffered them not; [8] and
passing by Mysia, they came down to Troas. [9] And a vision
appeared to Paul in the night: There was a man of Macedonia
standing, beseeching him, and saying, Come over into Macedonia,
and help us. [10] And when he had seen the vision, straightway
we sought to go forth into Macedonia, concluding that God had
called us to preach[3] the gospel unto them.

[11] Setting sail therefore from Troas, we made a straight course
to Samothrace, and the day following to Neapolis; [12] and from
thence to Philippi, which is a city of Macedonia, the first of the
district, a *Roman* colony: and we were in this city tarrying certain
days. [13] And on the sabbath day we went forth without the gate
by a river side, where[4] we supposed there was a place of prayer; and
we sat down, and spake unto the women that were come together.
[14] And a certain woman named Lydia, a seller of purple, of the
city of Thyatira, one that worshipped God, heard us: whose heart
the Lord opened to give heed unto the things which were spoken
by Paul. [15] And when she was baptized, and her household, she
besought us, saying, If ye have judged me to be faithful to the Lord,
come into my house, and abide *there*. And she constrained us.

[16] And it came to pass, as we were going to the place of prayer,
that a certain maid having a[5] spirit of divination met us, who
brought her masters much gain by soothsaying. [17] The same
following after Paul and us cried out, saying, These men are
servants[6] of the Most High God, who proclaim unto you the[7] way of
salvation. [18] And this she did for many days. But Paul, being
sore troubled, turned and said to the spirit, I charge thee in the
name of Jesus Christ to come out of her. And it came out that
very hour.

[19] But when her masters saw that the hope of their gain was
gone,[8] they laid hold on Paul and Silas, and dragged them into the

[2] Or, *Phrygia and the region of Galatia.*
[3] Gr. *bring the good tidings.* See ch. 5. 42.
[4] Many authorities read *where was wont to be &c.*
[5] Gr. *a spirit, a Python.* [6] Gr. *bondservants.* [7] Or, *a way.* [8] Gr. *come out.*

marketplace before the rulers, [20] and when they had brought them unto the magistrates,[9] they said, These men, being Jews, do exceedingly trouble our city, [21] and set forth customs which it is not lawful for us to receive, or to observe, being Romans. [22] And the multitude rose up together against them: and the magistrates[9] rent their garments off them, and commanded to beat them with rods. [23] And when they had laid many stripes upon them, they cast them into prison, charging the jailor to keep them safely: [24] who, having received such a charge, cast them into the inner prison, and made their feet fast in the stocks. [25] But about midnight Paul and Silas were praying and singing hymns unto God, and the prisoners were listening to them; [26] and suddenly there was a great earthquake, so that the foundations of the prison-house were shaken: and immediately all the doors were opened; and every one's bands were loosed. [27] And the jailor, being roused out of sleep and seeing the prison doors open, drew his sword and was about to kill himself, supposing that the prisoners had escaped. [28] But Paul cried with a loud voice, saying, Do thyself no harm: for we are all here. [29] And he called for lights and sprang in, and, trembling for fear, fell down before Paul and Silas, [30] and brought them out and said, Sirs, what must I do to be saved? [31] And they said, Believe on the Lord Jesus, and thou shalt be saved, thou and thy house. [32] And they spake the word of the[10] Lord unto him, with all that were in his house. [33] And he took them the same hour of the night, and washed their stripes; and was baptized, he and all his, immediately. [34] And he brought them up into his house, and set food[11] before them, and rejoiced greatly, with all his house, having[12] believed in God.

[35] But when it was day, the magistrates[13] sent the serjeants,[14] saying, Let those men go. [36] And the jailor reported the words to Paul, *saying,* The magistrates[13] have sent to let you go: now therefore come forth, and go in peace. [37] But Paul said unto them, They have beaten us publicly, uncondemned, men that are Romans, and have cast us into prison, and do they now cast us out privily? nay verily; but let them come themselves and bring us out. [38]

[9] Gr. *prætors:* comp. ver. 22, 35, 36, 38.
[10] Some ancient authorities read *God.* [11] Gr. *a table.*
[12] Or, *having believed God.* [13] Gr. *prætors.* See ver. 20. [14] Gr. *lictors.*

And the serjeants[14] reported these words unto the magistrates:[13] and they feared when they heard that they were Romans; [39] and they came and besought them; and when they had brought them out, they asked them to go away from the city. [40] And they went out of the prison, and entered into *the house of* Lydia: and when they had seen the brethren, they comforted[15] them, and departed.

XVII

[1] Now when they had passed through Amphipolis and Apollonia, they came to Thessalonica, where was a synagogue of the Jews: [2] and Paul, as his custom was, went in unto them, and for three sabbath[1] days reasoned with them from the scriptures, [3] opening and alleging that it behooved the Christ to suffer, and to rise again from the dead; and that this Jesus, whom, *said he,* I proclaim unto you, is the Christ. [4] And some of them were persuaded, and consorted with Paul and Silas; and of the devout Greeks a great multitude, and of the chief women not a few. [5] But the Jews, being moved with jealousy, took unto them certain vile fellows of the rabble, and gathering a crowd, set the city on an uproar; and assaulting the house of Jason, they sought to bring them forth to the people. [6] And when they found them not, they dragged Jason and certain brethren before the rulers of the city, crying, These that have turned the[2] world upside down are come hither also; [7] whom Jason hath received: and these all act contrary to the decrees of Cæsar, saying that there is another king, *one* Jesus. [8] And they troubled the multitude and the rulers of the city, when they heard these things. [9] And when they had taken security from Jason and the rest, they let them go.

[10] And the brethren immediately sent away Paul and Silas by night unto Berœa: who when they were come thither went into the synagogue of the Jews. [11] Now these were more noble than those in Thessalonica in that they received the word with all readiness of mind, examining the scriptures daily, whether these things were so. [12] Many of them therefore believed; also of the Greek women of honorable estate, and of men, not a few. [13] But when the Jews

[15] Or, *exhorted.*
[1] Or, *weeks.* [2] Gr. *the inhabited earth.*

of Thessalonica had knowledge that the word of God was proclaimed of Paul at Berœa also, they came thither likewise, stirring
up and troubling the multitudes. [14] And then immediately the
brethren sent forth Paul to go as far as to the sea: and Silas and
Timothy abode there still. [15] But they that conducted Paul
brought him as far as Athens: and receiving a commandment unto
Silas and Timothy that they should come to him with all speed,
they departed.

[16] Now while Paul waited for them at Athens, his spirit was
provoked within him as he beheld the city full of idols. [17] So he
reasoned in the synagogue with the Jews and the devout persons,
and in the marketplace every day with them that met him. [18]
And certain also of the Epicurean and Stoic philosophers encoun-
tered him. And some said, What would this babbler say? others, He
seemeth to be a setter forth of strange[3] gods:[4] because he preached[5]
Jesus and the resurrection. [19] And they took hold of him, and
brought him unto[6] the[7] Areopagus, saying, May we know what this
new teaching is, which is spoken by thee? [20] For thou bringest
certain strange things to our ears: we would know therefore what
these things mean. [21] (Now all the Athenians and the strangers
sojourning there spent[8] their time in nothing else, but either to tell
or to hear some new thing.) [22] And Paul stood in the midst of
the Areopagus, and said,

Ye men of Athens, in all things I perceive that ye are very[9]
religious. [23] For as I passed along, and observed the objects of
your worship, I found also an altar with this inscription, TO AN
UNKNOWN GOD. What therefore ye worship in ignorance, this I set
forth unto you. [24] The God that made the world and all things
therein, he, being Lord of heaven and earth, dwelleth not in
temples[10] made with hands; [25] neither is he served by men's
hands, as though he needed anything, seeing he himself giveth to
all life, and breath, and all things; [26] and he made of one every
nation of men to dwell on all the face of the earth, having determined *their* appointed seasons, and the bounds of their habitation;
[27] that they should seek God, if haply they might feel after him

[3] Or, *foreign divinities*. [4] Gr. *demons*.
[5] See marg. note on ch. 5. 42. [6] Or, *before*. [7] Or, *the hill of Mars*.
[8] Or, *had leisure for nothing else*. [9] Or, *somewhat superstitious*. [10] Or, *sanctuaries*.

and find him, though he is not far from each one of us: [28] for in him we live, and move, and have our being; as certain even of your own poets have said,

For we are also his offspring.

[29] Being then the offspring of God, we ought not to think that the[11] Godhead is like unto gold, or silver, or stone, graven by art and device of man. [30] The times of ignorance therefore God overlooked; but now he commandeth[12] men that they should all everywhere repent: [31] inasmuch as he hath appointed a day in which he will judge the[13] world in righteousness by[14] the[15] man whom he hath ordained; whereof he hath given assurance unto all men, in that he hath raised him from the dead.

[32] Now when they heard of the resurrection of the dead, some mocked; but others said, We will hear thee concerning this yet again. [33] Thus Paul went out from among them. [34] But certain men clave unto him, and believed: among whom also was Dionysius the Areopagite, and a woman named Damaris, and others with them.

XVIII

[1] After these things he departed from Athens, and came to Corinth. [2] And he found a certain Jew named Aquila, a man of Pontus by race, lately come from Italy, with his wife Priscilla, because Claudius had commanded all the Jews to depart from Rome: and he came unto them; [3] and because he was of the same trade, he abode with them, and they wrought; for by their trade they were tent-makers. [4] And he reasoned in the synagogue every sabbath, and persuaded[1] Jews and Greeks.

[5] But when Silas and Timothy came down from Macedonia, Paul was constrained by the word, testifying to the Jews that Jesus was the Christ. [6] And when they opposed themselves and blasphemed,[2] he shook out his raiment and said unto them, Your blood *be* upon your own heads; I am clean: from henceforth I will go unto the Gentiles. [7] And he departed thence, and went into the house of a certain man named Titus Justus, one that worshipped

[11] Or, *that which is divine.* [12] Some ancient authorities read *declareth to men.*
[13] Gr. *the inhabited earth.* [14] Gr. *in.* [15] Or, *a man.*
[1] Gr. *sought to persuade.* [2] Or, *railed.*

God, whose house joined hard to the synagogue. [8] And Crispus,
the ruler of the synagogue, believed[3] in the Lord with all his house;
and many of the Corinthians hearing believed, and were baptized.
[9] And the Lord said unto Paul in the night by a vision, Be not
afraid, but speak and hold not thy peace: [10] for I am with thee,
and no man shall set on thee to harm thee: for I have much people
in this city. [11] And he dwelt *there* a year and six months, teaching
the word of God among them.

[12] But when Gallio was proconsul of Achaia, the Jews with one
accord rose up against Paul and brought him before the judgment-
seat, [13] saying, This man persuadeth men to worship God contrary to the law. [14] But when Paul was about to open his mouth,
Gallio said unto the Jews, If indeed it were a matter of wrong or of
wicked villany, O ye Jews, reason would that I should bear with
you: [15] but if they are questions about words and names and
your own law, look to it yourselves; I am not minded to be a judge
of these matters. [16] And he drove them from the judgment-seat.
[17] And they all laid hold on Sosthenes, the ruler of the synagogue,
and beat him before the judgment-seat. And Gallio cared for none
of these things.

[18] And Paul, having tarried after this yet many days, took his
leave of the brethren, and sailed thence for Syria, and with him
Priscilla and Aquila: having shorn his head in Cenchreæ; for he
had a vow. [19] And they came to Ephesus, and he left them there:
but he himself entered into the synagogue, and reasoned with the
Jews. [20] And when they asked him to abide a longer time, he
consented not; [21] but taking his leave of them, and saying, I will
return again unto you if God will, he set sail from Ephesus.

[22] And when he had landed at Cæsarea, he went up and saluted
the church, and went down to Antioch. [23] And having spent
some time *there,* he departed, and went through the region of
Galatia, and Phrygia, in order, establishing all the disciples.

[24] Now a certain Jew named Apollos, an Alexandrian by race,
an[4] eloquent man, came to Ephesus; and he was mighty in the
scriptures. [25] This man had been instructed[5] in the way of the
Lord; and being fervent in spirit, he spake and taught accurately

[3] Gr. *believed the Lord.* [4] Or, *a learned man.* [5] Gr. *taught by word of mouth.*

the things concerning Jesus, knowing only the baptism of John: [26] and he began to speak boldly in the synagogue. But when Priscilla and Aquila heard him, they took him unto them, and expounded unto him the way of God more accurately. [27] And when he was minded to pass over into Achaia, the brethren encouraged him, and wrote to the disciples to receive him: and when he was come, he helped[6] them much that had believed through grace; [28] for he powerfully confuted the Jews, *and*[7] *that* publicly, showing by the scriptures that Jesus was the Christ.

XIX

[1] And it came to pass, that, while Apollos was at Corinth, Paul having passed through the upper country came to Ephesus, and found certain disciples: [2] and he said unto them, Did ye receive the Holy Spirit when ye believed? And they *said* unto him, Nay, we did not so much as hear whether the[1] Holy Spirit was *given*. [3] And he said, Into what then were ye baptized? And thev said, Into John's baptism. [4] And Paul said, John baptized with the baptism of repentance, saying unto the people that they should believe on him that should come after him, that is, on Jesus. [5] And when they heard this, they were baptized into the name of the Lord Jesus. [6] And when Paul had laid his hands upon them, the Holy Spirit came on them; and they spake with tongues, and prophesied. [7] And they were in all about twelve men.

[8] And he entered into the synagogue, and spake boldly for the space of three months, reasoning and persuading *as to* the things concerning the kingdom of God. [9] But when some were hardened and disobedient, speaking evil of the Way before the multitude, he departed from them, and separated the disciples, reasoning daily in the school of Tyrannus. [10] And this continued for the space of two years; so that all they that dwelt in Asia heard the word of the Lord, both Jews and Greeks. [11] And God wrought special miracles[2] by the hands of Paul: [12] insomuch that unto the sick were carried away from his body handkerchiefs or aprons, and the diseases departed from them, and the evil spirits

[6] Or, *helped much through grace them that had believed.* [7] Or, *showing publicly.*
[1] Or, *there is a Holy Spirit.* [2] Gr. *powers.*

went out. [13] But certain also of the strolling Jews, exorcists, took
upon them to name over them that had the evil spirits the name of
the Lord Jesus, saying, I adjure you by Jesus whom Paul preacheth.
[14] And there were seven sons of one Sceva, a Jew, a chief priest,
who did this. [15] And the evil spirit answered and said unto them,
Jesus I know,[3] and Paul I know; but who are ye? [16] And the
man in whom the evil spirit was leaped on them, and mastered
both of them, and prevailed against them, so that they fled out of
that house naked and wounded. [17] And this became known to
all, both Jews and Greeks, that dwelt at Ephesus; and fear fell upon
them all, and the name of the Lord Jesus was magnified. [18] Many
also of them that had believed came, confessing, and declaring their
deeds. [19] And not a few of them that practised magical arts
brought their books together and burned them in the sight of all;
and they counted the price of them, and found it fifty thousand
pieces of silver. [20] So mightily grew the word of the Lord and
prevailed.

[21] Now after these things were ended, Paul purposed in the
spirit, when he had passed through Macedonia and Achaia, to go to
Jerusalem, saying, After I have been there, I must also see Rome.
[22] And having sent into Macedonia two of them that ministered
unto him, Timothy and Erastus, he himself stayed in Asia for a
while.

[23] And about that time there arose no small stir concerning the
Way. [24] For a certain man named Demetrius, a silversmith, who
made silver shrines of Diana,[4] brought no little business unto the
craftsmen; [25] whom he gathered together, with the workmen of
like occupation, and said, Sirs, ye know that by this business we
have our wealth. [26] And ye see and hear, that not alone at
Ephesus, but almost throughout all Asia, this Paul hath persuaded
and turned away much people, saying that they are no gods, that
are made with hands: [27] and not only is there danger that this
our trade come into disrepute; but also that the temple of the great
goddess Diana[4] be made of no account, and that she should even
be deposed from her magnificence whom all Asia and the[5] world
worshippeth. [28] And when they heard this they were filled with

[3] Or, *recognize.* [4] Gr. *Artemis* [5] Gr. *the inhabited earth.*

wrath, and cried out, saying, Great *is* Diana[4] of the Ephesians. [29] And the city was filled with the confusion: and they rushed with one accord into the theatre, having seized Gaius and Aristarchus, men of Macedonia, Paul's companions in travel. [30] And when Paul was minded to enter in unto the people, the disciples suffered him not. [31] And certain also of the Asiarchs,[6] being his friends, sent unto him and besought him not to adventure himself into the theatre. [32] Some therefore cried one thing, and some another: for the assembly was in confusion; and the more part knew not wherefore they were come together. [33] And[7] they brought Alexander out of the multitude, the Jews putting him forward. And Alexander beckoned with the hand, and would have made a defence unto the people. [34] But when they perceived that he was a Jew, all with one voice about the space of two hours cried out, Great *is* Diana[4] of the Ephesians. [35] And when the townclerk had quieted the multitude, he saith, Ye men of Ephesus, what man is there who knoweth not that the city of the Ephesians is temple-keeper of the great Diana,[4] and of the *image* which fell down from Jupiter?[8] [36] Seeing then that these things cannot be gainsaid, ye ought to be quiet, and to do nothing rash. [37] For ye have brought *hither* these men, who are neither robbers of temples nor blasphemers of our goddess. [38] If therefore Demetrius, and the craftsmen that are with him, have a matter against any man, the[9] courts are open, and there are proconsuls: let them accuse one another. [39] But if ye seek anything about other matters, it shall be settled in the regular assembly. [40] For indeed we are in danger to be accused[10] concerning this day's riot, there being no cause *for it:* and as touching it we shall not be able to give account of this concourse. [41] And when he had thus spoken, he dismissed the assembly.

XX

[1] AND after the uproar ceased, Paul having sent for the disciples and exhorted them, took leave of them, and departed to go into Macedonia. [2] And when he had gone through those parts, and

[6] That is, officers having charge of festivals &c. in the Roman province of Asia.
[7] Or, *And* some *of the multitude instructed Alexander.*
[8] Or, *heaven.* [9] Or, *court* days *are kept.*
[10] Or, *accused of riot concerning this day.*

had given them much exhortation, he came into Greece. [3] And when he had spent three months *there,* and a plot was laid against him by the Jews as he was about to set sail for Syria, he determined to return through Macedonia. [4] And there accompanied him as[1] far as Asia, Sopater of Berœa, *the son* of Pyrrhus; and of the Thessalonians, Aristarchus and Secundus; and Gaius of Derbe, and Timothy; and of Asia, Tychicus and Trophimus. [5] But these had[2] gone before, and were waiting for us at Troas. [6] And we sailed away from Philippi after the days of unleavened bread, and came unto them to Troas in five days; where we tarried seven days.

[7] And upon the first day of the week, when we were gathered together to break bread, Paul discoursed with them, intending to depart on the morrow; and prolonged his speech until midnight. [8] And there were many lights in the upper chamber where we were gathered together. [9] And there sat in the window a certain young man named Eutychus, borne down with deep sleep; and as Paul discoursed yet longer, being borne down by his sleep he fell down from the third story, and was taken up dead. [10] And Paul went down, and fell on him, and embracing him said, Make ye no ado; for his life is in him. [11] And when he was gone up, and had broken the bread, and eaten, and had talked with them a long while, even till break of day, so he departed. [12] And they brought the lad alive, and were not a little comforted.

[13] But we, going before to the ship, set sail for Assos, there intending to take in Paul: for so had he appointed, intending himself to go by[3] land. [14] And when he met us at Assos, we took him in, and came to Mitylene. [15] And sailing from thence, we came the following day over against Chios; and the next day we touched at Samos; and the[4] day after we came to Miletus. [16] For Paul had determined to sail past Ephesus, that he might not have to spend time in Asia; for he was hastening, if it were possible for him, to be at Jerusalem the day of Pentecost.

[17] And from Miletus he sent to Ephesus, and called to him the

[1] Many ancient authorities omit *as far as Asia.*
[2] Many ancient authorities read *came, and were waiting.*
[3] Or, *on foot.*
[4] Many ancient authorities insert *having tarried at Trogyllium.*

elders[5] of the church. [18] And when they were come to him, he said unto them,

Ye yourselves know, from the first day that I set foot in Asia, after what manner I was with you all the time, [19] serving the Lord with all lowliness of mind, and with tears, and with trials which befell me by the plots of the Jews; [20] how I shrank not from declaring unto you anything that was profitable, and teaching you publicly, and from house to house, [21] testifying both to Jews and to Greeks repentance toward God, and faith toward our Lord Jesus Christ.[6] [22] And now, behold, I go bound in the spirit unto Jerusalem, not knowing the things that shall befall me there: [23] save that the Holy Spirit testifieth unto me in every city, saying that bonds and afflictions abide me. [24] But I hold not my life of any account as dear unto myself, so[7] that I may accomplish my course, and the ministry which I received from the Lord Jesus, to testify the gospel[8] of the grace of God. [25] And now, behold, I know that ye all, among whom I went about preaching the kingdom, shall see my face no more. [26] Wherefore I testify unto you this day, that I am pure from the blood of all men. [27] For I shrank not from declaring unto you the whole counsel of God. [28] Take heed unto yourselves, and to all the flock, in which the Holy Spirit hath made you bishops,[9] to feed the church of the[10] Lord which he purchased[11] with his own blood. [29] I know that after my departing grievous wolves shall enter in among you, not sparing the flock; [30] and from among your own selves shall men arise, speaking perverse things, to draw away the disciples after them. [31] Wherefore watch ye, remembering that by the space of three years I ceased not to admonish every one night and day with tears. [32] And now I commend you to God,[12] and to the word of his grace, which is able to build *you* up, and to give *you* the inheritance among all them that are sanctified. [33] I coveted no man's silver, or gold, or apparel. [34] Ye yourselves know that these hands ministered unto my necessities, and to them that were with me. [35]

[5] Or, *presbyters*. [6] Many ancient authorities omit *Christ*.
[7] Or, *in comparison of accomplishing my course*.
[8] Or, *good tidings*. [9] Or, *overseers*.
[10] Some ancient authorities, including the two oldest manuscripts, read *God*.
[11] Gr. *acquired*. [12] Some ancient authorities read *the Lord*.

In all things I gave you an example, that so laboring ye ought to help the weak, and to remember the words of the Lord Jesus, that he himself said, it is more blessed to give than to receive.

[36] And when he had thus spoken, he kneeled down and prayed with them all. [37] And they all wept sore, and fell on Paul's neck and kissed him, [38] sorrowing most of all for the word which he had spoken, that they should behold his face no more. And they brought him on his way unto the ship.

XXI

[1] And when it came to pass that we were parted from them and had set sail, we came with a straight course unto Cos, and the next day unto Rhodes, and from thence unto Patara: [2] and having found a ship crossing over unto Phœnicia, we went aboard, and set sail. [3] And when we had come in sight of Cyprus, leaving it on the left hand, we sailed unto Syria, and landed at Tyre; for there the ship was to unlade her burden. [4] And having found the disciples, we tarried there seven days: and these said to Paul through the Spirit, that he should not set foot in Jerusalem. [5] And when it came to pass that we had accomplished the days, we departed and went on our journey; and they all, with wives and children, brought us on our way till we were out of the city: and kneeling down on the beach, we prayed, and bade each other farewell; [6] and we went on board the ship, but they returned home again.

[7] And when we had finished the voyage from Tyre, we arrived at Ptolemais; and we saluted the brethren, and abode with them one day. [8] And on the morrow we departed, and came unto Cæsarea: and entering into the house of Philip the evangelist, who was one of the seven, we abode with him. [9] Now this man had four virgin daughters, who prophesied. [10] And as we tarried there some days, there came down from Judæa a certain prophet, named Agabus. [11] And coming to us, and taking Paul's girdle, he bound his own feet and hands, and said, Thus saith the Holy Spirit, So shall the Jews at Jerusalem bind the man that owneth this girdle, and shall deliver him into the hands of the Gentiles. [12] And when we heard these things, both we and they of that place besought him not to go up to Jerusalem. [13] Then Paul answered, What do ye,

weeping and breaking my heart? for I am ready not to be bound only, but also to die at Jerusalem for the name of the Lord Jesus. [14] And when he would not be persuaded, we ceased, saying, The will of the Lord be done.

[15] And after these days we took[1] up our baggage and went up to Jerusalem. [16] And there went with us also *certain* of the disciples from Cæsarea, bringing[2] *with them* one Mnason of Cyprus, an early disciple, with whom we should lodge.

[17] And when we were come to Jerusalem, the brethren received us gladly. [18] And the day following Paul went in with us unto James; and all the elders were present. [19] And when he had saluted them, he rehearsed one by one the things which God had wrought among the Gentiles through his ministry. [20] And they, when they heard it, glorified God; and they said unto him, Thou seest, brother, how many thousands[3] there are among the Jews of them that have believed; and they are all zealous for the law: [21] and they have been informed concerning thee, that thou teachest all the Jews who are among the Gentiles to forsake Moses, telling them not to circumcise their children, neither to walk after the customs. [22] What is it therefore? they will certainly hear that thou art come. [23] Do therefore this that we say to thee: We have four men that have a vow on them; [24] these take, and purify thyself with them, and be at charges for them, that they may shave their heads: and all shall know that there is no truth in the things whereof they have been informed concerning thee; but that thou thyself also walkest orderly, keeping the law. [25] But as touching the Gentiles that have believed, we wrote,[4] giving judgment that they should keep themselves from things sacrificed to idols, and from blood, and from what is strangled, and from fornication. [26] Then Paul took[5] the men, and the next day purifying himself with them went into the temple, declaring the fulfilment of the days of purification, until the offering was offered for every one of them.

[27] And when the seven days were almost completed, the Jews from Asia, when they saw him in the temple, stirred up all the multitude and laid hands on him, [28] crying out, Men of Israel,

[1] Or, *made ready.* [2] Or, *bringing* us to *one Mnason &c.*
[3] Gr. *myriads.* [4] Or, *enjoined.* Many ancient authorities read *sent*
[5] Or, *took the men the next day, and purifying himself &c.*

help: This is the man that teacheth all men everywhere against the people, and the law, and this place; and moreover he brought Greeks also into the temple, and hath defiled this holy place. [29] For they had before seen with him in the city Trophimus the Ephesian, whom they supposed that Paul had brought into the temple. [30] And all the city was moved, and the people ran together; and they laid hold on Paul, and dragged him out of the temple: and straightway the doors were shut. [31] And as they were seeking to kill him, tidings came up to the chief[6] captain of the band,[7] that all Jerusalem was in confusion. [32] And forthwith he took soldiers and centurions, and ran down upon them: and they, when they saw the chief[6] captain and the soldiers, left off beating Paul. [33] Then the chief[6] captain came near, and laid hold on him, and commanded him to be bound with two chains; and inquired who he was, and what he had done. [34] And some shouted one thing, some another, among the crowd: and when he could not know the certainty for the uproar, he commanded him to be brought into the castle. [35] And when he came upon the stairs, so it was that he was borne of the soldiers for the violence of the crowd; [36] for the multitude of the people followed after, crying out, Away with him.

[37] And as Paul was about to be brought into the castle, he saith unto the chief[6] captain, May I say something unto thee? And he said, Dost thou know Greek? [38] Art thou not then the Egyptian, who before these days stirred up to sedition and led out into the wilderness the four thousand men of the Assassins? [39] But Paul said, I am a Jew, of Tarsus in Cilicia, a citizen of no mean city: and I beseech thee, give me leave to speak unto the people. [40] And when he had given him leave, Paul, standing on the stairs, beckoned with the hand unto the people; and when there was made a great silence, he spake unto them in the Hebrew language, saying,

XXII

[1] Brethren and fathers, hear ye the defence which I now make unto you.

[6] Or, *military tribune*. Gr. *chiliarch*. [7] Or, *cohort*.

[2] And when they heard that he spake unto them in the Hebrew language, they were the more quiet: and he saith,

[3] I am a Jew, born in Tarsus of Cilicia, but brought up in this city, at the feet of Gamaliel, instructed according to the strict manner of the law of our fathers, being zealous for God, even as ye all are this day: [4] and I persecuted this Way unto the death, binding and delivering into prisons both men and women. [5] As also the high priest doth bear me witness, and all the estate of the elders: from whom also I received letters unto the brethren, and journeyed to Damascus to bring them also that were there unto Jerusalem in bonds to be punished. [6] And it came to pass, that, as I made my journey, and drew nigh unto Damascus, about noon, suddenly there shone from heaven a great light round about me. [7] And I fell unto the ground, and heard a voice saying unto me, Saul, Saul, why persecutest thou me? [8] And I answered, Who art thou, Lord? And he said unto me, I am Jesus of Nazareth, whom thou persecutest. [9] And they that were with me beheld indeed the light, but they heard not the voice of him that spake to me. [10] And I said, What shall I do, Lord? And the Lord said unto me, Arise, and go into Damascus; and there it shall be told thee of all things which are appointed for thee to do. [11] And when I could not see for the glory of that light, being led by the hand of them that were with me I came into Damascus. [12] And one Ananias, a devout man according to the law, well reported of by all the Jews that dwelt there, [13] came unto me, and standing by me said unto me, Brother Saul, receive thy sight. And in that very hour I looked[1] up on him. [14] And he said, The God of our fathers hath appointed thee to know his will, and to see the Righteous One, and to hear a voice from his mouth. [15] For thou shalt be a witness for him unto all men of what thou hast seen and heard. [16] And now why tarriest thou? arise, and be baptized, and wash away thy sins, calling on his name. [17] And it came to pass, that, when I had returned to Jerusalem, and while I prayed in the temple, I fell into a trance, [18] and saw him saying unto me, Make haste, and get thee quickly out of Jerusalem; because they will not receive of thee testimony concerning me. [19] And I said, Lord, they themselves

[1] Or, *received my sight* and looked *upon him.*

know that I imprisoned and beat in every synagogue them that believed on thee: [20] and when the blood of Stephen thy witness was shed, I also was standing by, and consenting, and keeping the garments of them that slew him. [21] And he said unto me, Depart: for I will send thee forth far hence unto the Gentiles.

[22] And they gave him audience unto this word; and they lifted up their voice, and said, Away with such a fellow from the earth: for it is not fit that he should live. [23] And as they cried out, and threw off their garments, and cast dust into the air, [24] the chief[2] captain commanded him to be brought into the castle, bidding that he should be examined by scourging, that he might know for what cause they so shouted against him. [25] And when they had tied him up with[3] the thongs, Paul said unto the centurion that stood by, Is it lawful for you to scourge a man that is a Roman, and uncondemned? [26] And when the centurion heard it, he went to the chief[2] captain and told him, saying, What art thou about to do? for this man is a Roman. [27] And the chief[2] captain came and said unto him, Tell me, art thou a Roman? And he said, Yea. [28] And the chief[2] captain answered, With a great sum obtained I this citizenship. And Paul said, But I am *a Roman* born. [29] They then that were about to examine him straightway departed from him: and the chief[2] captain also was afraid when he knew that he was a Roman, and because he had bound him.

[30] But on the morrow, desiring to know the certainty wherefore he was accused of the Jews, he loosed him, and commanded the chief priests and all the council to come together, and brought Paul down and set him before them.

XXIII

[1] And Paul, looking stedfastly on the council, said, Brethren, I have lived before God in all good conscience until this day. [2] And the high priest Ananias commanded them that stood by him to smite him on the mouth. [3] Then said Paul unto him, God shall smite thee, thou whited wall: and sittest thou to judge me according to the law, and commandest me to be smitten contrary to the law? [4] And they that stood by said, Revilest thou God's

[2] Or, *military tribune*. Gr. *chiliarch*. [3] Or, *for*.

high priest? [5] And Paul said, I knew not, brethren, that he was high priest: for it is written, Thou shalt not speak evil of a ruler of thy people. [6] But when Paul perceived that the one part were Sadducees and the other Pharisees, he cried out in the council, Brethren, I am a Pharisee, a son of Pharisees: touching the hope and resurrection of the dead I am called in question. [7] And when he had so said, there arose a dissension between the Pharisees and Sadducees; and the assembly was divided. [8] For the Sadducees say that there is no resurrection, neither angel, nor spirit; but the Pharisees confess both. [9] And there arose a great clamor: and some of the scribes of the Pharisees' part stood up, and strove, saying, We find no evil in this man: and what if a spirit hath spoken to him, or an angel? [10] And when there arose a great dissension, the chief[1] captain, fearing lest Paul should be torn in pieces by them, commanded the soldiers to go down and take him by force from among them, and bring him into the castle.

[11] And the night following the Lord stood by him, and said, Be of good cheer: for as thou hast testified concerning me at Jerusalem, so must thou bear witness also at Rome.

[12] And when it was day, the Jews banded together, and bound themselves under a curse, saying that they would neither eat nor drink till they had killed Paul. [13] And they were more than forty that made this conspiracy. [14] And they came to the chief priests and the elders, and said, We have bound ourselves under a great curse, to taste nothing until we have killed Paul. [15] Now therefore do ye with the council signify to the chief[1] captain that he bring him down unto you, as though ye would judge of his case more exactly: and we, before he comes near, are ready to slay him. [16] But Paul's sister's son heard of their lying in wait, and[2] he came and entered into the castle and told Paul. [17] And Paul called unto him one of the centurions, and said, Bring this young man unto the chief[1] captain; for he hath something to tell him. [18] So he took him, and brought him to the chief[1] captain, and saith, Paul the prisoner called me unto him, and asked me to bring this young man unto thee, who hath something to say to thee. [19] And the chief[1]

[1] Or, *military tribune.* Gr. *chiliarch.*
[2] Or, *having come in* upon them, *and he entered &c.*

captain took him by the hand, and going aside asked him privately, What is it that thou hast to tell me? [20] And he said, The Jews have agreed to ask thee to bring down Paul to-morrow unto the council, as though thou wouldest inquire somewhat more exactly concerning him. [21] Do not thou therefore yield unto them: for there lie in wait for him of them more than forty men, who have bound themselves under a curse, neither to eat nor to drink till they have slain him: and now are they ready, looking for the promise from thee. [22] So the chief[1] captain let the young man go, charging him, Tell no man that thou hast signified these things to me. [23] And he called unto him two of the centurions, and said, Make ready two hundred soldiers to go as far as Cæsarea, and horsemen threescore and ten, and spearmen two hundred, at the third hour of the night: [24] and *he bade them* provide beasts, that they might set Paul thereon, and bring him safe unto Felix the governor. [25] And he wrote a letter after this form:

[26] Claudius Lysias unto the most excellent governor Felix, greeting. [27] This man was seized by the Jews, and was about to be slain of them, when I came upon them with the soldiers and rescued him, having learned that he was a Roman. [28] And desiring to know the cause wherefore they accused him, I[3] brought him down unto their council: [29] whom I found to be accused about questions of their law, but to have nothing laid to his charge worthy of death or of bonds. [30] And when it was shown to me that there would be a plot against[4] the man, I sent him to thee forthwith, charging his accusers also to speak against him before thee.[5]

[31] So the soldiers, as it was commanded them, took Paul and brought him by night to Antipatris. [32] But on the morrow they left the horsemen to go with him, and returned to the castle: [33] and they, when they came to Cæsarea and delivered the letter to the governor, presented Paul also before him. [34] And when he had read it, he asked of what province he was; and when he understood that he was of Cilicia, [35] I will hear thee fully, said he, when thine accusers also are come: and he commanded him to be kept in Herod's palace.[6]

[3] Some ancient authorities omit *I brought him down unto their council.*

[4] Many ancient authorities read *against the man on their part, I sent him to thee. charging &c.* [5] Many ancient authorities add *Farewell.* [6] Gr. *Prætorium.*

XXIV

[1] And after five days the high priest Ananias came down with certain elders, and *with* an orator, one Tertullus; and they informed the governor against Paul. [2] And when he was called, Tertullus began to accuse him, saying,

Seeing that by thee we enjoy much peace, and that by thy providence evils are corrected for this nation, [3] we accept it in all ways and in all places, most excellent Felix, with all thankfulness. [4] But, that I be not further tedious unto thee, I entreat thee to hear us of thy clemency a few words. [5] For we have found this man a pestilent fellow, and a mover of insurrections among all the Jews throughout the[1] world, and a ringleader of the sect of the Nazarenes: [6] who moreover assayed to profane the temple: on whom also we laid hold:[2] [8] from whom thou wilt be able, by examining him thyself, to take knowledge of all these things whereof we accuse him. [9] And the Jews also joined in the charge, affirming that these things were so.

[10] And when the governor had beckoned unto him to speak, Paul answered,

Forasmuch as I know that thou hast been of many years a judge unto this nation, I cheerfully make my defence: [11] seeing that thou canst take knowledge that it is not more than twelve days since I went up to worship at Jerusalem: [12] and neither in the temple did they find me disputing with any man or stirring up a crowd, nor in the synagogues, nor in the city. [13] Neither can they prove to thee the things whereof they now accuse me. [14] But this I confess unto thee, that after the Way which they call a sect, so serve I the God of our fathers, believing all things which are according to the law, and which are written in the prophets; [15] having hope toward God, which these also themselves look[3] for, that there shall be a resurrection both of the just and unjust. [16] Herein[4] I also exercise myself to have a conscience void of offence toward God and men always.

[1] Gr. *the inhabited earth.*

[2] Some ancient authorities insert *and we would have judged him according to our law.* 7 *But the chief captain Lysias came, and with great violence took him away out of our hands,* 8 *commanding his accusers to come before thee.* [3] Or, *accept.*

[4] Or, *On this account.*

[17] Now after some years I came to bring alms to my nation, and offerings: [18] amidst[5] which they found me purified in the temple, with no crowd, nor yet with tumult: but *there were* certain Jews from Asia—[19] who ought to have been here before thee, and to make accusation, if they had aught against me. [20] Or else let these men themselves say what wrong-doing they found when I stood before the council, [21] except it be for this one voice, that I cried standing among them, Touching the resurrection of the dead I am called in question before you this day.

[22] But Felix, having more exact knowledge concerning the Way, deferred them, saying, When Lysias the chief[6] captain shall come down, I will determine your matter. [23] And he gave order to the centurion that he should be kept in charge, and should have indulgence; and not to forbid any of his friends to minister unto him.

[24] But after certain days, Felix came with Drusilla, his[7] wife, who was a Jewess, and sent for Paul, and heard him concerning the faith in Christ Jesus. [25] And as he reasoned of righteousness, and self-control, and the judgment to come, Felix was terrified, and answered, Go thy way for this time; and when I have a convenient season, I will call thee unto me. [26] He hoped withal that money would be given him of Paul: wherefore also he sent for him the oftener, and communed with him. [27] But when two years were fulfilled, Felix was succeeded by Porcius Festus; and desiring to gain favor with the Jews, Felix left Paul in bonds.

XXV

[1] FESTUS therefore, having[1] come into the province, after three days went up to Jerusalem from Cæsarea. [2] And the chief priests and the principal men of the Jews informed him against Paul; and they besought him, [3] asking a favor against him, that he would send for him to Jerusalem; laying a plot to kill him on the way. [4] Howbeit Festus answered, that Paul was kept in charge at Cæsarea, and that he himself was about to depart *thither* shortly. [5] Let them therefore, saith he, that are of power among you go down with me, and if there is anything amiss in the man, let them accuse him.

[5] Or, *in* presenting *which.* [6] Or, *military tribune.* Gr. *chiliarch.*
[7] Gr. *his own wife.* [1] Or, *having entered upon his province.*

[6] And when he had tarried among them not more than eight or ten days, he went down unto Cæsarea; and on the morrow he sat on the judgment-seat, and commanded Paul to be brought. [7] And when he was come, the Jews that had come down from Jerusalem stood round about him, bringing against him many and grievous charges which they could not prove; [8] while Paul said in his defence, Neither against the law of the Jews, nor against the temple, nor against Cæsar, have I sinned at all. [9] But Festus, desiring to gain favor with the Jews, answered Paul and said, Wilt thou go up to Jerusalem, and there be judged of these things before me? [10] But Paul said, I am standing before Cæsar's judgment-seat, where I ought to be judged: to the Jews have I done no wrong, as thou also very well knowest. [11] If then I am a wrong-doer, and have committed anything worthy of death, I refuse not to die; but if none of those things is *true* whereof these accuse me, no man can give[2] me up unto them. I appeal unto Cæsar. [12] Then Festus, when he had conferred with the council, answered, Thou hast appealed unto Cæsar: unto Cæsar shalt thou go.

[13] Now when certain days were passed, Agrippa the king and Bernice arrived at Cæsarea, and[3] saluted Festus. [14] And as they tarried there many days, Festus laid Paul's case before the king, saying, There is a certain man left a prisoner by Felix; [15] about whom, when I was at Jerusalem, the chief priests and the elders of the Jews informed *me,* asking for sentence against him. [16] To whom I answered, that it is not the custom of the Romans to give[2] up any man, before that the accused have the accusers face to face, and have had opportunity to make his defence concerning the matter laid against him. [17] When therefore they were come together here, I made no delay, but on the next day sat on the judgment-seat, and commanded the man to be brought. [18] Concerning whom, when the accusers stood up, they brought no charge of such evil things as I supposed; [19] but had certain questions against him of their own religion,[4] and of one Jesus, who was dead, whom Paul affirmed to be alive. [20] And I, being perplexed how to inquire concerning these things, asked whether he would go to Jerusalem

[2] Gr. *grant me by favor:* and so in ver. 16.
[3] Or, *having saluted.* [4] Or, *superstition.*

and there be judged of these matters. [21] But when Paul had appealed to be kept for the decision of the[5] emperor, I commanded him to be kept till I should send him to Cæsar. [22] And Agrippa *said* unto Festus, I also could[6] wish to hear the man myself. To-morrow, saith he, thou shalt hear him.

[23] So on the morrow, when Agrippa was come, and Bernice, with great pomp, and they were entered into the place of hearing with the chief[7] captains and the principal men of the city, at the command of Festus Paul was brought in. [24] And Festus saith, King Agrippa, and all men who are here present with us, ye behold this man, about whom all the multitude of the Jews made suit to me, both at Jerusalem and here, crying that he ought not to live any longer. [25] But I found that he had committed nothing worthy of death: and as he himself appealed to the[5] emperor I determined to send him. [26] Of whom I have no certain thing to write unto my lord. Wherefore I have brought him forth before you, and specially before thee, king Agrippa, that, after examination had, I may have somewhat to write. [27] For it seemeth to me unreasonable, in sending a prisoner, not withal to signify the charges against him.

XXVI

[1] And Agrippa said unto Paul, Thou art permitted to speak for thyself. Then Paul stretched forth his hand, and made his defence:

[2] I think myself happy, king Agrippa, that I am to make my defence before thee this day touching all the things whereof I am accused by the Jews: [3] especially[1] because thou art expert in all customs and questions which are among the Jews: wherefore I beseech thee to hear me patiently. [4] My manner of life then from my youth up, which was from the beginning among mine own nation and at Jerusalem, know all the Jews; [5] having knowledge of me from the first, if they be willing to testify, that after the straitest sect of our religion I lived a Pharisee. [6] And now I stand *here* to be judged for the hope of the promise made of God unto our fathers; [7] unto which *promise* our twelve tribes, earnestly serving

[5] Gr. *the Augustus.* [6] Or, *was wishing.* [7] Or, *military tribunes.* Gr. *chiliarchs.*
[1] Or, *because thou art especially expert.*

God night and day, hope to attain. And concerning this hope I am accused by the Jews, O king! [8] Why is it judged incredible with you, if God doth raise the dead? [9] I verily thought with myself that I ought to do many things contrary to the name of Jesus of Nazareth. [10] And this I also did in Jerusalem: and I both shut up many of the saints in prisons, having received authority from the chief priests, and when they were put to death I gave my vote against them. [11] And punishing them oftentimes in all the synagogues, I strove to make them blaspheme; and being exceedingly mad against them, I persecuted them even unto foreign cities. [12] Whereupon[2] as I journeyed to Damascus with the authority and commission of the chief priests, [13] at midday, O king, I saw on the way a light from heaven, above the brightness of the sun, shining round about me and them that journeyed with me. [14] And when we were all fallen to the earth, I heard a voice saying unto me in the Hebrew language, Saul, Saul, why persecutest thou me? it is hard for thee to kick against the[3] goad. [15] And I said, Who art thou, Lord? And the Lord said, I am Jesus whom thou persecutest. [16] But arise, and stand upon thy feet: for to this end have I appeared unto thee, to appoint thee a minister and a witness both of the things wherein[4] thou hast seen me, and of the things wherein I will appear unto thee; [17] delivering thee from the people, and from the Gentiles, unto whom I send thee, [18] to open their eyes, that[5] they may turn from darkness to light and from the power of Satan unto God, that they may receive remission of sins and an inheritance among them that are sanctified by faith in me. [19] Wherefore, O king Agrippa, I was not disobedient unto the heavenly vision: [20] but declared both to them of Damascus first, and at Jerusalem, and throughout all the country of Judæa, and also to the Gentiles, that they should repent and turn to God, doing works worthy of repentance.[6] [21] For this cause the Jews seized me in the temple, and assayed to kill me. [22] Having therefore obtained the help that is from God, I stand unto this day testifying both to small and great, saying nothing but what the prophets and Moses did say should come; [23] how[7] that the Christ must[8]

[2] Or, *On which errand.* [3] Gr. *goads.*
[4] Many ancient authorities read *which thou hast seen.* [5] Or, *to turn them.*
[6] Or, *their repentance.* [7] Or, *if.* Or, *whether.* [8] Or, *is subject to suffering.*

suffer, *and* how[7] that he first by the resurrection of the dead should proclaim light both to the people and to the Gentiles.

[24] And as he thus made his defence, Festus saith with a loud voice, Paul, thou art mad; thy much learning is[9] turning thee mad. [25] But Paul saith, I am not mad, most excellent Festus; but speak forth words of truth and soberness. [26] For the king knoweth of these things, unto whom also I speak freely: for I am persuaded that none of these things is hidden from him; for this hath not been done in a corner. [27] King Agrippa, believest thou the prophets? I know that thou believest. [28] And Agrippa *said* unto Paul, With[10] but little persuasion thou wouldest fain make me a Christian. [29] And Paul *said,* I would to God, that whether[11] with little or with much, not thou only, but also all that hear me this day, might become such as I am, except these bonds.

[30] And the king rose up, and the governor, and Bernice, and they that sat with them: [31] and when they had withdrawn, they spake one to another, saying, This man doeth nothing worthy of death or of bonds. [32] And Agrippa said unto Festus, This man might have been set at liberty, if he had not appealed unto Cæsar.

XXVII

[1] AND when it was determined that we should sail for Italy, they delivered Paul and certain other prisoners to a centurion named Julius, of the Augustan band.[1] [2] And embarking in a ship of Adramyttium, which was about to sail unto the places on the coast of Asia, we put to sea, Aristarchus, a Macedonian of Thessalonica, being with us. [3] And the next day we touched at Sidon: and Julius treated Paul kindly, and gave him leave to go unto his friends and refresh[2] himself. [4] And putting to sea from thence, we sailed under the lee of Cyprus, because the winds were contrary. [5] And when we had sailed across the sea which is off Cilicia and Pamphylia, we came to Myra, *a city* of Lycia. [6] And there the centurion found a ship of Alexandria sailing for Italy; and he put us therein. [7] And when we had sailed slowly many days, and were come with

[9] Gr. *turneth thee to madness.* [10] Or, *In a little* time *thou &c.*
[11] Or, *both in little and in great,* i. e., in all respects.
[1] Or, *cohort.* [2] Gr. *receive attention.*

difficulty over against Cnidus, the wind not further[3] suffering us,
we sailed under the lee of Crete, over against Salmone; [8] and with
difficulty coasting along it we came unto a certain place called Fair
Havens; nigh whereunto was the city of Lasea.

[9] And when much time was spent, and the voyage was now
dangerous, because the Fast was now already gone by, Paul admonished them, [10] and said unto them, Sirs, I perceive that the
voyage will be with injury and much loss, not only of the lading
and the ship, but also of our lives. [11] But the centurion gave more
heed to the master and to the owner of the ship, than to those
things which were spoken by Paul. [12] And because the haven
was not commodious to winter in, the more part advised to put to
sea from thence, if by any means they could reach Phœnix, and
winter *there; which is* a haven of Crete, looking north-east[4] and
south-east. [13] And when the south wind blew softly, supposing
that they had obtained their purpose, they weighed anchor and
sailed along Crete, close in shore. [14] But after no long time there
beat down from it a tempestuous wind, which is called Euraquilo:
[15] and when the ship was caught, and could not face the wind,
we gave way *to it,* and were driven. [16] And running under the lee
of a small island called Cauda,[5] we were able, with difficulty, to
secure the boat: [17] and when they had hoisted it up, they used
helps, under-girding the ship; and, fearing lest they should be cast
upon the Syrtis, they lowered the gear, and so were driven. [18]
And as we labored exceedingly with the storm, the next day they
began to throw *the freight* overboard; [19] and the third day they
cast out with their own hands the tackling[6] of the ship. [20] And
when neither sun nor stars shone upon *us* for many days, and no
small tempest lay on *us,* all hope that we should be saved was now
taken away. [21] And when they had been long without food, then
Paul stood forth in the midst of them, and said, Sirs, ye should have
hearkened unto me, and not have set sail from Crete, and have
gotten this injury and loss. [22] And now I exhort you to be of good
cheer; for there shall be no loss of life among you, but *only* of the
ship. [23] For there stood by me this night an angel of the God

[3] Or, *suffering us to get there.*
[4] Gr. *down the south-west wind and down the north-west wind.*
[5] Many ancient authorities read *Clauda.* [6] Or, *furniture.*

whose I am, whom also I serve, [24] saying, Fear not, Paul; thou must stand before Cæsar: and lo, God hath granted thee all them that sail with thee. [25] Wherefore, sirs, be of good cheer: for I believe God, that it shall be even so as it hath been spoken unto me. [26] But we must be cast upon a certain island.

[27] But when the fourteenth night was come, as we were driven to and fro in the *sea of* Adria, about midnight the sailors surmised that they were drawing near to some country: [28] and they sounded, and found twenty fathoms; and after a little space, they sounded again, and found fifteen fathoms. [29] And fearing lest haply we should be cast ashore on rocky ground, they let go four anchors from the stern, and wished[7] for the day. [30] And as the sailors were seeking to flee out of the ship, and had lowered the boat into the sea, under color as though they would lay out anchors from the foreship, [31] Paul said to the centurion and to the soldiers, Except these abide in the ship, ye cannot be saved. [32] Then the soldiers cut away the ropes of the boat, and let her fall off. [33] And while the day was coming on, Paul besought them all to take some food, saying, This day is the fourteenth day that ye wait and continue fasting, having taken nothing. [34] Wherefore I beseech you to take some food: for this is for your safety: for there shall not a hair perish from the head of any of you. [35] And when he had said this, and had taken bread, he gave thanks to God in the presence of all; and he brake it, and began to eat. [36] Then were they all of good cheer, and themselves also took food. [37] And we were in all in the ship two hundred threescore and sixteen souls. [38] And when they had eaten enough, they lightened the ship, throwing out the wheat into the sea. [39] And when it was day, they knew not the land: but they perceived a certain bay with a beach, and they took counsel whether they could drive[8] the ship upon it. [40] And casting off the anchors, they left them in the sea, at the same time loosing the bands of the rudders; and hoisting up the foresail to the wind, they made for the beach. [41] But lighting upon a place where two seas met, they ran the vessel aground; and the foreship struck and remained unmoveable, but the stern began to break up by the violence *of the waves*. [42] And the

[7] Or, *prayed*. [8] Some ancient authorities read *bring the ship safe to shore*.

soldiers' counsel was to kill the prisoners, lest any *of them* should
swim out, and escape. [43] But the centurion, desiring to save Paul,
stayed them from their purpose; and commanded that they who
could swim should cast themselves overboard, and get first to the
land; [44] and the rest, some on planks, and some on *other* things
from the ship. And so it came to pass, that they all escaped safe to
the land.

XXVIII

[1] AND when we were escaped, then we knew that the island was
called Melita.[1] [2] And the barbarians showed us no common kindness: for they kindled a fire, and received us all, because of the
present rain, and because of the cold. [3] But when Paul had
gathered a bundle of sticks and laid them on the fire, a viper came
out by[2] reason of the heat, and fastened on his hand. [4] And when
the barbarians saw the *venomous* creature hanging from his hand,
they said one to another, No doubt this man is a murderer, whom,
though he hath escaped from the sea, yet Justice hath not suffered
to live. [5] Howbeit he shook off the creature into the fire, and took
no harm. [6] But they expected that he would have swollen, or
fallen down dead suddenly: but when they were long in expectation
and beheld nothing amiss come to him, they changed their minds,
and said that he was a god.

[7] Now in the neighborhood of that place were lands belonging
to the chief man of the island, named Publius; who received us,
and entertained us three days courteously. [8] And it was so, that
the father of Publius lay sick of fever and dysentery: unto whom
Paul entered in, and prayed, and laying his hands on him healed
him. [9] And when this was done, the rest also that had diseases
in the island came, and were cured: [10] who also honored us with
many honors; and when we sailed, they put on board such things
as we needed.

[11] And after three months we set sail in a ship of Alexandria
which had wintered in the island, whose sign was The[3] Twin
Brothers. [12] And touching at Syracuse, we tarried there three

[1] Some ancient authorities read *Melitene*. [2] Or, *from the heat*.
[3] Gr. *Dioscuri*.

days. [13] And from thence we made[4] a circuit, and arrived at Rhegium: and after one day a south wind sprang up, and on the second day we came to Puteoli; [14] where we found brethren, and were entreated to tarry with them seven days: and so we came to Rome. [15] And from thence the brethren, when they heard of us, came to meet us as far as The Market of Appius and The Three Taverns; whom when Paul saw, he thanked God, and took courage.

[16] And when we entered into Rome, Paul[5] was suffered to abide by himself with the soldier that guarded him.

[17] And it came to pass, that after three days he called together those[6] that were the chief of the Jews: and when they were come together, he said unto them, I, brethren, though I had done nothing against the people, or the customs of our fathers, yet was delivered prisoner from Jerusalem into the hands of the Romans: [18] who, when they had examined me, desired to set me at liberty, because there was no cause of death in me. [19] But when the Jews spake against it, I was constrained to appeal unto Cæsar; not that I had aught whereof to accuse my nation. [20] For this cause therefore did I entreat[7] you to see and to speak with *me:* for because of the hope of Israel I am bound with this chain. [21] And they said unto him, We neither received letters from Judæa concerning thee, nor did any of the brethren come hither and report or speak any harm of thee. [22] But we desire to hear of thee what thou thinkest: for as concerning this sect, it is known to us that everywhere it is spoken against.

[23] And when they had appointed him a day, they came to him into his lodging in great number; to whom he expounded *the matter,* testifying the kingdom of God, and persuading them concerning Jesus, both from the law of Moses and from the prophets, from morning till evening. [24] And some believed the things which were spoken, and some disbelieved. [25] And when they agreed not among themselves, they departed after that Paul had spoken one word, Well spake the Holy Spirit through Isaiah the prophet unto your fathers, [26] saying,

[4] Some ancient authorities read *cast loose.* [5] Some ancient authorities insert *the centurion delivered the prisoners to the Chief of the camp: but &c.*

[6] Or, *those that were of the Jews first.*

[7] Or, *call for you, to see and to speak with* you.

Go thou unto this people, and say,
By hearing ye shall hear, and shall in no wise understand;
And seeing ye shall see, and shall in no wise perceive:
[27] For this people's heart is waxed gross,
And their ears are dull of hearing,
And their eyes they have closed;
Lest haply they should perceive with their eyes,
And hear with their ears,
And understand with their heart,
And should turn again,
And I should heal them.

[28] Be it known therefore unto you, that this salvation of God is
sent unto the Gentiles: they will also hear.[8]

[30] And he abode two whole years in his own hired dwelling,
and received all that went in unto him, [31] preaching the kingdom of God, and teaching the things concerning the Lord Jesus
Christ with all boldness, none forbidding him.

[8] Some ancient authorities insert ver. 29, *And when he had said these words, the Jews departed, having much disputing among themselves.*